International Law and the Global South

Perspectives from the Rest of the World

This book series aims to promote a complex vision of contemporary legal developments from the perspective of emerging or developing countries and/or authors integrating these elements into their approach. While focusing on today's law and international economic law in particular, it brings together contributions from, or influenced by, other social sciences disciplines. Written in both technical and non-technical language and addressing topics of contemporary importance to a general audience, the series will be of interest to legal researchers as well as non-lawyers.
In referring to the "rest of the world", the book series puts forward new and alternative visions of today's law not only from emerging and developing countries, but also from authors who deliberately integrate this perspective into their thinking. The series approach is not only comparative, post-colonial or critical, but also truly universal in the sense that it places a plurality of well-informed visions at its center.

The Series

- Provides a truly global coverage of the world in reflecting cutting-edge developments and thinking in law and international law
- Focuses on the transformations of international and comparative law with an emphasis on international economic law (investment, trade and development)
- Welcomes contributions on comparative and/or domestic legal evolutions

More information about this series at http://www.springer.com/series/13447

Julien Chaisse · Tomoko Ishikawa
Sufian Jusoh
Editors

Asia's Changing International Investment Regime

Sustainability, Regionalization, and Arbitration

Springer

Editors
Julien Chaisse
School of Law
Chinese University of Hong Kong
Hong Kong
Hong Kong

Sufian Jusoh
Institute of Malaysian and International Studies (IKMAS)
National University of Malaysia
Bangi
Malaysia

Tomoko Ishikawa
Graduate School of International Development
Nagoya University
Nagoya
Japan

ISSN 2510-1420 ISSN 2510-1439 (electronic)
International Law and the Global South
Perspectives from the Rest of the World
ISBN 978-981-10-5881-3 ISBN 978-981-10-5882-0 (eBook)
DOI 10.1007/978-981-10-5882-0

Library of Congress Control Number: 2017950004

Printed on acid-free paper

This Springer imprint is published by Springer Nature
The registered company is Springer Nature Singapore Pte Ltd.
The registered company address is: 152 Beach Road, #21-01/04 Gateway East, Singapore 189721, Singapore

Foreword

The United Nation's 2030 Agenda for Sustainable Development, the Addis Ababa Action Agenda and the Paris Climate Agreement require bold action to improve people's well-being while protecting the environment. Measures to generate investment to tackle a range of economic, social and environmental challenges are central to this global agenda. A stable investment environment, supported by a strong, coherent legal framework governing international investments, is essential to its success. In Asia and the Pacific, reforms still need to be completed to deliver simpler, more transparent and equitable rules-based investment regimes.

This is important, because foreign direct investment (FDI) makes a vital contribution to growth and development in the Asia and the Pacific. In recent years, the region has received up to half of annual total global inflows. It continues to outperform the global average, and although starting from a low base, FDI to the region's least developed countries has trebled since 2005. Asia-Pacific countries are also becoming an important source of capital for financing outbound investments to our region and beyond. Outflows from developing Asian economies have increased significantly, compared with a decline in outflows from regional developed economies.

Regulatory frameworks need to keep up with the changing dynamics of the investment flows. Supporting investment has traditionally been the preserve of domestic policy. This has led countries to introduce different incentives and concessions which overtime have distorted tax regimes and lowered government revenues. At their worst, these distortions have led to unproductive investments, undermining sustainable growth. A multilateral response could support long-term sustainable investments and provide investors a clear framework in which to resolve commercial disputes, in particular in the context of International Investment Agreements (IIAs).

To support sustainable development, IIAs need to reflect economic, environmental and social concerns. Their increased number has done much to imbue investment policy with an international dimension. Their interaction with existing domestic policies and with each other needs to be actively managed to avoid duplication and inconsistency. Many now include provisions on investment promotion and cooperation as well as requirements to harmonise investment rules and regulations. The ASEAN Comprehensive Investment Agreement (ACIA) is a good example. Wider regional trade or economic partnership agreements could be even more far-reaching.

As we work to support free trade as a positive force for competition, growth and development, the design of Investor-State Dispute Settlement (ISDS) mechanisms is critical. Well-designed IIAs mechanisms are integral to improving the multilateral governance of international investment regimes. Yet the increase of treaty-based ISDS cases, 40% of which are against developed economies, is well known. It has highlighted the need for a delicate balance to be struck between the investors' right to protection and states' sovereign right to regulate their markets. The United Nations has been active in supporting policy development in this area with this in mind.

The United Nations Commission on International Trade Law laid out *Rules on Transparency in Treaty-based Investor-States Arbitration*. These provide for open hearings for arbitrations brought under IIAs concluded after April 2014 when the rules came into force. The United Nations General Assembly adopted the *Convention on Transparency in Treaty-Based Investor-State Arbitration* to provide a mechanism for those countries wanting to adopt these rules for agreements signed prior to this date. The United Nations Conference on Trade and Development provides policy guidance in negotiating IIAs under its Investment Policy Framework for Sustainable Development.

Reform of IIAs could make a major contribution to improving international investment regimes. Tight definitions of the scope of investment investor are vital, and the scope and principle of fair and equitable treatment should be clearly set out. We need to consider limiting the Full Protection and Security provision to "physical" security and protection, and make the level of protection commensurate with the country's level of development. Precise definitions of the application and scope of expropriation should be formulated and the notion of indirect expropriation clarified. Adequate policy advice is needed to ensure countries in receipt of FDI are able to effectively adjust their domestic regulatory and governance regimes. And provisions for sustainable development, responsible investment and business practices, and social and environmental protection need to be mainstreamed.

The scope of consent given to ISDS needs to be qualified up front in IIAs, procedures made more transparent and arbitral tribunals made to take into account standards of investor behaviour when settling investor-state disputes. Where possible, the role of domestic judicial systems needs to be increased. Overall, IIAs should be flexible enough to be adapted when necessary.

These are some of the areas of reform which deserve serious consideration as we work to deliver on the 2030 Agenda for Sustainable Development. This book provides some of the detail and solid analysis we need to inform work to reform international investment regimes. I hope we can build on it to deliver results as we work to deepen economic cooperation and integration across Asia and the Pacific.

June 2017

Dr. Shamshad Akhtar
Under-Secretary-General of the United Nations
Executive Secretary of the Economic
and Social Commission for Asia and the Pacific
United Nations Sherpa for the G20
Bangkok, Thailand

Contents

About the Editors

Julien Chaisse is a Professor of Law at the Chinese University of Hong Kong (CUHK), Faculty of Law, Hong Kong. He is an award-winning scholar of international law with a special focus on the regulation and development of economic globalisation. Prior to joining the CUHK in 2009, Dr. Chaisse was a Senior Research Fellow at the World Trade Institute (Switzerland). Dr. Chaisse has served as Director of the CUHK's Centre for Financial Regulation and Economic Development since 2013. He has established forward-looking legal projects and events at the CUHK, including the series "Asia FDI Forum", which has become the most prominent conference on foreign investment regulation in Asia. In addition to his professorship, Dr. Chaisse is an experienced arbitrator and a leading consultant to international organisations, governments, multinational law firms and private investors. He is also a member of the World Economic Forum's International Trade and Investment Council.

Tomoko Ishikawa is an Associate Professor at Nagoya University in Japan. She is a member of the Legal Advisory Committee of the Energy Charter Treaty and an arbitrator at Shenzhen Court of International Arbitration. Her professional experience includes serving as a Judge at the Tokyo District Court and holding the position of Deputy Director at the International Legal Affairs Bureau of the Ministry of Foreign Affairs of Japan. Her most recent publications include: 'Provisional Application of Treaties at the Crossroads between International and Domestic Law' 31(2) ICSID Review pp. 270–289 (2016); 'The Rise of the Notion of Illegitimate Debt' 6(3) 'Accounting, Economics and Law' pp. 189–217 (2016) and 'Restitution as a "Second Chance" for Investor-State Relations: Restitution and Monetary Damages as Sequential Options' Vol. 3 McGill Journal of Dispute Resolution pp. 154–175 (2017).

Sufian Jusoh is the Deputy Director and a Senior Fellow at the Institute of Malaysia and International Studies, Universiti Kebangsaan Malaysia. Dr. Jusoh has been a consultant to many countries and international organisations such as the World Bank, the Asian Development Bank, ASEAN, the World Trade Organisation and the World Intellectual Property Organisation. He plays a key role in the reform of the investment laws in Myanmar, Timor Leste, Laos and the Federated States of Micronesia. Dr. Jusoh holds an LL.B from Cardiff Law School, an LL.M from University College London and a Ph.D. in Law from University of Bern, Switzerland. He is the co-author of the book "The ASEAN Comprehensive Investment Agreement The Regionalisation of Laws and Policy on Foreign Investment" (Elgar 2016).

Introduction

Julien Chaisse, Tomoko Ishikawa and Sufian Jusoh

1 An Introduction

This book is motivated by the rapid evolution of the international investment regime in the Asia-Pacific region that has occurred over the last few years. The objective of this book is to provide perspectives to help predict the future regulatory framework for foreign investment in the region, and how the regional trends affect the development of global rules for foreign investment. It does so by inviting a number of leading experts to comment on the main problems confronting the actors involved in international investment law and policy.

The changing dynamics in the flow of investment into and out of Asia[1] require a close look at the operation of international investment law in the Asia-Pacific region. Until the latter part of the twentieth century, developing Asian countries had been the recipient of capital or foreign direct investments (FDI) from the more developed economies. As the economies of developing Asian countries grew, many of these countries started to become the source of capital and started to commit to outward foreign direct investment (OFDI). The World Investment Report issued by

[1]For the present purposes, 'Asia' includes those countries grouped as Eastern Asia, Southern Asia and South-Eastern Asia, as defined by the United Nations Conference on Trade and Development (UNCTAD).

J. Chaisse (✉)
CFRED, School of Law, The Chinese University of Hong Kong, Sha Tin, Hong Kong
e-mail: Julien.chaisse@cuhk.edu.hk

T. Ishikawa
Nagoya University, Nagoya, Japan
e-mail: mane@tkc.att.ne.jp

S. Jusoh
National University of Malaysia, Bangi, Malaysia
e-mail: sufianjusoh@gmail.com

J. Chaisse et al. (eds.), *Asia's Changing International Investment Regime*,
International Law and the Global South, DOI 10.1007/978-981-10-5882-0_1

the United Nations Conference on Trade and Development (UNCTAD) observes that developing Asia emerged as the largest investing region in 2014.[2] To name a few, the People's Republic of China (China), South Korea, Malaysia, Singapore, Taiwan and Thailand joined the list of countries offering to invest in other countries. At the beginning, these countries' investments were directed to other countries in the global South, but now many of these countries are also investing in the developed economies that used to be their primary sources of investment.

The changes in the dynamics of investment flows have shifted the direction of international investment agreements (IIAs).[3] Traditionally, an IIA was an instrument by which the developed economies sought to protect the interests of their investors in developing Asian countries. This was reflected in the structure and content of these investment treaties, which generally offer strong protection for foreign investments and consist of simpler and a smaller number of provisions than modern investment treaties. As the sources of capital have started to diversify, developing Asian countries as exporters of capital are now seeking the protection of their investors and investments in the same way as the more developed economies do. Accordingly, developing Asian countries are starting to re-examine the way IIAs have been designed, and to revisit certain provisions in these treaties. Hence, there is an increasing need to have more balanced and negotiated terms in future IIAs.

The advent of the new generation of regional trade agreements also demands a re-examination of the way IIAs are negotiated and concluded. As cross-border investment and trade are intrinsically linked and inter-dependent, modern regional trade agreements also contain an investment chapter. At the same time, a trade in services chapter in trade agreements affects foreign investment activities, which largely overlap with the provision of services through commercial presence.[4] The close relationship between investment and trade has also directed many countries to seek a higher level of liberalisation or market access for their investors and this is reflected in the new generation IIAs and regional trade agreements.

The new dynamics of investment flows has also resulted in the increase in the number of investor-state dispute settlement (ISDS)[5] claims filed against Asian countries. This has started to influence the mindsets of these countries towards the ISDS mechanism. On the one hand, some affected countries perceive the ISDS mechanism as an unfair system that leads to the victimisation of the capital-importing states, and are reviewing their existing IIAs and their domestic laws, as well as starting to take a harder line on the use and access to ISDS in future IIAs. On the other hand, they also recognise the importance of the mechanism being

[2]UNCTAD (2016, p. 7). It should be noted that their FDI outflows declined in 2015 reflecting the global and regional economic slowdown (ibid 50).

[3]For the purposes of this proposal, the term 'IIAs' includes bilateral investment treaties (BITs) and investment chapters in preferential trade agreements (PTAs).

[4]For the 'convergence factors' between investment and trade law, see Kurtz (2016, pp. 10–20).

[5]Following the terminology used by the UNCTAD, for the purpose of this research ISDS will be use to refer to international arbitration in treaty-based claims, given its predominance as an investor-state dispute settlement mechanism; UNCTAD (2015, p. 106).

available to their own investors, resulting in a state where there is a plurality of different positions and practices on the ISDS mechanism.

Against this background, this introductory chapter examines how the changes in the structure and dynamics of investment flows in developing Asian countries have influenced the way in which investment treaties are drafted, negotiated and concluded.

The book is structured as follows. Part I sets the scene and provides a detailed analysis of the current global forces that shape international investment law with regard to rule-making, dispute resolution and economics. Part II focuses on the regionalization of investment rules in Asia. It examines the key features of these rules and their precedent-setting role for future investment law and policy in this region. Part III refines the analysis by investigating current trends in investor state dispute settlement.

2 Setting the Scene: Regional Trends in an Evolving Global Landscape

Part I provides the backdrop to the remaining sections of the text. In order to explain the increasingly important role of the Asia-Pacific region in global investment and trade, Part I presents the key features of global trends in investment rule-making, investment arbitration and economic trends before contrasting hem with regional trends in the Asia-Pacific context.

In Chapter "The Changing Patterns of Investment Rule-Making Issues and Actors", the book editors examine how the changes in the structure and dynamics of investment flows in developing Asian countries have influenced the way in which investment treaties are drafted, negotiated and concluded.

In Chapter "Shaping Globalization: Recent Trends in Asia-Pacific Foreign Direct Investment", Bekzod Abdullaev and Douglas H. Brooks examine the recent trends in both inward and outward FDI flows in the Asia-Pacific region. This chapter first examines global FDI trends and observes that, with regard to the levels of FDI flows, there is a demonstrable link between the lifting of FDI restrictions and a dramatic increase of world FDI inflows. With regard to the modes of entry of FDI, it demonstrates that since the end of the 1990s, cross-border mergers and acquisitions have been dominant in Europe, while growth in greenfield investments has been led by Asian players, and has also been on the rise in Latin America and the Caribbean since 2010. The chapter proceeds to examine the sectoral trends in FDI flows and demonstrates that in the last two decades, developed and developing economies have experienced a sectoral shift in foreign capital flows from manufacturing towards services sectors. It then reviews recent trends in FDI flows by region, national income level, economic bloc and sectors, with particular attention to developments in the Asia-Pacific region. The examination demonstrates that the nature of FDI in the Asia-Pacific region has been undergoing major transformations, and more FDI is now directed towards the service sector than towards the manufacturing and primary sectors combined. The chapter concludes by stressing the importance of the availability of FDI data and greater evidence-based analysis in order to heighten the efficacy of policy formulation.

In Chapter "Reforming the International Investment Regime: Two Challenges", Karl P. Sauvant addresses two challenges in relation to the reform of the international investment law and policy regime that have a strong policy resonance in the Asian region: how to encourage the flow of substantially higher amounts of sustainable FDI and how to bring about a more widely accepted dispute-settlement approach. On the former, this chapter stresses the need to launch an international support program for sustainable investment facilitation, and proposes several options for a sustainable FDI support program. On the latter, this chapter proposes the establishment of an Advisory Centre on International Investment Law as a way to provide administrative and legal assistance to developing respondent states. This chapter concludes by stressing that the international investment law and policy regime needs further improvements, and governments in Asia that actively negotiate IIAs have the opportunity to contribute significantly to the further development of the investment regime.

In Chapter "Investment Protection and Host State's Right to Regulate in Indian Model Bilateral Investment Treaty 2015: Lessons for Asian Countries", Prabhash Ranjan provides an analysis of the background, content and challenges of the new Indian model BIT of 2015, which can provide helpful lessons to the Chinese BIT programme. This chapter first observes that although the Indian BIT programme is one of the biggest amongst developing countries, most existing Indian BITs are one-sided treaties that give massive protection to foreign investment yet contain limited space for the host state's right to regulate, as illustrated by the 2003 Indian model BIT. This chapter proceeds to examine the factors which prompted the Indian government to re-think its BIT programme, including the recent instances of foreign investors suing India under different BITs. It then critically discusses key provisions of the new Indian model BIT of 2015 from the standpoint of whether a suitable balance has been struck between investment protection and host state's right to regulate. The analysis focuses on several key provisions and is carried out by comparing the final version with the draft version unveiled earlier and in light of the recommendations made by the Law Commission of India on the draft model BIT. The analysis reveals several issues with the new model, including: some provisions are tilted in favour of the host State's right to regulate at the expense of investment protection; and that the model is not in sync with the other plans of the Indian government to attract foreign investors like 'Make in India'. This chapter concludes by observing that with this model India will face difficulty in drawing its existing treaty partners or new countries to the negotiating table, which underlies the need for a more balanced model BIT which would have found more takers in the international community.

In Chapter "China's Regulation of Foreign Direct Investment", Leon Trakman gives an overview of China's recent foray into BITs. This chapter begins with an outline of China's BIT program by looking at its model investment treaties and analysing some of the BITs that have been concluded by China with other states. It proceeds to examine the operation of China's BITs by analysing the claims brought under these agreements. It then examines China's contemporary approaches to the regulation of FDI in light of the recently concluded FTA with Australia and the global regulatory climate. This chapter concludes that, while China will likely restrict the rights of investors in its future BITs, it will be unlikely to deviate significantly from established regulatory practices.

3 The Regionalization of Investment Law and Policy in the Asia-Pacific Region

Part II explores a key feature of investment rule-making in the Asia-Pacific region, namely the increased regionalisation of investment pacts. There are two forms of IIAs that exist in practice: BITs and investment chapters in the PTAs.[6] Important examples of PTAs which have been concluded or signed in the Asia-Pacific region include the ACIA and the TPPA. The RCEP and the Pacer Plus Agreement among the Pacific Island Nations, which also include investment chapters, are currently under negotiation. At the bilateral level, there are several significant developments such as the Myanmar–EU BIT negotiations, which are expected to open and liberalise Myanmar's economy (which sits in ASEAN and borders China and India), and the China–US BIT negotiations. Part II also analyses the emergence of China as a rule-maker on investment matters in the international community. China's interests lie in providing substantive protection for its investors abroad as well as in opening new investment opportunities, while consolidating, through the undertaking of international obligations, internal reforms conducive to promoting domestic market opening and a stable business environment. As a major capital-exporting state, it may not come as a surprise that China has also adopted an aggressive BIT policy: China has signed 131 such treaties, being outdone only by Germany, with the world's highest number—137 BITs. On the other hand, China's BIT policy also reflects the need to effectively implement its economic reforms, and the concerns over the possibility of investment agreements interfering with its key domestic policy objectives.

In Chapter "Ten as One? Explaining ASEAN Regulation on Foreign Investment", Julien Chaisse and Sufian Jusoh discuss the role of the ACIA. This chapter acknowledges the ACIA as one of the most important legal documents in the formation and functioning of the ASEAN Economic Community (AEC), especially from the perspective of the regionalisation of investment law and policy in the Asia-Pacific region. Having analysed the content of the ACIA, this chapter argues that the ACIA responds to the concerns of foreign business about the potentially capricious nature of regulatory change in an efficient, transparent, and legally binding manner. It then examines issues surrounding the implementation of the

[6]Chaisse (2013, p. 188).

ACIA and argues that some ASEAN member states will have to make further improvements in lifting foreign investment limits in some sectors in order to enhance overall investment facilitation and create better collaboration between the ASEAN member states. It concludes by providing future prospects of the integration of the ASEAN regional economy. They include: (a) in the post-2015 period, ASEAN will continue to deepen and enhance economic integration in areas covered in the AEC 2015 blueprint; (b) this will include the enhancement of the investment environment by introducing effective, efficient, coherent and responsive regulations and good regulatory practice; and (c) ASEAN will also ensure that ACIA will contribute towards the further integration of ASEAN into the global economy by adopting a more coherent approach with a view to adopting a common position in regional and global economic fora.

In Chapter "China-Japan-Korea Trilateral Investment Treaty Implications for Future Investment Negotiations in Asia", Shintaro Hamanaka examines the China–Japan–Korea trilateral investment treaty. This chapter begins with the explanation of the background of the analysis as follows. The China–Japan relationship is key to economic cooperation in Asia, particularly in the negotiation of regional economic agreements. Among the negotiation items in economic agreements, it is investment, rather than trade or tariffs, that has been the central issue for China and Japan. Since the two countries have adopted distinct investment treaty practice, agreeing upon the modality of discipline on investment policy is not easy. The existing difference in stance in investment negotiations between the two countries will be likely to constitute an obstacle to ongoing and future negotiations for economic agreements in Asia. Against this background, this chapter examines the content of the China–Japan–Korea investment treaty and concludes that while it is more comprehensive than the old China–Japan bilateral treaty, its scope is still limited. This chapter then examines the ongoing negotiations of the China–Japan–Korea FTA, which includes an investment chapter, and explains the difference in stance between China and Japan in this context as follows. From the Chinese perspective, investment is a done deal and Beijing is of the view that its investment chapter should basically follow what was agreed in the trilateral investment treaty. From the Japanese perspective, given its strong interest in investment issues, it is pointless to sign a trilateral FTA unless its investment chapter shows a significant improvement on the trilateral investment treaty. The chapter also observes that a similar argument is applicable to the negotiations for the RCEP. The chapter concludes by examining the implication of the ongoing negotiation for the United States–China BIT with respect to Japan's attitude towards investment negotiation vis-à-vis China, focusing on the effect of the comparative weakness of its bargaining power vis-à-vis China in investment negotiations, especially in relation to the United States, which has an investment screening process for Chinese investment.

In Chapter "A Baseline Study for RCEP's Investment Chapter: Picking the Right Protection Standards", Junianto James Losari analyses the multiple IIAs existing in the Asia-Pacific region with a view to suggesting the appropriate investment protection standards for the RCEP. This chapter does so by examining the level of protection granted to foreign investors and policy space granted to state parties in the various IIAs between the negotiating states of the RCEP. It also compares the existing IIA provisions with those in the recent investment agreements such as the investment chapter of the TPPA and the EU–Canada Comprehensive Economic and Trade Agreement (CETA). Based on these analyses, this chapter suggests the standards that should be considered by the negotiators of the RCEP, including the innovations that can be found in recent investment agreements such as the investment chapters of the TPPA and CETA. The chapter concludes that, by refining and adding more clarity to the provisions as well as ensuring the proper balance between investment protection and the right of states' to regulate, the RCEP may add more value to the existing investment protection regimes in the region.

In Chapter "'One Belt, One Road': China's New Big Plan and Its Impact on FDI", He Jun examines the 'One Belt, One Road' (OBOR) policy, which has become one of the most topical issues since the announcement of the 'Silk Road Economic Belt and 21st-Century Maritime Silk Road' by Chinese President Xi Jinping in 2013, with a focus on China's Agricultural FDI in Asia. This chapter explains that OBOR is a strategy to connect the vibrant East Asia group of economies at one end and the developed European economies at the other by enhancing mutual cooperation and promoting common development among these countries. It proceeds to identify the main features of China's Agricultural FDI in Asia, including that: investment coverage is broad and refers to integral industrial structure; agricultural investment in Asia is concentrated in six countries; the average investment scale in this field is lower than that in other areas; and this investment has obtained good results generally and enjoys remarkable geographical advantages. The chapter concludes by identifying the challenges FDI in agriculture typically faces such as capital shortage, financing difficulty, lack in experience of global operation and various investment risks compared with other industries, and by providing certain suggestions for China's future FDI in agriculture in Asia to address these issues. They include: to accelerate top-level design; to play an effective role in multilateral and bilateral cooperation mechanisms in Asia; to cultivate investors in enterprises and enhance investment cooperation between host countries and multinational enterprises; to innovate in terms of the mode of investment in external agriculture and reinforce governmental public service; and to constantly improve enterprises' operational ability in international markets.

In Chapter "The Role of Pacific Rim FTAs in the Harmonization of International Investment Law: Towards a Free Trade Area of the Asia-Pacific", Mark Feldman and Cristián Rodríguez Chiffelle argue that the Pacific Rim region provides the building blocks for the harmonization of the international investment law regime. This chapter first identifies the five elements that establish the Pacific Rim region as the natural centre of gravity for a rapidly harmonizing international investment law regime, including that: in the near future, five major agreements could govern a very substantial share of global investment (the US–China BIT, the EU–China BIT, and the three mega-regional free trade agreements—the Transatlantic Trade and Investment Partnership (TTIP), the TPP and the RCEP); and that a convergence in state practice across treaties is contributing to the harmonization of international investment law. Having examined the context of the harmonization of the international investment law through BITs and FTAs in the Pacific Rim region, this chapter then argues that significant gains in investment liberalization are being made in the region. In particular, it observes that the TPP and RCEP agreements can serve as pathways to a Free Trade Area of the Asia-Pacific (FTAAP); a US–China BIT can bridge remaining differences between the TPP and RCEP; and APEC—including the APEC IEG—can play a key role in supporting harmonization efforts in the region. The chapter concludes by identifying challenges to harmonization such as provisions on performance requirements, free transfers, state-owned enterprises and transparency of documents and hearings, and providing potential strategies for Pacific Rim States to respond to such challenges.

4 Towards a Greater Practice of Investment Arbitration in the Asia-Pacific Region

Part III focuses on the practice of investment arbitration in the Asia-Pacific region. The international investment regime has never been exempt from criticism and at the present time it might be reaching a turning point.[7] These criticisms are primarily addressed at investment arbitration, and they raise the concern that such procedures might favour the investor's interests above those of the host state, restricting the states' regulatory powers, and that the arbitral rulings lack consistency and predictability.[8] A legal approach[9] to such allegations requires paying closer attention to the arbitral awards to see how the tribunals understand and apply the international investment regime, and in particular how they apply the standards of protection for foreign investments. In order to address these concerns **Part III** investigates recent developments in the Asian practice of investment arbitration.

In Chapter "The Future of Investor-State Arbitration: Revising the Rules?", Rahul Donde and Julien Chaisse review current trends, concerns and recent developments in investment arbitration in the Asian region. This chapter first examines the remarkable expansion of investor-state disputes in the Asian context. It observes that Asia has witnessed a startling increase of the number of investor-state disputes, and accordingly about 20% of all known investment disputes involve Asian states, with further growth of the number of disputes involving

[7]For a good summary of the history of the FDI regime, the arguments in favour and against it, and proposed paths for its reform, see UNCTAD (2015).

[8]Henckels (2015, p. 1).

[9]International investment entails not only the legal aspects, but also the economic, political and cultural factors that shape and affect the regime. The complexity of the international investment regime allows for several approaches, each of which might permit a closer look at its different aspects. For an analysis of which types of political risk lead to ISDS in oil and gas, see Dupont et al. (2015, p. 337); for an analysis on the role of development in arbitration outcomes, see Franck (2009).

Asia in the future being predicted by several authors. This chapter proceeds to examine the precarious situation of investor-state arbitration in the Asia-Pacific region. While arbitration remains the preferred dispute-resolution mechanism for resolving investor-state disputes, a number of Asian states, disenchanted with investor-state arbitration, have started to step back from the investor-state arbitration system. A few states have denounced investor-state arbitration entirely, while others have significantly reformed the dispute resolution provisions of their investment agreements. Vietnam and Canada have agreed to dispense with the inclusion of investor-state arbitration in their respective investment agreements with the EU. Against the backdrop of this tumultuous state of affairs, this chapter reviews the current trends and recent developments in the ISDS framework, and considers their effects on both Asian states and Asian investors. The chapter concludes by arguing that the considerable evolution (and, perhaps maturity) in the international investment law framework in Asian countries bodes well for the region. It also stresses the importance of adopting and adapting to recent international developments concerning the ISDS framework in the Asian context.

In Chapter "Investor-State Dispute Settlement (ISDS) Cases in the Asia-Pacific Region—The Record", Martina Francesca Ferracane provides a macro-analysis of investor-state dispute settlement cases in Asia. This chapter analyses the ISDS cases involving countries in the Asia-Pacific region by examining the growth of dispute intensity, country and sectorial distribution of the claims, and the outcome of the cases such as the amount ratio in awards in favour of the investor in ISDS cases against Asia-Pacific countries. This chapter then discusses the controversies over the inclusion of ISDS mechanisms in international agreements, and concludes that the discussions on concrete proposals to improve the ISDS system should adapt to a new reality of increasingly growing investment stemming from developing countries as well as the globalized nature of investment, especially in the case of multinational corporations.

In Chapter "Breaking the Market Dominance of ICSID? An Assessment of the Likelihood of Institutional Competition, Especially from Asia, in the Near Future", Andrea Bjorklund and Bryan Druzin examine the possibility of the emergence of an Asian centre for investment arbitration—a very much debated, if not favoured, option in Asian policy circles—from a law and economics angle. This chapter argues that, given the current market dominance of ICSID in the investment arbitration service world, the emergence of such a centre should be constrained by network effects. It explains how network effects create a monopoly-type situation that prevents potential rivals from successfully challenging the market dominance of the prevailing standard, and argues that the dominance of ICSID generates network effects that bolster and entrench this market dominance, limiting and even precluding competition from Asia (or elsewhere). Having observed the discernible impact of network effects in the current investment arbitration environment, this chapter proceeds to argue that certain exogenous events could substantially reduce or altogether annihilate the network effects. It argues that, while network effects suggest that the emergence of an Asian centre for investment arbitration would prove extremely difficult, given several unknown factors, it remains a possibility.

The first such factor is the inclusion of a 'permanent' court and Appellate Body in the EU–Vietnam FTA and in the Comprehensive Trade and Economic Agreement between Canada and the EU, and the EU's proposal for the inclusion of a similar body in the TTIP, which gives rise to the possibility that any number of institutions may be selected to host it. Also considered are regional 'prejudices', which may lead to displacing the market dominance of the ICSID. It concludes that network effects are indeed currently at play and powerfully reinforce the market dominance of ICSID, but the long-term continuation of ICSID's dominance in the market for investment arbitration is by no means guaranteed.

This work is the result of considerable collective effort, which started with the Asia FDI Forum held in Hong Kong on November 5–6, 2015, an event jointly organized by the CUHK Law Faculty and the Columbia University Centre for Sustainable Investment (CCSI), which has been generously supported by the CUHK Faculty of Law and Oxfam HK. The work has benefited immensely from contributions from many sources, both at the institutional as well as at the individual level. We are delighted at the final result and would sincerely like to express our gratitude to all who have contributed to this project in one way or the other. Thanks must also be extended to our research assistants Ms. Rachel Xu Qian and Mr. Faliq. We also want to express sincere thanks to the many members of the CUHK Law Faculty who have played an important role in bringing this volume to fruition, namely Prof. Christopher Gane (Dean of CUHK Law), Prof. Gregory Gordon, Prof. Bryan Mercurio, Prof. Samuli Seppänen, Prof. Lutz-Christian Wolff, Prof. Chao Xi, and Prof. Mimi Zou. We are also sincerely thankful to Springer for their efficient preparation of the final text for publication.

References

Chaisse, J. 2013. Assessing the exposure of Asian states to investment claims. *Contemporary Asia Arbitration Journal* 6: 188.

Dupont, Chaisse, et al. 2015. Types of political risk leading to investment arbitrations in the oil and gas sector. *The Journal of World Energy Law & Business* 8: 337.

Franck, Susan D. 2009. Development and outcomes of investment treaty arbitration. *Harvard International Law Journal* 50.

Henckels, Caroline. 2015. *Proportionality and deference in investor-state arbitration: Balancing investment protection and regulatory autonomy*, 1. Cambridge: Cambridge University Press.

Kurtz, Jürgen. 2016. *The WTO and international investment law: Converging systems*, 10–20. Cambridge: Cambridge University Press.

UNCTAD. 2015. World investment report 2015. Reforming International Investment Governance.

UNCTAD. 2016. World investment report 2016, 7. http://unctad.org/en/PublicationsLibrary/wir2016_en.pdf. Accessed 5 Sept 2016.

Part I
Setting the Scene: Regional Trends in an Evolving Global Scenario

The Changing Patterns of Investment Rule-Making Issues and Actors

Julien Chaisse, Tomoko Ishikawa and Sufian Jusoh

1 Introduction

Foreign investment plays a pivotal role in most countries' development in many ways. The benefits of inward investment include, amongst others, the following: developing a sound economic structure; increasing and diversifying manufacturing; offering novel and more developed services; creating employment; and bringing innovative technology. Conversely, outward investment can bring long-term capital gains to the home country, help to build economic and political ties with other nations, and, in some cases, to ensure access to critical natural resources. In order to encourage cross-border capital flows, countries have taken various steps such as reforming their domestic legal frameworks to liberalise rules on inward and outward investment and to create special regimes which provide incentives and protection for foreign investment. The reform of domestic legal frameworks has taken place in many countries in Asia, ranging from the more developed countries such as China, the Philippines, Malaysia and Thailand to emerging economies such as Lao PDR, Myanmar and Timor Leste. Alongside the developments in domestic law, countries have also taken action in the international sphere, including entering into bilateral and multilateral trade and/or investment agreements.

A history of the development of international investment law can be briefly summarised as follows. The practice in the 19th century was to protect the alien

J. Chaisse (✉)
CFRED, School of Law, The Chinese University of Hong Kong, Sha Tin, Hong Kong
e-mail: Julien.chaisse@cuhk.edu.hk

T. Ishikawa
Nagoya University, Nagoya, Japan
e-mail: mane@tkc.att.ne.jp

S. Jusoh
National University of Malaysia, Bangi, Malaysia
e-mail: sufianjusoh@gmail.com

J. Chaisse et al. (eds.), *Asia's Changing International Investment Regime*,
International Law and the Global South, DOI 10.1007/978-981-10-5882-0_2

property by reference to the domestic laws of the host state, so that aliens would be given equal treatment to nationals. Later on, the United States of America (USA), particularly in its relation with the Latin American states, sought to externalise the norms that governed a state's responsibility for injuries to aliens and their property. The USA claimed an international minimum standard with which the foreigner should be treated including the investor's right to prompt, adequate and effective compensation (known as the Hull formula),[1] and the right to settle disputes beyond the domestic courts of the host state. European countries endorsed the international minimum standard of treatment of foreign investment after their colonies became independent, a move which was in opposition to 'nationalist fervour'. Against this backdrop, in the 1960s and the 1970s, developing countries sought to establish the so-called the 'New international Economic Order'. This movement produced a series of United Nations General Assembly Resolutions, including Resolution 3281 which contains the Charter of Economic Rights and Duties of States.[2] The Charter adopted a standard for compensation which is lower than the Hull formula, that is, the standard of 'appropriate compensation',[3] but this standard did not gain support. Consequently, in spite of political and ideological disparities, by the end of the twentieth century the international regime of foreign investment had taken firm root.[4] Since the conclusion of the first Bilateral Investment Treaty (BIT) in 1959 between Germany and Pakistan, IIAs have significantly increased both in number and importance. As of the end of 2015, there are over 3,300 IIAs.[5]

The primary purpose of IIAs is to protect and promote foreign investment by providing legal stability and security for the operation of foreign investors and their investments. With a view to attracting investment inflows and receiving the benefits of the assumed consequent economic development, the states in exchange agree to limit their sovereign power to regulate the activities by foreign investors.[6] This purpose is in principle consistent with the host state policies to protect and enhance the public interest. Indeed, in developing countries, the former may well be a necessary condition for the latter, as foreign investment brings prosperity that 'inevitably engenders much higher societal expectations for environmental quality of life—and makes available the resources required to afford the pursuit of such expectations'.[7]

---

[1]Olmos Giupponi (2015, p. 113).

[2]UNGA Res 3281 (XXIX) (12 December 1974) UN Doc. A/RES/29/3281 (1974).

[3]Id., Article 2(c): 'Each State has the right: …To nationalize, expropriate or transfer ownership of foreign property, in which case appropriate compensation should be paid by the State adopting such measures, taking into account its relevant laws and regulations and all circumstances that the State considers pertinent'.

[4]Pauwelyn (2014, p. 372).

[5]According to the UNCTAD World Investment Report (2016), as of the end of 2015 the total number of IIAs is 3,304. UNCTAD (2016, p. 101).

[6]Salacuse (2010, p. 427).

[7]Wälde and Kolo (2001, p. 811).

2 The Rise of Investment Disputes

Nonetheless, in practice, IIAs entail conflicts of interest between the investor and the host state over the nature of the control that could be exercised over the foreign investment. Essentially, the investor's interest is to control its investment within a stable and predictable legal regime, while the host state seeks to exert its sovereign power to define its policies. This conflicting interest poses a big challenge to the policy-makers in Asian countries, because in developing their economies there is the greater need for the governments to adopt a milder approach of progressive liberalisation. In other words, policy-makers in developing countries need to retain greater policy space than that in developed countries so that they can formulate policies in a flexible manner as the countries develop. Also the concern over the loss of sovereignty is relevant in this context—with respect to the pre-establishment phase, the starting point of general international law on foreign investment is that sovereign states have the right to decide whether to open their economies to foreign investors and to determine the modalities for its admission and establishment, which is a 'prerogative deriving from national sovereignty'.[8] With the rapid development of international investment law, increasing attention is paid to the need for the balance between the domestic and international legal frameworks seeking to promote foreign investment on the one hand, and the laws and policies necessary to regulate the conduct of investors and investments to protect legitimate public interests, on the other.[9]

At the centre of this issue, there are concerns over investor-state arbitration. While the investment regime has been construed largely through bilateral, rather than multilateral, negotiations, an increasing number of investment treaties have similar structures, purposes, and principles in part due to the fact that individual negotiations have proceeded on the basis of treaty models prepared by capital-exporting countries. The most significant similarities include the provision of international arbitration as the ISDS mechanism. Investment arbitration is deemed to be a crucial feature of foreign investment protection because it provides access to a neutral forum for the settlement of disputes. Investor-state arbitration was welcomed not only as an alternative to the domestic courts of the host state, but also as a technique that 'depoliticises' the disputes, by removing them from the intergovernmental political relationship between the home state and the host state.[10] On the other hand, investor-state arbitration that operates outside the domestic legal

[8]Sacerdoti (2000, p. 105).

[9]Recent discussions about investor-state dispute settlement in the context of the negotiation of the Transatlantic Trade and Investment Partnership (TTIP) most vividly demonstrate this point. See, e.g., Opinion of the European Economic and Social Committee, see Investor Protection and Investor to State Dispute Settlement in EU Trade and Investment Agreements with Third Countries, REX/411. www.eesc.europa.eu/?i=portal.en.rex-opinions.35922. Accessed May 27, 2015. See also Waibel et al. (2010).

[10]Shihata (1986, p. 1). Cf. Roberts (2014, p. 1).

framework of the host state can be considered to be an unwarranted interference with the sovereignty of the host state. This is especially so given that investor-state disputes have evolved from traditional expropriation cases to conflicts arising out of regulatory interference with various aspects of the investment, and therefore they are now considered to be 'regulatory disputes within the public law sphere'.[11]

3 Rules and Dispute Settlement: Relevance to Asia-Pacific Region

As noted, recent years have witnessed the rapidly changing dynamics of foreign investment and trade in Asia. Countries such as China, India, Thailand, Vietnam, Malaysia, Singapore, and South Korea are now increasingly investing abroad; at the same time, many developing countries in the region such as Myanmar, Indonesia and the Philippines continue to leverage foreign investment for economic growth. These trends raise new policy questions for the home and host countries which are seeking to maximise the benefits of such outward and inward investment, while also mitigating the potential social and environmental costs. The new opportunities and risks set a challenge for policy-makers, researchers and civil society to develop effective and innovative governance frameworks in order to achieve sustainable and inclusive growth.

Foreign investment has become increasingly important in shaping the international economic landscape.[12] Asia is now the world's centre for foreign investment. FDI inflows into the region have surpassed half a trillion dollars, establishing its status as the largest recipient region of the world.[13] Last year, developing Asian states saw inflows increase by 16% to USD 541 billion—a record.[14] Additionally, Asian economies have made significant contributions to global investment outflows.[15] Between 2009 and 2016 developing Asia contributed to an average of 23.5% of total global FDI outflow, the highest being 30.2% in 2014 and the lowest percentage 20.2% in 2009. The top five home economies for OFDI as of 2015 in developing Asia are as follows: China at USD 127.6 billion (an increase of 3.6% compared to 2014); Hong Kong China at USD 55.1 billion (a decrease of 55.9% compared to 2014); Singapore at USD 35.5 billion (a decrease of 9.3% compared to

[11]Kingsbury et al. (2005, p. 15). See also Van Harten (2007), ch. I; Burke-White and von Staden (2010, p. 283), Hansen (2010, p. 523). Burke-White and Staden provide a definition of public law arbitrations as 'arbitrations for which the critical issue on which the outcome turns to be whether the state has the power and legal ability to undertake regulation in the public interest' (Burke-White and von Staden 2010, p. 285).

[12]Elkins and Simmons (2006, pp. 811, 843).

[13]http://unctad.org/en/PublicationsLibrary/wir2016_Overview_en.pdf.

[14]http://unctad.org/en/PublicationsLibrary/wir2016_Overview_en.pdf.

[15]Vivienne Bath and Luke Nottage.

2014); Republic of Korea at USD 27.6 billion (a decrease of 1.4% compared to 2014); and Taiwan at USD 14.8% (an increase of 16.2% compared to 2014).[16]

At the basis of their growing international significance there exist the efforts by Asian states to attract and retain foreign investment.[17] Such efforts include the reform of domestic legal frameworks towards further liberalisation and removal of FDI restrictions in increasingly sensitive sectors, and notably the establishment of the Asian Infrastructure Investment Bank.[18] The development of regional trade and investment links within Asia has also expanded rapidly, with Asia now being second only to Europe in terms of the volume of intra-regional trade.[19]

Asian States have also concluded a prolific number of IIAs[20] including mega regional trade agreements with investment chapters like the Trans-Pacific Economic Partnership Agreement (TPPA), the ASEAN Comprehensive Investment Agreement (ACIA) and the continued negotiation of the Regional Cooperation Economic Partnership (RCEP) involving ASEAN Member States and parties to the ASEAN + 6 regional trade agreements.[21] Indeed, more than a third of IIAs currently in existence involve Asian signatories.[22]

4 Explaining Concerns and Criticism

Having said this, the growing number of investment arbitration cases has also generated increasing concerns over the ISDS system. Some of the most controversial cases that underlie these concerns involve countries in the Asia-Pacific

---

[16]See *World Investment Report* 2016 (UNCTAD 2016). http://unctad.org/Sections/dite_dir/docs/WIR2016/wir16_fdi_Asia_en.pdf. Accessed 15 October 2016.

[17]http://unctad.org/en/pages/newsdetails.aspx?OriginalVersionID=1218&Sitemap_x0020_Taxonomy=UNCTAD%20Home;#6;#Investment and Enterprise.

[18]See Asian Infrastructure Investment Bank, *Articles of Agreement* (2015). http://www.aiib.org/html/aboutus/Basic_Documents/; ASEAN *Master Plan on ASEAN Connectivity* (2011). http://www.asean.org/resources/publications/asean-publications/item/master-plan-on-asean-connectivity-2; National Development and Reform Commission, Ministry of Foreign Affairs, Ministry of Commerce of People's Republic of China, *Vision and Actions on Jointly Building Silk Road Economic Belt and 21st-Century Maritime Silk Road* (2015). http://en.ndrc.gov.cn/newsrelease/201503/t20150330_669367.html; Ministry of Foreign Affairs of Republic of Korea, *EurAsia Initiative* (2015). http://www.mofa.go.kr/ENG/image/common/title/res/0707_eurasia_bro.pdf. See also http://unctad.org/en/pages/newsdetails.aspx?OriginalVersionID=1218&Sitemap_x0020_Taxonomy=UNCTAD%20Home;#6;#Investmentand Enterprise.

[19]'Connecting with Asia: How do we Deepen our Integration into the Region?' *Speech by the Secretary to the Treasury of New Zealand* (2016). http://www.treasury.govt.nz/publications/media-speeches/speeches/connectingwithasia.

[20]Bath and Nottage (2011, p. 1).

[21]For some discussion on the investment chapters in the ASEAN + 6 regional trade agreements and the ACIA, see Chaisse and Jusoh (2016).

[22]China has concluded the largest number of investment treaties, followed by South Korea and India. Chaisse and Hamanaka (2014, p. 3), Bryan Cave (2015).

region. In Philip Morris Asia v. Australia, Australia's plain packaging regime for the sale of tobacco products was challenged as a breach of investment protection obligations under the Hong Kong—Australia BIT. In particular, the claimant alleged that the plain packaging deprives it of the value of its investments—its brands, branding, and intellectual property—in Australia, and constitutes expropriation. While the claim was dismissed at the jurisdictional phase,[23] this case sparked a discussion about the so-called 'regulatory chill' as a possible result of the threat of investor-state arbitration.[24] Abaclat v. Argentina,[25] Ambiente v. Argentina[26] and Alemmani v. Argentina[27] are the cases brought by the holders of Argentina's sovereign bonds. The majority of the tribunals in Abaclat and Ambiente cases concluded that the rights under financial instruments that are governed by foreign law and not related to specific economic projects in the host state still qualify as investment under the Italy–Argentina BIT. This reading of the definition of investment has been criticised for being overly broad and leading to the unwarranted expansion of the scope of subject-matter jurisdiction of investment arbitration tribunals.[28]

Some stakeholders argue that the system unduly favours the interests of foreign investors, and borders encroachment into the sovereignty of the host state. However, as examined in Chapter "China's Regulation of Foreign Direct Investment", the oft-stated concern over the pro-investor bias amongst arbitral tribunals is not well substantiated by evidence. On the other hand, the lack of consistent reasoning that sufficiently demonstrates their deferential approach might well be observed in the investment arbitration case law,[29] which has led to the argument that investment treaties and tribunal decisions do not take into account the

---

[23]Philip Morris Asia Limited v. The Commonwealth of Australia, UNCITRAL, PCA Case No. 2012-12, Award on Jurisdiction and Admissibility of 17 December 2015.

[24]Opinion of the European Economic and Social Committee, see Investor Protection and Investor to State Dispute Settlement in EU Trade and Investment Agreements with Third Countries (2015) OJ C/332/45, para 7.9: '7.9 The mere threat of a case under ISDS can create a regulatory chill which dissuades governments from regulating in the public interest for fear of litigation and resulting penalty charges. For example, the New Zealand government has put on hold its own tobacco plain packaging law pending the decision on the Philip Morris case against Australia.'.

[25]*Abaclat & Others v. Argentina*, ICSID Case No. ARB/07/5, Decision on Jurisdiction and Admissibility (4 August 2011).

[26]*Ambiente Ufficio S.p.A. & Others v. Argentina*, ICSID Case No. ARB/08/9, Decision on Jurisdiction and Admissibility (8 February 2013). The proceedings were discontinued on 28 May 2015, for lack of payment of the costs of the arbitration by the claimant investors (Regulation 14 (3) (d) of the ICSID Administrative and Financial Regulations).

[27]*Giovanni Alemanni & Others v. Argentina*, ICSID Case No. ARB/07/8, Decision on Jurisdiction and Admissibility (17 November 2014). The proceedings were discontinued on 14 December 2015 for the same reason as Ambiente v. Argentina.

[28]Abaclat and Ambiente decisions were accompanied by strong dissenting opinions from Abi-Saab and Torres Bernárdez, respectively. See generally Waibel (2011). See also Ishikawa (2015, p. 115).

[29]Kurtz (2012, pp. 686, 688).

need of the government to develop policies to meet the development needs of these countries. Accordingly, there is also the argument that the issues concerning the host state's regulatory power should be brought to the domestic legal system rather to an international tribunal.

With all these concerns, some countries are seeking to reform the way investment treaties are drafted and negotiated and to some extent terminate investment treaties which are expiring. For example, as examined in Chapter 16, India now seeks to re-open negotiations of the existing BITs on the basis of its new model BIT of 2015. Indonesia has also terminated, or expressed its intention to terminate, existing BITs with several countries. The objective of their new IIA policy is to provide for a balanced provision taking into account the reality of current investment flows, investment needs and the importance of flexibility in the policy-making of the host countries. Nevertheless, despite the criticisms of the ISDS, many of the new IIAs, including the mega regional trade agreements, continue to adopt ISDS provisions, with some innovative provisions, such as the fork-in-the road clause, qualifications of members of the tribunal and the need for the hearing to be open to public. Some new and future IIAs may also limit the application of ISDS to certain types of claims only, leaving the rest of the claims to be referred to the domestic court.

5 The Current Situation in Asia

The book aims to provide a detailed analysis of the contemporary Asian situation, i.e. the current trends and changes in the Asia-Pacific region with regard to existing investment rules, rule-making, and investment arbitration.

While a number of important studies have been published concerning the meaning and scope of investment standards, the practice of a few countries, and the practice of investor-state arbitration, there is rather limited literature on the regional trends in Asia and the Pacific. This is so even though this region of the world is highly important both in terms of rule-making with respect to foreign investment but also in terms of foreign investment expansion.

In terms of investment rule-making the Asia-Pacific region is pioneering innovative approaches in the twenty-first century and high-standard IIAs either in the form of BITs or free trade agreements (FTAs). For example, in February this year 12 countries in the Asia-Pacific region signed the Trans-Pacific Economic Partnership Agreement (TPPA). While its entry into force depends on ratification by the signatory states, the signing of the TPPA is one of the most significant events in economic, political and legal terms in the region since the beginning of the twenty-first century. Its importance extends well beyond the economic impact: it is significant that 12 member states that are in different stages of development and have different legal, economic and political systems have successfully agreed on a set of rules and principles governing international trade and investment. Interest is also being shown by other APEC members who are seeking to join the wide regional pact. The TPPA's investment chapter not only liberalises investment sectors in the signatory states but also introduces more detailed investor-state dispute settlement provisions that seek to address the concerns over the system, such as the role of the TPPA Commission in treaty interpretation, the qualifications of arbitrators, and the opening of hearings to the public. In addition, the Asia-Pacific region is seeing the negotiation of another mega FTA containing an investment chapter, in the form of the RCEP. The RCEP consists of ASEAN member states and its regional dialogue partners, namely, Australia, China, India, Japan, South Korea, and New Zealand. It is interesting to see how the RCEP will further develop investment rule-making in the region, where many of the RCEP negotiating parties are also parties to the TPPA. There could be convergence of international investment rules in the two mega agreements. In addition to the TPPA and the RCEP, the negotiations of a BIT between the largest and the second largest economy in the world, that is the USA and China, are in progress.

Looking at the ASEAN, the next ten years will see the transformation of the ASEAN region into an ASEAN Community; this process will include the plan to make ASEAN an investment hub and a major player in the global economy through the ASEAN Community 2025 Blueprint 'Forging Ahead Together'.[30] ASEAN plans to be a major investment and economic powerhouse through its own ASEAN Community Blueprint. In addition, ASEAN member states are also part of the TPPA and the RCEP. Newer ASEAN member states, such as Lao PDR, Myanmar, and Vietnam, are also opening and modernising their economies, to attract more investment and to enhance their economic competitiveness. Moreover, one should not forget that small countries such as Timor-Leste aim to be part of ASEAN, and the Pacific Island Nations are also working on their own trade and investment arrangements through PACER Plus negotiations. These recent trends and developments in the Asia-Pacific region form an important context in the discussions on IIAs in the region.

6 Conclusion

Developing Asia continues to be account for an important part of global investment, both as the main recipient of FDI and as one of the major contributors to OFDI. The changes in the nature of FDI flows in developing Asia has also led to changes in the nature of the investment regime in these countries. In the earlier phase of development, mainly in the 1960s and 1970s, many of these countries had to accept the terms of the IIAs imposed on them by the capital exporting countries, causing many of the Asian countries to accept one-sided deals that were designed to protect the interests of foreign investors and their investments. However, in recent times, the increased number of ISDS cases against Asian states and the increase in OFDI from

[30]See, for example, Jusoh (2014).

Asian states to other parts of the world, including to the developed nations who were previously the exporters of capital to the Asian states, have changed the dynamic of the global investment regimes. Asian states are more careful about providing protection to investors and their investments whilst looking for a higher level of flexibility in the treaty language in order to allow a higher flexibility in policy making. Asian states which are sources of OFDI are also looking towards a higher level of liberalisation and market access in the countries where they are investing, although the sectors of economy they invest in are more limited compared to investors from the developed economies. As the Asian economies continue to prosper, many of these countries are busy in treaty-making, either in the form of IIAs or an investment chapter in the mega regional trade agreements. Among the treaties being negotiated are the RCEP, Malaysian–EU FTA, Japan–EU Economic Partnership Agreement, and Japan–China–Korea FTA. Next in the pipeline is the potential of a Free Trade Agreement of Asia and the Pacific under the auspices of APEC, which will cover all the 27 APEC economies. If the TPPA takes many years to negotiate, an APEC-wide FTA will take longer to negotiate and to implement and it will probably be the second half of the 21st century before it is being fully implemented.

Although there is more focus on the mega regional trade agreements, the actual action on the changes and reform to take place will be more at the regional or sub-regional level based on existing treaties. In ASEAN for example, the ASEAN Comprehensive Investment Agreement, or ACIA, is the standard bearer in several areas, such as liberalisation, protection of investors and their investments, and investment facilitation and transparency. ACIA has introduced several innovative provisions such as the qualification of arbitrators in the ISDS arbitral tribunal, the formation of consultation between host state and home state on the question of taxation policy and expropriation and what are the conditions for an indirect expropriation to take place as outlined in Annex 2 of the Agreement. The ongoing investment policy reforms in the newer ASEAN member states including Myanmar, Lao PDR and Cambodia use ACIA as the benchmark. The recently passed Myanmar Investment Law adopts most of the standards set in ACIA into domestic investment policy. Even Timor-Leste which is an ASEAN candidate country uses ACIA as the benchmark in their investment policy reform. However, for further research, it will be important to find out how the ASEAN 6 and Vietnam view ACIA's provisions in these countries' investment policy reforms. Most of the ASEAN 6 and Vietnam are both the recipient of FDIs and also contribute to the OFDI into many ASEAN Member States. It is also important to note that most of the ASEAN 6, apart from Indonesia, do not have a specific law on investments. Any examination of the need to adopt ACIA into domestic investment regimes will involve deeper research by looking at an array of laws, such as the Investment Promotion Law, the law in incentives and the Constitution.

References

ASEAN. 2011. Master plan on ASEAN connectivity. http://www.asean.org/resources/publications/asean-publications/item/master-plan-on-asean-connectivity-2.

Asian Infrastructure Investment Bank. 2015. Articles of agreement. http://www.aiib.org/html/aboutus/Basic_Documents/.

Bath, Vivienne, and Luke Nottage. 2011. Introduction. In *Investment law and dispute resolution law and practice in Asia*, ed. Vivienne Bath and Luke Nottage, 1. UK: Routledge.

Bath, Vivienne, and Luke Nottage, Asian investment and the growth of regional investment agreements. In *Routledge handbook of Asian law*, ed. Christoph Antons. UK: Routledge (forthcoming).

Burke-White, William W., and Andreas, von Staden. 2010. Private litigation in a public law sphere: The standard of review in investor-state arbitrations. *Yale Journal of International Law* 35: 283.

Bryan Cave. 2015. International investment arbitration in Asia—Year in review.

Chaisse, Julien, and Shintaro Hamanaka. 2014. The investment version of Asian noodle bowl-proliferation of agreements, 3. Asian Development Bank, Working paper No. 128.

Chaisse, Julien, and Shintaro Jusoh. 2016. *The ASEAN comprehensive investment agreement: The regionalisation of laws and policy on foreign investment*. London: Elgar.

Connecting with Asia. 2016. How do we deepen our integration into the region? Speech by the Secretary to the Treasury of New Zealand. http://www.treasury.govt.nz/publications/media-speeches/speeches/connectingwithasia.

Elkins, Zachary, Guzman Andrew T., and Beth A., Simmons. 2006. Competing for capital: The diffusion of bilateral investment treaties, 1960–2000. *International Organization* 60: 811, 843.

Hansen, Robin F. 2010. Parallel proceedings in investor-state treaty arbitration: Responses for treaty-drafters, arbitrators and parties. *The Modern Law Review* 73: 523.

Investor protection and investor to state dispute settlement in EU trade and investment agreements with third countries, REX/411. www.eesc.europa.eu/?i=portal.en.rex-opinions.35922. Accessed 27 May 2015.

Ishikawa, Tomoko. 2015. Keeping interpretation in investment treaty arbitration "on track": The role of state parties. In *Reshaping the investor-state dispute settlement system: Journeys for the 21st century*, ed. J. Kalicki and A. Joubin-Bret, 115. The Netherlands: Brill/Nijhoff.

Jusoh, Sufian. 2014. ASEAN investment agreements: A tool of economic diplomacy in the meeting the objectives of ASEAN economic community blueprint. *Journal of Diplomacy and Foreign Relations*.

Kingsbury, Benedict, et al. 2005. The emergence of global administrative law. *Law and Contemporary Problems* 68: 15.

Kurtz, Jürgen. 2012. The shifting landscape of international investment law and its commentary. *American Journal of International Law* 106 (686): 688.

Ministry of Foreign Affairs of Republic of Korea. 2015. EurAsia initiative. http://www.mofa.go.kr/ENG/image/common/title/res/0707_eurasia_bro.pdf.

National Development and Reform Commission, Ministry of Foreign Affairs, Ministry of Commerce of People's Republic of China. 2015. Vision and actions on jointly building silk road economic belt and 21st-century maritime silk road. http://en.ndrc.gov.cn/newsrelease/201503/t20150330_669367.html.

Olmos Giupponi, Belén Olmos. 2015. The protection of foreign direct investment in Latin America: Where do we stand on international arbitration? *Journal of International Arbitration* 32: 113.

Pauwelyn, Joost. 2014. At the edge of chaos? *ICSID Review: Foreign Investment Law Journal* 29: 372.

Roberts, Anthea. 2014. State-to-state investment treaty arbitration: A hybrid theory of interdependent rights and shared interpretive authority. *Harvard International Law Journal* 51: 1.

Sacerdoti, Giorgio. 2000. The admission and treatment of foreign investment under recent bilateral and regional treaties. *The Journal of World Investment: Law, Economics, Politics* 1: 105.

Salacuse, Jeswald W. 2010. The emerging global regime for investment. *Harvard International Law Journal* 51: 427.

Shihata, Ibrahim F.I. 1986. Towards a greater depoliticization of investment disputes: The roles of ICSID and MIGA. *ICSID Review* 1: 1.

UNCTAD. 2016. World investment report 2016, 101.

Van Harten, Gus. 2007. *Investment treaty arbitration and public law*, Ch I. Oxford: Oxford University Press.

Waibel, Michael. 2011. *Sovereign defaults before international courts & tribunals*. Cambridge: Cambridge University Press.

Waibel, Michael, et al. (eds.). 2010. *The backlash against investment arbitration*. The Netherlands: Kluwer.

Wälde, Thomas, and Abba Kolo. 2001. Environmental regulation, investment protection and "regulatory taking" in international law. *ICLQ* 50: 811.

World Investment Report. 2016. UNCTAD. http://unctad.org/Sections/dite_dir/docs/WIR2016/wir16_fdi_Asia_en.pdf. Accessed 15 Oct 2016.

Shaping Globalization: Recent Trends in Asia-Pacific Foreign Direct Investment

Bekzod Abdullaev and Douglas H. Brooks

1 Introduction

Foreign direct investment (FDI) plays an important role in achieving economic growth in developing economies, especially in economies with insufficient domestic capital. FDI acts as a potential source of capital, foreign exchange, skills, market access, employment, and linkages for growth in other areas of the host (and possibly source) economy. It potentially increases connectivity in the host economy and opportunities to participate in global value chains. The chances of realizing FDI's potential depend on the investment climate, the host economy's stage(s) in the development process and its macroeconomic stability, and the nature of the FDI itself. FDI may be from a private or public sector source (including state owned enterprises), may take the form of greenfield investments or mergers and acquisitions (M&As), and may be motivated by a search for natural resources, greater efficiency, expansion of markets, linkages, or strategic benefits. All of these factors influence the degree to which, and the point(s) at which, the investment process is amenable to policy influence.

Until the 1980s FDI by multinational corporations was generally viewed as impinging on national sovereignty and security in developing economies.[1] However, over the last four decades restrictions on FDI have been significantly eased in response to deregulation, technological change, expansion of trade and production networks, establishment of economic blocs and globalisation, as well as increasing evidence of FDI's potentially positive effects on the host economy. Some

[1]Brooks et al. (2003).

B. Abdullaev (✉) · D.H. Brooks
Australian APEC Study Centre, RMIT University, Melbourne, Australia
e-mail: b.abdullaev@outlook.com

D.H. Brooks
e-mail: dofrobro@gmail.com

J. Chaisse et al. (eds.), *Asia's Changing International Investment Regime*,
International Law and the Global South, DOI 10.1007/978-981-10-5882-0_3

East and Southeast Asian economies (Hong Kong, Singapore and Malaysia) liberalised their investment regimes in the 1960s, while other Asian economies (Republic of Korea, China and India) and Latin America economies liberalised their markets in the 1980s and 1990s. African economies followed, deregulating investment policies to attract more FDI in the 1990s.[2] These changes enabled M&As to be attractive in the telecommunications, electricity, other public utilities and financial services sectors, and government privatisation programmes provided opportunities for international greenfield investments.

The empirical literature on the impact of FDI on a host economy provides mixed views. Not all of the effects of FDI are positive, and impacts are often amplified for local communities where the investments occur. Studies supporting the positive effects of FDI on economic growth postulate that FDI stimulates technological change through the adoption of foreign technology[3] and know-how leading to technological spillovers, increasing returns to specialisation,[4] productivity growth[5,6] and economic growth within the host economy. Other research[7,8,9] finds that FDI may crowd out domestic investment, heighten vulnerability to external shocks and dependence, distort resource allocation[10] and lead to uncompetitive practices by foreign affiliates and domestic firms. Particular concerns have arisen concerning the impacts of FDI on local communities.[11,12,13] Nevertheless, the consensus is that FDI aligned with host economy-specific advantages has the potential to increase consumer welfare and employment, raise labour and environmental standards, and contribute to improved living standards and poverty alleviation.[14,15]

Global FDI flows experienced a five-fold expansion from US$204 billion in 1990 to US$1.2 trillion in 2014 and are currently the largest form of cross-border capital flows (Fig. 4). But the trajectory during this period was not uniform or continuous. A rapid surge was observed until 2000, a reduction until the mid-2000s and an upward trend afterwards. North-North FDI flows were dominant from the 1990s through the dotcom boom period and North-South flows trended upwards from the early 2000s. Developing economies, especially from Asia, appeared

[2]Miyake and Sass (2000).

[3]Findlay (1978, pp. 1–16).

[4]Rivera-Batiz and Rivera-Batiz (1991, pp. 287–307).

[5]Helpman et al. (2004, pp. 300–16).

[6]Yeaple (2008).

[7]Kentor (1998, pp. 1024–1046).

[8]Aitken and Harrison (1999, pp. 605–618).

[9]Braunstein and Epstein (2002).

[10]Boyd and Smith (1992, pp. 409–32).

[11]Brooks and Hill (2004).

[12]Figlio and Blonigen (2000, pp. 48: 338–63).

[13]Organisation for Economic Co-operation and Development (OECD) (2002).

[14]Rugman and Doh (2008).

[15]Sauvant and Mallampally (2015, pp. 237–268).

noticeable on the world stage as international investors on a larger scale from 2002 onwards. Since 2010, developing economies began receiving more than half of the world's FDI inflows, reflecting the gradual shift of the global economy's center of gravity toward developing countries, globalization of capital markets and the growing prominence of developing economies in global supply chain linkages. As indicated in Fig. 1, inflows and outflows from developing economies have been more steadily increasing in recent decades than those from more developed economies, signalling one contribution from developing economies to macroeconomic stability during the global financial crisis.

This chapter reviews recent trends in FDI flows by region, national income level, economic bloc, and sectors with particular attention to developments in the Asia-Pacific region. It is structured as follows. Section 2 provides background information about macro trends in FDI by region, modes of entry and sector. Section 3 focuses the discussion on FDI trends in Asia-Pacific economies by economy and economic blocks. This is followed by an overview of FDI diversity in Sect. 4, based on a new measure of such diversity. Section 5 concludes the chapter.

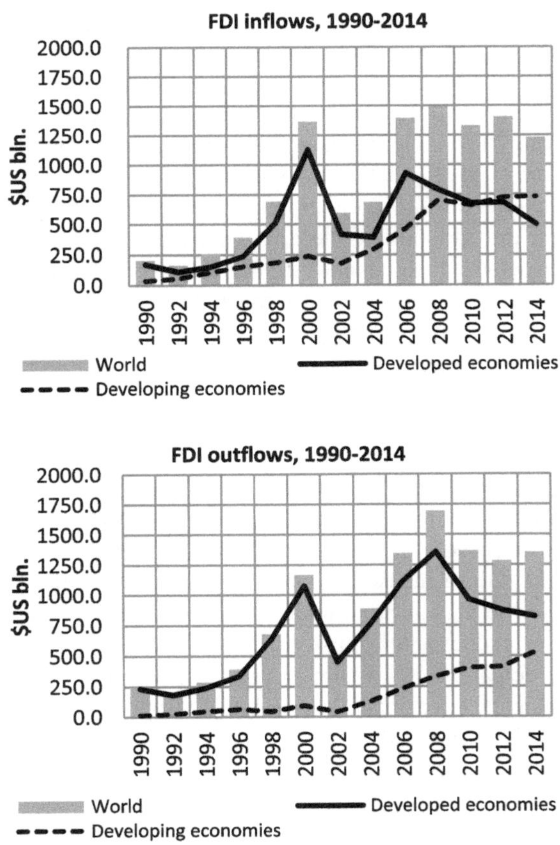

Fig. 1 FDI inflows and outflows, 1990–2014. *Source* UNCTADStat, 2015; Authors' calculations

2 Macro-trends in FDI

2.1 Regional Developments

The levels of FDI flows across different regions have changed significantly over time. Inflows of FDI have increasingly favoured Asia over the past two and a half decades with a slight reduction observed in the developed world, though with differences across economies. Developing Asia now invests more abroad than any other region. Meanwhile, East and Southeast Asia continues to be the largest recipient region. China has come to play a particularly important role in FDI during recent decades, both as a destination and as a source. In 2014, the latest year with available data at time of writing, China was the largest recipient of FDI inflows, receiving US$ 129 billion. At the same time its FDI outflows were nearly as large, reaching US$ 116 billion.

Figure 2 reflects changes in FDI stocks between 1990 and 2014, taking into account net new flows, valuation changes, write-offs, reclassifications and other adjustments. By 2014 European economies held almost half of the world's FDI inward stock, followed by North America, Asia, Latin America and the Caribbean, Oceania, Africa and Middle East. Compared to 1990, a significant rise was observed in Asia from 14 to 20% of the global FDI stock, a slight increase in Latin America and the Caribbean from 5 to 7%, substantial reductions in North America from 29 to 23%, and a relative decline in Europe from 44 to 42% and in Oceania from 4 to 3% between 1990 and 2014. The African share of FDI stock hasn't changed despite Africa's regional approach to enhancing economic development and the adoption of the Lagos Plan of Action in 1980. In general, Africa's challenges with peace and security; free movement of persons, goods, capital and services; agriculture; and infrastructure and energy have kept FDI policy reforms a relatively lower priority.[16]

2.2 Modes of Entry

The value of international cross-border M&A and greenfield investment activity experienced a rapid increase from the 1990s, and especially during the 2000s, not only due to internalisation benefits, operational synergies and strategic value but also the change in attitude in some economies towards take-overs, easing of barriers, reduction of transaction costs, deregulation of financial markets and a greater participation of investment banks in M&A deals. Moreover, technological developments have made it possible for multinational firms to manage cross-border supply chains and centralized purchasing for more than one economy, especially in

[16]UNCTAD (2012).

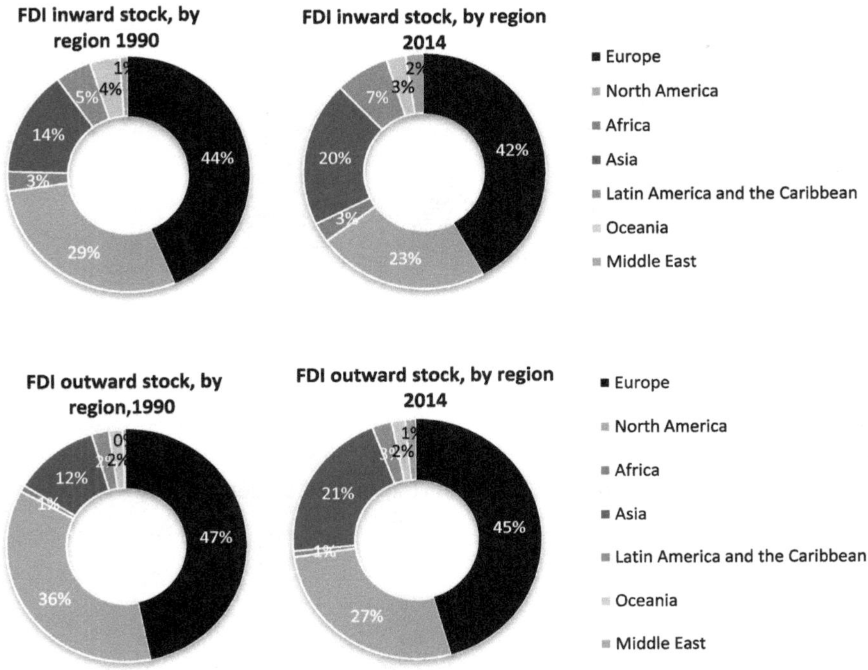

Fig. 2 FDI inward and outward stock, by region. *Source* UNCTADStat, 2015; Authors' calculations

the retail sector, and increasing returns to scale in R&D accelerated M&A activities in the pharmaceutical and chemical industries.[17]

Levels of cross-border M&A and greenfield investments since 1990 are shown in Fig. 3, distinguished between M&A and greenfield modes of entry. The value of international cross-border M&A activity rose very rapidly to attain record levels in 1999, followed by a sharp reduction until 2004. The trend was dominated by Europe and North America and the gradual emergence of the Asia Pacific region in the mid-2000s with the key investors being from Japan, followed by Singapore, Hong Kong and China.

As Fig. 3 reveals, greenfield investments expanded gradually and reached US $1.5 trillion before the Global Financial Crisis beginning in 2008, but then declined to average pre-crisis levels by 2013–2014. In contrast to M&A, destinations of greenfield investments were led by Asia, followed by Europe, North America, Oceania, Middle East and Africa with investments in Africa showing promising signs of expansion. Developing economies now account for about two thirds of greenfield FDI inflows.

---

[17]Miyake and Sass (2000).

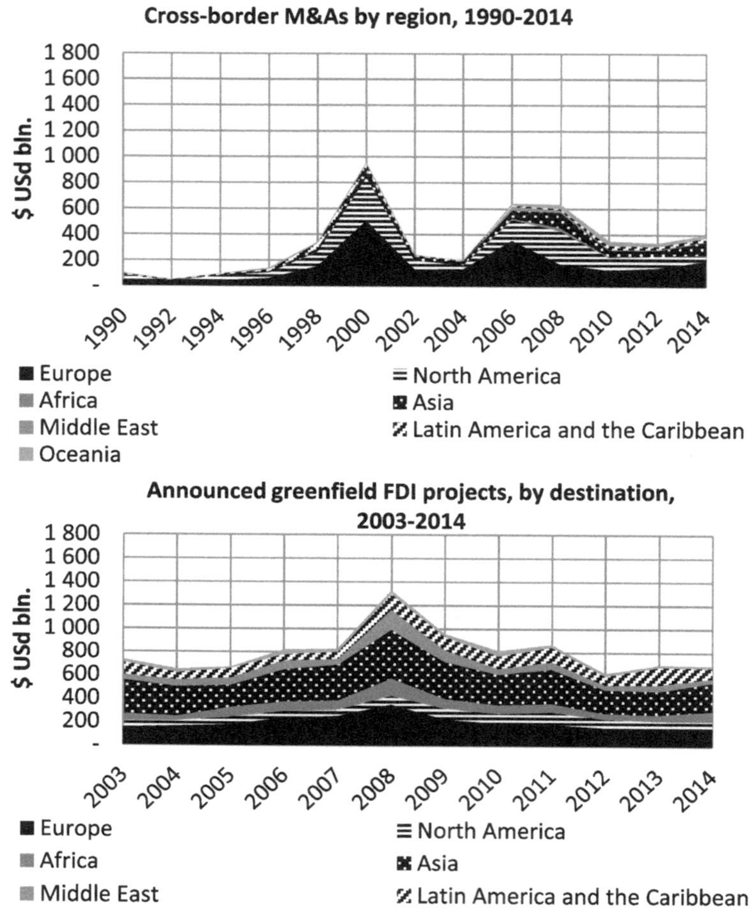

Fig. 3 FDI inflows by mode of entry, by region. *Source* UNCTADStat; fDi markets database, 2015; Authors' calculations

Figure 4 presents the distribution of M&A and greenfield investments across primary, manufacturing and service sectors, again separated by mode of entry. M&As were mainly concentrated in the service sectors (e.g. telecommunications) during 1990–2014 whereas manufacturing was attractive for greenfield investments over the same period, although in the mid-2000s service sector greenfield investments overtook those in primary and manufacturing sectors. There has been a shift over time towards service sector FDI due to liberalization in the sector, increasing tradability of services, growth of global value chains, and the normal development process of structural transformation with increasing shares of services in output and employment. By 2012, services accounted for about 63% of the global FDI stock, more than twice manufacturing's 26% share.

Fig. 4 FDI inflows by mode of entry, by sector. *Source* UNCTADStat; fDi markets database, 2015; Authors' calculations

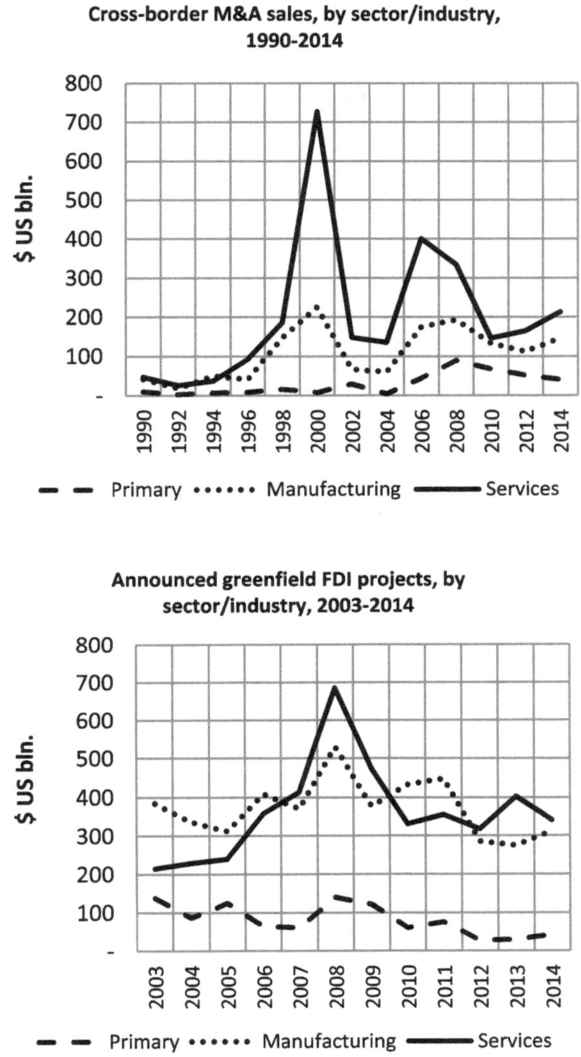

2.3 *Global Sectoral Trends*

The composition of FDI flows has shifted from natural resource seeking FDI towards knowledge-intensive/service based activities. Table 1 shows estimated global inflows into primary, manufacturing and service sectors in 1990–92 and 2010–12. FDI was already skewed towards manufacturing and services in 1990–92, partly reflecting food security concerns related to FDI in agriculture, but increasingly towards services over the past 20 years. This was especially true in developing economies, while there was a slight reduction in developed economies' share of global services FDI. Economies such as India have been able to attract increasing amounts of FDI in high value-added services, and other developing economies (e.g. Philippines), have also attracted FDI in particular service sectors such as contact centers.

East Asia and South-East Asian economies have been able to attract significantly more efficiency-seeking FDI in manufacturing (electronics, textiles) than other developing economies. Meanwhile, a number of Latin American and Caribbean economies have attracted large-scale natural resource-seeking FDI and services FDI through privatizations, and efficiency-seeking FDI in labor intensive manufacturing. Africa has attracted mainly natural resource-seeking FDI, though some economies attracted relatively more manufacturing (e.g. FDI in the automobile industry in South Africa; garment factories in Lesotho).[18]

Over the twenty five years following the collapse of the Soviet Union, transition economies carried out massive reforms aimed at establishing open market economies. Economies in the former Soviet Union (FSU) bloc underwent three main stages: (i) stabilization and structural adjustment programs; (ii) reform of their legal and regulatory framework; and (iii) implementing industrial competitiveness and regional cooperation policies to reap economies of scale in production and to increase firm-level capability building. Investment liberalization prompted by the obsolescence of older capital assets began in the mid- to late-1990s after liberalization of trade and other international transactions.[19] During the early years of transition FDI inflows were concentrated in the primary (natural resource-based) sector, but even then service sector FDI increased from 0.1 to 3.3% of global inward FDI from 1990–92 to 2010–12.

Many developing economies look to FDI as a means of promoting structural transformation. In this context it has traditionally been thought of as primarily aimed at low-skill and low-wage manufacturing and assembly activities, such as textiles, garments, and electronics assembly. In reality, most FDI in developing economies targets more advanced industrial sectors, and its skill-intensity has been accelerating over time.[20]

As shown in Table 2, the ratio of FDI flows to semi-skilled relative to low-skilled sectors in developing economies was nearly nine, or nearly three times greater in 2010–2012 than it was twenty years earlier (when it was already over three). Semi-skilled sectors include those such as industrial machinery, transportation equipment, medical devices and scientific instruments. The ratio of FDI flows to high-skilled relative to low-skilled sectors in developing economies was over 14, or more than twice the ratio twenty years earlier. These ratios are still well below those in developed economies, suggesting substantial room for even greater

---

[18]UNDESA, World Economic and Social Survey 2005: financing for development, (2005). United Nations Publications.

[19]UNCTAD (2012).

[20]Moran (2015, pp. 21–31).

Table 4.1 Estimated global inward FDI flows, by sector, 1990–1992 and 2010–2012

	1990–1992				2010–2012			
Sector	Developed countries (%)	Developing economies (%)	Transition economies (%)	World (%)	Developed countries (%)	Developing economies (%)	Transition economies (%)	World (%)
Total	74.8	24.4	0.8	100.0	57.7	37.3	5.0	100.0
Primary	5.1	2.6	0.5	8.2	4.3	4.6	0.8	9.7
Manufacturing	20.8	8.8	0.1	29.7	9.8	10.2	0.8	20.8
Services	44.0	11.1	0.1	55.1	40.6	21.9	3.3	65.7

Source UNCTAD, 2014

Table 4.2 Estimated global inward FDI flows in manufacturing sector by skill level, 1990–1992 and 2010–2012, mln USD

	1990–1992				2010–2012			
Sector/industry	Developed countries	Developing economies	Transition economies	World	Developed countries	Developing economies	Transition economies	World
Low skill sectors	2800	723	1	3524	620	2164	558	3342
Semi-skill sectors	5257	2396	43	7696	37,417	18,786	2746	58,949
High skill sectors	17,220	4482	74	21,777	70,387	31,604	7833	109,824
Ratio of semi skill to low skill	1.9	3.3	41.7	2.2	60.3	8.7	4.9	17.6
Ratio of high skill to low skill	6.1	6.2	71.3	6.2	113.4	14.6	14.1	32.9

Source UNCTAD, 2014

contributions to the structural transformation process. In part their growth reflects the rapid growth in global value chains, especially among Asia-Pacific economies, as a means of their exports and economic development.

3 FDI Trends in Asia-Pacific Economies

While Asia-Pacific remains the favoured destination for FDI among developing regions, and China remains by far the most significant destination in the region for aggregate flows, closer examination of the data reveals a more nuanced picture. The first panel in Table 3 shows the tremendous increase in FDI flows to top Asia-Pacific destinations. It also shows the emergence of India (and Kazakhstan) among the more prominent locations. The aggregate flows can be considered a rough proxy for FDI's contribution of foreign exchange, among the other potential benefits mentioned above.

Upon examining the second panel of Table 3 we see that the importance of China as a destination largely reflects the size of its population and hence (together with its rapidly rising income per capita) the size of its market. Measured by inflows per capita, a number of smaller economies have done relatively well in attracting FDI, and shown substantial improvement over time. Similarly, the bottom panel of Table 3 reflects the importance of FDI in supplementing domestic investment, as indicated by its share in gross fixed capital formation. Again, performance differs according to the measure used, but substantial increase over time is apparent.

3.1 Performance of Economic Blocs

Since the mid-2000s, FDI performance has varied across economic blocs. FDI inflows to the APEC, ASEAN and the proposed Regional Comprehensive Economic Partnership (RCEP) areas (all entirely or substantially in Asia-Pacific) have gradually increased as the economies in these regions became major and competitive global production centers, and at the same time have developed large intermediate and final demand for a wider range of products and services.

Inward FDI shrank by half between 2005 and 2014 in EU and the Transatlantic Trade and Investment Partnership (TTIP) regions. Other more developed economic blocs, including the Trans-Pacific Partnership (TPP), G20 (a grouping of larger economies rather than a trading bloc) and NAFTA, also experienced downturns during the same period (Table 4).

As for FDI outflows (Table 5), APEC, ASEAN and RCEP's shares in world FDI outflows more than doubled from their pre-crisis average, from 34 to 71%, from 3 to 6% and from 10 to 26%, respectively, by 2014. The shares of global investments from G20, NAFTA, and TPP also increased, albeit at a slower pace. Among

Table 4.3 Top ten destinations for FDI in developing Asia, 1990–2014

Average annual total FDI inflows (mln. USD)			
Economy	1990–1995		2010–2014
China	19610.5	China	122442.0
Singapore	6307.6	Hong Kong, China	82969.9
Hong Kong, China	4859.1	Singapore	58410.6
Malaysia	4654.8	India	30083.9
Indonesia	2164.3	Indonesia	18709.2
Thailand	2003.5	Kazakhstan	11728.8
Korea, Republic of	1326.4	Malaysia	10682.2
Taiwan	1221.8	Korea, Republic of	10286.3
Philippines	1028.3	Thailand	9218.3
Viet Nam	946.7	Viet Nam	8397.4
FDI as % of gross fixed capital formation			
Viet Nam	33.5	Hong Kong, China	135.5
Singapore	31.3	Singapore	79.6
Kazakhstan	23.9	Mongolia	60.5
Malaysia	19.4	Cambodia	56.9
Hong Kong, China	14.9	Kyrgyzstan	30.0
Cambodia	14.5	Brunei Darussalam	29.9
Kyrgyzstan	11.7	Kazakhstan	26.3
China	9.7	Myanmar	22.9
Maldives	7.7	Viet Nam	21.7
Philippines	6.4	Malaysia	14.8
Average FDI inflow per capita (USD)			
Singapore	1915.1	Hong Kong, China	11667.4
Hong Kong, China	810.3	Singapore	11006.6
Brunei Darussalam	349.4	Brunei Darussalam	1666.2
Malaysia	237.6	Mongolia	968.0
Taiwan	59.0	Kazakhstan	698.7
Kazakhstan	46.4	Turkmenistan	634.5
Thailand	34.6	Malaysia	368.0
Korea, Republic of	30.2	Korea, Republic of	207.3
Maldives	28.9	Thailand	137.0
Turkmenistan	25.1	Cambodia	109.6

Source UNCTADStat, 2015; Authors' calculations

economic blocs, the EU and TTIP shares in global outward FDI dropped from 55 to 21% and from 70 to 46%, respectively.

A number of recent and new regional cooperation initiatives are helping to boost Asia-Pacific's share. The Greater Mekong Subregion and the ASEAN Economic Community are contributing to formation of a large, more unified market in Southeast Asia which can join in triangular trade with the massive emerging

Table 4.4 Percentage share in global FDI inflows by trading bloc

	2005–07 average	2008	2009	2010	2011	2012	2013	2014
APEC	39	54	41	49	48	49	57	53
ASEAN	5	3	4	8	6	8	9	11
EU	43	21	33	27	28	26	23	21
G20	59	65	55	56	56	51	61	52
NAFTA	20	27	16	19	19	16	24	14
RCEP	14	20	19	22	21	23	24	30
TPP	26	35	24	29	28	29	35	28
TTIP	56	41	45	42	43	38	38	28

Source UNCTADStat, 2015

Table 4.5 Percentage share in global FDI outflows by trading bloc

	2005–07 average	2008	2009	2010	2011	2012	2013	2014
APEC	34	46	60	53	58	66	70	71
ASEAN	3	2	4	4	4	4	5	6
EU	55	44	32	34	33	25	22	21
G20	59	69	70	62	67	66	64	64
NAFTA	19	23	31	24	29	30	30	29
RCEP	10	17	20	18	18	24	25	26
TPP	25	34	43	34	40	44	44	43
TTIP	70	62	58	54	58	49	47	46

Source UNCTADStat, 2015

markets in China and India. China has introduced its "one belt, one road" initiative, supported by formation of the Asian Infrastructure Investment Bank and the New Development Bank (BRICS bank). Korea has introduced a Eurasia initiative for interregional cooperation and Japan has announced a US$ 110 billion initiative for infrastructure development, expected to be primarily in the region.[21] All of these new activities should contribute to growth and diversification in Asia-Pacific.

4 Diversity of FDI in the Asia-Pacific Region

The effects of FDI on the host economy depend on factors such as absorptive capacity, policy parameters and economic structure. FDI's contributions to production of new and/or advanced products may have direct effects on the composition of the host country's exports and make them more diversified and

[21]UNCTAD (2015).

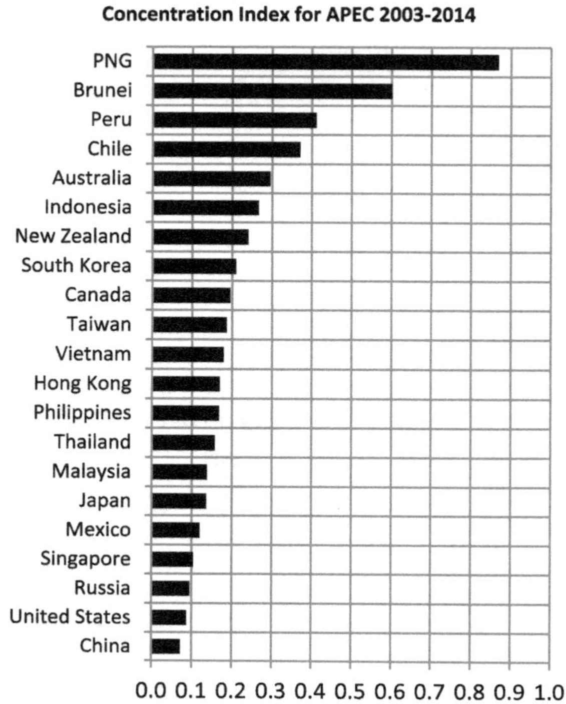

Fig. 5 Greenfield FDI concentration index 2003–2014. *Source* fDi markets (2015); Authors' calculations

sophisticated.[22] This can also lead to the transfer of new and/or more sophisticated productive capabilities to local firms.[23] Thus, it is more likely that diversified FDI will have positive spill-over effects, enhance a country's export potential, and help it integrate into Global Value Chains. Further, a limited based of FDI may signify lack of competiveness, raise vulnerability concerns of the concentrated sector(s) to external shocks, and jeopardize the stability of economic growth.

A simple FDI concentration index for APEC economies is presented below. The FDI concentration index is calculated according to the formula:

$$CI_{FDI} = \sum_{i=1}^{39} w_i^2$$

where i is the sector and w is the share of the sector's investments in total FDI. The results of calculating the FDI concentration index for APEC economies during 2003–2014 are presented in Fig. 5. Based on available information, a value of less

[22]Tadesse and Shukralla (2011, pp. 141–59).

[23]Manabu and Nabeshima (2012).

than 0.05 suggests FDI is not concentrated; a value between 0.05 and 0.10, moderately concentrated FDI; a value between 0.10 and 0.20, highly concentrated FDI; and a value more than 0.20, extremely concentrated FDI.[24]

According to the results, greenfield investments in Papua New Guinea, Brunei, Peru, Chile, Australia, Indonesia, New Zealand and South Korea are extremely concentrated, followed by high concentration in Canada, Taiwan, Vietnam, Hong Kong, Philippines, Thailand, Malaysia, Japan, Mexico, and Singapore. Greenfield investments in Russia, United States and China were moderately concentrated with none of the economies scoring diversified greenfield FDI.

APEC's Regional investment analytical group (RIAG)[25] is continuing to explore the implications of concentration and diversification among regional FDI. Better understanding of the advantages and disadvantages, and factors that contribute to the attraction of FDI and its impacts can heighten the efficacy of policies intended to maximize the net benefits.

5 Conclusion

Foreign direct investment, globally and particularly in Asia-Pacific, has been helping to transform the global economy. At the same time, the nature of FDI in Asia-Pacific has been undergoing major transformations. More FDI now occurs in service sectors than in manufacturing and primary sectors combined.

Foreign direct investment can have both negative and positive impacts but is generally viewed as making positive net contributions to the host and source economies. Besides its direct contributions to productive capacity, FDI promotes numerous linkages where it occurs. Variation in the relative importance of these effects in a host economy can be seen when FDI is measured gross, per capita, or a share of total investment. For developing economies, FDI's potential links to trade, participation in global value chains, and structural transformation make it particularly attractive.

The Asia-Pacific region has emerged as the leading source, as well as the leading destination region for FDI, capitalizing on and adding to its prominence in global value chains. The strength of intraregional FDI highlights the role of building policy coherence through regional cooperation. New developments in the availability of FDI data and more granular analysis will support improvements in policy formulation, but also underscores the potential further benefits from greater evidence-based analysis.

---

[24]These ranges are marginally different than those for the conventional Herfindahl-Hirschman index of industrial concentration. A conventional index value below 0.1 is 'unconcentrated'; those between 0.1 and 0.18 are considered 'moderately concentrated', and those above 0.18 are 'highly concentrated'.

[25]For more information on RIAG, see Abdullaev et al. (2015, pp. 88–97).

References

Abdullaev, Bekzod, Douglas Brooks, and Ken Waller. 2015. Investment policy in APEC: Developments and a look forward. In *Current issues in Asia Pacific foreign direct investment*, 88–97. The Australian APEC Study Centre at RMIT.

Aitken, Brian, and Ann Harrison. 1999. Do domestic firms benefit from direct foreign investment? Evidence from Venezuela. *American Economic Review* 89: 605–618.

Boyd, John, and Bruce Smith. 1992. Intermediation and the equilibrium allocation of investment capital: Implications for economic development. *Journal of Monetary Economics* 30: 409–432.

Braunstein, Elissa, and Gerald Epstein. 2002. Bargaining power and foreign direct investment in China: Can 1.3 billion consumers tame the multinationals? CEPA Working Paper 2002/13. New York: Center for Economic Policy Analysis.

Brooks, Douglas H., and Hal Hill (eds.). 2004. *Managing FDI in a globalizing economy: Asian experiences*. London: Palgrave Macmillan.

Brooks, Douglas H., Emma Fan, and Lea Sumulong. 2003. Foreign direct investment in developing Asia: Trends, effects, and likely issues for the forthcoming WTO negotiations. ERD Working Paper No. 38, Manila: Asian Development Bank.

Figlio, David, and Bruce Blonigen. 2000. The effects of foreign direct investment on local communities. *Journal of Urban Economics* 48: 338–363.

Findlay, Ronald. 1978. Relative backwardness, direct foreign investment, and the transfer of technology: A simple dynamic model. *Quarterly Journal of Economics* 92: 1–16.

Helpman, Elhanan, Mark Melitz, and Steven Yeaple. 2004. Export versus FDI with heterogeneous firms. *American Economic Review* 94: 300–316.

Kentor, Jeffrey. 1998. The long-term effects of foreign investment dependence on economic growth, 1940–1990. *American Journal of Sociology* 103: 1024–1046.

Manabu, Iwamoto, and Kaoru Nabeshima. 2012. Can FDI promote export diversification and sophistication of host countries? Dynamic panel system GMM analysis. Discussion Paper No. 347, Institute of Developing Economies.

Miyake, Maiko, and Magdolna Sass. 2000. Recent trends in foreign direct investment. OECD Financial Market Trends, No. 76.

Moran, Theodore. 2015. Foreign direct investment, supply chain creation, and structural transformation: Lessons for APEC. In *Current issues in Asia Pacific foreign direct investment*, 21–31. The Australian APEC Study Centre at RMIT.

Organisation for Economic Co-operation and Development (OECD). 2002. *Foreign direct investment for development: Maximising benefits, minimising costs*. Paris: OECD.

Rivera-Batiz, Francisco, and Luis Rivera-Batiz. 1991. The effects of direct foreign investment in the presence of increasing returns due to specialization. *Journal of Development Economics* 34: 287–307.

Rugman, Alan, and Jonathan Doh. 2008. *Multinationals and development*. New Haven: Yale University Press.

Sauvant, Karl, and Padma Mallampally. 2015. Policy options for promoting foreign direct investment in the least developed countries. *Transnational Corporations Review* 7: 237–268.

Tadesse, Bedassa, and Elias Shukralla. 2011. The impact of foreign direct investment on horizontal export diversification: Empirical evidence. *Applied Economics* 45: 141–159.

UNCTAD. 2012. Regional integration and foreign direct investment in developing and transition economies, Geneva.

UNCTAD. 2015. World investment report 2015: Reforming international investment governance. Geneva: United Nations Publications.

UNDESA. 2005. World economic and social survey 2005: Financing for development. United Nations Publications.

Yeaple, Stephen. 2008. Firm heterogeneity and the structure of U.S. multinational activity: An empirical analysis. NBER Working Paper No. 14072, National Bureau of Economic Research.

Reforming the International Investment Regime: Two Challenges

Karl P. Sauvant

1 Introduction

This short contribution addresses two challenges in relation to the reform of the international investment law and policy regime, namely how to encourage the flow of substantially higher amounts of sustainable foreign direct investment (i.e., investment that makes a maximum contribution to development) and how to bring about a more widely accepted dispute-settlement approach. These challenges are part of the broader context within which governments in Asia negotiate international investment agreements, and which they may want to keep in mind in future negotiations.

The reform of the investment law and policy regime needs to be seen against the background of intensive international discussions of the strengths and weaknesses of that regime. In fact, ideas that would have been cast away only five years ago as being unrealistic (such as a world investment court) are now firmly inscribed in the international agenda. The investment regime is in flux, and it is therefore an appropriate time to seek substantial improvements that would make that regime more widely accepted by all stakeholders.

Karl P. Sauvant is Resident Senior Fellow at the Columbia Center on Sustainable Investment, a joint center of Columbia Law School and the Earth Institute at Columbia University. This text draws on Karl P. Sauvant, *The Evolving International Investment Law and Policy Regime: Ways Forward.* E15 Task Force on Investment Policy–Policy Options Paper (Geneva: International Centre for Trade and Sustainable Development and World Economic Forum, E15 Initiative, 2016), available at http://works.bepress.com/karl_sauvant/428/, http://e15initiative.org/wp-content/uploads/2015/09/WEF_Investment_Law_Policy_regime_report_2015_1401.pdf and http://ccsi.columbia.edu/files/2015/08/E-15-Investment-policy-options-published-Jan-16.pdf. The full Policy Options Paper provides a detailed discussion of the two proposals outlined here.

K.P. Sauvant (✉)
Columbia Center on Sustainable Investment, New York, USA
e-mail: karlsauvant@gmail.com

J. Chaisse et al. (eds.), *Asia's Changing International Investment Regime*, International Law and the Global South, DOI 10.1007/978-981-10-5882-0_4

It is not surprising that these discussions are ongoing, as the regime, in its current form, is a relative young construct. It has evolved, and continues to do so, in response to experiences, pressures and changing interests. And it has shown its impact through its investor-State dispute-settlement mechanism.

To a certain extent, some of the regime's weaknesses are a legacy issue. The regime was framed at a time of significant power asymmetries between the principal capital exporting (mostly developed) and most capital importing (mostly developing) countries, and long involved overwhelmingly unidirectional (i.e., North-South) foreign direct investment (FDI) flows. Today, however, it exists in an environment marked by the imperative to promote sustainable development, including the need to halt climate change; growing economic inequality; far greater economic and political interdependence, with FDI increasingly a two-way street; far greater public involvement in policy and rule-making; and a desire for the preservation of policy space and balanced rights and responsibilities on the part of governments and international investors.

The reformist quest for carefully balancing the regime should be welcome, as it reflects changing circumstances: it is a sign of greater maturity and fairness in international economic relations, even if it might complicate the search for consensus in rule-making.

Any discussion of the reform of the investment regime needs to begin with an identification of the regime's purpose, whether in relation to bilateral, regional or multilateral investment agreements. In a world in which all United Nations members just adopted, in September 2015 and at the highest political level, the Sustainable Development Goals, it appears logical that the purpose of the regime should be to encourage the flow of substantially higher amounts of sustainable FDI in the framework of a widely accepted enabling investment framework that regulates the relationships between governments and international investors in a balanced manner.

A good part of the international discussions about the investment regime revolve around some of the elements of the regime's purpose. This contribution focuses on two of these elements. The first one addresses the need to encourage the flow of substantially higher amounts of sustainable FDI by launching an international support program for sustainable investment facilitation, suggesting also alternative ways in which such an objective could be achieved (Sect. 2). The second one deals with the quest for a more widely accepted enabling investment framework and, in particular, its dispute-settlement mechanism that is at its core, proposing the establishment of an independent Advisory Centre on International Investment Law (Sect. 3).

2 Encouraging the Flow of Sustainable Investment: The Need for an International Support Program for Sustainable Investment Facilitation

Why is there a need to encourage the flow of sustainable investment?
The answer is straight-forward: The world's investment needs are tremendous: to upgrade the physical infrastructure for the 21st century; to enhance skills; to build the science, technology and innovation capacity required to advance the frontier of knowledge; to transition to a low-carbon world economy to halt climate change; and, ultimately, to create employment, advance growth and development and create better living conditions worldwide—in brief, to meet the Sustainable Development Goals. This will require, annually, trillions of dollars of new investment.

While the public purse has to provide most of the required funds, FDI can make an important contribution as well. However, world FDI inflows declined substantially from their peak of US$2 trillion in 2007 as a result of the financial crisis. Flows need not only to recover, but surpass this earlier record. There is no economic reason why FDI flows could not be substantially higher than what they were in 2007.

However, the issue is not only more FDI, but better FDI. "Better" FDI is investment that has certain "sustainability characteristics" in terms of contributing as much as possible to the economic, social and environmental development of host countries and take place in the framework of fair governance mechanisms while remaining commercially viable—in brief: sustainable FDI for sustainable development.

There is of course the challenge of defining FDI's "sustainability characteristics". (Note that the focus here is on the characteristics of individual FDI projects, as opposed to the overall behavior of international investors as capture, e.g., in the "responsible business conduct" instruments of the OECD.) An international organization or a non-governmental organization could establish a working group to prepare, in a multi-stakeholder process, an indicative list of FDI sustainability characteristics. Individual governments seeking to attract sustainable FDI could draw on that list for guidance purposes. A "sustainable FDI" definition is also needed for investor-state disputes, as arbitral tribunals consider, as they should, an investment's development impact when adjudicating claims and, therefore, need evaluation criteria. The same applies as more international investment agreements make reference to "sustainable development" or "sustainable investments". Such a working group could also identify mechanisms to encourage specifically sustainable investment flows.

To obtain considerably higher sustainable FDI flows requires that the FDI determinants at the country level are right. And that means that countries themselves have to be at the forefront of improving the FDI determinants: they need to strengthen the crucial economic determinants of their economies (e.g., the quality of human resources, of the science, technology and innovation capacity, of the physical infrastructure), their regulatory frameworks for FDI and their investment promotion capacities.

Many countries, however, and especially the 48 least developed countries, can do only so much on their own. They simply lack the capacity to compete successfully in the highly competitive FDI world market to attract the required funds. Hence, they need assistance, not only to strengthen their economic FDI determinants (including through official development assistance), but also their FDI regulatory frameworks and investment promotion capacities.

Accordingly, future international investment agreements should incorporate binding commitments that aim at encouraging higher sustainable investment flows. Some investment agreements already contain commitments by the treaty partners that seek to further this objective, for instance by requiring consultations on the promotion of investment flows between them. But few contain binding commitments in this respect. Notable exceptions are the 2015 Brazilian investment treaties with Angola and Mozambique: among other things, they mandate the establishment of "thematic agendas" for cooperation and investment facilitation. This is an approach that should be emulated in other international investment agreements.

But one should also consider going further and launch an international support program for sustainable investment facilitation, with national investment promotion agencies as the focal points. A sustainable FDI support program would complement the World Trade Organization (WTO)-led Aid-for-Trade Initiative and the WTO Trade Facilitation Agreement, which focus on trade. In a world of global value chains, these two instruments address one side of the equation, namely trade, while a sustainable FDI support program would address the other side of the equation, namely investment. Analogue to the WTO efforts, a sustainable FDI support program would be entirely technical in nature, focusing on practical actions to encourage sustainable investment flows to developing countries.

One option to create such a program is to extend the Aid-for-Trade Initiative to cover investment. The initial emphasis could be on investment in services, given the WTO's General Agreement on Trade in Services and that services account for nearly two-thirds of the world's FDI stock. Alternatively, the Aid-for-Trade Initiative could be complemented with a separate Aid-for-Investment Initiative.

Another option is to expand the Trade Facilitation Agreement to cover sustainable investment. A subsidiary body of the Committee on Trade Facilitation could provide the platform to consult on the operation of what would be a sustainable investment module within the Trade Facilitation Agreement.

A third option is for all governments to launch a Sustainable Investment Facilitation Understanding. The WTO could work on such an Understanding as part of a post-Doha agenda, but work could also begin in another international organization with experience in FDI matters, especially UNCTAD, the OECD or the World Bank. Or leading outward FDI countries could launch a plurilateral initiative, initiated by the G20. (The top ten outward FDI economies, which include four emerging markets, accounted for four-fifths of world FDI outflows in 2014.)

If governments want to meet the world's future investment needs and, in particular, the Sustainable Development Goals, they need to help countries through an international effort to attract more sustainable FDI, helping in this manner also to put the world on a sustainable development path.

3 Improving Dispute Settlement: The Need for an Advisory Centre on International Investment Law

The investor-State dispute-settlement mechanism constitutes the heart of the international investment law and policy regime. It makes the regime effective. And it is precisely for this reason that a number of its shortcomings are being criticized in various quarters. There is a pressing need to improve the investor-State dispute-settlement mechanism. The proposal of the European Commission (the Commission) to create a world investment court and appeals mechanism is laudable in this respect, and it is to be hoped that the Commission will be able to convince member States, the European Parliament and its partner countries to move forward in this direction. Institutionalizing investor-State dispute settlement in this manner would enhance the investment regime's legitimacy.

Even if a world investment court system should be established, however, it would not alleviate another serious shortcoming of the regime, namely that poor countries (and especially the least developed among them), including in Asia, typically do not have the human and financial resources adequately to defend themselves as respondents in international investment disputes. And a dispute-settlement mechanism that does not provide a level playing field for the disputing parties is compromised, undermining its very legitimacy and, with that, the legitimacy of the international investment regime.

This is particularly important as claims against host country governments can reach hundreds of millions of dollars, host country regulations may be challenged, law-making may be chilled, and the reputation of a country as an investment location may be at stake. Moreover, litigating claims is expensive, especially as disputes are becoming more complex. There is also the risk that governments may have to assume the litigation costs of the claimants if they lose a case. The advent of third-party funding further accentuates the imbalance for more vulnerable countries, as such funders typically do not provide funding to (State) respondents but only to claimants.

This puts many countries in an asymmetric situation whenever disputes arise, beginning with a possible readiness to settle disputes in which they could potentially prevail, or knowing when to settle during an early stage of a dispute when they usefully could do so, simply because they do not have the required sophistication or the resources to defend themselves.

An independent Advisory Centre on International Investment Law would help to establish a level playing field by providing administrative and legal assistance to respondents that face investor claims and are not in a position to defend themselves adequately.

It is useful, in this context, to look at the experience of the Advisory Centre on WTO Law. When, after the creation of the WTO, the number of disputes brought before this institution rose, the independent WTO Advisory Centre was established in 2001. It advises its developing country members on all issues relating to WTO law. This includes assisting its members through all stages of the WTO's regular panel and Appellate Body proceedings as complainants, respondents and third parties. The WTO Advisory Centre provides its services through its own staff or through outside counsel at reduced rates.

Something similar could be envisaged in relation to the international investment regime. Naturally, establishing an Advisory Centre on International Investment Law raises a host of issues that would need to be considered carefully. And the closer any assistance comes to actual participation in litigation, the more difficult it may become for some countries to support such an initiative—although, as in the case of the WTO Advisory Centre, a group of individual countries interested in furthering the legitimacy of the regime could go ahead on their own.

In any event, the central challenge is to identify acceptable ways that give all countries a fair chance to defend themselves adequately in disputes to which they are party. Hence, as in the case of the WTO Advisory Centre, the difficulties associated with establishing an Advisory Centre on International Investment Law should not be insurmountable. And doing so would indisputably strengthen the legitimacy of the international investment law and policy regime in its function to enable substantially higher flows of sustainable FDI.

4 Conclusion

The international investment law and policy regime is in flux, and a number of its aspects are being challenged. Improvements have been made as governments learn from their past experience, but more improvements need to be made. Governments in Asia have the opportunity to contribute significantly to the further development of the investment regime, given that they are participating in a host of bilateral and regional investment treaty negotiations. Moreover, China chairs the G20 in 2016. This gives that country the opportunity to initiate an exploratory process on how to move the reform of the regime forward, perhaps even in the direction toward a plurilateral or multilateral investment framework.

Investment Protection and Host State's Right to Regulate in the Indian Model Bilateral Investment Treaty: Lessons for Asian Countries

Prabhash Ranjan

In recent years, investment treaty arbitration (ITA) has come under scathing criticism for failing to balance rights of foreign investors (investment protection) with host country's right to regulate (regulation).[1] In view of this, many countries have adopted new bilateral investment treaty (BIT) practice aimed at ensuring that foreign investment is protected from arbitrary state action without undermining the ability of host states to regulate in public interest.[2] Given this, the objective of this chapter is to analyse the new Indian Model BIT 2016[3] to examine whether it

I am grateful to Sanjeevi Seshadri for providing able research assistance for writing this chapter.

[1]L.T. Wells, 'Backlash to Investment Arbitration: Three Causes' in M. Waibel et al. (eds), *The Backlash Against Investment Arbitration* (Kluwer 2010) 341. See also S. Schill, 'Enhancing International Investment Law's Legitimacy: Conceptual and Methodological Foundations of a New Public Law Approach' (2011) 52 Va. J. Int'l L. 57, 69. Schill states: "the extent to which investment treaties limit a state's regulatory powers and subject the exercise of such powers to liability claims by foreign investors may become the litmus test for the future viability of the system". B. Choudhary, 'Recapturing Public Power: Is Investment Arbitration's Engagement of the Public Interest Contributing to the Democratic Deficit?' (2008) 41 Vand. J. Transnat'l L. 775.
[2]See S. Spears, 'The Quest for Policy Space in New Generation of International Investment Agreements' (2010) 13 JIEL 1037; M. Sornarajah, 'Mutations of Neo Liberalism in International Investment Law' (2011) 3 TL&D, 203, 229. For recent treaty practice aimed at rebalancing see UNCTAD, *World Investment Report: Global Value Chains: Investment and Trade for Development* (United Nations 2013). See also F. Ortino, 'Refining the Content and Role of Investment 'rules' and 'standards': A new Approach to International Treaty Making' (2013) 28 ICSID Rev—FILJ, 152, 157.
[3]Model Text for the Indian Bilateral Investment Treaty 2016. http://www.finmin.nic.in/reports/ModelTextIndia_BIT.pdf. Important to keep in mind that the Indian Model BIT contains two dates—28 December 2016 given in the letter accompanying the text; and 14 January 2016 on the website of the Ministry of Finance, Government of India as the date of adoption of the Model BIT. In this paper, we use the 14 January 2016 date, and thus call the Model BIT as 2016 Model BIT and not 2016 Model BIT.

P. Ranjan (✉)
Faculty of Law, South Asian University, New Delhi, India
e-mail: prabhash.ranjan@sau.ac.in

J. Chaisse et al. (eds.), *Asia's Changing International Investment Regime*, International Law and the Global South, DOI 10.1007/978-981-10-5882-0_5

balances investment protection with host State's right to regulate as claimed by the Indian government.[4] A Model BIT acts as a template for future BIT negotiations and is usually the first step in a country's investment treaty practice. India wishes to use the new Model as the basis to renegotiate its existing 80 odd BITs and sign new BITs. The chapter will critically discuss the main provisions of the new Indian Model BIT of 2016 from the standpoint of whether it reconciles investment protection and host state's right to regulate. The chapter is organised as follows: Part I gives the background by briefly discussing the developments that led to the adoption of the 2016 Model BIT. Subsequent parts of the chapter discuss the following key provisions of the 2016 Model BIT: definition of investment (Part II), most favoured nation (Part III), fair and equitable treatment (Part IV), full protection and security (Part V), non precluded measure clause (Part VI), taxation as an exception (Part VII) and investor-state dispute settlement provision (Part VIII). Part IX concludes by providing some indication of future direction.

1 Background to the Indian Model BIT 2016

India started signing BITs, or bilateral investment promotion agreements (BIPAs), as called in India, in the early 1990s. This signing of BITs was part of India's overall strategy of economic liberalisation unleashed in 1991 and had the clear objective of attracting foreign investment.[5] India signed the first BIT with the United Kingdom (UK) in 1994. This BIT served as the template for India to negotiate further BITs.[6] In fact, the Indian Model BIT of 2003[7] is very similar to the India-UK BIT. Since 1994 India has entered into BITs with more than 80 countries, out of which more than 70 have already come into force.[8] India is also negotiating a BIT with the US.[9]

---

[4]Government of India, Ministry of Commerce and Industry, 25 July 2016 http://www.dipp.gov.in/English/questions/25072016/lu1290.pdf. Accessed 5 January 2017.

[5]For a full discussion of India's BIT programme, including its origin and evolution, see Prabhash Ranjan, 'India and Bilateral Investment Treaties—A Changing Landscape' (2014) 29 ICSID Rev—FILJ 419.

[6]Dev Krishan, 'India and International Investment Law' in Bimal Patel (ed), *India and International Law* (Martinus Nijhoff 2008) 277.

[7]Indian Model Text of Bilateral Investment Promotion and Protection Agreement. http://finmin.nic.in/the_ministry/dept_eco_affairs/icsection/Indian%20Model%20Text%20BIPA.asp?pageid=1. Accessed 10 October 2016.

[8]The full list of India's BITs is available at http://finmin.nic.in/bipa/bipa_index.asp?pageid=2. Accessed 10 October 2016.

[9]Prabhash Ranjan, 'Reviving the Indo-US BIT Dialogue', *The Financial Express* (New Delhi, 26 January 2016). http://www.financialexpress.com/article/fe-columnist/reviving-the-indo-us-bit-dialogue/34946/. Accessed 5 March 2016.

Towards the end of 2011, a tribunal in *White Industries v India*[10] found that India violated its obligations under the India-Australia BIT[11] (see Part III for more details on this case). This award is significant because it is the first known ITA adverse award against India and a watershed moment in the history of Indian BITs. After this award, many foreign corporations slapped ITA notices against India: *Vodafone* issued an arbitral notice to India under the India-Netherlands BIT for a retrospective taxation measure[12]; Cairn Energy has also dragged India to arbitration under the India-UK BIT for a retrospective taxation measure[13]; Germany's *Deutsche Telekom* has issued a notice of arbitration to India under the India-Germany BIT over a cancellation of a satellite venture[14]; France's *Louis Dreyfus Armateurs* (LDA) brought a case against India under the India-France BIT challenging a series of measures adopted by the Indian government that allegedly prevented the implementation of a joint venture project to modernise the port in Haldia in Kolkata, India[15]; *Tenoch Holdings*, another foreign investor, has issued an arbitral notice against India under the India-Russia and India-Cyprus BIT for withdrawal of approval to grant telecom licenses.[16] Recently, the Permanent Court of Arbitration (PCA), in a dispute between Devas multimedia's Mauritian investors and India,[17] concluded that India violated the India-Mauritius BIT.[18] This dispute arose due to India annulling a contract signed in 2005 between Antirx, the

---

[10]*White Industries Australia Limited v Republic of India*, UNCITRAL, Final Award (30 November 2011).

[11]Ibid para 16.1.1 (a).

[12]*Vodafone v. India*, UNCTIRAL, Notice of Arbitration (not public), (17 April 2014). http://italaw.com/cases/2544. Accessed 10 January 2016.

[13]*Cairn Energy PLC v India*, http://investmentpolicyhub.unctad.org/ITA/Details/691. Accessed 20 February 2016. In this case, an arbitration tribunal has been constituted.

[14]*Deutsche Telekom v. India*, ICSID Additional Facility, Notice of Arbitration (not public), (2 September 2013). http://italaw.com/cases/2275. Accessed 7 March 2016.

[15]*Louis Dreyfus Armateurs SAS v The Republic of India*, http://investmentpolicyhub.unctad.org/ITA/Details/600. Accessed 20 February 2016. See also Bhushan Satish and Shreyas Jayasimha, 'Indian Courts First Blush with Investment Treaty Arbitration: Taking Some Lessons from the Calcutta High Court' http://kluwerarbitrationblog.com/2016/03/16/indian-courts-first-brush-with-investment-treaty-arbitration-taking-some-lessons-from-the-calcutta-high-court. Accessed 20 February 2016. In this case, also an arbitration tribunal has been constituted.

[16]*Tenoch Holdings Limited, Mr Maxim Naumchenko and Mr Andre Poluektov v The Republic of India*, PCA Case No 2013-23, http://investmentpolicyhub.unctad.org/ITA/Details/491. Accessed 7 March 2016. Some other notices of arbitration include Strategic Infrasol Foodstuff LLC and *The Joint Venture of Thakur Family Trust UAE with Ace Hospitality Management DMCC UAE v Republic of India*, Notice of Arbitration, 8 October 2016. http://www.italaw.com/sites/default/files/case-documents/italaw7082.pdf. Accessed 7 March 2016.

[17]*CC/Devas (Mauritius) Ltd., Devas Employees Mauritius Private Limited, and Telcom Devas Mauritius Limited v. Republic of India*, PCA Case No 2013-09.

[18]'Antrix-Devas Deal: Permanent Court of Arbitration rules against Indian government' *The Indian Express*, (Bengaluru, 27 July 2016). http://indianexpress.com/article/business/business-others/antrix-devas-deal-hague-international-tribunal-rules-against-indian-govt/. Accessed 25 September 2016.

marketing arm of the Indian Space Research Organisation (ISRO), a government entity, with Devas Multimedia, a multimedia services provider.[19] As per this contract, Antrix was supposed to provide 70 MHz of S-band satellite spectrum to Devas for providing multimedia services.[20] However, the government hurriedly cancelled the contract citing that it needs to use the satellite spectrum for national purposes.[21] While a full legal analysis of this case is not possible because the award has not been made public, reportedly India has been found guilty of having violated the provisions on expropriation and fair and equitable treatment.[22] Worth noting that India had challenged the appointment of arbitrators in this case.[23] India challenged the appointment of the Presiding Arbitrator (Hon. Marc Lalonde) and Co-Arbitrator (Professor Francisco Orrego Vicuna), 'on the ground that the arbitrators served together on two tribunals which took a position on a legal issue (the "essential security interests" clause) expected to arise in the present proceedings. India's challenge as regards the Presiding Arbitrator didn't sustain whereas the challenge regarding the co-Arbitrator was upheld.[24]

This adverse BIT arbitral ruling and scores of other ITA notices served to India by many foreign corporations triggered demands to revisit BITs by different actors, including academia, parliamentarians, and civil society organisations. In the academic community, few commentators have argued for a critical assessment of India's BITs even before the *White Industries* case.[25] Demands have become stronger after the *White Industries* case.[26] Before, the *White Industries* case, the Indian Parliament rarely debated BITs. However, post-*White Industries*, BITs have started attracting greater attention in the Indian Parliament. For example, the *White Industries* award has been criticised as 'attack on the sovereignty of the Indian Judiciary.'[27] Similarly, civil society organisations are now demanding a review of

---

[19]Ibid.

[20]Ibid.

[21]Ibid.

[22]Ibid.

[23]*CC/Devas (Mauritius) Ltd, Devas Employees Mauritius Private Limited, and Telecom Devas Mauritius Limited v The Republic of India*, PCA Case No 2013-09, (Decision on the Respondent's Challenge to the Hon. Marc Lalonde as Presiding Arbitrator and Prof. Francisco Orrego Vicuna as Co-Arbitrator), (30 September 2013), (*Devas v India*), para 3 http://italaw.com/cases/1962. Accessed 10 October 2016.

[24]Ibid paras 65–67.

[25]See Prabhash Ranjan, 'International Investment Agreements and Regulatory Discretion: Case Study of India' (2008) 9 JWIT 209.

[26]See Ranjan (n 5), Biswajit Dhar, Reji Joseph and James TC, 'India's Bilateral Investment Agreements: Time to Review' (2012) XLVII EPW 113; Smitha Francis and Murli Kallummal, 'India's Comprehensive Trade Agreements: Implications for Development Trajectory' (2013) XLVIII EPW 109.

[27]Statement by P. Rajeeve, Member of Parliament (India), Transcript of the Proceedings of the Rajyasabha (22 May 2012) 52. For more on this issue see Ranjan (n 5).

India's existing BIT programme,[28] arguing that the threat of BIT arbitrations 'will have a chilling effect on the ability of different ministries (of the Indian government) to regulate various social and economic needs.'[29]

As a result, India started the process of developing a new Model BIT, which would act as the template for future BIT negotiations. India first released a draft version of the Model BIT in April 2015, which attracted considerable attention.[30] Finally, in January 2016, India adopted the new Model BIT.[31] The 2016 Model is very detailed containing 38 articles running into close to 30 pages as against the 15 articles in just seven pages of the 2003 Model,[32] which contains elaborate substantive and procedural assurances for protection of foreign investment, except the right to establishment, with limited exceptions, reservations and carve-out provisions.[33] It is claimed that the Indian Model BIT is aimed at balancing investment protection with host State's right to regulate.[34] We now turn to analysing some of the key provisions in India's Model BIT 2016 to test this claim.

2 Definition of Investment

The definition of investment in a BIT plays a very important role in determining the scope of application of rights and obligations under the treaty and to the establishment of jurisdiction of ITA tribunal.[35] Most Indian BITs provide a broad

[28]An open letter to the Indian Prime Minister on India-US BIT. http://www.madhyam.org.in/admin/tender/August_7_Letter_to_PM%20(1).html. Accessed 26 August 2014.

[29]Letter written by many civil society organisations to the Indian Prime Minister expressing concerns about India's BITs, Dated 13 June 2012. http://donttradeourlivesaway.files.wordpress.com/2012/06/civil-society-letter-on-us-india-bit.pdf. Accessed 10 October 2016.

[30]The Law Commission of India prepared a report on the draft Model BIT—Government of India, Law Commission of India, Report No 260, Analysis of the Draft Model Indian Bilateral Investment (August 2016). http://lawcommissionofindia.nic.in/reports/Report260.pdf. Accessed 9 October 2016, Grant Hanessian and Kabir Duggal, 'The 2016 Indian Model BIT: Is This Change the World Wishes to See?' (2016) 30 ICSID Rev 729, 729–740; Prabhash Ranjan, 'Comparing Investment Provisions in India's FTAs with India's Stand Alone BITs: Contributing to the Evolution of New Indian BIT Practice', (2016), 16 JWIT 899.

[31]Also see Grant Hanessian & Kabir Duggal, *The Final 2015 Indian Model BIT: Is This the Change the World Wishes to See*, ICSID Review (2017); Aniruddha Rajput, *India's shifting treaty practice: a comparative analysis of the 2003 and 2015 Model BITs*, 7(2) Jindal Global Law Review (2016) 201–226.

[32]See above n 8.

[33]Prabhash Ranjan, 'India's International Investment Agreements and India's Regulatory Power as a Host Nation' (PhD thesis, King's College London 2012). https://kclpure.kcl.ac.uk/portal/files/13524464/Studentthesis-Prabhash_Ranjan_2013.pdf. Accessed 9 October 2016.

[34]See above n 5.

[35]OECD, *International Investment Law: Understanding Concepts and Tracking Innovations* (OECD 2008). https://www.oecd.org/investment/internationalinvestmentagreements/40471468.pdf. Accessed 9 October 2016. On definition of investment, see also Rudolf Dolzer and

asset-based definition of 'investment', where every kind of asset, established or acquired by the foreign investor is an investment.[36]

The 2016 Model BIT has moved away from a broad-asset based definition of investment and provides for an enterprise-based definition of investment where an enterprise is to be taken together with its assets.[37] In the 2016 Model BIT, investment means an enterprise that has been constituted, organised and operated in good faith by an investor in accordance with the domestic laws of the country. Article 1.4 also provides a non-exhaustive list of assets that an enterprise may posses.[38] Further, certain characteristics of investment 'such as' commitment of capital or other resources, certain duration (the period is not specified), the expectation of gain or profit, the assumption of risk and significance for the development of the country where the investment is made, should also be satisfied.

The requirement that investment should be significant for the development of the country to be eligible for treaty protection has been criticised as being too subjective.[39] Also, as the tribunal in *LESI SpA v Algeria* held, it is difficult to ascertain whether investment has contributed to development of the host State.[40] For instance, it is not clear how sizeable or successful should the investment be to conclude that it has contributed to development of host State?[41] While some tribunals suggest that it is enough if the investment contributes in one way or another,[42] other tribunals have held that this contribution should be 'significant'.[43] This reveals that the Indian Model BIT grants significant discretion to arbitral tribunals.

(Footnote 35 continued)

Christoph Schreuer, *Principles of International Investment Law* (2nd edn, OUP 2012), 60–78; Jeswald W. Salacuse, *The Law of Investment Treaties* (OUP 2010) 166–186; Mavluda Sattorova, 'Defining Investment under the ICSID Convention and BITs: Of Ordinary Meaning, Telos, and Beyond' (2012) 2 Asian J. Int. Law, 267.

[36]See 2003 Indian Model BIT (n 7) Article 1(b).

[37]See 2016 Indian Model BIT (n 4) Article 1.4 *"investment" means an enterprise constituted, organised and operated in good faith by an investor in accordance with the law of the Party in whose territory the investment is made, taken together with the assets of the enterprise, has the characteristics of an investment such as the commitment of capital or other resources, certain duration, the expectation of gain or profit, the assumption of risk and a significance for the development of the Party in whose territory the investment is made....*".

[38]Ibid Article 1.4 (a) to (h).

[39]Dolzer and Schreuer (n 44).

[40]LESI SpA v Algeria, 72(iv).

[41]See Mr. Patrick Mitchell v. The Democratic Republic of Congo, ICSID Case No. ARB/99/7, Annulment proceeding 33 (Feb. 9, 2004), http://www.italaw.com/sites/default/files/case-documents/ita0537.pdf.

[42]Ibid.

[43]Malaysian Historical Salvors v Malaysia, ICSID Case No ARB/05/10, Award on Jurisdiction 124 (17 May 17, 2007), http://www.italaw.com/sites/default/files/case-documents/ita0496.pdf.

Moreover, from Article 1.4 it is not very clear whether the characteristics of investment are to be satisfied just by an enterprise or also by its assets? This can be understood with the help of following example—let us assume that a foreign pharmaceutical enterprise, legally constituted in India for last 10 years, gets a patent on a drug. After say, just six months of granting the patent, the Indian government revokes the patent for some reason, which the enterprise wishes to challenge before an arbitral tribunal. Here, will the 'characteristics test' of investment be required to be satisfied by the asset (patent right) or by the enterprise or both? If it is the patent right, then it might be difficult to satisfy the 'characteristics test' due to short duration for which the asset has been in existence. If, on the other hand, the 'characteristics test' has to be satisfied by the enterprise, it will be relatively easier to fall under the definition of 'investment' and the short duration for which the patent right has been in existence will not matter.

Instead of having this convoluted approach to defining investment, from the standpoint of reconciling investment protection with host State's right to regulate, it would have been much better for India to adopt the definition of investment, which is given in the Investment chapters of India's FTAs. Investment chapters in these FTAs also define investment as every kind of asset owned or controlled by the investor.[44] However, India's FTAs provide additional factors that have to be satisfied for an asset to be an investment. These FTAs state that for an asset to be an investment it should posses certain characteristics of investment like commitment of capital or other resources, the expectation of gains or profits or the assumption of risk.[45] These characteristics can be referred to as pertaining to the economic dimension of an investment.[46] In other words, where an asset lacks economic characteristics of an investment, it is not an investment no matter what form the asset may take.[47] Consequently, an ITA tribunal will not have jurisdiction over a dispute involving an asset, owned and controlled by a foreign investor, that does not satisfy the economic characteristics of investment like commitment of capital or assumption of risk. From the perspective of India's regulatory power, the requirement that an investment should satisfy economic characteristics to be eligible for treaty protection will provide India greater regulatory freedom to deal with short term financial flows that do not satisfy economic characteristics of investment

[44]See Article 3 (i) of the Comprehensive Economic Partnership Agreement between Japan and The Republic Of India (India-Japan FTA) (signed on 16 February 2011, entered into force on 01 August 2011); Article 10.2(d) of the Comprehensive Economic Cooperation Agreement between the Government of Malaysia and the Government of Republic of India (India-Malaysia FTA) (signed on 24 September 2010, entered into force on 01 July 2011); Article 10.1 of India-Korea Comprehensive Economic Partnership Agreement (India-Korea FTA) (signed on 07 August 2009, entered into force on 01 January 2010); Article 6.1(1) of India-Singapore FTA. Comprehensive Economic Cooperation Agreement between the Republic of India and the Republic of Singapore (India-Singapore FTA) (signed on 29 June 2005, entered into force on 01 August 2005).

[45]Ibid Article 10.2 (d) of the India Malaysia FTA; Article 10.1 of India-Korea FTA.

[46]See N. Rubins, 'The Notion of Investment in International Investment Arbitration' in N Horn (ed) *Arbitrating Foreign Investment Disputes* (OUP 2004) 283.

[47]Article 3(i) Note 2 of India-Japan FTA (n 51).

like commitment of capital or assumption of risk. From the perspective of foreign investment, such a definition will ensure that genuine investments shall enjoy treaty protection without getting into the complexity of whether the asset or the enterprise has to satisfy the 'characteristics test'.

3 Most Favoured Nation (MFN)

The MFN clause obligates the State granting MFN treatment to extend to the beneficiary State the treatment accorded to a third state, in case this treatment is more favourable in comparison to the treatment under the basic treaty.[48] While there is largely an agreement that a properly worded MFN provision will allow for the importation of substantive protections from the secondary BIT into the primary BIT, controversy exists as to whether the MFN provision also applies to procedural issues of investor-state dispute settlement[49] including 'admissibility-related access restrictions to investor-state dispute settlement', such as a waiting periods[50] and incorporating the host State's more favourable consent to arbitration.[51]

The Indian Model BIT 2016 does not contain the MFN provision. India, in its statement, at UNCTAD's World Investment Forum stated that the MFN provision in BITs has proved to be disadvantageous because it disturbs the various strategic, diplomatic and political reasons behind negotiating bilateral treaties.[52] India's concerns about MFN directly stem from the *White Industries v India* case.[53] In *White Industries v India*, the Australian investor, relying on the MFN provision of India-Australia BIT, argued for the importation of a favourable substantive provision related to '*effective means of asserting claims and enforcing rights*' given in India-Kuwait BIT into the India-Australia BIT.[54] The MFN provision in India-Australia BIT is as follows:

---

[48]Endre Ustor 'Most-Favoured-Nation Clause' in Bernhardt and Macalister-Smith (eds.), *Encyclopedia of Public International Law* (vol. III, North-Holland Publishing 1997) 468; S.W. Schill, *Multilateralization of International Investment Law* (CUP 2009).

[49]Salacuse (n 44), 253.

[50]Cf *Emilio Augustine Maffezini v The Kingdom of Spain*, ICSID Case No ARB/97/7, Award (13 November 2000), paras 38–64 and *Wintershall Aktiengesellschaft v Argentine Republic*, ICSID Case No ARB/04/14, Award (8 December 2008), paras 159–168.

[51]*Wintershall,* Ibid para 163.

[52]Statement of India 2014 (n 27).

[53]Ibid.

[54]*White Industries v India*, paras 11.1.1–11.1.5. For more details on this case, see Prabhash Ranjan, 'The White Industries Arbitration: Implications for India's Investment Treaty Programme' (*Investment Treaty News*, 13 April 2012). https://www.iisd.org/itn/2012/04/13/the-white-industries-arbitration-implications-for-indias-investment-treaty-program/; Manu Sanan, 'The White Industries Award: Shades of Grey' (2012) 13 JWIT, 661.

A Contracting Party shall at all times treat investments in its own territory on a basis no less favourable than that accorded to investments or investors of any third country.

India contended such importation arguing that such importation would '*fundamentally subvert the carefully negotiated balance of the BIT*'.[55] However, the tribunal did not agree with India and allowed for the importation of the substantive provision from the secondary BIT into the primary BIT.[56] The tribunal held that an importation of the substantive provision into the primary BIT would serve the purpose for which countries have incorporated the MFN provision in the BIT.[57]

As a result of this case, India's major concern with MFN provision is the use of this provision by foreign investors to borrow beneficial substantive and procedural provisions from third-country BITs. However, not having the MFN provision is not the right way to address this concern. This concern could have been addressed by limiting the scope of the MFN treatment in the BIT. EU-Canada Comprehensive Economic and Trade Agreement (CETA)[58] shows how this can be done. Article 8.7 (1) of the EU-Canada CETA contains the MFN provision, which puts both sides under an obligation not to accord treatment less favourable to a foreign investor than accorded in like situations to investors of a third country with respect to the establishment, acquisition, expansion, conduct etc. This clearly means that host States cannot discriminate between foreign investors in the application of domestic regulatory measures. In order to limit the scope of the MFN provision so as to exclude first situation discussed above, Article 8.7(4) states that 'treatment' referred to in Article 8.4(1) does not include 'procedures for the resolution of investment disputes between investors and States provided for in other international investment treaties' and that 'substantive obligations in other international investment treaties and other trade agreements do not in themselves constitute 'treatment' and thus cannot give rise to a breach of this Article [MFN]' unless a host State has adopted or maintained measures pursuant to those obligations.[59] This clarification makes it very clear that investors cannot use the MFN provision to borrow beneficial procedural provisions or beneficial substantive provisions, unless it can be shown that host State has adopted or is maintaining a domestic measure in accordance with some substantive provision given in the BIT, from a third country BIT. India should have followed this approach.[60] Not having the MFN provision will expose foreign

---

[55]Ibid para 11.2.1.

[56]Ibid paras 11.2.2–11.2.8. see also *Bayindir v Islamic State of Pakistan*, ICSID Case No ARB/03/29, Decsion on Jurisdiction, (14 November 2005); *MTD Equity v Republic of Chile*, ICSID Case No ARB/01/7, Award, (25 May 2004).

[57]Ibid para 11.2.4. See also the ILC Draft Articles on Most Favoured Nation Clauses with commentaries available at http://legal.un.org/ilc/texts/instruments/english/commentaries/1_3_1978.pdf.

[58]CETA.

[59]CETA.

[60]Prabhash Ranjan 'Most Favoured Nation Provision in Indian Bilateral Investment Treaties—A Case for Reform' (2016) 55 IJIL 39–64. See also UNCTAD 'Most Favoured Nation Treatment,

investors to the risk of discriminatory treatment by the host State in application of domestic measures.[61] Thus, absence of the MFN provision gives precedence to State's right to regulate over investment protection and thus fails to reconcile investment protection with host State's right to regulate.

4 Fair and Equitable Treatment

Fair and equitable treatment (FET) has emerged as the most important standard of treatment in BITs[62] and has attracted considerable scholarly attention.[63] FET has become a catch-all provision capable of sanctioning many legislative, regulatory and administrative actions of the host state due to a largely unresolved scope and content of the FET provision.[64] One major reason for FET becoming a catch-all kind of provision is that it often occurs in almost all BITs[65] without much guidance about its meaning and content.[66] This has given rise to a debate regarding the meaning of the FET provision, specifically whether the meaning of FET is restricted to customary international law standard or is the meaning broader and autonomous.[67] An important reason for this debate is that some BITs link FET to customary international law[68] whereas in some BITs FET appears as an autonomous

(Footnote 60 continued)

UNCTAD Series on Issues in International Investment Agreements II' (United Nations 2010). http://unctad.org/en/Docs/diaeia20101_en.pdf. Accessed 9 October 2016.

[61] Ranjan, ibid.

[62] Andrew Newcombe and Lluis Paradell '*Law and Practice of Investment Treaties*' (Kluwer 2009) 254; Salacuse (n 44) 219, Salacuse describes FET as the *grundnorm* or basic norm of the investment treaty system.

[63] Salacuse (n 44); K Vandevelde '*Bilateral Investment Treaties: History, Policy and Interpretation*' (OUP 2010); 43.

[64] Surya Prasad Subedi, *International Investment Law* (Hart Publishing 2008), 172–173; see also Gus Van Harten, *Investment Treaty Arbitration and Public Law* (OUP 2007), 89.

[65] Newcombe and Paradell (n 67) 254.

[66] Scholars have described FET as wide, tenuous and imprecise—See M. Sornarajah '*The International Law on Foreign Investment*' (2nd edn, CUP 2004) 332; Vaughan Lowe 'Regulation or Expropriation' (2002) 55 CLP 447. Christoph Schreuer 'Fair and Equitable Treatment in Arbitral Practice' (2005) 6 JWIT 364; Salacuse (n 44), 221; Vandevelde (n 68), 69.

[67] Dolzer and Schreuer (n 44), 134.

[68] For example, Article 10.4 (1) of the investment chapter of India-Korea FTA states—'*Each Party shall accord to an investment of an investor of the other Party in its territory "fair and equitable treatment" and "full protection and security." The concepts of "fair and equitable treatment" and "full protection and security" do not require treatment in addition to or beyond that which is required by the customary international law minimum standard of treatment of aliens*'.

standard.[69] Even in BITs that link FET to customary international law, the debate is whether the FET standard is based on the Neer standard[70] or has it evolved.[71]

Interestingly, the 2016 Model BIT does not contain a FET provision. The reason for not including the FET provision can be gauged from India's statement issued in 2014, where India expressed its unhappiness about the FET provisions being interpreted very broadly by arbitration tribunals and thus, by implication, suggesting that these broad interpretations restrict host State's right to regulate.[72] Instead, the Model BIT contains a provision entitled 'Treatment of Investments'.[73] As part of this, Article 3.1 prohibits a country from subjecting foreign investments to measures that constitute a violation of customary international law 'through' denial of justice, which covers both judicial and administrative proceedings; or fundamental breach of due process; or targeted discrimination on manifestly unjustified grounds such as gender, race or religious belief or manifestly abusive treatment.[74] It is not clear from the text whether the purpose of providing these four instances is to enumerate that State can violate customary international law with respect to foreign investment only if State's egregious behaviour falls under one of these instances? If the purpose is to limit the meaning of customary international law to just these four instances, then this is distinct even from than the standard formulated under the 1926 *Neer* award.[75]

A key omission in Article 3.1 of the Indian Model BIT is the ground of arbitrariness to challenge hosts State's regulatory measure. Many ITA tribunals[76] including NAFTA tribunals that have held that if a State acts in a manifestly

---

[69]For example, 2003 Indian Model BIT (n 7) Article 3 (2) provides the FET provision as —'*Investments and returns of investors of each Contracting Party shall at all times be accorded fair and equitable treatment in the territory of the other Contracting Party*'. There is no reference to customary international law.

[70]*LFH Neer and Pauline Neer (USA) v United Mexican States* (15 October 1926) reprinted in (2006) 4 UNRIAA 60. See also *Glamis Gold v The United States of America*, UNCITRAL, Award, (8 June 2009) para 614.

[71]See Merrill and Ring v Canada, paras 205–211; ADF Group Inc. v. United States of America, ICSID Case No. ARB (AF)/00/1, Award 179 (Jan. 9, 2003). http://www.italaw.com/sites/default/files/case-documents/ita0009.pdf. Also see *Gold Reserve Inc v Bolivia*, ICSID Case No ARB(AF)/09/1, Award, (22 September 2014), para 567.

[72]Ibid (n 59).

[73]See 2016 Model BIT (n 4) Article 3.

[74]Ibid, Article 3.1 provides—No Party shall subject investments made by investors of the other Party to measures which constitute a violation of customary international law through:

(i) Denial of justice in any judicial or administrative proceedings; or
(ii) fundamental breach of due process; or
(iii) targeted discrimination on manifestly unjustified grounds, such as gender, race or religious belief; or
(iv) manifestly abusive treatment, such as coercion, duress and harassment.

[75]See Hanessian and Duggal (n 30).

[76]Saluka v. The Czech Republic, 284; Metaplar v Argentina, Award, 6 January 2008, 187; AES v Hungary, Award, 23 September 2010, 9.3.40.

arbitrary manner, it breaches the international minimum standard.[77] The ICJ, in the ELSI case[78] gave some guidance regarding the meaning of arbitrary action—the court said arbitrariness 'is not so much something opposed to a rule of law, as something opposed to the rule of law … It is a wilful disregard of due process of law, an act which shocks, at least surprises, a sense of juridical propriety'.[79] Non-inclusion of something like 'manifest arbitrariness' in the Indian Model BIT as one of the grounds to challenge host State's regulatory conduct leaves a gap for protection of foreign investment. Inclusion of 'manifest arbitrariness' would have meant that while the host State's regulatory conduct would be judged using a high standard and thus provide enough regulatory latitude, it would also ensure that foreign investors have a recourse when host States acts in bad faith or in an irrational or manifestly unreasonable manner.

5 Full Protection and Security

Another major treaty provision found in most BITs is 'full protection and security' (FPS). As part of this provision, host States undertake an obligation to provide FPS to foreign investment. However, BITs, like the FET provision, do not usually define meaning of FPS. This has given rise to debate whether FPS is confined to physical safety and protection of investments or does it also include other kinds of protection.[80] Many tribunals have interpreted FPS to mean that it puts the host State under an obligation to ensure physical safety and protection of foreign investment.[81] Some arbitral tribunals have expanded the meaning of FPS from physical protection to also include regulatory and legal security.[82] For example, in *CME v Czech Republic*, the tribunal while analysing the obligation of 'full security and protection' held that '*the host State is obligated to ensure that neither by amendment of its laws nor by actions of its administrative bodies is the agreed and approved security and protection of the foreign investor's investment withdrawn or devalued*'.[83] We still have some

---

[77]International Thunderbird v Mexico, 197. Also see Glamis Gold v Mexico, 625; Cargil v Mexico, 298.

[78]Case Concerning Electronica Sicula S.p.A. (ELSI) (U.S.A. v. Italy), Judgement, 1989 I.C.J. Rep. 1989 (July 20).

[79]Ibid, para 31.

[80]Dolzer and Schreuer (n 44), 160–61.

[81]*AAPL v Sri Lanka* ICSID Case No ARB/87/3, Final Award, (27 June 1990); *AMT v Zaire* ICSID Case No ARB/93/1, Award, (21 February 1997).

[82]Newcombe and Paradell (n 67), 310.

[83]*CME Czech Republic v The Czech Republic*, UNCITRAL, Partial Award, 913 September 2001), para 613. see also *Azurix v Argentina*, ICSID Case No ARB/01/12, Award, (14 July 2006), paras 406–408; *Siemens v Argentina*, ICSID Case No. ARB/02/8, Award, (6 February 2007), para 303; *National Grid v Argentina*, UNCITRAL, Award, (3 November 2008), paras 187–90; *Total S.A. v Argentine Republic*, ICSID Case No. ARB/04/1, Decision on Liability, (27 December 2010), para 343.

tribunals that have held that FPS only provides for protection to foreign investment from physical injury and does not encompass other kinds of regulatory protection such as maintenance of stable and legal commercial or business environment.[84]

The 2016 Model BIT provides that foreign investment and investors shall be accorded full protection and security.[85] Further, the Model provides that FPS is restricted to physical security for foreign investment and investors and does not extend to '*any other obligation whatsoever*'.[86] Given the arbitral maze on the actual scope of the FPS provision, this clarity in the Indian Model BIT will help curb arbitral discretion. It also reconciles investment protection with host State's regulatory power. On the one hand, it puts the host State under an obligation to provide physical security to foreign investment, and at the same time, ensures that adoption of host State's regulatory measures that might impact the business or legal environment cannot be challenged as violation of FPS though such regulatory measures may be challengeable under other BIT provisions.

6 Non-precluded-Measures (NPM) Clause

Non Precluded Measures (NPM) provisions in a BIT, also known as General Exceptions clause (starting with words like—'*nothing in this agreement precludes…*') provide the regulatory latitude to host countries to deal with threats to important national interests.[87] NPM provisions provide flexibility to countries to deviate from the substantive obligations in certain circumstances that warrant giving preference to non-investment policy goals over investment protection. Given the debate on conflict between investment protection and host country's regulatory power, NPM provisions in BITs are useful tools that allow a host country to adopt measures for the pursuance of non-investment objectives without incurring any liability under international law.

---

[84]*AWG Group v The Argentine Republic*, ICSID Case No. ARB/03/19, Decision on Liability, (30 July 2010), para 179. Also see *Saluka Investments BV v The Czech Republic*, UNCITRAL, Partial Award, (17 March 2006), para 484; *BG Group Plc. v The Republic of Argentina*, UNCITRAL, Final Award, (24 December 2007), paras 323–326; *Crystallex International Corporation v. Bolivarian Republic of Venezuela*, ICSID Case No. ARB(AF)/11/2, Award, (10 March 2016) para 632.

[85]See 2016 Model BIT (n 4) Article 3.2.

[86]Ibid, Article 3.2 provides: *For greater certainty, "full protection and security" only refers to a Party's obligations relating to physical security of investors and to investments made by the investors of the other Party and not to any other obligation whatsoever*".

[87]Salacuse (n 44) 343; Andrew Newcombe "General Exceptions in International Investment Agreements" in Marie-Claire C. Segger et al. (eds), '*Sustainable Development in World Investment Law*' (Kluwer 2011), 355, 356–357.

NPM provisions in BITs were put to a test when a spate of arbitration cases were brought against Argentina for adopting measures aimed at addressing an economic crisis in early 2000.[88] For example, US investors claimed that the regulatory measures adopted by Argentina violated many provisions of the US-Argentina BIT; whereas Argentina relied on the NPM provision given in Article XI of the BIT[89] as a defence for these claims.[90] These cases, despite similar facts and law, have resulted in conflicting decisions with some ITA tribunals concluding that Argentina's action cannot be condoned under Article XI[91] whereas some have held otherwise.[92]

A NPM provision has two main elements—first, the permissible objectives; and second, the nexus requirement. Permissible objectives means those objectives mentioned in the NPM provision for which the host state can deviate from its treaty obligations. Important to note that a host state will be able to deviate from its BIT obligations, relying on the NPM provision, only for those objectives that are contained in the NPM provision and not for other objectives.[93] Nexus requirement in a NPM provision is the link between adopted measures and the permissible objective to be achieved through that measure. Words such as 'necessary' require a

[88]For more on the Argentine economic crisis and subsequent IIA disputes see—J. Alvarez and K. Khamsi 'The Argentine Crisis and Foreign Investors' in Sauvant K. (ed), *Yearbook on International Investment Law and Policy 2008-2009* (OUP 2009) 379.

[89]Article XI provides—'*This treaty shall not preclude the application by either party of measures necessary for the maintenance of public order, the fulfillment of its obligations with respect to the maintenance or restoration of international peace or security, or the protection of its own essential security interests*'.

[90]See *CMS Gas Transmission Co v Argentina*, (n 33); *CMS Gas Transmission Company v Argentina*, ICSID Case No ARB/01/8 (Annulment Proceedings); *Enron Corporation Ponderossa Assets v Argentine Republic*, ICSID Case No ARB/01/3; *Enron Creditors Recovery Corp v Argentina* ICSID Case No ARB/01/3 (Annulment Proceeding); *Sempra Energy International v Argentina*, ICSID Case No ARB/02/16; *Sempra Energy International v Argentina,* ICSID Case No ARB/02/16 (Annulment Proceedings); *LG&E Energy Corporation v Argentina*, ICISD Case No ARB/02/1, Decision on Liability, (03 October 2006); *Continental Casualty Company v Argentina*, ICSID Case No ARB/03/9, (05 September 2008); *El Paso v Argentina*, ICSID Case No. ARB/03/15, (31 October 2011).

[91]*CMS Gas Transmission Co v Argentina*, (n 33); *Enron Corporation v Argentina*, ICSID Case No ARB/01/3; *Sempra Energy International v Argentina*, ICSID Case No ARB/02/16.

[92]Ibid (n 109), *LG&E Energy Corporation v Argentina*; *Continental Casualty Company v Argentina*.

[93]For more discussion on this see William Burke-White and Andreas Von Staden, "Investment Protection in Extraordinary Times: The Interpretation and Application of Non-Precluded Measures Provisions in Bilateral Investment Treaties" (2008) 48 Va. J. Int'l L. 314. For a discussion on NPM provision in Indian BITs see Prabhash Ranjan 'Non Precluded Measures in Indian International Investment Agreements and India's Regulatory Power as a Host Nation' (2012) 2 Asian J. Int. Law, 29. For a different view point on the inclusion of General Exception clauses in BITs, see A Newcombe, 'The Use of General Exceptions in IIAs: Increasing Legitimacy or Uncertainty?' in A. de Mestral and C. Lévesque (eds), *Improving International Investment Agreements* (London, Routledge, 2013) 267.

stronger connection between the regulatory measure and permissible objective compared to words like 'related to'.

The 2016 Model BIT contains a separate chapter on exceptions covering both general and security exceptions. Article 32 contains general exceptions with a long list of permissible objectives, which includes protection of public morals[94]; maintenance of public order[95]; protection of human, animal or plant life or health[96]; protection and conservation of the environment[97]; to ensure compliance with domestic laws that are not inconsistent with the provisions of the treaty.[98] The inclusion these permissible objectives will provide opportunities to reconcile investment protection with the host State's right to regulate.

Another interesting aspect of the NPM provision is that it contains 'necessary' as the only next requirement for all the above-mentioned permissible objectives. Furthermore, the treaty, in footnote 6, provides guidance to the arbitral tribunal in how to determine whether a measure is 'necessary'.[99] Footnote 6 provides that in considering whether a measure is necessary, the tribunal shall take into account whether there was no less restrictive alternative measure reasonably available to the country or not. This author has already argued for this interpretation of necessary to be put in the text.[100] This interpretation of 'necessary' has the following advantages. First, it will serve host State's regulatory power better by dissuading the arbitral tribunal from judging the relative importance of host State's regulatory objective with the restriction on foreign investment.[101] Second, it will also ensure that an arbitral tribunal shall not conflate the treaty based defence of 'necessity' with the 'necessity' defence under customary international law.[102] Third, by requiring that only least investment restrictive measure, which is reasonably available to the host country be adopted, this test will also ensure that foreign investment is not unduly restricted.

However, a major textual flaw in Article 32 is the absence of a chapeau, which would have ensured that host State's measures are applied in a manner that do not constitute a misuse or abuse of the NPM provisions. To make sure that host State's

---

[94]2016 Indian Model BIT, (n 4) Article 32.1 (i).

[95]Ibid.

[96]2016 Indian Model BIT, (n 4) Article 32.1 (ii).

[97]2016 Indian Model BIT, (n 4) Article 32.1 (iv).

[98]2016 Indian Model BIT, (n 4) Article 32.1 (iii).

[99]2016 Indian Model BIT, (n 4) footnote 6.

[100]Ranjan (n 32), 33–34.

[101]Relative judging of the host State's regulatory objective with the restriction on foreign investment will take place if the arbitral tribunal adopts a proportionality kind of analysis. For more on this see Ranjan (2011).

[102]Article 25 of the ILC Articles provides the 'necessity' defence under customary international law. Some tribunals have adopted this methodology such as CMS v Argentina (n 33); see also Kurtz (n 35).

don't abuse their regulatory power, the NPM provisions should contain a chapeau specifying that there shall be no unjustifiable discrimination or that there shall be no disguised restriction, as is the case with Article XX of GATT.[103]

7 Taxation Is Outside the Scope of the BIT

Article 2.4(ii) states that the treaty shall not apply to '*any law or measure regarding taxation, including measures taken to enforce taxation obligations*'. This article further provides that host State's decision that a particular regulatory measure is related to taxation, whether made before or after the commencement of arbitral proceedings, shall be non-justiciable.[104] No arbitral tribunal shall be able to review such decision.[105]

It is quite evident that India has decided to keep taxation measures outside the purview of the BIT in response to Vodafone and Cairn challenging India's retrospective application of taxation law under different BITs, as mentioned before. Excluding taxation measures completely means that foreign investors shall not be able to challenge such measures under BITs under any circumstance. Moreover allowing host State to have the last word on whether a regulatory matter pertains to taxation or not might lead to regulatory abuse. In any case, excluding taxation measures altogether from the purview of the BIT is a disproportionate reaction especially when it has been argued that taxation is part of a State's police power and thus it justifies non-compensation even in cases of deprivation of foreign investment.[106] Though one concedes that the actual scope of claiming that that taxation is part of State's police powers and is thus non-compensable is far from settled,[107] it is also true that arbitral tribunals shall give due deference to host states while adjudicating on host State's taxation-related regulatory measures. For example, the tribunal in *EnCana v Ecuador* recognised that if a tax law 'is extraordinary, or

[103]The significance of the chapeau in context of Article XX of GATT has been repeatedly asserted by the WTO Appellate Body. see Appellate Body Report—*United States: Standards for Reformulated and Conventional Gasoline,* WTO Doc. WT/DS2/AB/R (adopted April 29, 2016); Appellate Body Report—*United States: Import Prohibition of certain Shrimp and Shrimp Products*, WTO Doc. WT/DS58/AB/R (October 12, 1998). Also see Article 28.3 of the EU-Canada CETA.

[104]2016 Indian Model BIT (n 4), Article 2.4(ii).

[105]Ibid.

[106]Newcombe and Paradell (n 67), 358. See also Brownlie (2008), Louis B. Sohn and R.R. Baxter, 'Harvard Draft Convention on the International Responsibility of States for Injuries to Aliens' (1961) AJIL 55, Article 105.

[107]Prabhash Ranjan and Pushkar Anand 'Determination of Indirect Expropriation and Doctrine of Police Power in International Investment Law: A Critical Appraisal' in Leila Choukroune (ed), *Judging the State in International Trade and Investment Law* (Springer 2016), Forthcoming.

'punitive in amount', a claim of indirect expropriation can be made.[108] On the same line, the tribunal in *Burlington v Ecuador*, observed that 'confiscatory taxation constitutes an expropriation without compensation and is unlawful'.[109]

8 Investor State Dispute Settlement

The Indian Model BIT allows for investor-state dispute settlement or ITA. In terms of scope, ITA shall apply to a dispute between the host State and foreign investor only if the dispute arises out of an alleged breach of an obligation of the host State under Chapter II of this Treaty, other than the obligation under Articles 9 and 10 of this Treaty.[110] However, the foreign investor must submit the dispute first to local courts[111] and only after exhausting local remedies for at least a period of five years from the date when the foreign investor first acquired knowledge of the measure in question.[112] The requirement to exhaust local remedies shall not be applicable '*if the investor can demonstrate that there are no available domestic legal remedies capable of reasonably providing any relief in respect of the same measure*'.[113]

The foreign investor, after exhausting all local remedies for five years, if no satisfactory resolution has been reached, can commence the arbitral process by transmission of a notice of dispute to the host State.[114] This 'notice of dispute' will be accompanied by another six months of attempts by the investor and the State to resolve the dispute through meaningful negotiation, consultation or other third party procedures.[115] In case there is no amicable settlement of the dispute, the investor can submit a claim to arbitration,[116] subject to the following additional conditions—first, not more than six years have elapsed from the date on which the investor first

[108] *EnCana Corporation* v. *Ecuador*, LCIA Case No. UN3481, UNCITRAL, Award, (3 February 2006) para 177.

[109] *Burlington Resource Inc v Republic of Equador*, ICSID Case No. ARB/08/5, Decision on Liability, (14 Decembar 2012); see also *Occidental Exploration and Production Company v Republic of Equador*, LCIA Case No UN3467, UNCITRAL, Award, (1 July 2004) para 85, where it was said that 'Taxation can result in expropriation as can other types of regulatory measures'; *Link-Trading Joint-Stock Company v Republic of Moldova*, UNCITRAL, Final Award, (18 April 2002) para 64 (As a general matter, fiscal measures only become expropriatory when they are found to be an abusive taking. Abuse arises where it is demonstrated that the Slate has acted unfairly or inequitably towards the investment, where it has adopted measures that are arbitrary or discriminatory in character or in their manner of implementation, or where the measures taken violate an obligation undertaken by the State in regard to the investment').

[110] Ibid Article 13.2.

[111] 2016 Indian Model BIT, (n 4) Article 15.1.

[112] 2016 Indian Model BIT, (n 4) Article 15.2.

[113] 2016 Indian Model BIT, (n 4) Article 15.1.

[114] 2016 Indian Model BIT, Article 15.2.

[115] 2016 Indian Model BIT, Article 15.4.

[116] 2016 Indian Model BIT, Article 16.

acquired or should have acquired knowledge of the measure in question[117]; and/or, second, not more than 12 months have elapsed from the conclusion of domestic proceedings[118]; third, before submitting the claim to arbitration, a minimum of 90 days' notice has to be given to host state[119]; fourth, the investor must waive the 'right to initiate or continue any proceedings' under the domestic laws of the host state.[120] Additionally, in cases where the claim is submitted by a foreign investor in respect of loss or damage to a juridical person owned or controlled by the former, the juridical person shall have to waive its right to initiate or continue any proceedings under the laws of the host state.[121] All these conditions make it quite difficult for foreign investors to initiate investment treaty arbitration against the host State, and thus, tilt the balance in favour the host State.

9 Conclusion

India's decision to adopt a new Model BIT especially in light of the growing debate on how to reconcile investment protection with host State's right to regulate, should be welcomed. India, at last, woke up, courtesy foreign investors suing India under different BITs, to the reality that broad and vague investment protection standards can be interpreted in manners that give precedence to investment protection over host State's right to regulate. There are two critical lessons that other Asian countries, especially the ones in the South Asian region, can learn from India's experience. First, a country need not wait to be hit by a BIT claim to begin the process of reviewing its BITs. Second, a country can be critical of the BIT regime and yet remain continuously engaged in. The fact that India has adopted a new Model BIT that continues to give the right to foreign investors to challenge India's regulatory measures under ITA is proof of this.

However, a critical aspect is the terms of this engagement. The terms of engagement with the ITA system should be such that it balances investment protection with host State's right to regulate and not go to the other end of spectrum of tilting the scale in favour of host State's right to regulate. As the discussion in this chapter demonstrates, the Indian Model BIT, barring some of the provisions like FPS, has not quite been able to balance the twin objectives of investment protection and State's regulatory power. Narrow definition of investment, an extremely narrow FET-type provision, exclusion of a MFN clause and of taxation measures from the purview of the BIT, a NPM provision without a chapeau and a complicated and sequential investor state dispute settlement, tilt the scale towards host State's right

[117]2016 Indian Model BIT, Article 15.5(i).

[118]2016 Indian Model BIT, Article 15.5(ii). Also see Hanessian and Duggal (2017), 7.

[119]2015 Indian Model BIT, Article 15.5(v).

[120]2015 Indian Model BIT, Article 15.5(iii).

[121]2015 Indian Model BIT, Article 15.5(iv).

to regulate. Furthermore, although the attempt of the Model BIT is to reduce arbitral discretion, as the discussion in the chapter shows, many provisions still remain undefined and thus, continue to grant significant discretion to arbitral tribunals. Consequently, whether a balance would be struck between investment protection and host State's right to regulate would depend on the approach adopted by an arbitral tribunal. Thus, Asian countries that wish to develop new Model BITs should strike a balance between investment protection and host State's right to regulate and also define the BIT provisions with as much precision as possible so as to minimize arbitral discretion.[122]

[122]Henckels (2016).

China's Regulation of Foreign Direct Investment

Leon E. Trakman

1 Introduction

China has grown into the second largest economy in the world. It is the largest recipient of foreign direct investment ('FDI') and fifth in outward FDI, recently overtaking the United States as the world's largest trading nation.[1] A Special Report of the Asia Society indicates that FDI from China to the USA is more than doubling annually.[2] China's projected investment is expected to reach close to US$2 trillion by 2020. China's investments are diverse and global. It is a net importer of, among other products, oil, gas, and coal. It is investing significantly in Africa, Asia and South America to meet its energy supply needs.[3]

China's growth as an importer and exporter of FDI in the last two decades is also reflected in its investment and related contractual practices.[4] While it employs a Model BIT which guides its investment treaty practices, its treaties are also adapted

---

[1]See e.g., China Eclipses US as Biggest Trading Nation. Bloomberg News (2013). www.bloomberg.com/news/articles/2013-02-09/china-passes-u-s-to-become-the-world-s-biggest-trading-nation. Accessed 1 November 2014. Also see World Investment Report (2010). UNCTAD (2010). www.unctad.org. Accessed 1 November 2014.

[2]See Rosen and Hanemann (2011, p. 35).

[3]See Gu et al. (2008, p. 274), Neumayer and Laura (2005, p. 1567).

[4]On the growth in Chinese FDI, see Statistics of FDI In January–July 2012. Ministry of Commerce, People's Republic of China (2012). http://english.mofcom.gov.cn/aarticle/statistic/foreigninvestment/201208/20120808295811.html. Accessed 1 November 2014. On China's growing leadership in international investment law and practice generally, see Wang (2009, p. 575), see also Schill (2007, p. 73).

L.E. Trakman (✉)
Faculty of Law, University of New South Wales, Sydney, Australia
e-mail: l.trakman@unsw.edu.au

J. Chaisse et al. (eds.), *Asia's Changing International Investment Regime*,
International Law and the Global South, DOI 10.1007/978-981-10-5882-0_6

to the circumstances of its treaty partners. Initially concerned primarily about regulating inbound investment to protect itself from foreign investors, China's treaties increasingly focus on outbound investments given the growth of outbound investment, including but not limited to investments by state owned enterprises ('SOEs') abroad.[5]

The result is that China has concluded the second largest number of BITs to date, following Germany.[6] This is a significant development considering that China concluded its first BIT in 1982 with Sweden and its second BIT in 1989. It ratified the International Centre for Settlement of Investment Disputes Convention in 1993 ('ICSID Convention').[7] Equally striking is the development of China's three Model BITs, the first was initiated in the early 1980s, the second was developed in the mid-1990s, and the third was in 1998. A notable feature of the current Model BIT is in the emphasis that it gives to the investor the protection over market accession, China's endorsement of investor-state arbitration under the ICSID Convention and the United Nations Commission on International Trade Law's ('UNCITRAL') ad hoc rules of arbitration, and China's sanctioning of umbrella clauses which protects the rights of investors from treaty partner states.[8]

China's BITs extend across the globe. Among them are close to 30 BITs with African countries including, among others, Egypt, Ghana, Kenya, Mali, Mozambique, South Africa and Tunisia.[9] China also has BITs with various Western countries, such as with Germany concluded in 2004. It is currently negotiating BITs with the Gulf Cooperation Council, ASEAN, the South African Customs Union and Closer Economic Partnerships with Hong Kong and Macao, and for some years, with the US. It recently entered into an investment agreement with Korea and Japan, as well as with Canada. Accentuating its BIT programme, China has entered into thirteen new free trade agreements ('FTA') in the last decade, with others under

---

[5]See Yang (2012, p. 6), Qing (2012, p. 18). See generally, Poulsen (2012).

[6]The number of Chinese and German BITs are not exceptional in themselves, given that BITs have grown from 1 in 1959 to well over 3,000 today. See 'Caseload–Statistics (Issue 2012–2)' *ICSID* (2012). http://icsid.worldbank.org/ICSID/FrontServlet?requestType=ICSIDDocRH&actionVal=CaseLoadStatistics. Accessed 1 November 2014; UNCTAD (2012). See generally Trakman (2014a, b, p. 367).

[7]See, e.g., 'List of contracting states and other signatories of the convention' *ICSID* (2012), http://ICSID.worldbank.org/ICSID/FrontServlet?requestType=ICSIDDocRH&actionVal=ShowDocument&language=English. Accessed 1 November 2014. See too Willems (2011, p. 1). Schreuer (2011).

[8]An example of China's endorsement of ISA under the ICSID and UNCITRAL is contained in Article 5 and 9 of the Germany-China BIT which came into force on December 11 2005. Article 10(2) of that BIT provides an umbrella clause, providing that each state party shall respect its treaty obligations relating to investors from the other state party. On the provisions in China's Model BIT, see Shan and Gallagher (2009a, b).

[9]For a list of China's BITs, see 'Full list of Bilateral Investment Agreements concluded, 1 June 2013' *UNCTAD* (2013). www.unctad.org/sections/dite_pcbb/docs/bits_china.pdf. Accessed October 13, 2014; The text of each BIT is available at www.unctadxi.org/templates/docsearch_779.aspx. Accessed 13 October 2014; On China's investment treaty partners, see https://ICSID.worldbank.org/ICSID/FrontServlet. Accessed 13 October 2014. See too Kragelund (2009, p. 479).

negotiation. It has negotiated a free trade agreement with Australia and has further FTAs with the EU, India and Switzerland under consideration.[10]

This introductory chapter canvasses China's recent foray into BITs. It begins with an outline of China's BIT program by looking at its model investment treaties and analyses some of the BITs that were concluded by China with other states. Second, the chapter examines the operation of China's BITs by analysing the claims brought under these agreements. Finally, the chapter examines China's contemporary approaches to the regulation of FDI in light of the recently concluded FTA with Australia and the global regulatory climate. The chapter concludes that while China will likely restrict the rights of investors in its future BITs, it will be unlikely to deviate significantly from the established regulatory practices.

2 China's BIT Program

China's early BITs only permitted disputes to proceed to arbitration on the basis of the amount of compensation sought for expropriation rather than based on a determination of whether China had engaged in an expropriation. The underlying assumption was that China's regulation of foreign investment was not subject to legal challenge under the doctrine of sovereign immunity.[11] China also did not include, in its earlier BITs, substantive national treatment obligations, directed at according foreign investors the same treatment as its nationals.[12]

Broadly, China adhered to a two-tier policy in its early BIT program while it was predominantly an inbound investment destination and not yet a major exporter of capital. It concluded BITs with developed states primarily to build its economic infrastructure through inbound and increasingly, outbound investment. It signed BITs with developing countries primarily to build diplomatic alliances and to satisfy its resource needs and only with the secondary objective of promoting outbound investment in the short term. This dual track approach is understandable. China sought to establish an effective international investment regime at a time in which it was undergoing significant transformation, economically, politically and socially.[13]

---

[10]On China's various bilateral investment agreements, see 'China—Bilaterals.org' www.bilaterals.org/spip.php?rubrique118. Accessed 13 October 2014. China has also signed over ninety Double Taxation Avoidance Treaties (DTTs), See www.chinatax.gov.cn/n8136506/n8136593/n8137537/n8687294/8688432.html. Accessed October 13, 2014. On the announcement of an EU-China BIT in 2013, see http://europa.eu/rapid/press-release_IP-14-33_en.htm. On the first round of EU-China BIT negotiations, see http://ec.europa.eu/trade/policy/countries-and-regions/countries/china/.

[11]On China's early BIT practice of providing for ISA only in respect of compensation, as distinct from the State's right to regulate property, see Chinese Model BIT, reprinted in Shan and Gallagher (2009a, b). See too e.g., art 12(3) of the Singapore-China Free Trade Agreement.

[12]See generally, Li (2010, p. 1).

[13]See e.g., China-Romania BIT (1983), China-Thailand (1985), China-Sri Lanka (1986) and China-Poland (1988). Li (2010, p. 114).

Consequently, during its first generation of BITs commencing in 1982, China reserved extensive regulatory powers and accorded limited protections to inbound investors. For example, in acceding to the ICSID Convention in 1993, China restricted the scope of investor-state arbitration ('ISA') under its first and second Model BITs.[14] China also stipulated that foreign investors had to resort to domestic administrative review before referring disputes to ISA. In addition, it imposed a waiting period of three to nine months in order to provide parties with the opportunity to reach a settlement. Only after having exhausted local remedies and these waiting periods, could foreign investors initiate ISA proceedings against a host state.[15] The requirement is also found in selected newer Chinese BITs including the China–Korea BIT (2009).

China gradually modified its negotiated BITs after it adopted its 'Going Abroad' strategy in 1999 and propagated its 2001 Outline of the Tenth Five-Year Plan for National Economy and Social Development,[16] including a focus on outbound investment.[17] Threshold influences on its BIT practice stemmed from its accession to the ICSID in 1993, its inclusion of ISA in its BITs, and providing that foreign investors receive national treatment in its more recent BITs.[18]

China became active as an inbound and outbound participant in the later stages of the global development of BITs,[19] with a meteoric rise to pre-eminence as the country with the most BITs, of which the significant majority are still in force.[20]

Nevertheless, the liberalization of Chinese BITs under its current third Model BIT may be reversed in the near future. In particular, while China's fourth Model treaty is still in the drafting stages and expected within a year, commentators believe that it will restrict investors' rights and access to ISA more than its current Model BIT which grants significant protections to foreign investors.[21]

China will not be alone in restricting investor protections. The latest US Model BIT upon which the Chinese Model BIT is likely to draw, has extended the scope of a state's right to engage in regulatory expropriation. The US Model BIT

[14]On the development of China's Model investment agreements, see Shan and Gallagher (2013).

[15]Trakman (2012a, b, c, 2014a, b).

[16]The Outline of this Plan is available at *The State Council, The People's Republic of China*. http://english.gov.cn/official/2005-07/29/content_18334.htm. Accessed 2 November 2014. For some of the effects of China's 'Going Abroad' Policy, see 'China's go abroad policy produces effects' *People* Daily (2011). http://english.peopledaily.com.cn/90001/90778/90861/7443645.html. Accessed 1 November 2014.

[17]See Cai (2006, p. 62).

[18]See Shan and Gallagher (2009a, b, ss 1.77–1.82).

[19]See Ministry of Commerce, People's Republic of China, Department of Treaty and Law, http://tfs.mofcom.gov.cn/column/2010.shtml. Accessed 2 November 2014.

[20]Li (2010, p. 1).

[21]See, e.g., Shan and Zhang (2013, p. 1), Shan et al. (2012, p. 120, para 229). But see the US-China BIT, which subjects the admission of FDI to both MFN and national treatment clauses. See Dolzer et al. (1995, p. 49).

has restricted the rights of foreign investors under standards of fair and equitable treatment, minimum standards of justice and national treatment and has provided a subjective national security test by which state parties to BITs define their own national interests, as distinct from being based on objective criteria.[22] Still, China faces a particular dilemma in restricting investor protections. As a developing country, it is conceivably cautious of ISA as a means by which foreign investors can mount investment claims against developing countries under international investment laws that accord better protection to those investors than Chinese domestic law.[23] However, ISA is also attractive to inbound investors who want to limit risks when they invest in developing countries. Thus, in recent years China has expanded the scope of ISA, particularly in its bilateral agreement with Canada and its trilateral agreement with Japan and Korea, extending investor protections to protect its growing outbound investors from the regulatory defences of other host states.[24]

China's policy dilemma is reflected in its Model BITs and the subsequent agreements concluded with resource rich states. These developments are analysed below.

2.1 China's Model BITs

China's accession to over 140 BITs has rekindled interest in China's current Model BIT and what provisions it may include in its fourth Model BIT. This interest gives rise to several questions.[25] First, how distinctive is China's current Model BIT from the Model BITs adopted by other countries, such as the United States and Canada? Second, to what extent does China incorporate its Model BIT into its negotiated BITs, and how do its negotiated BITs vary from its current Model BIT? Thirdly, what inferences can one draw from China's short but intensive Model BIT history?

China's negotiated BITs have gone through generational changes, mostly in accordance with its changing Model BITs. First it is important to appreciate that China's first Model BIT did not provide for ISA. Its second Model BIT provides for ISA, but China chose not to incorporate ISA in all its ensuing BITs that were otherwise based on that Model BIT. China's third and current Model BIT provides

---

[22]See United States Model Bilateral Investment Treaty (2012) at www.ustr.gov/sites/default/files/BIT%20text%20for%20ACIEP%20Meeting.pdf. Accessed 1 November 2014. On the illustrative measure of "investment" in the US Model BIT, see Gudgeon (2012, p. 105).

[23]See Shan (2013).

[24]On China's shifting position in regard to investment arbitration, see generally Bath and Luke (eds) (2011).

[25]China has over 140 BITs, surpassing Germany that had signed the most BITs until recently. For an overview of China's BITs, see generally, 'FTA News Release' *China FTA Network*. http://fta.mofcom.gov.cn/english/index.shtml. Accessed 1 November 2014.

for ISA for all investor-state disputes, which it also embodies in its negotiated agreements.

Second, China's first generation of Model BITs limited investor claims to compensation, as distinct from claims relating to the nature of an expropriation. China's current Model BIT entertains claims based on both the nature of an expropriation and the extent of compensation.

Despite this change in the treatment of expropriation, ISA tribunals are likely to interpret the scope of expropriation narrowly, particularly in relation to an indirect expropriation. However, it is difficult to argue with conviction that the absence of ISA awards to date against China under its current Model BIT is due to the tradition of ISA tribunals construing BITs narrowly.[26]

An analysis of China's current Model BIT provides a number of observations. The preamble includes three principles: (i) to facilitate and attract investment; (ii) to contribute to the prosperity of both contracting states; and (iii) to cooperate on the basis of equality and mutual benefit.[27]

Article 1(1) of the Model BIT adopts an asset-based definition of investment that is comparable to definitions of investment adopted in the West. It states: 'The term 'investment' means *every kind of asset invested* by investors of one Contracting Party *in accordance with the laws and regulations of the other Contracting Party* in the territory of the latter',[28] followed by a non-exhaustive list of different asset classes of such investments.

One can question the nature and non-exhaustive character of investments. One can also query the reference to, 'in accordance with the laws and regulations' of the host state. Despite these criticisms, open-ended language in defining or circumscribing the scope of an investment, including through a list of asset classes, is not uncommon in BITs, notwithstanding the paucity of ISA disputes interpreting that language under a Chinese BIT in particular.[29]

China's Model BIT also does not include an objective measure of an 'investment'. However, it does provide illustrations of investments from which ISA tribunals can draw in determining the boundaries of an investment, such as in distinguishing between movable and immovable property, interests in companies, contractual rights, intellectual property rights and business concessions. In extending its application beyond the 2012 US Model BIT, it also adopts an illustrative measure of an "investment". There is also ISA jurisprudence in which tribunals have implied an objective measure of an investment, involving third-party BITs and FTAs.[30]

---

[26]See Shan and Gallagher (2013), ch 4.

[27]See Preambles in the three versions of the Chinese Model BITs respectively.

[28]Emphasis added.

[29]See e.g., Cole and Anuj Kumar (2011, p. 305).

[30]See United States Model Bilateral Investment Treaty (2012). www.ustr.gov/sites/default/files/BIT%20text%20for%20ACIEP%20Meeting.pdf. Accessed 1 November 2014. On the illustrative measure of 'investment' in the US Model BIT, see Gudgeon (2012, p. 105). On different methods of determining an 'investment' in international investment law, see Gaillard (2009, p. 403), Yannaca-Small (2010, p. 248).

Regulations concerning the administration of investment are provided in Article 2 of China's Model BIT. The article delineates fundamental standards for the promotion and protection of FDI, the principles governing the admission of an investment, provision for constant protection and security measures, and obligations of non-discrimination. There is nothing particularly unusual about this Article. The principles governing the admission of investments that focus less on market access to FDI than on subjecting FDI to the traditional sovereignty rights of the host state are not peculiar to China.[31]

Article 3(1) of the Model BIT provides that foreign investors enjoy the constant protection and security in the territory of the other Contracting Party. This is also unremarkable. Nor is Article 3(2), providing for 'national treatment' of investors from home partner states, unusual.[32] What is noteworthy, however, is that the 'national treatment' of foreign investors is not invariably included in Chinese BITs.[33] One explanation is that China historically resisted a national treatment standard, despite incorporating it into its current Model BIT, and that China continues to resist incorporating it into specific BITs. Another explanation is that China sometimes accords foreign investors more than national treatment; and indeed, rejects a minimal standard of treatment accorded to foreign investors as imperialist and colonialist and in conflict with contemporary international law.[34] It is clear that the purpose is not only to enhance trade and investment, but also to add to the prosperity of the contracting states. Other Model BITs adopted by North American and European countries may not articulate their national interest in similar language, but it is reasonable to infer that the prosperity of the host state is likely to be identified with the national interest of any state party to a BIT.[35]

Article 4 provides for expropriation. It is probably the most controversial article in the Model BIT. It sets out four conditions to legitimate an expropriation. The expropriation must (i) be in the public interest; (ii) be in accordance with domestic legal procedure; (iii) be undertaken on a non-discriminatory basis; and (iv) provide for compensation.

It is likely that, in setting out these four conditions governing an expropriation, the Model BIT purports to legitimate other forms of regulatory action over foreign investors that fall short of such an expropriation. This would effectively restrict the range of actions that foreign investors can bring against a host state under a

---

[31]See e.g., Shan (2013, p. 219). But see the US-China BIT which subjects the admission of FDI to both MFN and national treatment clauses; Dolzer et al. (1995, p. 49). See generally, Goldhaber (2003, p. 22).

[32]'Without prejudice to its laws and regulations, each Contracting Party shall accord to investments and activities associated with such investments by the investors of the other Contracting Party treatment not less favorable than that accorded to the investments and associated activities by its own investors.'

[33]Shan (2013, p. 233).

[34]Yao (1987, p. 334), cited in Shan (2013, p. 232). See too Shan et al. (2012, p. 120).

[35]On distinctive 'national interest' and 'national security' issues relating to FDI in Asia and China in particular, see Bath (2012, p. 5).

Chinese BIT. Article 4 also does not specifically accord due process of law to a foreign investor. What is also uncertain is the extent to which the requirement that an expropriation be in accordance with 'domestic legal procedure' replicates a due process standard. If that 'procedure' guarantees a foreign investor procedural justice, it would mirror some aspects of due process as an American constitutional lawyer might conceive of due process. Even if a 'domestic legal procedure' falls short of such due process, that deficiency arguably would be offset somewhat by the requirement that an expropriation should not be discriminatory under Article 2 and that compensation should be paid under Article 4(iv) of the Chinese Model BIT.[36] It may also be overcome to some extent if the BIT included an article provided for the national treatment of foreign investors.

Finally, two provisions in China's Model BIT deal with dispute resolution. Article 8 regulates the settlement of disputes between contracting parties. Article 9 deals with the settlement of disputes between host states and foreign investors. Neither provision is particularly unusual. Article 8 provides that state parties must first attempt to settle their dispute through consultation. Failing that, provision is made for an ad hoc arbitration. Should that also fail, resort can be had to the International Court of Justice. Such an incremental approach to resolving disputes between states is conventional, and arguably, is quite defensible in relation to investment disputes between state parties.

Regarding investor-state disputes, Article 9(2) requires the parties to try to settle their dispute amicably through negotiations. Should that fail, an investor can apply to a competent court of the contracting party, or to the ICSID.[37] Providing an investor with the choice of bringing a claim to a domestic court is investor friendly; however, it is also strategic. Chinese investors abroad may well appreciate the option of applying to a domestic court, depending on such factors as the reputation of that court, and the time, cost and convenience of proceeding there. Foreign investors in China may do the same. Again, there is little experience upon which to draw any definitive conclusions about which path foreign investors will choose in the absence of significant litigation or ISA under BITs based on China's Model BIT.[38]

A controversial issue historically involving China's 1992 Model BIT was that ISA tribunals would only determine the amount of compensation on the request of an investor which itself did not explicitly provide for prompt, adequate, and effective compensation. All other matters beyond compensation could only be submitted to ISA with the consent of both parties. The presupposition was that a state was entitled to exercise its sovereign authority in expropriating; and that such action was not itself subject to a legal challenge, unless that state so consented. It would seem, albeit not with certainty, that the current Model BIT resolves that issue

[36]On limitations associated with compensation in ISA proceedings and in international investment law generally, see Muthucumaraswamy (2003, p. 1).

[37]Article 13 provides for the settlement of disputes between investors and a contracting party.

[38]See Trakman and Kunal (2016).

in favour of ISA tribunals being empowered to make both determinations. However, China is not obliged to follow its own Model BIT and may decide, depending on the context, to vary from it in specific investment treaties. Much will also depend on how such a provision is interpreted by arbitration tribunals, should ISA claims against China eventuate.

2.2 *China's Impending Fourth Model BIT*

How will a new Chinese Model BIT change its negotiating practices? The dual dilemma for China in adopting a fourth Model BIT is in being seen as liberalizing its BITs generally in the interests of the free flow of FDI, but also in protecting its national interests from inbound foreign investors.

In practice, China may follow a pragmatic pathway in which it liberalizes its negotiated BITs incrementally and not necessarily generally. In particular, it is likely to agree to more extensive protection for foreign investors in treaties in which its primary purpose is to benefit its outbound investors in discrete partner states. It is likely to limit such protection in treaties in which its primary purpose is to regulate FDI flows into China. A Chinese BIT with a developing African country in which China is focused on building a diplomatic alliance and acquiring raw materials, is also likely to include state exemptions and investor protections that are quite different to a BIT China concludes with Canada, Australia, or Singapore. What is clear is that China is a great student of history and has learnt from the BIT practices of the West including about their economic, political and legal consequences.

Indeed, much has changed on the FDI landscape globally as well as for China since it devised its current Model BIT 15 years ago. In particular, newer models of BITs, including in Asia but also in the United States, provide more elaborate defences to investor claims. This is typified in the NAFTA case of *Methanex v. United States of America*,[39] in the US and Canadian Model Treaties,[40] and in the India-Singapore Economic Cooperation Agreement.[41] In particular, each treaty includes defences to investor claims on such extensive grounds as public health,

[39]See *Methanex Co v* US, Final Award, (7 August 2005). www.state.gov/documents/organization/51052.pdf. Accessed 2 November 2014; see also Methanex Corporation and the United States of America, NAFTA Claims. www.naftaclaims.com/disputes_us_6.htm. Accessed 2 November 2014; Kirkman (2002, p. 343).

[40]See United States Trade Representative, '2012 US Model Bilateral Investment Agreement'. www.ustr.gov/sites/default/files/BIT%20text%20for%20ACIEP%20Meeting.pdf. Accessed 1 November 2014. This replaces the Treaty between the Government of the United States of America and the Government of [Country] Concerning the Encouragement and Reciprocal Protection of Investment, '2004 Model BIT'. www.state.gov/documents/organization/117601.pdf. Accessed 1 November 2014.

[41]See 'Comprehensive Economic Cooperation Agreement between the Republic of India and the Republic of Singapore'. http://commerce.nic.in/ceca/toc.htm. Accessed 2 November 2014.

public morality, social welfare and sustainable development.[42] ICSID tribunals have also accommodated these defences.[43] They have rejected investor claims that such defences deny foreign investors fair and equitable treatment, or that a signatory state has exceeded the limits of the margin of appreciation in protecting its public interests over the investment interests of foreign investors.[44]

It is conceivable that China will reframe its fourth Model BIT to accommodate these developments, including by widening the scope of state exemptions and by further narrowing the ambit of an "expropriation". However, China may decide not to follow the lead of the West, not only to maintain its independence pathway as an inbound and outbound investment regime. It may appreciate the economic and political benefit of further liberalizing its international investment regime in contradistinction to Western countries that have retreated from such liberalization. Moreover, insofar as the articles in China's impending Model BIT are comparable, in whole or in part, to provisions in Model BITs devised by developed Western countries, ISA tribunals may apply determinations arising out of the latter BITs by analogy to Chinese BITs. This practice is subject to the observation that there is no formal precedent in international ISA jurisprudence and therefore no duty of ISA tribunals to adhere to prior decisions.[45]

What is arguable is that China's current Model BIT potentially provides foreign investors with as much protection as does the 2012 US Model BIT.[46] The 2012 US Model BIT restricts the scope of its earlier 2004 US Model BIT in linking a regulatory expropriation to the fair and equitable treatment of foreign investors, to a minimum standard of justice, and to an equal treatment of domestic and foreign investors.[47] The 2012 US Model BIT also includes subjective national security provisions and more expansive measures taken by governments to protect public

---

[42]See Newcombe (2008, p. 4).

[43]A series of cases illustrate these variable conceptions of 'fair and equitable' treatment. See *Maffezini v Kingdom of Spain* ICSID Case No.. ARB/97/7, award on the Merits, s 64 (Nov 13, 2000), http://italaw.com/documents/Maffezini-Award-English.pdf. Accessed 1 November 2014; *MTD Equity Sdn Bhd & MTD Chile SA v Chile*, ICSID Case No.. ARB/01/7, s 178 (May 25, 2004). http://italaw.com/documents/MTD-Award.pdf. Accessed 1 November 2014. Laird (2004, p. 4).

[44]See generally Macdonald (1993), Bakircioglu (2008, p. 711), Shany (2005, p. 907).

[45]On the absence of binding precedents, at least in principle, in international investment law, see Schreuer and Matthew (2012, p. 1188). See generally 'Current International Investment Issues: OECD Investment Committee' *Foreign Investment Review Board*. www.firb.gov.au/content/international_investment/current_issues.asp?NavID=60. Accessed 2 November 2014.

[46]United States Model Bilateral Investment Treaty (2012). www.ustr.gov/sites/default/files/BIT%20text%20for%20ACIEP%20Meeting.pdf. Accessed 1 November 2014. See also Vandevelde (2004, p. 307), cf American Model Bilateral Investment Treaty (2004). www.state.gov/documents/organization/117601.pdf. Accessed 1 November 2014. On Canada's Model Investment Treaty, see Newcombe (2004).

[47]On the application of minimal standards of treatment to a variety of specific defenses in earlier US Model BITs, see Dumberry (2002, p. 657); see also Directorate for Financial and Enterprise Affairs, 'Fair and Equitable Treatment Standard in International Investment Law' (Organization for Economic Co-operation and Development, Working Paper No. 2004/3 2004) 11. www.oecd.org/dataoecd/22/53/33776498.pdf. Accessed 2 November 2014.

health and related public interests.[48] These developments are embodied in recent US BITs such as Chapter 11 of the US-Peru Free Trade Agreement.[49] They demonstrate a desire by the US to retain greater regulatory control over inbound investment, somewhat in response to intrusive investor claims brought against developed countries.[50]

In contrast, China's current Model BIT, arguably, has less invasive national security, public order and financial exigency exemptions. It also does not link the protection accorded to foreign investors so explicitly to these regulatory defenses.[51]

Nevertheless, China's Model BIT does adhere to a restrictive definition of investment, directed at limiting the scope and application of asset classes.[52] Some investor protections in the current Model BIT have also not found their way into all of China's BITs, notably the national standard of treatment.[53] Some of China's negotiated BITs also include more elaborate national interest protections than China's Model BIT, such as more elaborate protection of the environment directed at sustainable development, public health and human rights.[54] In addition, some BITs provide for the interpretation of investment treaties through interpretative committees set up by the parties which bind ISA tribunals. This is also more likely to narrow than widen the scope of investor protection.[55]

These developments are understandable as China tailors variations in its BITs to its relationships with different BIT partners, making or extracting concessions as the case justifies.[56] Most importantly, the present analysis concludes that China does

[48]On the application of minimal standards of treatment to a variety of specific defenses in earlier US Model BITs, see Dumberry 2002, p. 657); see also Directorate for Financial and Enterprise Affairs, 'Fair and Equitable Treatment Standard in International Investment Law' (Organization for Economic Co-operation and Development, Working Paper No. 2004/3 2004) 11. www.oecd.org/dataoecd/22/53/33776498.pdf. Accessed 2 November 2014.

[49]See Peru Trade Promotion Agreement, US-Peru, 12 April 12 2006 (entered into force 1 Feb 2009) art 10.21; Free Trade Agreement, US-Colombia, 22 November 2006 (anticipated entry into force, 2012) art 10.21; Free Trade Agreement, Korea-US, 30 June 2007 (Approved by Congress, 12 October 2011) art 11.21.

[50]See generally Kantor (2004, p. 383).

[51]See e.g., Kurtz (2010, p. 325).

[52]The Department of Foreign Trade of the Ministry of Commerce ('MOFCOM') identifies two categories of investment. First, FDI includes equity joint ventures, contractual joint ventures, wholly foreign-owned enterprises, holding companies with foreign investment, joint exploration and others). Second, 'other foreign investments' includes shares, international lease, compensation trade and processing and assembling. See further, 'Investment in China, Statistics about Utilisation of Foreign Investment in China from Jan to Oct 2010' (2010) www.fdi.gov.cn/pub/FDI/wztj/wstztj/lywztj/t20101116_128338.htm. Accessed Nov 1st, 2014.

[53]Shan (2013, p. 20) (word version).

[54]See generally Peterson (2009), Van Harten (2007).

[55]For an empirical study on trends, and biases, in the behavior of investment arbitrators, see Van Harten (2012, p. 211).

[56]See Weeramantry (2012, p. 192).

not bind itself to its model investment treaties and negotiates its agreements pragmatically.

2.3 *ISA Claims Against China*

To date, there have been few ISA claims against China and none of these claims succeeded. There are various explanations for the paucity of such claims. First, foreign investors do not want to proceed against China and jeopardize their future dealings there, or risk a run-in with the Chinese legal system, such as happened with the Stern Hu case, albeit in distinctive circumstances.[57] As an EU Report of 7 March 2012 reflects, initiating ISA against China is likely to be a 'last resort'.[58] Second, China is well-resourced to defend itself against foreign investors including by engaging in costly, dilatory and fractious ISA proceedings. Thirdly, at least under first generation Chinese BITs, foreign investors could only claim compensation, but could not raise a claim based on the fact that expropriation has occurred.[59] As a result, any investor claim against a host state would likely fail *ab initio* on grounds that, given the exclusion of a legally determined expropriation, an ISA tribunal would lack jurisdiction to hear the investor's claim. Adding to this absence of ISA jurisdiction are tribunal decisions involving BIT treaty language that restricts compensation claims by investors against state parties to those BITs.

Ekran Berhad v. China is an illustration of an ISA claim against China under the Rules of the ICSID Convention which was first suspended and then withdrawn.[60] That claim was brought by a Malaysian construction company. In issue was the right of the local government to revoke the claimant's license to construct on leasehold property of 90,000 ha of land in the Hainan Province of China. The Malaysian claimant subsequently withdrew the claim and the case was suspended.[61]

Had the case proceeded to an award, it would have required an ISA tribunal to consider the meaning and significance of a provision in the China-Malaysia BIT, based on the China Model BIT, under which an ISA Tribunal is required to follow 'domestic legal procedure' in engaging in a direct or indirect expropriation.[62] Much would also have hinged on the Tribunal's interpretation of Article 7(4) of the

[57]Stern Hu, an Australian businessman of Chinese origins, was found guilty in 2010 by a Chinese court of stealing commercial secrets and accepting bribes. See Bath (2010).

[58]See Rubinacci (2012). See 'Public consultation on the future relationship between the EU and China', (European Commission 2011). http://trade.ec.europa.eu/consultations/?consul_id=153. Accessed 1 November 2014.

[59]See Smith (2010).

[60]ICSID Case ARB/11/15.

[61]ICSID Case ARB/11/15 proceedings suspended pursuant to the Parties' agreement on 22 July 2011. See http://ICSID.worldbank.org. Accessed 1 November 2014.

[62]The provision for an ISA tribunal to adhere to 'domestic legal procedure' is contained in Article 4(ii) of China's Model BIT.

China-Malaysia BIT, particularly in relation to the nature and limits of a compensation claim.[63]

If the withdrawn claim signifies anything, it is that a single foreign investor was willing to initiate a claim against China; China may have responded aggressively; and the investor withdrew the claim.[64] Drawing any salutary conclusion from this case would be suspect, except to lend some credence to the assumption that China is likely to be a tenacious adversary; and that only a well-financed foreign investor would likely prevail in a potentially protracted and costly dispute with China. However, much would also depend on the nature and terms of the investment treaty in issue, the specific claim and defence. In issue would also be a tension between China's need to demonstrate its willingness to defend the national good from foreign intrusion and its countervailing interest in mollifying skittish foreign investors who might retreat from investing in China to avoid its regulatory regime.[65]

Another more recent claim was brought against China under China–Republic of Korea BIT, for RMB100 million in damages by a South Korean investor in the PRC, Ansung Housing Co Ltd ('Ansung'). In proceeding under the ICSID, Ansung alleged that, due to various alleged arbitrary and illegal actions and omissions by the Shenyang-Xian government, it had been deprived of the use and enjoyment of its investment and that its investment plans were frustrated. It alleged that such actions forced it to dispose of its entire investment to a Chinese purchaser at a price significantly lower than its initial investment. An ICSID Tribunal, appointed to hear the case, decided in favour of China on 9 March 2017.[66]

What remains unclear is whether these cases are exceptional on grounds that China is too formidable a state against which to proceed through ISA. A more salutary realisation is that China is unlikely to insulate itself indefinitely from foreign investor claims, given Chinese BITs that provide extensive protection to foreign investors, not least of all to protect China's outbound investors. This argument is reinforced by the observation that rich states, including the US, Germany, Canada and Australia, are or have been subject to significant ISA claims. Included among these is the successful ISA claim brought against Germany, *Vattenfall AB, Vattenfall Europe AG, Vattenfall Europe Generation AG v. Federal Republic of* Germany.[67] Pending claims brought by multinationals against developed states include *Eli Lilly* and *Company v. The Government of* Canada.[68]

---

[63]This BIT article is modeled on Article 4(iv) of China's Model BIT providing for compensation.

[64]The terms of any settlement reached by the disputing parties is not publicly known.

[65]*Ansung Housing Co, Ltd. v People's Republic of China* (ICSID Case No. ARB/14/25).

[66]See https://www.italaw.com/cases/5391. See too

[67]ICSID Case ARB/09/6.

[68]UNCITRAL, ICSID Case No. UNCT/14/2.

2.4 ISA Claims by Chinese Investors Against Host States

Given the geometric increase in outbound investments by Chinese investors including Chinese state enterprises, it is reasonable to expect a comparable increase in claims brought by Chinese investors against host BIT states. The extent to which these observations are borne out in practice is analysed below.[69]

An initial caution is to avoid overstating the volume of ISA arbitrations in general. For example, the ICSID caseload has grown geometrically, from a single case in 1972 to approximately 10 cases in 1990, to 38 new cases filed between January and July 2012.[70] However, despite this growth, the absolute number of ICSID cases is limited compared to international commercial arbitration cases. For example, by the middle of 2013 1,435 claims had been filed with the China International Economic and Trade Arbitration Commission ('CIETAC'), 994 cases with the International Center for Dispute Resolution and 795 cases with the International Chamber of Commerce.[71] Thus, the limited number of decided ISA cases also makes it difficult to draw definitive conclusions about the application of ISA to claims by outbound Chinese investors against host states and claims by foreign investors against China in particular.

Chinese foreign investors have brought only a few ISA cases against host states under BITs. Included among claims by Chinese outbound investors is the 2011 ICSID case of *Tza Yap Shum v. Peru* brought by a Hong-Kong resident against Peru.[72] There, the investor, purporting to expand a fish factory in Peru, alleged that the Peruvian taxation authority had breached the expropriation provision in the China-Peru BIT of 1994[73] by investigating his business and levying liens on his firm's bank accounts that 'ended up destroying [his] business operations and economic viability.'[74] He claimed that this constituted an 'indirect expropriation.'[75]

[69]For background discussion of these issues, see Shan and Gallagher (2009a, b), Shan (2005), Moser (2007), Montt (2009), Kong (2008, p. 105), Shan et al. (2012, p. 120).

[70]See 'The ICSID Caseload—Statistics' *World Bank* (2012). http://ICSID.worldbank.org/ICSID/FrontServlet?requestType=ICSIDDocRH&actionVal=CaseLoadStatistics. Accessed 1 November 2014.

[71]'The ICSID Caseload—Statistics' *World Bank* (2012). http://ICSID.worldbank.org/ICSID/FrontServlet?requestType=ICSIDDocRH&actionVal=CaseLoadStatistics. Accessed 1 November 2014; see also Steingruber (2012).

[72]ICSID Case No. ARB/07/6, 'Decision on Jurisdiction and Competence', June 19, 2009, Award on Merits, July 7, 2011 ('Tza Yap Shum'). See also Eliasson (2011).

[73]Agreement between the Government of the Republic of Peru and the Government of the People's Republic of China Concerning the Encouragement and Reciprocal Protection of Investments done at Beijing on 9 June 1994, entered into force 1 February 1995, 1901 UNTS 257 (hereafter 'Peru-China BIT') art 1(2)(a).

[74]ICSID Case No. ARB/07/6, 'Decision on Jurisdiction and Competence', 19 June 2009, Award on Merits ('Tza Yap Shum') s 31.

[75]ICSID Case No. ARB/07/6, 'Decision on Jurisdiction and Competence', 19 June 2009, Award on Merits ('Tza Yap Shum') s 31.

The case raised jurisdictional issues, namely, whether a Hong Kong national was qualified as an investor under the Peru-China BIT[76]; whether a prescribed waiting period of six months for amicable settlement had taken place[77]; and whether the claimant was required to exhaust local remedies before proceeding to ISA.[78] The Tribunal also considered the significance of the MFN clause in Article 3(2) of the China-Peru BIT, providing that 'the treatment and protection referred to in Paragraph 1 of this Article [the fair and equitable guarantee] shall not be less favourable than that accorded to investments and activities associated with such investments of investors of a third State.'[79]

Peru lost the case. The tribunal decided that the claimant, a resident of Hong Kong, was a national of the People's Republic of China for the purpose of bringing a claim under the ICSID. It ruled that interim measures imposed by the tax authority of Peru were arbitrary in failing to comply with Peru's own internal procedures.[80] It ruled further that the provision in Article 8(3) of the Peru-China BIT 'involving the amount of compensation for expropriation' included a determination whether the property was actually expropriated, in addition to the amount of compensation.[81] In its decision on the merits on 7 July 2011, the Tribunal awarded the claimant over US$700,000 in damages and US$200,000 in interest.[82] Peru filed to have the award annulled.[83]

In reaching a determination that the Peruvian authorities had expropriated the claimant's property, the Tribunal construed the China-Peru BIT expansively. However, the Tribunal construed the specific wording of Article 8(3) in that BIT governing MFN treatment, restrictively. This flies in the face of the general application of an MFN clause, namely, that investors are entitled to the most favourable treatment accorded to investors under any other BIT to which the host state, here Peru, is a signatory. Insofar as the treatment Peru accorded to Tza Yap Shum fell below the MFN treatment accorded to investors from any other BIT

---

[76]ICSID Case No. ARB/07/6, 'Decision on Jurisdiction and Competence', 19 June 2009, Award on Merits ('Tza Yap Shum') s 32.

[77]Agreement between the Government of the Republic of Peru and the Government of the People, ch 10, art 126.

[78]ICSID Convention, Regulations and Rules, art 26.

[79]ICSID Case No. ARB/07/6, 'Decision on Jurisdiction and Competence', 19 June 2009, Award on Merits ('Tza Yap Shum') art 3(5). See also Eliasson (2011).

[80]ICSID Case No. ARB/07/6, 'Decision on Jurisdiction and Competence', 19 June 2009, Award on Merits ('Tza Yap Shum') s 218.

[81]ICSID Case No. ARB/07/6, 'Decision on Jurisdiction and Competence', 19 June 2009, Award on Merits ('Tza Yap Shum') s 88.

[82]ICSID Case No. ARB/07/6, 'Decision on Jurisdiction and Competence', June 19, 2009, Award on Merits, July 7, 2011 ('Tza Yap Shum').

[83]ICSID Case No. ARB/07/6, 'Decision on Jurisdiction and Competence', June 19, 2009, Award on Merits, July 7, 2011 ('Tza Yap Shum').

partner state that ought to have served as a further basis for deciding in favour of the claimant.[84]

In the case of *Heilongjiang v. Mongolia*,[85] a Chinese investor brought a claim against Mongolia under the China-Mongolia BIT. The issue before the ISA tribunal was whether that tribunal had jurisdiction to determine that an expropriation had occurred in a first generation Chinese BIT that did not provide a claim for expropriation, but only for compensation. The Permanent Court of Arbitration decided in favour of Mongolia on 30 June 2017.[86]

A formidable, but ultimately unsuccessful, claim was lodged by Chinese insurance company, Ping An, under the ICSID against Belgium in 2012.[87] Ping An, China's second largest insurer, lost approximately US$3 billion when failed Belgo-Dutch bank, Fortis, was nationalized and sold during the 2008 financial crisis. The collapse of the price of Fortis Bank and its subsequent sale significantly diminished Ping An's interest in the European financial services of the Bank.

Ping An was unsuccessful in its claim, albeit on preliminary jurisdictional grounds.[88] Yet, the case is significant because this was the first mainland Chinese company to file a claim in the ICSID. It was also the first claim by a Chinese national against the government of a developed economy.

In December of 2014 a new investment claim was brought by Beijing Urban Construction Investment Development against Yemen based on the China–Yemen BIT signed in 1998.[89] In 2006, the claimant signed a US$114 million contract with the Yemeni civil aviation and meteorology authority to build an international airport in Sana'a, with completion anticipated in 2008. The claimant alleged that the project was subject to substantial delays and was not completed as a result of the Yemen Government's actions. In its decision on jurisdiction delivered on 31 May 2017, the Tribunal appointed under the ICSID Rules largely denied its jurisdiction to hear the matter.[90]

In summary, to date no ISA case involving a Chinese outbound investor proceeding against one of China's BIT partner states has significantly embellished

---

[84]On the general applicability of an MFN clause, see '*Renta 4 SVSA v The Russian Federation*', SCC Case No. arb V024/2007, at § 101; *Ros Invest Co UK Ltd v The Russian Federation*, SCC Case No. arb V079/2005, at s 130.

[85]*China Heilongjiang International Economic & Technical Cooperative Corp, et al v Mongolia*, PCA Case (China-Mongolia BIT 1991). www.pca-cpa.org/showpage.asp?pag_id=1378. Accessed 13 October 2014.

[86]See https://pcacases.com/web/view/48. See further *China Heilongjiang International Economic & Technical Cooperative Corp, et al v Mongolia*, PCA Case (China-Mongolia BIT 1991). www.pca-cpa.org/showpage.asp?pag_id=1378. Accessed 13 October 2014. See art 8 of the China-Mongolia BIT. See too art 4(iv) of China's Model BIT, discussed in Section III above.

[87]For a detailed examination of this case, *see* Chapter 20 of this book written by Clair Wilson, 'Protecting Chinese investments under the investor-state dispute settlement regime: a review in light of *Ping An v Belgium*'.

[88]On the denial of Ping An's Claim, see www.italaw.com/cases/3088. Accessed 14 August 2015.

[89]*Beijing Urban Construction Group Co Ltd* v *Republic of Yemen* (ICSID ARB/14/30).

[90]On the Tribunal's decision, see https://www.italaw.com/cases/5904 finalised 31/05/2017.

investment arbitration jurisprudence. None to date, other than the Ping An claim against Belgium, has involved substantial claims for compensation. What the cases do demonstrate is the greater willingness of Chinese foreign investors to mount claims against host states. It would be more telling if a Chinese national, particularly a state enterprise, were to bring a multimillion dollar claim against a host state, focusing on the nature and impact of an expropriation upon that complainant under a treaty based on China's Model BIT. The probability of this occurring presumably will also depend somewhat on the prospects of China's BIT partners negotiating with large scale Chinese investors to avoid formal ISA claims brought by those investors against them. The Ping An case may also represent a turning point in the readiness of large Chinese companies to bring substantial claims against China's BIT partners.

2.5 *China-Australia Free Trade Agreement*

China and Australia have recently concluded a free trade agreement that entered into force in December of 2015. The context in which this agreement was concluded provides great insights into China's policy towards investment protection.

Although Australia has recently announced that it will negotiate ISA selectively in its investment facilitation agreement,[91] the China-Australia FTA makes provision for ISA. In the official press release following its negotiations with China, Australia noted that "[ISA] will enable Australians to invest in China with greater confidence".[92]

Presumably Australia favoured providing for ISA to protect its outbound investors from Chinese courts, an approach it has adopted in negotiating other treaties with developing countries. However, it is equally likely that China also favoured ISA, due to its concerns that Australian courts might deny the claims of Chinese investors on national interest grounds. Supporting this view is a statement by Australian Department of Foreign Affairs and Trade that "the ICSID provisions contain strong safeguards to protect the Australian Government's ability to regulate in the public interest and pursue legitimate welfare objectives in areas such as health, safety and the environment".[93] The inferred result is that both Australia and China agreed to ISA under the rules of the ICSID Convention on strategic grounds, because the perceived economic benefits of so agreeing outweighed the perceived cost.

Unofficial reports of negotiators further suggest that China insisted on including ISA in the FTA. China's current economic model may explain this instance on including ISA. China is a resource-reliant country that employs various powerful state owned entities in searching for investment opportunities abroad. These entities

---

[91]See Trakman and Sharma (2015, p. 1).

[92]KAFTA art 11.16 para 1 (a), (b), (c) and (d); JAEPA art 14.6 paras 1 and 2. See, Robb, Andrew AO MP (2014).

[93]Ibid.

are viewed with suspicion by host states and conceivably by domestic courts. This explains in part why China wishes to arbitrate in a neutral third party forum, notably through ISA, rather than before foreign domestic courts, including Australian courts.

In summary, China-Australia FTA provides multiple insights into China's current approaches to the administration and regulation of FDI. Concerned with securing natural resources, China encourages its enterprises to build trade networks abroad. These state sponsored entities are viewed with suspicion and may be challenged by host states. However, by allowing for ISA, China will likely face claims by foreign investors operating within its jurisdiction. Thus, China is attempting to balance these two conflicting priorities in its current agreements, as is reflected in the FTA with Australia.

2.6 China and the Future of ISA

Considering recent backlashes against ISA, it is important to examine whether China is likely to reject ISA in its future agreements.[94] For example, China could insist, in regard to inbound FDI, that investor-state claims against it should be resolved by Chinese arbitration institutions, administrative agencies, or by Chinese courts. It could also decline to include ISA provisions in its BITs, impacting on both inbound and outbound investors. It could do so on grounds that ISA favours developed states and their investors; and that international investment law and practice is biased against developing states and their investors, including China.[95]

The prospect of China requiring domestic courts to decide investor-state disputes has some foundation, as distinct from providing foreign investors with the option of proceeding to a domestic court or to ISA. China could insist that, as a sovereign state, its domestic courts ought to preside over claims brought against Chinese enterprises within its territorial jurisdiction; and that Chinese courts have the jurisdiction, legal competence and substantive knowledge to decide such disputes under Chinese law.

A difficult issue is to determine the influence of the institution and process of dispute resolution upon which the result of an investor-state claim is determined. In particular, there is perceptible global support for using ISA to resolve investor-state disputes, notably under the rules of the ICSID and the UNCITRAL,[96] and limited

---

[94]Trakman and Musayelyan (2015, p. 1).

[95]See e.g., Jishnu (2012). In this interview, Van Harten observes that developing countries sometimes are the target of treaties directed at enhancing opportunities for foreign investors from other states and on occasions, leading to significant losses for those target countries. See too Trakman (2012a, b, c, p. 603).

[96]The UNCITRAL Rules are a general set of rules that can be applied flexibly and in an ad hoc manner to resolve any type of international dispute and are adopted widely globally, including for the resolution of investor-state disputes. Some of the 2010 amendments to the UNCITRAL rules

resort to international commercial arbitration.[97] The extent to which China follows this global development is difficult to determine conclusively. This is due, in part, to China's limited exposure to publicly known investor-state disputes. It is also because of the sometimes blurred line between foreign and domestic investment under Chinese law, and also because disputes with some foreign elements are heard confidentially by the China International Economic and Trade Arbitration Commission, and the Beijing International Arbitration Centre, among other arbitration centres within China.[98]

What is clear, however, is that China's most recent BITs provide generally for a choice between domestic courts and ISA under the ICSID Convention, or under the UNCITRAL Rules.[99] China has also not negotiated BITs that provide exclusively for recourse to domestic courts, as was adopted by Australia's Labour Government in 2010 and then changed when the Abbott Government declared that it would negotiate ISA selectively.[100] However, Chinese domestic law is likely to influence international investment law arising from investor-state disputes with some foreign elements which foreign investors choose to submit to Chinese domestic courts under an applicable BIT.[101] Again, the prospect of Chinese courts and domestic law influencing the interpretation of investment treaty law is not peculiar to China. The domestication of international investment law pervades investment jurisprudence generally.[102]

Concerns are also likely to arise about the conduct of ISA proceedings in which China is the respondent, such as over China's reluctance to permit third party intervention in proceedings, its possible refusal to consent to hold public hearings, and its insistence on confidential documentation and unpublished awards.[103]

Although China's size and economic might heightens these concerns, transparency concerns arising from such action is not an indictment peculiar to China.

(Footnote 96 continued)

were inspired by the rising use of the Rules in ISA. See UNCITRAL Arbitration Rules, UNCITRAL (2010). www.uncitral.org/uncitral/en/uncitral_texts/arbitration/2010Arbitration_rules.html. Accessed 3 November 2014. On the flexibility of UNCITRAL proceedings, see UNCITRAL Arbitration Rules, UNCITRAL (2010). www.uncitral.org/uncitral/en/uncitral_texts/arbitration/2010Arbitration_rules.html. Accessed 1 November 2014. For the text of the UNCITRAL Model Law and in particular, art 34, see www.uncitral.org/pdf/english/texts/arbitration/ml-arb/07-86998_Ebook.pdf. Accessed 3 November 2014.

[97]On similarities and differences between international commercial arbitration and investment arbitration, see Nottage and Miles (2009).

[98]See generally Tao (2012), Leung (2011).

[99]On the case for investor-state arbitration, see generally Dugan et al. (2008), Muchlinski et al. (2008), McLachlan et al. (2008), Kahn and Walde (eds) (2007), Van Harten (2007).

[100]See Emerson (2014). See Trakman (2013), Kurtz (2012, p. 1), Trakman (2012a, b, c, p. 83).

[101]Shan (2013, p. 221).

[102]See Vandevelde (2005, p. 157). See also 'United Nations Conference on Trade and Development, World Investment Report 2010. xxv' *UNCTAD* (2010). http://unctad.org/en/pages/DIAE/World%20Investment%20Report/WIR-Series.aspx. Accessed 1 November 2014.

[103]See too Moser (1998, p. 27).

Other states have adopted comparable measures in the past.[104] ISA is initiated with the consent of both direct parties to ISA disputes. Third parties, such as public interest groups, until comparatively recently were not permitted to participate in ISA proceedings, such as under the ICSID.[105] Nor could ISA awards ordinarily be published without the consent of both ISA parties.[106] Typically, the Secretary General of the ICSID could publish reports of conciliation commissions or awards rendered by arbitral tribunals in ICSID proceedings, but only 'with the consent of both disputing parties'.[107] There were also explanations, and not always convincing ones, for limiting the transparency of ISA proceedings and awards. For example, in *Suez Sociedad General de Aguas de Barcelona s.a. and Vivendi Universal s.a. v. Republic of Argentina*, the arbitration tribunal acknowledged that the case 'potentially involved matters of public interest and human rights' and that public access 'would have the additional desirable consequence of increasing the transparency of ISA'.[108] It nevertheless declined to permit public participation under the petition.

---

[104]See generally Yackee and Wong (2006) (discussing transparency in international investment arbitration); Marian (2010, p. 275) (discussing transparency in international investment arbitration).

[105]*Suez Sociedad General de Aguas de Barcelona SA and Vivendi Universal SA v the Republic of Argentina* (Order in Response to a Petition by Five Non-Governmental Organizations for Permission to Make an Amicus Curiae Submission), ICSID Arbitral Tribunal, Case No. ARB/03/19, 12 February 2007; (Order in Response to a Petition for Transparency and Participation as Amicus Curiae) ICSID Arbitral Tribunal, Case No. ARB/03/19, 19 May 2005. The petition challenged the decision of the Government of Argentina to accede to the ICSID treaty on grounds that it violated the constitutional guarantees of citizens of Argentina to participate in proceedings. While the government of Argentina was willing to hear the petition, the complainant company was not. However, the Attorney General of Argentina published on the internet the information in his possession on the related cases. See too Alfaro and Lorenti (2005, p. 417).

[106]See e.g., *GEA Group Aktiengesellschaft v Ukraine* (Award) (ICSID Arbitral Tribunal, Case No. ARB/08/16, 31 March 2011); *Talsud, SA v United Mexican States* (Award) (ICSID Arbitral Tribunal, Case No. ARB (AF)/04/4, 16 June 2010); Gemplus, *SA, SLP, SA and Gemplus Industrial, SA DE* CV *v United Mexican States* (Award) (ICSID Arbitral Tribunal, Case No. ARB (AF)/04/3, 16 June 2010).

[107]See e.g., *GEA Group Aktiengesellschaft v Ukraine* (Award) (ICSID Arbitral Tribunal, Case No. ARB(AF)/04/4, 16 June 2010); *Gemplus, SA, SLP, SA and Gemplus Industrial,* SA *DE CV v United Mexican States* (Award) (ICSID Arbitral Tribunal, Case No. ARB(AF)/04/3, 16 June 2010). *Aguas del Tunari, SA v Republic of Bolivia (Order Taking Note of Discontinuance)* (ICSID Case No. ARB/02/3, 28 March 2006). http://ita.law.uvic.ca/documents/AguasdelTunari-jurisdiction-eng_000.pdf. Accessed 1 November 2014. These requirements, replicated on the ICSID website, are http://ICSID.worldbank.org/ICSID/FrontServlet?requestType=CasesRH&actionVal=ShowHome&pageName=Cases_Home. Accessed 3 November 2014. See too ICSID Procedural Order of 2 February 2011 inviting third parties to apply to submit amici curiae briefs under ICSID Arbitration Rule 37(2). See further Vandevelde, Kenneth J, '*Aguas del Tunari, SA v Republic of Bolivia*', (2007) 101 Am J Int'l L 179 (providing an overview and analysis of the case); Gramont (2006, p. 3).

[108]Order in Response to a Petition for Transparency and Participation as Amicus Curiae (ICSID Case No. ARB/03/19, 19 May 2005) [19], [22].

An equally difficult issue is how ISA tribunals will decide disputes in which inbound foreign investors claim that China has used its economic and politial power to take advantage of them.[109] However, if the liberalization of international investment law is to be truly even-handed, it also needs to focus on the functional advantages of large-scale Western investors, rather than focusing solely on the functional advantages countries like China may give to their state owned enterprises and multinational corporations.

A further concern is that China will use diplomatic measures to pressure foreign states into submitting to claims by outbound Chinese state enterprises. This has currently arisen in China's reaction to Australia's exclusion of Huawei, a Chinese telecommunication company, from Australia's broadband program on the alleged grounds that Huawei engaged in cybercrimes against foreign companies and cyber-espionage on behalf of the Chinese government.[110] This was followed by the US and EU blacklisting Huawei as a security risk, and the UK investigating whether to maintain its relationship with Huawei.[111] China's reaction to the Australian Government's decision was that Huawei was a highly regarded international telecommunications company; it had passed an intense security clearance in the UK; members of its Board included past members of the Australian Government; and that China was considering retaliating against Australia for its treatment of Huawei.[112]

A key issue is to determine when and to what degree China is likely to intervene, diplomatically or otherwise, on behalf of private outbound investors. In the Huawei case, the alleged economic loss of the Australian broadband contract alone exceeded US$1 billion. The political risk included damage to China's reputation on alleged grounds that it collaborated with Huawei in cyberespionage. In choosing whether to intervene diplomatically, China undoubtedly will engage in a cost-benefit analysis, in weighing the benefit of defending a prominent outbound investor, together with China's reputation in the multilateral community, against the cost of antagonizing the Australian and other Governments that followed suit and also blacklisted Huawei.[113]

---

[109]See Bath (2011), Yang (2012).

[110]See China Giant banned from NBN, Australian Financial Review (2012). www.afr.com/p/technology/china_giant_banned_from_nbn_9U9zi1oc3FXBF3BZdRD9mJ. Accessed 1 November 2014; Good Reason for Ban on Huawei, The Australian (2012). www.theaustralian.com.au/national-affairs/opinion/good-reason-for-ban-on-huawei/story-e6frgd0x-1226503441514. Accessed 1 November 2014.

[111]See EU Report urges action against Chinese telecom firms, Yahoo News (2012). http://au.news.yahoo.com/thewest/a/-/world/15623498/eu-report-urges-action-againstchinese-telecom-firms/. Accessed 3 November 2014; www.guardian.co.uk/technology/2012/oct/10/huawei-international-blacklisting. Accessed 1 November 2014.

[112]See Chinese government plays no role in Huawei, execs insist. Australian Financial Review (2012). www.afr.com/p/national/chinese_govt_plays_no_role_in_huawei_SJEkkWcm6e4VS8Iqf4kbVO. Accessed 1 November 2014.

[113]Chinese government plays no role in Huawei, execs insist. Australian Financial Review (2012). www.afr.com/p/national/chinese_govt_plays_no_role_in_huawei_SJEkkWcm6e4VS8Iqf4kbVO. Accessed 1 November 2014.

A further concern is that a well-resourced country like China will use conflict prevention and avoidance measures to force inbound investors into submission, including following an ISA claim against it. The ancillary view is that such negotiations will take place privately and will lead to take-it-or leave it results dictated by China that may have occurred in *Ekran Berhad v. People's Republic of China.*[114] However, investor-state negotiations ordinarily do not take place on a level playing field. Nor is it unusual for a BIT to require investor-state parties to first attempt to resolve their differences through negotiation, or failing that, conciliation, before resorting to arbitration.[115] The purpose in requiring negotiation and conciliation measures is to encourage conflict avoidance albeit complicated by structural bargaining disparities between investor-state parties.[116] The fact that a state party may enjoy a positional bargaining advantage over an inbound investor in such negotiations or conciliation inheres in international investment practice, not unlike the positional advantage enjoyed by multinational corporations over many developing states.[117]

Taking all of these factors into consideration, it is likely that China will continue to rely on ISA for the resolution of investment related disputes but it may do so by rebalancing its treaties to provide for greater regulatory control to host states. There appears to be no indication within China that there is displeasure with ISA. On the contrary, ISA is preferred by Chinese investors operating abroad. Furthermore, foreign countries concluding treaties with China will likely prefer to rely on ISA on the account of China's developing legal system.

3 Conclusion

A particular challenge for China relates to lingering concerns over whether, despite its recent flurry of bilateral and regional activism, it has adequately liberalized its international investment regime, in a global setting in which developed states such as the US are retreating from investment liberalization.

---

[114]ICSID Case No. ARB/11/15. Proceedings were suspended pursuant to the Parties' agreement on 22 July 2011. See 'ICSID' http://ICSID.worldbank.org. Accessed 3 November 2014.

[115]See Tang (2005, p. 547).

[116]UNCTAD, Investor–State Disputes: Prevention and Alternatives to Arbitration, UNCTAD Series on International Investment Policies for Development (May 2010), xxiii. www.unctad.org/en/docs/diaeia200911_en.pdf. Accessed 3 November 2014; See UNCTAD (2010), xvii–xix. http://unctad.org/en/docs/diaeia200911_en.pdf. Accessed 3 November 2014. See also Franck and Anna (2010). On the UNCTAD's most recent report on investor state dispute settlement, see UNCTAD (2014).

[117]See e.g. art 12(3) of the Singapore–China BIT which provides: 'if a dispute involving the amount of compensation resulting from expropriation, nationalization or other measures having effect equivalent to nationalization or expropriation cannot be settled within six months after resort to negotiation. It may be submitted to an international arbitral tribunal established by both parties.' The Singapore–China BIT came into force on 7 February 1986.

A traditional criticism is that China has taken an unduly restrictive view of the rights of foreign investors to receive national treatment.[118] China is reproached for imposing rigid constraints upon foreign investors, notably a one-by-one method of approving applications for FDI.[119] This practice is sometimes criticized for leading to a dilatory and selective investment entry process through which Chinese regulatory authorities evaluate each FDI project, in apparent order, before approving them. A related concern is that China conceives of sovereign immunity and state privilege, not limited to state enterprises, too expansively and as a measure of regulating not only the entry, but also the day-to-day activities of inbound foreign investors.[120] In contention is China's alleged failure to enshrine the "liberty" of inbound investors and for supposedly unduly interfering with their "rights" as investors.[121]

A contrary view is that foreign investors have less reason to bring ISA against China because China often accords foreign investors better than "national treatment", offsetting concerns that they receive less than fair and equitable treatment or are subject to indirect expropriations.[122] China has also committed itself to recognizing and enforcing arbitration awards, inter alia, as a signatory to the New York Convention on the Recognition and Enforcement of Foreign Arbitration Awards ('New York Convention').[123] It has undertaken to submit ISA disputes to the ICSID and acceded to the ICSID Convention.[124] Perhaps most importantly, China has an image to project and protect, namely, as being "friendly" towards foreign investors including being perceived to be fair; while foreign investors in China have usually received handsome returns on their investments there.[125]

Whatever the criticisms that are directed at China's image in relation to foreign investment, China has succeeded in attracting huge amounts of FDI over several decades and is perceived as economically and politically positioned to further extend its global influence over FDI markets.[126]

---

[118] See e.g., Shearman and Sterling (2012) which maintains that China's National Development and Reform Commission (NDRC), a major regulatory authority in charge of foreign investments in the PRC, has recently denied 'national treatment' to RMB funds in the form of a limited liability partnership with a foreign-invested company as general partner ('GP') and with only PRC domestic investors as limited partners ('LP')S.

[119] See *Shan* (n 22) 228. [K: Requires full references].

[120] On China's conception of absolute sovereign immunity, see *Shan* (n 22) 228.[K: Requires full references].

[121] See Trakman (2011a, b, p. 775).

[122] See Shan and Zhang (2013, p. 1), Trakman (2011a, b), Kinnear (2009).

[123] See Xia (2011, p. 20).

[124] But see Rooney (2007, p. 704) (arguing that, even after China's accession to the Washington Convention became effective, it was some years before China provided for ICSID arbitration in early BITs).

[125] See Nottage and Weeramantry (2011, p. 25).

[126] On China's shifting position in regard to investment arbitration, see Bath (2011).

The challenge for it is in accommodating its status as a predominantly capital importer to now being a global capital importer and exporter.[127] As a capital importer, China had significant historical reasons to regulate inbound capital including through BITs, domestic laws, administrative regulation, its court system and commercial arbitration. As a growing capital exporter today, China has the countervailing need to extend BIT protections for the benefit of its outbound investors in BIT partner states, not least of all due to concern of host states challenging inbound Chinese SOEs.

China's growing interest in concluding FTAs and BITs that enable its outbound investors to profit abroad is also consistent with the aspirations of other capital exporters.[128] Nor should one expect otherwise, from China or any other capital exporter. Investment protectionism is the other side of the investment liberalization coin. It is a coin that liberal states of the West repeatedly flip when it comes to the rights of foreign investors. It is not a coin whose use should be treated as abhorrent because China is increasingly flipping that coin.[129]

At the same time, it would be misleading to suggest that China has not continued to adopt a protectionist stance towards vulnerable sectors of its economy, notably its struggling rural sectors.[130] For example, the Supreme Peoples' Court of China has affirmed the virtue of such protectionism in principle in the national interest and beyond the demands of China's rural sector.[131]

In contrast, the tide of investor-state claims brought by Chinese investors against China's BIT partners is changing significantly. Historically, outbound Chinese investors brought only a small number of claims and only against developing states. However, the recent claim by Ping An represents a significant increase in the quantum of a claim from an outbound Chinese investor and in targeting a developed state. It is reasonable to expect a growing number of large scale Chinese investors, including state owned enterprises, to bring other substantial claims against China's BIT partners in the future.

The fact that China has expanded the grounds for investor claims in its more recent BITs beyond compensation is a sign of investment liberalization that benefits Chinese investors in foreign host states. Whether China will further liberalize investor protections, *inter alia*, to protect its capital exporters in its fourth Model BIT, remains uncertain. However it frames its Model BIT, China is likely to rely on its capacity to dissuade inbound investors from lodging investor claims against it, either by accommodating foreign investor interests, or by demonstrating its formidable capacity and tenacity in defending against such claims.

---

[127]See, e.g., Planfker (2008), Li and Jonathan (2006).

[128]On the history of this division between capital exporter and importer states, see generally Muthucumaraswamy (2010, p. 142).

[129]On the history of this division between capital exporter and importer states, see generally Muthucumaraswamy (2010, p. 142).

[130]See Sauvant et al. (2011), pt 2, Schutter and Peter (2011).

[131]See, e.g., Wolff (2010, p. 1001) (noting China's protectionism); see also Wei (2010, p. 164) (discussing limits placed on complainants under bilateral investment agreements with China).

What remains to be seen is whether China will be able to rely on ISA tribunals to adopt an expansive interpretation of a government taking action based on 'necessity' under a Chinese BIT to legitimate its expropriation of a foreign investment in response to a national, or indeed international, economic misadventure. If the current global economic slowdown continues, such a necessity defence is all the more likely to eventuate on grounds that China cannot reasonably avert the need to impose more rigorous restraints on inbound investment.

References

Alfaro, Carlos E., and Pedro M. Lorenti. 2005. The growing opposition of Argentina to ICSID arbitral tribunals: A conflict between international and domestic law? *Journal of World Investment & Trade*, 6.

Bath, Vivienne. 2010. The Chinese legal system and the Stern Hu case, East Asia Forum. http://www.eastasiaforum.org/2010/03/28/the-chinese-legal-system-and-the-stern-hu-case/.

Bath, Vivienne. 2011. The quandary for Chinese regulators: Controlling the flow of investors into and out of China. In *Foreign investment and dispute resolution law and practice in Asia*, ed. Vivienne Bath and Luke Nottage. Routledge.

Bath, Vivienne. 2012. Foreign investment, the national interest and national security: Foreign direct investment in Australia and China. *Sydney Law Review*, 34.

Bath, Vivienne, and Luke Nottage (eds.). 2011. *Foreign investment and dispute resolution law and practice in Asia*. Routledge.

Bakircioglu, Onder. 2008. The application of the margin of appreciation doctrine in freedom of expression and public morality cases. *German Law Journal* 8: 711.

Cai, Congyan. 2006. Outward foreign direct investment protection and the effectiveness of Chinese BIT practice. *Journal of World Investment and Trade* 7: 62.

Caseload–Statistics (Issue 2012–2). ICSID. 2012. http://icsid.worldbank.org/ICSID/FrontServlet?requestType=ICSIDDocRH&actionVal=CaseLoadStatistics. Accessed 1 Nov 2014.

China Eclipses US as Biggest Trading Nation. 2013. Bloomberg news. http://www.bloomberg.com/news/articles/2013-02-09/china-passes-u-s-to-become-the-world-s-biggest-trading-nation.

Cole, Tony, and Anuj Kumar Vaksha. 2011. Power-conferring treaties: The meaning of 'investment' in the ICSID convention. *Leiden Journal of International Law* 24: 305.

Directorate for Financial and Enterprise Affairs. 2004. Fair and equitable treatment standard in international investment law. Organization for Economic Co-operation and Development, Working Paper No. 2004/3, 11. www.oecd.org/dataoecd/22/53/33776498.pdf.

Dolzer, Rudolf, and Margrete Stevens. 1995. *Bilateral investment treaties*. Martinus Nijuhoff Publishers.

Dugan, Christopher, et al. 2008. *Investor-state arbitration*. Oxford: Oxford University Press.

Dumberry, Patrick. 2002. The quest to define 'fair and equitable treatment' for investors under international law: The case of the NAFTA. Chapter 11 Pope & Talbot Awards. *Journal of World Investment*, 3.

Eliasson, Nils. 2011. China's investment treaties: A procedural perspective. In *Foreign investment and dispute resolution law and practice in Asia*, ed. Vivienne Bath and Luke Nottage. Taylor & Francis Group.

Emerson, Craig. Trading our way to more jobs and prosperity, Department of Foreign Affairs and Trade. http://www.dfat.gov.au/publications/trade/trading-our-way-to-more-jobs-and-prosperity.html#investorstate.

European Commission. 2011. Public consultation on the future relationship between the EU and China. http://trade.ec.europa.eu/consultations/?consul_id=153.

Franck, Susan D., and Anna Joubin-Bret. (eds.). 2010. UNCTAD, investor-state disputes: prevention and alternatives to arbitration II. In *Proceedings of the Washington and Lee University and UNCTAD joint symposium on international investment and alternative dispute resolution*, Lexington, Virginia, UNCTAD. www.unctad.org/en/docs/webdiaeia20108_en.pdf.

Gramont, Alexandre. 2006. After the water war: The battle for jurisdiction in Aguas Del Tunari, S.A. v. Republic of Bolivia. *Transnational Dispute Management*, 3. www.crowell.com/documents/After-the-Water-War_The-Battle-for-Jurisdiction-in-Aguas-del-Tunari_v_Bolivia.pdf.

Gaillard, Emmanuel. 2009. Identify or define? Reflections on the evolution of the concept of investment in ICSID practice. In *International investment law for the 21st century essays in honour of Christoph Schreuer*, 403, ed. Christina Binder. Oxford: Oxford University Press.

Gu, Jing, et al. 2008. Global governance and developing countries: The implications of the rise of China. *World Development* 36: 274.

Gudgeon, K.Scott. 2012. United States bilateral investment treaties: Comments on their origin, purposes, and general treatment standards. *Berkeley Journal of International Law* 4: 105.

Goldhaber, Michael D. 2003. Big arbitrations. *The American Lawyer*, 22. www.americanlawyer.com/focuseurope/bigarbitrations.html.

Jishnu, Latha. 2012. Secretive tribunals, hidden damages, Interview. www.downtoearth.org.in/content/secretive-tribunals-hidden-damages.

Kahn, Philippe, and Thomas W. Walde. (eds.). 2007. *New aspects of international investment law*. Brill.

Kantor, Mark. 2004. The new draft Model U.S BIT: Noteworthy developments. *Journal of International Arbitration*, 21.

Kirkman, Courtney. 2002. Fair and equitable treatment: Methanex v. United States and the narrowing scope of NAFTA Article 1105. *Law & Policy in International Business* 34: 343.

Kinnear, Meg. 2009. The continuing development of the fair and equitable treatment standard. In *Investment treaty law: Current issues III. Remedies in international investment*, ed. Bjorklund and others. BRIICL.

Kong, Qingjiang. 2008. Bilateral investment treaties: The Chinese approach and practice. *Asian Yearbook of International Law* 8: 105.

Kragelund, Peter. 2009. Knocking on a wide open door: Chinese investments in Africa. *The Review of African Political Economy* 36: 479.

Kurtz, Jurgen. 2010. Adjudging the exceptional at international investment law: Security, public order and financial crisis. *International and Comparative Law Quarterly*, 59.

Kurtz, Jurgen. 2012. Australia's rejection of investor-state arbitration: Causation, omission and implication. *ICSID Review*, 1.

Laird, Ian A. 2004. MTD Equity Sdn Bhd and MTD Chile S.A. v Republic of Chile—recent developments in the fair and equitable treatment standard. *Transnational Dispute Standard* 1: 4.

Leung, Raymond Hai Ming. 2011. *China arbitration handbook*. Sweet & Maxwell Limited.

Li, Ling. 2010. Chinese bilateral investment treaties: Practice and challenges. *Journal of International Economic Law* 17: 1.

Li, Yong, and Jonathan Reuvid. 2006. *Doing business with China*. GMB Publishing Ltd.

Macdonald, Ronald St. J. 1993. The margin of appreication'. In *The European system for the protection of human rights*, ed. Macdonald Matscher and Petzold. Martinus Nijhoff Publishers.

Marian, Cornel. 2010. Balancing transparency: The value of administrative law and Mathews-balancing to investment treaty arbitrations. *Pepperdine Dispute Resolution Law Journal*, 10.

McLachlan, Campbell et al. 2008. *International investment arbitration: Substantive principles*. Oxford: Oxford University Press.

Montt, Santiago. 2009. *State liability in investment treaty arbitration: Global constitutional and administrative law in the BIT generation*. Hart Publishing.

Moser, Michael. 2007. *Managing business disputes in today's China: Duelling with dragons*. Kluwer Law International.

Moser, Michal J. 1998. CIETAC arbitration: A success story? *Journal of International Arbitration* 15: 27.
Muchlinski, Peter and others (eds.) 2008. *Oxford handbook of international investment law*. Oxford: Oxford University Press.
Muthucumaraswamy, Sornarajah. 2003. The Norman Paterson School of International Affairs Simon Reisman Lecture in international trade policy: The clash of globalizations and the international law on foreign investment, Canadian Foreign Policy, 10.
Muthucumaraswamy, Sornarajah. 2010. *The international law on foreign investment*. Cambridge: Cambridge University Press.
Neumayer, Eric and Spess Laura. Do bilateral investment treaties increase foreign direct investment to developing countries? *World Development* 33: 1567.
Newcombe, Andrew. 2004. Canada's new model foreign investment protection agreement, Investment Treaty Arbitration. http://ita.law.uvic.ca/documents/CanadianFIPA.pdf.
Newcombe, Andrew. 2008. General exceptions in international investment agreements. BIICL Eighth Annual WTO Conference Draft Discussion Paper, 4. www.biicl.org/files/3866_andrew_newcombe.pdf.
Nottage, Luke, and Kate Miles. 2009. Back to the future for investor-state arbitrations: Revising rules in Australia and Japan to meet public interests, University of Sydney Legal Research Paper No 08/62. http://papers.ssrn.com/sol3/papers.cfm?abstract_id=1151167. Accessed 1 Nov 2014.
Nottage, Luke, and Romesh Weeramantry. 2011. Investment arbitration in Asia: Five perspectives on law and practice. In *Foreign investment and dispute resolution law and practice in Asia Routledge*, ed. Vivienne Bath and Luke Nottage.
Peterson, Luke Eric. 2009. Human rights and bilateral investment treaties: Mapping the role of human rights law within investor-state arbitration. International Center for Human Rights and Development. www.dd-rd.ca/site/_PDF/publications/globalization/HIRA-volume3-ENG.pdf.
Peterson, Luke Eric. 2014. China is hit with second ICSID claim, as Korean investor lodges arbitration, Investment Arbitration Reporter. www.iareporter.com/articles/20141106.
Planfker, Ted. 2008. *Doing business in China: How to profit in the world's fastest growing market*. Grand Central Publishing.
Poulsen, Lauge Skovgaard. 2012. Investment treaties and the globalisation of state capitalism: Opportunities and constraints for host states. In *Prospects in international investment law and policy*, ed. Echandi and Sauv. Cambridge University Press. http://papers.ssrn.com/sol3/papers.cfm?abstract_id=2050919. Accessed 13 Oct 2014.
Qing, Jiang Kong. 2012. U.S.-China bilateral investment treaty negotiations: Context, focus, and implications. *Asian Journal of WTO and International Health Law and Policy* 7: 18.
Rosen, Daniel, and Thilo Hanemann. 2011. An American open door? Maximizing the benefits of Chinese foreign direct investment, Center on U.S.-China Relations and Kissinger Institute on China and the United States, 35. www.ogilvypr.com/files/anamericanopendoor_china_fdi_study.pdf.
Rooney, Kim M. 2007. ICSID and BIT arbitrations and China. *Journal of International Law Arbitration*, 24.
Rubinacci, Leopoldo. 2012. EU-China investment relationship, update on state of play. DC Trade Civil Society Dialogue. http://trade.ec.europa.eu/doclib/docs/2012/march/tradoc_149185.pdf.
Sauvant, Karl P. et al. 2011. *FDI perspectives: Issues in international investment*. Vale Columbia Center on Sustainable International Investment.
Schreuer, Christoph. 2011. *The ICSID convention: A commentary*. Cambridge: Cambridge University Press.
Schreuer, Christoph, and Matthew Weiniger. 2012. A doctrine of precedent? In *The Oxford handbook of international investment law*, ed. Muchlinski Ortino, and Schreuer. Oxford: Oxford University Press.
Schutter, Olivier, and Peter Rosenblum. 2011. Large-scale investments in farmland: The regulatory challenge. In *Yearbook on international investment law & policy 2010–2011*. Oxford: Oxford University Press.

Shan, Wenhua, and Norah Gallagher. 2009a. *Chinese investment treaties: Policies and practice*. Oxford: Oxford University Press.
Shan, Wenhua, and Norah Gallagher. 2009b. Chinese investment treaties, policies and practice. In *Oxford international arbitration series*, ed. Mistelis. Oxford: Oxford University Press.
Shan, Wenhua, and Norah Gallagher. 2013. China. In *Commentaries on selected model investment treaties*, ed. Brown. Oxford: Oxford University Press.
Shan, Wenhua, and Zhang Sheng. 2013. An inquiry on US 2012 Model BIT and its acceptability for China. *Modern Law Science* 5: 1.
Shan, Wenhua, et al. 2012. National treatment for foreign investment in China: A changing landscape. *ICSID Review* 27: 120.
Shan, Wenhua. 2005. *The legal framework of EU-China investment relations: A critical appraisal*. Hart Publishing.
Shany, Yuval. 2005. Toward a general margin of appreciation doctrine in international law? *European Journal of International Law* 16: 907.
Shearman and Sterling LLP. 2005. *China NDRC denies the "National Treatment" for RMB Funds with Foreign GPs*. www.shearman.com/files/Publication/16515980-0f05-4aad-8ca1d74066eb8b90/Presentation/PublicationAttachment/0a664bc0-53c2-4b6c-b1f5-738c047ffa11/China-NDRC-Denies-the-%E2%80%9CNational-Treatment%E2%80%9D-for-RMB-Funds-with-Foreign-GPs-IF-071812.pdf.
Shen, Wei. 2010. Case note, beyond the scope of 'investor' and 'investment': who can make an arbitration claim under a Chinese BIT?—Some implications from a recent ICSID case. *Asian International Arbitration Journal* 6: 2.
Smith, Gordon. 2010. Chinese bilateral investment treaties restrictions on international arbitration. *Arbitration*, 76. www.kennedyslaw.com/files/Uploads/Documents/GordonSmithChineseBilateralInvestment_122010.pdf.
Steingruber, Andrea M. 2012. *Consent in international arbitration*. Oxford: Oxford University Press.
Schill, Stephan. 2007. Tearing down the Great Wall: The new generation investment treaties of the People's Republic of China. *Cardozo Journal of International and Comparative Law* 15: 73.
Tang, Houzhi. 2005. Combination of arbitration with conciliation: Arb/med. In *New horizons in international commercial arbitration and beyond*. ICCA Congress Series No. 12, ed. Jan van den Berg. Kluwer Law International.
Tao, Jingzhou. 2012. *Arbitration law and practice in China*. Kluwer Law International.
Trakman, Leon E. 2011a. The twenty-first century law merchant. *American Business Law Journal* 48.
Trakman, Leon E. 2011b. *Enter the dragon IV: China's proliferating investment treaty program*. UNSW Centre for Law, Markets and Regulation. www.clmr.unsw.edu.au/article/deterrence/public-v-private-enforcement/enter-dragon-iv-chinas-proliferatinginvestment-treaty-program.
Trakman, Leon. 2012a. China and investor-state arbitration. UNSW Law Research Paper No 2012-48. http://ssrn.com/abstract=2157387.
Trakman, Leon E. 2012b. The ICSID under siege. *Cornell International Law Journal* 45: 603.
Trakman, Leon E. 2012c. Investor-state arbitration or local courts: Will Australia set a new trend? *Journal of World Trade* 46: 83.
Trakman, Leon E. 2013. Investor-state arbitration: The Australian case. In *Regionalism in International Investment Law*, ed. Leon Trakman and Nicola Ranieri. Oxford: Oxford University Press.
Trakman, Leon. 2014a. China and investor-state arbitration. In *China, trade and investment*, ed. Picker Toohey, and Greenacre. Cambridge: Cambridge University Press.
Trakman, Leon. 2014b. The proliferation of free trade agreements: Bane or beauty? *Journal World Trade* 42.
Trakman, Leon, and David Musaleyan. 2015. The repudiation of investor-state arbitration and subsequent treaty practice: The resurgence of qualified investor-state arbitration. *ISCID Law Journal* 45: 1.

Trakman, Leon, and Kunal Sharma. 2015. Locating Australia on the Pacific Rim: Trade, investment and the Asian Century. *Transnational Dispute Management*, 1. www.transnational-dispute-management.com/article.asp?key=2178.

Trakman, Leon, and Kunal Sharma. (2016, forthcoming). Jumping back and forth between domestic courts and ISDS: Mixed signals from the Asia-Pacific Region. In ed. Hindelang, and Krajewski. Oxford: Oxford University Press.

UNCTAD. 2012. Total number of bilateral investment agreements concluded. UNCTAD (2012). www.unctad.org/sections/dite_pcbb/docs/bits_china.pdf. Accessed 1 Nov 2014.

Vandevelde, Kenneth. 2005. A brief history of international investment agreements. *UC Davis Journal of International Law and Policy* 12.

Van Harten, Gus. 2007. *Investment treaty arbitration and public law*. Oxford: Oxford University Press.

Van Harten, Gus. 2012. Arbitrator behaviour in asymmetrical adjudication: An empirical study of investment treaty arbitration. *Osgoode Hall Law Journal* 50: 211. http://papers.ssrn.com/sol3/papers.cfm?abstract_id=2149207.

Vandevelde, Kenneth J. 2004. Model bilateral investment treaties: The way forward. *Southwestern Journal of International Law* 18.

Vandevelde, Kenneth J. 2007. Aguas del Tunari, S.A. v. Republic of Bolivia. *American Journal of International Law* 101: 179.

Wang, Guiguo. 2009. China's practice in international investment law: From participation to leadership in the world economy. *Yale Journal of International Law* 34: 575.

Weeramantry, J. Romesh. 2012. Investor–state dispute settlement provisions in China's investment treaties, ICSID Review 27.

Wenhua, Shan. 2013. China and international investment law. In *Regionalism in international investment law*, ed. Leon Trakman and Nicola Ranieri. Oxford: Oxford University Press.

Willems, Jane. 2011. The settlement of investor state disputes and China—New developments on ICSID jurisdiction. *South Carolina Journal of International Law and Business* 8: 1.

Wolff, Lutz-Christian. 2010. Pathological foreign investment projects in China: Patchwork or trendsetting by the Supreme People's Court? *International Law* 44: 3.

World Investment Report. 2010. UNCTAD (2010). www.unctad.org.

Xia, Xiaohong. 2011. Implementation of the New York Convention in China. *International Commercial Arbitration Brief* 1(1): 20–24.

Yackee, Jason W., and Jarrod Wong. 2006. The 2006 procedural and transparency-related amendments to the ICSID arbitration rules: Model intentions, moderate proposals, and modest returns. In *Yearbook on international investment law & policy 2009–2010*, ed. Karl P. Sauvant. Oxford: Oxford University Press.

Yang, Shu-Dong. 2012. Investment arbitration and China: Investor or host state? Opinio Juris in Comparatione 2/2011 Paper no 6. http://papers.ssrn.com/sol3/papers.cfm?abstract_id=1973744.

Yannaca-Small, Katia. 2010. Definition of investment: An open-ended search for a balanced approach. In *Arbitration under international investment agreements: A guide to the key issues*, 248. ed. Yannaca-Small. Oxford: Oxford University Press.

Yao, Meizhen. 1987. *International investment law [in Chinese]*. Wuhan University Press.

Part II
The Regionalization of Investment Law and Policy in Asia-Pacific

Ten as One? Explaining ASEAN Regulation on Foreign Investment

Sufian Jusoh and Julien Chaisse

1 Introduction

This chapter discusses the role of the ASEAN Comprehensive Investment Agreement (ACIA), which is one of the most important legal documents in the formation and functioning of the ASEAN Economic Community (AEC),[1] especially from the perspective of the regionalisation of investment law and policy in the Asia-Pacific region.[2]

The AEC was officially launched at the end of 2015 with the declaration of the ASEAN Leaders Summit in Kuala Lumpur in November that year, through the new

[1]As explained elsewhere in this volume, the regionalisation of investment law and policy in the Asia-Pacific region can be illustrated by the Trans-Pacific Partnership (TPP), the Regional Comprehensive Economic Partnership (RCEP), and the Triangular Korea–Japan–China treaty. See also Chaisse (2015a, b, p. 563).

[2]This text draws on Julien Chaisse and Sufian Jusoh, *The ASEAN Comprehensive Investment Agreement. The Regionalization of Laws and Policy on Foreign Investment (London: Edward Elgar, International Investment Law Series edited by Andrea K. Bjorklund and August Reinisch, Chaisse* 2016 *265 p*). The book provides a full discussion of the many issues outlined here.

S. Jusoh (✉)
Institute of Malaysian & International Studies, Universiti Kebangsaan Malaysia, Bangi, Malaysia
e-mail: sufianjusoh@gmail.com

J. Chaisse
School of Law Chinese University of Hong Kong, Chinese University of Hong Kong, Hong Kong, Hong Kong
e-mail: Julien.chaisse@cuhk.edu.hk

J. Chaisse et al. (eds.), *Asia's Changing International Investment Regime*, International Law and the Global South, DOI 10.1007/978-981-10-5882-0_7

AEC 2025 Blueprint Forging Ahead Together.[3] ACIA plays an important role in the proper implementation of the AEC, because it promotes ASEAN (Association of Southeast Asian Nations) as a single investment destination, together with the free movement of investment and the freer flow of capital in the region. It also ensures that the ASEAN nations remain a competitive region for trade and investment, and it plays a prominent role in the "Global ASEAN."[4] In this respect, the chapter provides a comprehensive analysis of the drivers and issues that have guided the development of investment law and policy at the ASEAN level.

The chapter begins by discussing ASEAN as a single investment hub, followed by an outline of the history of the formation of ACIA. The chapter will then discuss ACIA and its role in the investment flow through the liberalisation of investment in ASEAN. This is followed by a discussion of the role of ACIA in shaping the policy on investment facilitation and transparency. The chapter will then discuss the role of ACIA in providing protection of investments. In explaining that ACIA is an important regional investment instrument, the chapter will then explore the relationship between ACIA and the investment decision-making process, followed by a discussion of the relationship between trade and investment, in particular the role of ACIA, the ASEAN Agreement in Trade in Goods (ATIGA) and the ASEAN Framework Agreement on Trade in Services (AFAS) in enhancing investment through trade. Before concluding, the chapter will discuss the remaining issues that need to be addressed by some ASEAN Member States to complete the ACIA implementation.

2 ASEAN as an Investment Destination

ASEAN was formed on 8th August, 1967 by Indonesia, Malaysia, the Philippines, Singapore and Thailand, these being the original members. ASEAN has since expanded to cover most of Southeast Asia including Brunei, Cambodia, Lao PDR,

[3]He ASEAN 2025: Forging Ahead Together comprise five (5) documents namely: 1.1 Kuala Lumpur Declaration on ASEAN 2025: Forging Ahead Together; 1.2 ASEAN Community Vision 2025; 1.3 ASEAN Political-Security Community (APSC) Blueprint 2025; 1.4 ASEAN Economic Community (AEC) Blueprint 2025; and 1.5 ASEAN Socio-Cultural Community (ASCC) Blueprint 2025. The first of these five documents, i.e. the Kuala Lumpur Declaration on ASEAN 2025: Forging Ahead Together, is a political document that was signed by the ASEAN Leaders during the 27th ASEAN Summit. The Declaration, amongst others, adopts the ASEAN Community Vision 2025 and the three Community Blueprints 2025 as well as contains directives of the Leaders on their implementation. The Declaration decides that the Initiative for ASEAN Integration (IAI) Work Plan III and the ASEAN Connectivity 2025, which will be adopted in 2016, shall be an integral part of the ASEAN 2025: Forging Ahead Together.

[4]For ASEAN's partners, ASEAN 2025 means a stronger, more visible and united ASEAN, with a greater role and voice in global economic fora and increased contribution to global economic governance. this is a concept of "Global ASEAN" was endorsed in "AEC 2025 Blueprint Forging Ahead Together" (paras 79 and 80).

Myanmar and Vietnam.[5] When ASEAN embarked on the ASEAN Vision 2020 in 1997, the ASEAN GDP was US$694 billion. Provided that ASEAN's Compound Annual Growth Rate (CAGR) is at 5% the ASEAN economy was intended to reach US$1 trillion by 2005 and US$2 trillion in 2020. ASEAN became a US$1 trillion economy in 2006, one year later than the predicted date. But ASEAN passed the US $2 trillion benchmark in 2011, nine years earlier than anticipated. By 2015, ASEAN's CAGR will almost reach the US$3 trillion point and it will be closer to US$4 trillion in 2020.[6]

ASEAN is a large market, with about 625 million people (this population is higher than North America or the European Union), 60% of whom are younger than 25 years old, and it has a gross domestic product of US$2.398 trillion ASEAN, and it is situated between two major economies, China and India, which are collaborators and competitors in the region, and it is situated within the old and new international trade routes, namely, the old Maritime Silk Road, which covered trade between the Middle East, China, Korea and Japan and the South China Sea, the Straits of Malacca and the Straits of Singapore, three of the busiest shipping lanes in the world.

Although ASEAN was formed in 1967, economic cooperation started in earnest with the creation of the ASEAN Free Trade Area (AFTA) through the Agreement on Common Effective Preferential Tariff of the ASEAN Free Trade Area (CEPT-AFTA) in 1992 which was replaced by the ATIGA, followed by the AFAS and the ASEAN Comprehensive Investment Agreement (ACIA).[7]

ASEAN as a whole remain a competitive and attractive destination for foreign direct investment (FDI). ASEAN economies have always been important destinations for FDI in the Asia-Pacific region. Despite economic difficulties in many parts of the world, such as those caused by the European and the American financial crisis, ASEAN continues to receive FDI and to invest in other countries in the form of Outward FDI (OFDI). The reasons for the continued interest of investors include

[5]Timor Leste is now an observer country and waiting for full membership of ASEAN. For more information about ASEAN, please refer to the ASEAN official website www.asean.org.

[6]IMF's Database on World Economic Outlook, July 2015.

[7]ASEAN's first step towards regional integration started with the signing of the Bali Accord [Is this Accord or Concord—the others are all Concord?] II, which was endorsed at the Nineth ASEAN Summit in October 2003. Bali Concord II consists of three pillars, namely, the ASEAN Security Community (now the ASEAN Political-Security Community), the ASEAN Economic Community, and the ASEAN Socio-Cultural Community. Bali Concord II was followed by the Bali Concord III with the theme of 'ASEAN Community in a Global Community of Nations'. Bali Concord III covers all the main pillars of ASEAN, namely, Political-Security Cooperation, Economic Cooperation, and Socio-cultural Cooperation. Bali Concord III promotes economic integration, which is: to enhance ASEAN's effective participation in regional and global economic initiatives impacting on the region; to promote economic stability in strengthening macroeconomic coordination and promoting financial cooperation at the regional and global level; and to promote economic development which is to strengthen cooperation with relevant international organisations in promoting higher level of economic dynamism, sustained prosperity, and inclusive growth.

the availability of resources, and export-oriented, market-seeking, and efficiency-seeking outlooks.[8] The launch of the AEC in 2015 and the AEC in 2025 may also be considered key drivers in the growth of FDI with ASEAN Member States.[9] In order to achieve the objective of achieving the AEC in 2015, ACIA is designed to enhance the flow of cross-border investment and to promote the freer flow of capital by making ASEAN a more competitive economy and a more attractive destination for FDI whilst increasing the intra-ASEAN investment both in goods and services.

Nevertheless, two main challenges remain for the ASEAN Economic Community including those in the investment sectors.[10] Firstly, due to the development gaps and investment climate positions, there is a big gap between the FDI received by Singapore compared with the rest of the other ASEAN Member States; Thailand, Malaysia, and Indonesia, which are economically always the most important after Singapore; The Philippines and Vietnam; and Cambodia, Lao PDR and Myanmar, where most of these countries' investments are resource-seeking given the wealth of minerals and water resources and a pool of relatively cheap labour.

Secondly, trade and investment between ASEAN Member States are still lower compared to trade and investment between ASEAN Member States and external partners. Except for Myanmar and Indonesia, ASEAN Member States received more FDI from non-ASEAN partners in 2014. According to the study in the International Investment Australia 2014, based on the data from UNCTAD Stats and the World Trade Organization (WTO), the World Bank and the IMF, two-way FDI made up of 80% of the total GDP of ASEAN in 2014—this is in stark contrast to about 20% in 1990.[11] Two-way (or mutual) investment is the sum of the stock of FDI into a country and the outward direct investment from a country. The contribution of the FDI to the GDP is almost the same with the contribution of trade to the GDP, which stood at about 100% of GDP, compared to more than 80% in 1990. The proportion of the FDI inflows to the GDP in ASEAN Member States between 2008 and 2013 is shown in Table 1.

At the same time extra-ASEAN trade formed about 73.4% of the total ASEAN trade in 2011. It is suggested that an increase in trade between ASEAN Member States will see an increase in the investment flow and stock between them. Trade and investment are seen as relying on each other; this is especially so in the age of global value chains where a finished product is made from various components

[8]OECD (2014).

[9]OECD (2014).

[10]OECD (2014).

[11]Economic Diplomacy, Trade Advocacy and Statistics Section, Department of Foreign Affairs and Trade, International Investment Australia 2014, Department of Foreign Affairs and Trade, Australia, September 2015, 16.

Table 1 The proportion of FDI inflows to the GDP in the ASEAN member states 2008–2013

Country	2008	2009	2010	2011	2012	2013
Brunei Darussalam	1.54	3.03	5.06	7.24	5.07	5.56
Indonesia	1.83	0.90	2.03	2.30	2.31	2.56
Cambodia	7.87	4.91	6.54	6.20	10.25	8.83
Lao PDR	4.18	5.46	3.88	3.63	3.15	3.81
Myanmar					1.79	3.84
Malaysia	3.28	0.06	4.40	5.23	3.19	3.70
Philippines	0.77	1.23	0.54	0.90	1.28	1.37
Singapore	6.35	12.38	23.30	17.43	19.54	21.44
Thailand	3.13	1.84	2.85	0.71	3.52	3.69
Vietnam	9.66	7.17	6.90	5.48	5.37	5.20

Source http://data.worldbank.org/indicator/BX.KLT.DINV.WD.GD.ZS/countries?display=default (last accessed on 15th January, 2016)

made in different locations. Thus, one would invest in a location to maximise return to produce a product or part of a product for export. The investor will have to be involved in trading, including by importing some parts or components and by exporting either some parts or components or the finished products.

The traditional notion of investment and trade relates only to main sectors or tangible products; this notion is slowly being eroded by the increase in the cross-border trade in services, thereby making investment in services through commercial presence ever more important. Thus, one can no longer keep a straight pigeon hole of trade in services separate from investment in the main sectors because investment in commercial presence is becoming an important component of FDI, hence the link to the flow between trade in goods and trade in services.

The level of FDI can be linked to the flow in the trade in goods and the trade in services; this is because efficiency-seeking and strategic-asset investors may export their products. FDI can be both a substitute and a complement to trade as efficiency-seeking firms look for the best location from which to produce and export their products,[12] whereas investment in services will contribute to the higher level of service supplies which may also contribute to the services export between the parties. Thus, it can be implied that strong growth in trade in goods and trade in services is one of the factors for the continued attractiveness of ASEAN Member States as investment destinations.

A study by Chaisrisawatsuk et al.[13] shows that there are strong positive and self-reinforcing relationships between bilateral trade and FDI flows, with trade

[12]OECD (2014).

[13]Chaisrisawatsuk and Chaisrisawatsuk (2007, p. 97).

inducing FDI as well as FDI inducing trade in the ASEAN and the OECD countries. In another study, it shows that in Asia, including ASEAN, the countries which export most are also the ones where FDI flows are the highest.[14] It has also been acknowledged that FDI has brought benefits to trade. For example, Austrade states that "*[I]nbound foreign direct investment into Australia over past decades, for example in the mining and food manufacturing industries has been a key driver of growth for Australia's exports, as well as growth of the domestic economy.*"[15]

3 The ASEAN Comprehensive Investment Agreement

To position ASEAN as an important economic and investment hub, ASEAN has developed ASEAN-wide investment frameworks that will work as a tool in economic diplomacy in ensuring that ASEAN becomes the single most important investment hub in the Asia-Pacific region.[16] ASEAN and ASEAN Member States have also negotiated and entered into various bilateral investment treaties (BIT) and preferential trade agreements (PTA)[17] with the aim of enhancing the ASEAN and ASEAN Member States' position as attractive investment destinations, either in natural-resource-seeking, market-seeking, efficiency-seeking or strategic-asset-seeking investment.[18]

The ACIA was signed by the ASEAN Economic Ministers (AEM) on 26th February, 2009. It consolidated two existing agreements: the ASEAN Investment Guarantee Agreement (ASEAN IGA), and the Framework Agreement on the ASEAN Investment Area (AIA). Beyond the mere consolidation of the earlier regional pacts, ACIA is an enhanced agreement that encompasses four pillars: liberalisation; facilitation; protection; and promotion. It also contains new features to further promote and encourage FDI inflows into ASEAN.

---

[14]Sjoholm (2013).

[15]Goodman, Austrade (2015).

[16]This section and some of the subsequent paragraphs draw from the monograph by Julien Chaisse and Sufian Jusoh (forthcoming, Edward Elgar).

[17]As stated by Lester and Mercurio, many of the so-called FTAs favour certain countries in trade relations and are basically discriminatory rather than 'free trade'. The term 'PTAs' [Should this be FTAs?] encompasses many different kinds of bilateral and regional trade agreements and it underscores their common denominator which is to establish preferences for the signatories over others in trade relations. See Lester and Mercurio (eds) (2009, p. 4).

[18]Jusoh (2014).

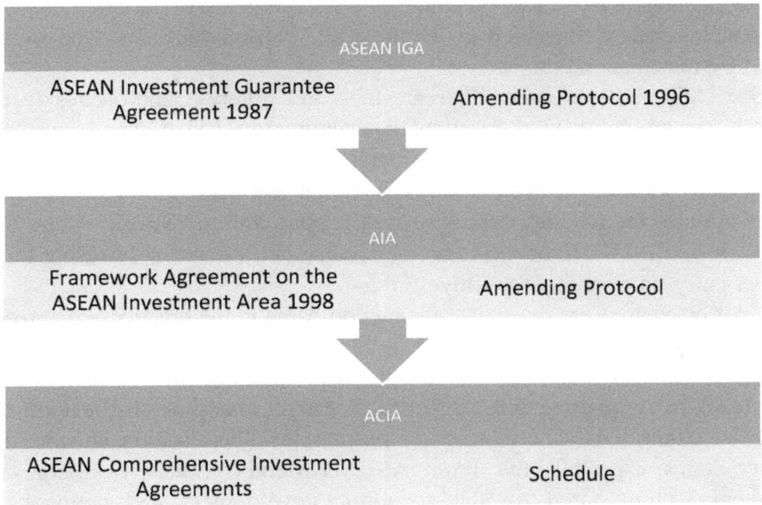

ACIA is an important pillar of the AEC and part of the ASEAN Community. ACIA is a result of the Cebu Declaration at the 12th ASEAN Summit in 2007 to transform ASEAN into a region with free movement of investments. ACIA complements two other important legal frameworks in the AEC, namely, ATIGA, which was signed in 2009 and came into force in 2010, and AFAS which came into force in 1995; these are designed to allow the free flow of goods and services and the freer flow of skilled labour, respectively. Since its establishment, ASEAN has striven for resilience, both individually as nations and as an international grouping. It spent time refining and fostering the concepts that defined ASEAN. The free flow of investment is a key component of the AEC.

4 ACIA and Investment Flow and Liberalisation in ASEAN

ACIA offers a platform for ASEAN Member States (AMS) to liberalise investment by lowering the entry and post-entry barriers faced by investors. The expectation is for ASEAN Member States to increase their economic and investment liberalisation over time in order to attract more investments into ASEAN and to ensure that ASEAN becomes an investment hub. The approach on the liberalisation of investments in ACIA is to remedy shortcomings in the earlier ASEAN investment agreements, namely, the ASEAN IGA and the ASEAN AIA. The liberalisation approach in the AIA was more complicated with the existence of the Temporary Exclusion List and the Sensitive List of Investments for ASEAN investors and foreign investors. The AIA agreement was also negotiated during the 1997–1998

Asian Financial Crisis and would not be progressive enough to handle post-financial crisis recovery efforts by the ASEAN Member States who were most affected by the financial crisis.

Hence, ACIA has to take different steps and different approaches to ensure economic sustainability in the region by encouraging ASEAN and non-ASEAN investments in the region. Investment liberalisation in ACIA responds to the needs of businesses looking to expand across national frontiers. Intra-ASEAN liberalisation facilitates the efficient deployment of capital within ASEAN. ACIA offers a platform for ASEAN Member States to liberalise investment by lowering the entry and post-entry barriers faced by investors.

ACIA's provisions are more liberalising compared to the predecessor agreements where ACIA provides for the progressive liberalisation of investment regimes and AMS have committed to progressively lift restrictions in the ten sectors covered under ACIA in accordance with a blueprint created to facilitate the development of the AEC (Article 9.4). The concept of progressive liberalisation allows ASEAN Member States, especially the newer ASEAN Member States, to liberalise their investment sectors based on the economic development and national policy objectives.[19]

The principle also includes the concept that once liberalisation of sectors occurs, the government should not backtrack on the liberalisation or reintroduce restrictions that have been removed. This section highlights the sectors covered for investment liberalisation under ACIA. ACIA's liberalisation of investment in ASEAN covers five main sectors, namely, manufacturing, fisheries, agriculture, forestry, and mining and quarrying and all the related services. ASEAN also agrees to further liberalise other areas subject to agreement by ALL Member States.[20]

ACIA has an expanded scope because it covers both FDI and portfolio investment (compared with AIA, which covers FDI only). Also, the benefits of ACIA are extended to ASEAN investors and foreign-owned ASEAN-based investors. Interestingly, ACIA remains flexible because it has a more comprehensive

---

[19]The principle of 'progressive liberalisation' follows the mechanism in use within the WTO especially in relation to the liberalisation of the services sector under the GATS, which approach is also adopted by ASEAN in the AFAS. On the notion of 'progressive liberalisation', see Chaisse and Chakraborty (2013, p. 44). GATS recognises the need for the developing countries to liberalise their economy and trade over time. Article XIX of the GATS calls for achieving progressive higher liberalisation and promoting the interests of all participants on a mutually advantageous basis and for securing an overall balance of rights and obligations. The mandate further states that negotiations shall have due regard for national policy objectives and the level of development of individual members, both overall and in individual sectors. It also states that there shall be appropriate flexibility for individual developing countries for opening fewer sectors, liberalising fewer types of market transactions, progressively extending market access in line with their development situation and flexibility of attaching market access conditions to foreign service suppliers.

[20]In terms of liberalisation, ACIA enshrines provisions, which accommodate the expansion of scope of this Agreement to cover other sectors in the future, such as the Article 3(3) (f) 'services incidental to manufacturing, agriculture, fishery, forestry, mining and quarrying; [Reaffirm our vision stated in AIA] and (g) any other sectors, as may be agreed upon by all Member States'.

Modification of Commitments under Article 10, which includes clear procedures on the modification of commitments and the inclusion of provision for compensatory adjustment to ensure balance of benefits.

ACIA also subscribes to the principles of non-discrimination which provides for National Treatment (NT) and Most Favoured Nation Treatment (MFN) to investors and covered investments within the ambit of ACIA. This means that, in general, ASEAN investors and their investments are not to be discriminated against in any of the ASEAN Member States where they invest or where their investment is located. At the same time, ACIA allows investors to select senior management irrespective of any nationality (SMBD), thereby allowing investors to seek the best talents in the various fields and to be able to work with people whom they can trust. ACIA also ensures that ASEAN Member States do not impose performance requirements which may put investors and their investment at a disadvantage over local investors or other third country investors.

The benefits flowing from NT, MFN and SMBD can be limited through the maintenance of restrictive measures inscribed in the list of limitations or the Schedule appended to ACIA. In the ten sectors, under Article 10, for a period of 12 months after the submission of a schedule and AMS may adopt measures or modify its reservations for prospective applications to investors and their investments provided that such measures or modifications shall not adversely affect any existing investors and investment.

5 ACIA, Facilitation and Transparency

Business always needs information on government measures within the territory in which it is investing, especially on information affecting businesses such as on investment measures, any new restrictions or liberalisation or licensing requirements. Thus, ACIA fits well with the expectation of businesses by providing a provision on transparency. Transparency could relate to the removal of barriers to investment, which are made meaningful 'to the extent that the members of the public know what laws, regulations, procedures and administrative ruling affect their interests, can participate in their development … and can request review of their application under domestic law ….'[21]

On the other hand, according to the United Nations Conference on Trade and Development (UNCTAD), which adopts a broader definition of transparency, the concept of transparency is closely associated with the 'promotion and protection in the field of international investment. In the present context, transparency denotes a state of affairs in which the participants in the investment process are able to obtain sufficient information from each other in order to make informed decisions and

[21]'APEC Leaders' Statement to Implement APEC Transparency Standards' (2002/2003), available at www.apec.org/apec/leaders__declarations/2003_leadersstmtimplapectranspstd.html.

meet obligations and commitments. As such, it may denote both an obligation and a requirement on the part of all participants in the investment process.'[22]

Transparency is linked to the level of political and business risks discussed above. It generally means that the higher is the level of transparency; the lower is the political and legal risk to the businesses. From a business point of view, 'transparency reduces risks and uncertainties, promotes patient investment, reduces opportunities for bribery and corruption, helps unveil hidden investment barriers and draws the line between genuine and less genuine policy objectives, assists investors dealing with "thin" rules, discourages "conflicting requirements" situations between home country or host country, contributes to the playing field among firms and facilitates sustainable development'.[23]

Business will benefit from ACIA because its Article 21 requires each ASEAN Member State to publish any international agreements to which it belongs and which pertain to investment, as well as all relevant measures pertaining to investment, be they laws, regulations or administrative guidelines. Such information shall be made available by each AMS to the ASEAN Investment Area Council. In order to ensure compliance with this obligation, each ASEAN Member State must establish an enquiry point at which all the information mentioned above in response to inquiries made by potential investors or other ASEAN Member States is made available.

Although ASEAN Member States agree to promote transparency to facilitate the flow of information to investors and their investments, the Member States retain a certain level of flexibility in order to safeguard certain types of information and state and business confidential information.

Under Article 21 (2) ACIA, an AMS is not obliged to disclose any confidential information, including that concerning particular investors or investments, if such disclosure would impede law enforcement, or be contrary to the public interest, or would prejudice legitimate commercial interests of particular public or private juridical persons.

6 ACIA and Protection of Investment

In terms of protection, ACIA has more comprehensive and clear provisions, and thus it ensures better protection compared to the previous ASEAN instruments. Investment protection relates to a series of minimum guarantees ensuring that established businesses will be treated in a non-discriminatory and fair manner. Such guarantees are keys to the long-term operation and growth of commercial operations across ASEAN. ACIA adopts the international best practices in providing investment protections to the investors and investments. It provides the following

---

[22]United Nations Conference on Trade and Development (UNCTAD) (2004).

[23]OECD (2003).

protections to investors and their investments, namely, fair and equitable treatment (FET), prohibition against expropriations without compensation, full protection and security, and free transfer of funds.

ASEAN Member States have agreed to extend FET to the covered investment of investors in the territory of the respective ASEAN Member States.[24] In the light of Article 11 ACIA and the case law developed in the context of similar treaties, the practical implications of the ACIA FET clause include that: the host AMS will be bound by the rule of law in exercising its power, and that such an exercise will not be arbitrary; the host AMS will have to ensure access to judicial or administrative tribunals or procedures for a review of such measures; and ASEAN investors who are parties to the proceeding must be given the opportunity to support or defend themselves, including having the right of legal representation, as well as the opportunity to appeal any adverse outcomes.

As provided under Article 11 of the ACIA, a host AMS will have to provide full protection and security of an investor's covered investment. Practically, this refers to the physical protection of the property of the investors from attacks (use of force) during riots or insurgence occurring in the territory of that AMS. One of the key substantive provisions commonly included in investment treaty texts is the obligation to provide 'full protection and security'. However, different variants are also found, such as 'full protection and full security', 'constant protection and security', 'protection and security', or 'physical protection and security'; these have not had much impact on the way in which the standard is applied.[25]

Through ACIA, AMS are committed to ensure that governments will not unlawfully expropriate or nationalise an investment without proper compensation. This protection for expropriation applies both to direct and indirect expropriation. It is important to note that each ASEAN Member State has the sovereign right to regulate investments in its territory. As such, not all government actions that interfere with foreign investors' investment can be deemed as indirect expropriation.

Annex 2, para 3 of the ACIA provides that for a measure or series of measures to be indirect expropriation, there must be a case-by-case, fact-based inquiry that considers at least the following cumulative factors: whether the action creates an adverse effect on the economic value of an investment; whether the action breaches the government's prior binding written commitment to the investor (by contract, licence, or other legal document); and whether the government action, including its objective, is disproportionate to the public purpose. Also, the measures imposed by the ASEAN Member State must be non-discriminatory, designed and applied to

[24]Article 11.

[25]The Parkerings v. Lithuania Award found that it is generally accepted that the variation of language between the formulation 'protection' and 'full protection and security' does not make a significant difference in the level of protection a host state is to provide. See *Parkerings-Compagniet AS v. Republic of Lithuania*, ICSID Case No. ARB/05/8, Award, 11th September, 2007, para 354.

protect legitimate public welfare objectives (such as public health, safety, and the environment).

A commitment of a host state to permit the transfer of funds into and out of a host state is a key consideration for an investor. For the host state, it is important to have policy space to monitor, regulate, and in some cases control the flight of capital and to regulate transfers in other circumstances. In the early treaties, there were no exceptions to the transfer of funds commitments, even though in certain circumstances, like in a balance of payments crisis, there are legitimate reasons to control capital flight.

Although IMF rules prohibit the controls on funds transfers related to current transactions, these rules do not apply to capital transactions (i.e., investment). The General Agreement on Trade in Services (GATS) provisions prohibit controls on capital flows in connection with sectors in which a state has made specific commitments in its national schedule of commitments. Disputes regarding the transfer of funds obligations rarely come up to investor–state arbitration.

This issue of a host state's legitimate reasons for restricting funds transfer has been addressed through specific treaty provisions in more recent agreements but with certain exceptions to the transfer of funds obligation.

Freedom to manage capital and funds is essential for any business operation. Article 13 ACIA guarantees that every ASEAN investor may freely and without delay conduct transfers relating to its investments into and out of the territory of the AMS where its investment is located. This includes the following transfers: contribution to capital; profits, capital gains, dividends, royalties, licence fees or any other fees, interest, or other income from the investment; proceeds from the total or partial sale or liquidation of its investments; payments under a contract, including a loan agreement; payments of compensation in cases of strife or lawful expropriation; payments from settlement of a dispute; and earnings or other remuneration of personnel who are employed and allowed to work in relation to the investment in that territory.

Additionally, ACIA guarantees that such transfers can be made in a freely usable currency at the market rate of exchange at the time of transfer. The term 'freely usable currency' simply means that the currency is in fact widely used to make payments for international transactions, and that is widely traded in the main exchange markets. There is no requirement for payment in a specific hard currency (e.g., Euro or US$) as it would be considered restrictive. Rather, ACIA guarantees that investors can freely determine the currency that they want in making any transfers.

There are several exceptions to the freedom of transfer of funds under Article 13, where an ASEAN Member State may prevent or delay the transfer of funds through an equitable, non-discriminatory, and good-faith application of its laws and regulations, with regard to bankruptcy, insolvency or the protection of the rights of creditors; trading in securities, futures, options or derivatives; criminal or penal offences and the recovery of proceeds of crime; financial reporting or record keeping of transfers when necessary to assist law enforcement or financial regulatory authority; ensuring compliance with the orders or judgements in judicial or administrative proceedings; taxation; social security, retirement, or compulsory saving schemes; severance for employees; and formalities imposed by the Central Bank or other relevant authorities of that ASEAN Member State.

ACIA also extends its protections to non-ASEAN Member States investors by them becoming an ASEAN investor. This can be done first by a non-ASEAN investor establishing a juridical entity which carries out substantial business in one of the ASEAN Member States. Then, this entity will become an ASEAN investor by establishing another juridical entity in its target destination of investment in another ASEAN Member State. The former entity must own or control the latter entity (i.e., have power to name a majority of its directors or to legally direct its actions), and the former entity must carry out substantive business operations in the ASEAN Member States where it was established.

Dispute settlement, meanwhile, responds to instances where host country decisions, actions, inactions or the inability to make decisions may nullify or impair the value of an investment. In this case, ASEAN provides concerned investors with direct access to dispute settlement procedures such as taking action in domestic courts, conciliation, mediation, or international arbitration.

7 Dispute Settlement Options in ACIA

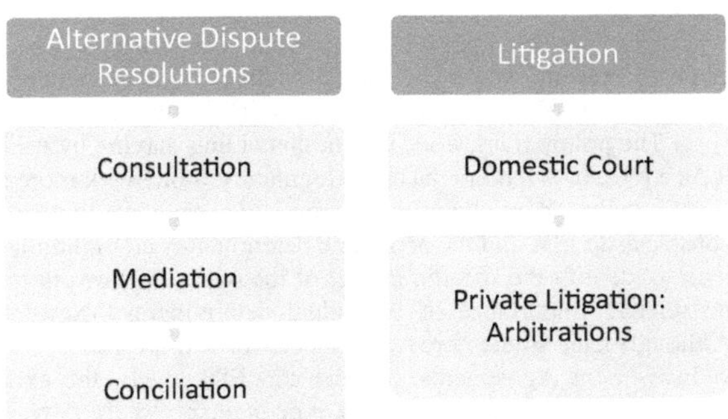

The ISDS provided in ACIA applies only to investment disputes arising after ACIA's coming into force, i.e., on 29th March, 2012. An investor may refer any dispute to a domestic court of the host country. However, it is not a requirement under ACIA for an investor to make use of domestic courts before requesting consultation or even filing for arbitration. Rather, investors are free to choose their preferred method of resolving any particular dispute.

If arbitration is seen to be the preferred dispute resolution procedure, however, the investor is required to waive in writing its right to initiate or continue any domestic court proceedings.

The one exception to this is that an investor will not be prevented from initiating or continuing an action that seeks interim measures of protection for the sole purpose of preserving the disputing investor's rights and interests and does not involve the payment of damages or resolution of the substance of the matter under dispute.

By committing to the protection guarantees, the AMS are making significant efforts to smooth the path for businesses to expand or diversify across regional borders. However, with more and more companies (whether big or small), entrepreneurs, and professionals viewing ASEAN as a single market, it is unrealistic to expect that there will never be disagreements between these ASEAN investors and their respective host states. ACIA recognizes this and therefore it contains a detailed chapter on dispute settlement.

8 ACIA and Investment Decision-Making Process

Various studies show that international investment agreements such as ACIA do not generally contribute to increased investment flows between the parties to the agreements.[26] This could be contributed by several factors. One of such factors is the lack of knowledge about the international investment agreements by the investors, especially by small and medium-sized enterprises, partly due to the lack

[26]Here, a few relatively recent examples should suffice to demonstrate this fact. Firstly, UNCTAD's World Investment Report (2003) held that 'BITs play a minor role in influencing global FDI flows. [...) The policy framework is at best enabling, having by itself little or no effect on FDI flows. [...] As a rule, IIAs tend to make the regulatory framework more transparent, stable, predictable and secure—that is, they allow the economic determinants to assert themselves. And when IIAs reduce obstacles to FDI and the economic determinants are right, they can lead to more FDI. But it is difficult to identify the specific impact of the policy framework on FDI flows, given the interaction and relative importance of individual determinants.' Newcombe and Paradell concluded that: 'Although later studies provide support for a more robust relationship between IIAs (International Investment Agreements, author) and FDI levels, the existence of a causal relationship and the strength of that relationship remain disputed. [...] Nevertheless, even if empirical evidence of a causal relationship is inconclusive, there remains strong competitive pressure for developing states to enter into IIAs and thereby signal to foreign investors that an enabling environment for foreign investment exists.' Newcombe and Paradell (2009). Thirdly, Büthe and Milner develop a more direct link between BITs and FDI: 'In sum, enforcement procedures established by (or as a consequence of) BITs enable foreign governments and private actors to impose higher economic and political costs on governments that renege on their policy commitments—and to do so more quickly—than in the absence of BITs. By increasing the likelihood and the time-discounted magnitude of the punishment for reneging, international institutions should reduce the time-inconsistency problem posed by FDI for developing country governments.' Büthe and Milner (2009, pp. 171–224) at 187. Fourthly, Busse et al., on the basis of their empirical analysis, go even further and conclude that 'BITs may even substitute for domestic institutions.' Busse et al. (2010, pp. 147–77). Finally, Tobin and Rose-Ackerman argue on the basis of empirical evidence that '... the global surge in BITs has weakened the treaties as a tool for attracting FDI to a particular country'. Tobin and Rose-Ackerman (2010, pp. 1–32), at 2. See also Chaisse and Bellak (2011, p. 3), Chaisse (2013, p. 187).

of resources among some of the respondents to arrange for information to enhance their understanding of the content of the agreements.

The second factor is that international investment agreements contribute to the complexity and confusion among businesses and investors because such agreements add to the complexity of too many PTAs and similar agreements and these agreements may not have standard terms and provisions. Businesses and investors would prefer some form of harmonisation among the PTAs and international investment agreements because different sets of provisions over the same subject matter will increase the cost of doing business, such as an increase in the complexity of trading arrangements and costs for commercial trading companies in understanding and complying with the administrative requirements of each agreement.

Nevertheless, there is a tendency for investors to utilise the PTAs and international investment agreements if they provide for an enhanced level of liberalisation and market access. This is consistent with the result of some of studies which show that PTAs and BITs do not stand high on the list of priorities of investors in making investment decisions, unless such PTAs or BITs also provide for investment liberalisation.

A study by Berger, Busse, Nunnenkamp and Roy which examines the potential impact of liberalisation and protection of foreign investment[27] found that liberal admission rules, such as NT provisions in the pre-establishment phase promote bilateral FDI.[28] Thus, market access liberalisation along with the provisions on non-discrimination[29] and the treatment of investors in an international investment agreement are important in attracting investors to invest in a particular destination.[30] Some studies show that an international treaty has a direct commerce-enhancing effect; i.e., by signing them, countries open up easier access to other markets and thus allow firms to benefit from low barriers to business with other countries and to easily export back to the home country.[31] Market access, either directly into the FDI destination or using the FDI destination as a route to access another market contributes towards the strong correlation between the signing of an investment treaty and the increase in the FDI flow.

In addition, the studies show that investment treaties like AANZFTA could contribute towards lowering the costs of production in the host country, such as by allowing access to cheaper materials and production inputs (e.g., new technologies) in efficiency-seeking investments. In short, the combination of signing international

[27]Berger et al. (2013, p. 247).

[28]Berger et al. (2013, p. 268).

[29]See Time [This seems a strange forename. Should it be Tim?] Büthe and Milner (2008, p. 741), Time [Ditto.] Büthe and Milner (2014, p. 88).

[30]Kenyon and Margalit (2014).

[31]See Busse et al. (2010, p. 147), Egger and Pfaffermay (2004, p. 788), Neumayer and Spess (2005, p. 1567), Salacuse and Sullivan (2005, p. 67), and Tobin and Rose-Ackerman (2011, p. 1).

treaties and implementing liberalising economic reforms leads to the most favourable assessment of the investment climate.[32]

9 ACIA's Relation with ATIGA and AFAS

In analysing investments, one should refer to both investments in the main sectors, such as manufacturing and mining, and investments in the commercial presence in trade in services, such as financial services, professional services, and accounting. This is mainly because FDI data consist both of investments in the main sectors and the commercial presence in trade in services.

ACIA has to be linked with ASEAN's trade in goods and trade in services agreement (ATIGA and AFAS) to make them in tandem as a set of interrelated instead of stand-alone agreements because the preferential trade component of a deep agreement with an investment chapter makes it comparatively cheaper for multinational corporations to secure supply chain inputs from the host country, while the investment protections protect against the political risks associated with large capital investments, such as expropriation, denial of justice, discriminatory treatment, and other governmental misconduct. These economies serve as part of the global chain of products and services, and the ASEAN agreements and the AEC serve to integrate the value chain between ASEAN Member States and the wider world.

In fact, ASEAN Member States are forming part of the Regional Value Chain (RVC), which is contributed by the expanding of operations by the multi-national companies, the increasing capacity of local firms in producing inputs used in the various stages of value chains in ASEAN, and the regional integration in ASEAN through the establishment of the ASEAN Economic Community in 2015.[33] The main industries forming part of the ASEAN RVC include automotive, electrical and electronics, and agriculture. It is reported that ASEAN value added inputs in the region's total exports are high and have been increasing, from 65% in 1995 to 69% in 2011. This development suggests that export-oriented foreign and local companies operating in the region have increased their sourcing of inputs from the region to use in producing or assembling subsequent components or finished products in the value chains they are associated with. This makes ASEAN an attractive destination for investors to invest in the existing RVC or even to create a new set of RVC within the ASEAN.

Agreement on Common Effective Preferential Tariff of the ASEAN Free Trade Area (CEPT-AFTA) 1992.[34] The main objective of ATIGA is to establish an

[32]Kenyon and Margalit (2014).

[33]ASEAN, *ASEAN Economic Report 2013–2014, FDI Development and Regional Value Chain* (ASEAN Secretariat Jakarta 2014).

[34]For a discussion on ATIGA, see Ke (2014, p. 414).

integrated market and production base with a free flow of goods by 2015, one of the goals of the formation of the AEC. ATIGA comprises several elements to ensure the realisation of the free flow of goods within ASEAN, including tariff liberalisation, removal of non-tariff barriers, rules of origin, trade facilitation, customs, standards and conformance, sanitary, and phytosanitary measures. To encourage transparency and predictability, Annex 2 of ATIGA provides the full Tariff Reduction Schedule (TRS) of each ASEAN Member State and it spells out the tariff rates to be applied on each product for each year up to 2015. ATIGA liberalises trade in goods through the elimination of both intra-regional tariffs and non-tariff barriers, which should increase the efficiency and competitiveness of ASEAN's manufacturing sector in the global market.

AFAS, which was signed in 1995, aims: to enhance cooperation in services between ASEAN Member States in improving the efficiency and competitiveness of ASEAN services industries; to diversify production capacity and supply, and the distribution of services; eliminate substantial barriers to trade in services; and liberalise trade in services by expanding the depth and scope of liberalisation beyond those undertaken under the GATS of the WTO.

AFAS adopts the definitions of the services trade in Article I.2 of GATS. The definition of services trade under AFAS, as in GATS, is four-pronged, depending on the territorial presence of the supplier and the consumer at the time of the transaction. Pursuant to Article I:2 of GATS, services trade include services supplied from the territory of one Member into the territory of any other Member (Mode 1—Cross-border trade); in the territory of one Member to the service consumer of any other Member (Mode 2—Consumption abroad); by a service supplier of one Member, through commercial presence, in the territory of any other Member (Mode 3—Commercial presence); and by a service supplier of one Member, through the presence of natural persons of a Member in the territory of any other Member (Mode 4—Presence of natural persons).

10 Issues in the Implementation of ACIA and Challenges Ahead

Although ACIA has been established as an important document in attracting investments into ASEAN, several important aspects of ACIA remain to be implemented. ASEAN has yet to produce a single comprehensive common investment policy document covering the region. Instead, investment policies remain within the domain of the individual ASEAN Member State, and investment policies and laws vary from one Member State to another.

The differences range from a Member State having a specific law dealing with investments to having different laws covering investments; investment promotion agencies and regulators; liberalisation of investment sectors and market access such as sector restrictions and foreign investors shareholding and participations;

admission of investments such as screening of investment proposals; incentives; protection of investments and investors; approach towards investor–state dispute settlement systems; grievance mechanisms; and an approach towards international investment agreements including BITs and investment chapters in the free trade agreements.

Another important step that ASEAN has to take is to socialise and promote ACIA as a tool for attracting FDI into ASEAN. ACIA is a unique agreement compared to other types of international investment agreement because it is a regional investment agreement, where the parties agree to certain steps to liberalise investment sectors whilst at the same time providing protections to ASEAN investors investing in all sectors. The socialisation of ACIA is important because international investment agreements may have a major impact on the investment decision-making process.[35] Investors generally do not take into account the existence of international investment agreement such as including investment chapters in the PTA or the existence of investor protections including the investor–state dispute settlement mechanism at the point of making the investment decision.

Thirdly, ASEAN needs to commence the joint promotion of ASEAN as a single investment destination, instead of individual ASEAN Member States promoting themselves as individual destinations.

Hence, there is a need for ASEAN Member States to start implementing the ASEAN Economic Community Blueprint 2025 as adopted in the ASEAN 2025: Forging Ahead Together. Under this document, ASEAN leaders envisioned that by 2025, ASEAN would be: highly integrated and cohesive; competitive, innovative and dynamic; with enhanced connectivity and sectoral cooperation; and a more resilient, inclusive, and people-oriented, people-centred community, integrated with the global economy.

ASEAN leaders undertake to achieve a highly integrated and cohesive regional economy that supports sustained high economic growth by: increasing trade, investment, and job creation; improving the regional capacity to respond to global challenges and mega trends; advancing a single market agenda through enhanced commitments in trade in goods, and through an effective resolution of non-tariff barriers; achieving deeper integration in trade in services; and ensuring a more seamless movement of investment, skilled labour, business persons, and capital.

AEC 2025 also envisions a competitive, innovative and dynamic community which fosters robust productivity growth. This will be done through: the creation and practical application of knowledge, supportive policies towards innovation, a science-based approach to green technology and development, and by embracing the evolving digital technology; the promotion of good governance, transparency and responsive regulations; effective dispute resolution; and a view towards enhanced participation in global value chains.

[35]See how some investors have structured or re-restructured their investments to size the benefits of investment treaties and/or arbitration Chaisse (2015a, b, pp. 225–306).

Furthermore, the ASEAN leaders envision that the AEC 2025 will provide enhanced connectivity and sectoral cooperation with improvements in regional frameworks. This will include: strategic sectoral policies vital to the effective operationalisation of the economic community; a resilient, inclusive, people-oriented and people-centred community that engenders equitable development and inclusive growth; a community with enhanced micro, small and medium enterprise development policies and cooperation to narrow the development gaps; and a community with effective business and stakeholder engagement, subregional development cooperation and projects, and greater economic opportunities that support poverty eradication.

The ASEAN leaders also envision that AEC 2025 will be 'A global ASEAN'. It will foster: a more systematic and coherent approach towards its external economic relations; a central and foremost facilitator and driver of regional economic integration in East Asia; and a united ASEAN with an enhanced role and voice in global economic fora in addressing international economic issues.

In 2015 and post 2015, ASEAN Member States will continue to work on the review of the ACIA built-in agenda items, including treatment on Permanent Resident and Prohibition Performance Requirements. Other items of interest to ASEAN are the Protocol to Amend ACIA, which provides the mechanism to facilitate amendment or modification of AMS's reservation list. This will be with especially respect to: their ongoing liberalisation efforts; the efforts of ASEAN to promote the region as a single investment destination; and to further improve their respective investment regimes through the ongoing projects relating to investment promotion and facilitation. The work on the built-in agenda items poses a big challenge because many ASEAN Member States still have some form of performance requirements in their investment policies, and ASEAN are, *de facto*, competitors for FDI.

11 Conclusion

ASEAN Member States value the growth and development dividends that can flow from increased economic integration. There is a consensus, reflected in ACIA, that cross-border investment has a positive role to play in all ten ASEAN Member States and that investors should be encouraged to maintain and expand their investments throughout the region. Likewise, there is hope that more investors will emerge in the coming years. This is the background to ACIA and it goes a long way towards explaining the way it offers potentially significant advantages for businesses doing business across the region.

ACIA facilitates the progressive liberalisation of investment in ten potentially profitable sectors: manufacturing; agriculture; fishery; forestry; mining; and related services. In other words, ACIA's investment liberalisation initiatives comprehensively consider the primary, secondary, and tertiary sectors.

In the liberalised sectors, ACIA commits ASEAN Member States to treat new investors and investments in accordance with the principles of NT and MFN treatment, discussed above. Limitations on the nationality of senior management and boards of directors are also reduced under ACIA. For example, through ACIA, AMS will be increasing their openness to cross-border exploration, production, and servicing in the oil and gas industry. There will also be fewer hurdles for cross-border supply chains in the textile industry with raw materials being harvested in one ASEAN Member State and processed in another so that a garment can be produced in a third ASEAN Member State.

In addition, ACIA offers a series of guarantees for ongoing regional businesses that government regulation will be fair and non-discriminatory. ACIA offers wider coverage than the previous investment instruments within ASEAN. The substantive protection and guarantees offered under ACIA are also clearer than those found in previous ASEAN investment instruments. This is especially true of ACIA's comprehensive application of NT and MFN treatment standards for the host-government regulation of investors and investments. One example is ACIA's non-discrimination provisions, both in relation to nationals and in relation to non-ASEAN origin investors. In addition, ACIA's definitions of additional guarantees, such as the criteria for lawful expropriation as well as the commitment to FET and to full protection and security, are clearer than under the previous agreements.

ACIA responds to the concerns of foreign business about the potentially capricious nature of regulatory change to be addressed in an efficient, transparent, and legally binding manner. The collective commitment of ASEAN Member States to a rules-based system of dispute settlement is a significant improvement over the previous approach where business people had to rely on the diplomatic protection of the home country governments. The provision of investor–state dispute settlement depoliticises potential conflicts between individual investors and host states, thereby allowing the former to prosecute alleged treaty breaches and to defend their property rights without soliciting the support of their governments.

The alternative dispute resolution procedures offered by ACIA include mediation, conciliation, and international arbitration. Of these, arbitration is most relevant to major disputes and thus is the subject of most of the ACIA's rules. Investor–state arbitration under ACIA offers the following additional advantages: arbitrators are independent from the host state and not subject to political pressures; enhanced predictability may stem from the recent rise in case law and arbitral awards; and, perhaps most importantly, arbitral awards result in binding decisions that can be enforced globally.

Thus, ASEAN Member States will have to make further improvements in raising foreign investment limits in some sectors in some ASEAN Member States; this will enhance overall investment facilitation and create better collaboration between the ASEAN Member States which are still dominated by competition in attracting FDIs.

In the post-2015 period, ASEAN will continue to deepen and enhance economic integration in areas covered in the AEC 2015 blueprint; this will include the enhancing the investment environment by introducing effective, efficient, coherent and responsive regulations and good regulatory practice. ASEAN will also ensure that ACIA will contribute towards the further integration of ASEAN into the global economy by adopting a more coherent approach with a view of adopting a common position in regional and global economic fora.

References

ASEAN. 2014. *ASEAN Economic Report 2013–2014*. FDI Development and Regional Value Chain: ASEAN Secretariat Jakarta.

Berger, A., et al. 2013. Do trade and investment agreements lead to more FDI? Accounting for key provisions inside the black box. *International Economics and Economic Policy* 10: 247.

Busse, Matthias, Jens Königer, and Peter Nunnenkamp. 2010. FDI promotion through bilateral investment treaties: More than a bit? *Review of World Economics* 146: 147–177.

Büthe, Tim., and Helen V. Milner. 2008. The politics of foreign direct investment into developing countries: Increasing FDI through international trade agreements? *American Journal of Political Science* 52: 741. (Time [This seems a strange forename. Should it be Tim?])

Büthe, Tim., and Helen Milner. 2009. Bilateral investment treaties and foreign direct investment: A political analysis. In *The effect of treaties on foreign direct investment*, ed. Karl P. Sauvant and Lisa E. Sachs, 171–224 at 187. USA: Oxford University Press.

Büthe, Time [Ditto.]., and Helen V. Milner. 2014. Foreign direct investment and institutional diversity in trade agreements: Credibility, commitment, and economic flows in the developing world, 1971–2007. *World Politics* 66: 88.

Chaisrisawatsuk, S., and W. Chaisrisawatsuk. 2007. Imports, exports and foreign direct investment interactions and their effects, chapter IV in ESCAP, towards coherent policy frameworks: Understanding trade and investment linkages, trade and investment studies, No. 62, United Nations, New York, 97.

Chaisse, Julien. 2013. Assessing the exposure of Asian states to investment claims. *Contemporary Asia Arbitration Journal* 6: 187.

Chaisse, Julien. 2015a. The shifting tectonics of international investment law—Structure and dynamics of rules and arbitration on foreign investment in the Asia-Pacific region. *George Washington International Law Review* 47: 563.

Chaisse, Julien. 2015b. The issue of treaty shopping in international law of foreign investment—Structuring (and restructuring) of investments to gain access to investment agreements. *Hastings Business Law Review* 11: 225–306.

Chaisse, Julien, and Christian Bellak. 2011. Do Bilateral investment treaties promote foreign direct investment? Preliminary reflections on a new methodology. *Transnational Corporations Review* 3: 3.

Chaisse, Julien, and Debashis Chakraborty. 2013. Deconstructing services and investment negotiations—A case study of India at WTO GATS and investment fora. *Journal of World Investment and Trade* 14: 44.

Chaisse, Julien., and Sufian Jusoh. 2016. The ASEAN comprehensive investment agreement: The regionalization of laws and policy on foreign investment. UK: Edward Elgar.

Egger, Peter, and Michael Pfaffermay. 2004. The impact of bilateral investment treaties on foreign direct investment. *Journal of Comparative Economics* 32: 788.

Goodman, Christina, Austrade. 2015. Overseas investment of Australian companies. Trade and Investment Note. www.austrade.gov.au/about-austrade/economics-at-austrade/overseas-investment-of-australian-companies. Accessed 18 May 2015.

Jusoh, Sufian. 2014. ASEAN investment agreements: A tool of economic diplomacy in meeting the objectives of ASEAN economic community blueprint. *Journal of Diplomacy and Foreign Relations*.
Ke, Jing Jia. 2014. Moving towards ASEAN economic community: A new era starting from ATIGA. *Global Trade and Customs Journal* 9: 414.
Kenyon, Tom., and Yotam Margalit. 2014. Does joining international treaties attract foreign investment? Experimental firm-level evidence. Columbia University Working Paper.
Lester, Simon., and Bryan Mercurio (ed). 2009. *Bilateral and regional trade agreements: Commentary and analysis,* 4. UK: Cambridge University Press.
Neumayer, Eric, and Laura Spess. 2005. Do bilateral investment treaties increase foreign direct investment to developing countries? *World Development* 33: 1567.
Newcombe, Andrew Paul, and Lluis Paradell. 2009. *Law and practice of international investment treaties*. Alphen aan den Rijn: Kluwer Law International.
OECD. 2003. *Public sector transparency and the international investor*. Paris.
OECD. 2014. *Southeast Asian investment policy perspectives*. OECD, Paris.
Salacuse, Jeswald, and Nicholas P. Sullivan. 2005. Do BITs really work? An evaluation of bilateral investment Treaties and their grand bargain. *Harvard International Law Journal* 46: 67.
Sjoholm, Fredrik. 2013. Foreign direct investments in Southeast Asia. Research Institute of Industrial Economics, Stockholm, IFN Working Paper No. 987.
Tobin, Jennifer, and Susan Rose-Ackerman. 2010. When BITs have some bite: The political-economic environment for bilateral investment treaties? *The Review of International Organizations* 6: 2.
Tobin, Jennifer, and Susan Rose-Ackerman. 2011. When BITs have some bite: The political economic environment for bilateral investment treaties. *The Review of International Organizations*, March 2011, 6(1): 1–32.
United Nations Conference on Trade and Development (UNCTAD). 2004. Transparency, Geneva.

China-Japan-Korea Trilateral Investment Treaty: Implications for Future Investment Negotiations in Asia

Shintaro Hamanaka

1 Introduction

Relations between China and Japan are central to economic cooperation in Asia, particularly when negotiating regional economic agreements. For both China and Japan, it is investment, not trade nor tariff that has been the central issue, amongst all negotiation items in economic agreements. The principal reason why Japan joins these agreements is not trade liberalization, but to secure non-discriminatory investment liberalization, including prohibiting various performance requirements. In contrast, China remains cautious against engaging pre-establishment (investment liberalization) national treatment (NT) as it may crimp industrial policy. Given these distinct investment goals, agreeing on the international disciplines to govern country investment policy is difficult. The difference in the negotiating stance of the two countries in investment will likely be the greatest obstacle to current and future negotiations for economic agreements in Asia.

China and Japan already spent much time negotiating international investment agreements (IIAs).[1] The Investment Protection Treaty between China and Japan was originally signed in 1989. But unlike other Chinese bilateral investment treaties (BITs), this treaty was not renegotiated. Then, there is the China-Japan-Korea Trilateral Investment Treaty (CJK investment treaty), which was signed in 2012 and became effective in 2014 despite the fact that the 1989 BIT remains in force. There are other current and future negotiations for IIAs that involve or will involve both China and Japan. In 2014, negotiations for China-Japan-Korea Free Trade

[1]In this chapter, IIAs refer both to investment treaties and investment chapters in free trade agreements (FTAs).

S. Hamanaka (✉)
Institute of Devoloping Economics (IDE-JETRO), Chiba, Japan
e-mail: shintaro_hamanaka@ide.go.jp

J. Chaisse et al. (eds.), *Asia's Changing International Investment Regime*, International Law and the Global South, DOI 10.1007/978-981-10-5882-0_8

Agreement (CJK FTA) were launched, with investment as one of its core chapters. Moreover, negotiations to establish Regional Comprehensive Economic Partnership (RCEP) among ASEAN+6 members[2] that includes investment chapter started in 2012. The Trans-Pacific Partnership (TPP), which includes Japan, was agreed in 2015. Whether China might join the TPP in the future is an important item on the regional economic agenda. The TPP includes a substantial investment chapter, which is largely based on the North America Free Trade Area (NAFTA) model. But it also incorporates the United States (US) post-NAFTA experience.[3]

This paper reviews the evolution of investment negotiation dynamics between China and Japan. It considers future prospects for IIAs in Asia, given the significance of the negotiation dynamics between the two largest economies in the region. In particular, we will closely examine the CJK investment treaty, which is one of few plurilateral investment treaties[4] in Asia. Interestingly, the CJK investment treaty is a relatively "Americanized" investment treaty signed by China, with the US not being a contracting party.[5] The CJK investment treaty gives some idea on the prospect of future Asian IIAs involving the two countries, including negotiations on the proposed CJK FTA investment chapter.

The paper is structured as follows. Section two briefly reviews the IIA policies of China and Japan and explains how they evolved over time. The third section reviews two investment treaties signed by China and Japan, the China-Japan BIT in 1989 and the 2012 CJK investment treaty. We compare the quality[6] of the CJK investment treaty with China-Japan BIT in 1989, as well as China-Korea BIT in 2007, and Japan-Korea BIT in 2003. The section also reviews the original positions of China and Japan on critical CJK investment treaty investment points (such as pre-establishment NT), and examines whose preference prevailed. Section four examines current negotiations over the CJK FTA investment chapter. It also touches on current negotiations on US-China BIT, China-Korea FTA, and European Union (EU)-China BIT and FTA. These IIAs impact China-Japan negotiations and IIAs in Asia, in general. The final section concludes.

[2]ASEAN+6 includes the 10 ASEAN members, China, Japan, Korea, Australia, New Zealand and India.

[3]Hodgson (2015).

[4]Plurilateral investment treaties have three or more signatories.

[5]Chi (2015).

[6]In this chapter, high quality investment treaties mean treaties that impose the high level of investment liberalization and the high level of investment protection.

2 IIA Policies of China and Japan

2.1 China's IIA Policies

Until 1978, China restricted inward foreign direct investment (FDI). The notion of private property was rejected under the planned economic system. The country wanted to establish its own control on economic development system rather than relying on foreign capital. Except for a limited number of joint ventures with former Soviet Union states, foreign investment was not allowed. Naturally, during this period, China did not sign any IIA either to attract FDI or to give protection to the limited investments made by foreign entities.

Economic reform started in late 1978 when a "socialist system with Chinese characteristics" was adopted. China began to understand how inward FDI could benefit economic development so its stance on inward FDI also changed. China signed its first BIT with Sweden in 1982 and during this "first phase", which lasted until 1998, it signed around 70 BITs. The majority were BITs with developed countries. They opted for limited investment protection through narrowly defined investor-state arbitration clauses.[7] China's first model BIT (formulated in 1984) did not include any NT provision. Dispute resolution was not included or limited to the amount of compensation for expropriation. The second model BIT (formulated in 1989) was of limited improvement; NT provisions were included, but its scope extremely limited. However, first phase BITs did include post-establishment (investment protection) most favored nation (MFN) status.

By the late 1990s, a second phase evolved as the Chinese government started to encourage outward investment, thereby significantly increasing investment outflows. In particular, it began investing heavily in resources sectors in developing countries, especially in Africa. In addition, China became then the largest investment recipients in the world. Naturally, Chinese IIA policies became more proactive. Accordingly, a third model BIT was formulated in 1997, including a comprehensive NT clause. Also, its dispute settlement provisions set clearer procedural guidelines than previous models. Between 1998 and 2007, China signed around 40 BITs. During this period, the majority of BITs with developed countries signed between 1982 and 1998 were also renegotiated and replaced with new ones, with the notable exception of Japan. Some BITs with developed countries included standstill commitments to non-conforming measures, meaning China would not increase discrimination toward foreign investors.

A third phase began after 2007 as China moved beyond being a prime destination for inflows and became a massive capital exporter. Chinese firms with strong political support and incentives began investing abroad and found the need to protect their investments.[8] Third generation IIA provisions are more detailed and

[7]Fan (2015).

[8]Berger (2008).

Table 1 Evolution of Chinese IIAs

	National treatment (NT)	Most favored nation (MFN)	Investor-state dispute settlement (ISDS)
First phase (1980s–1990s)	No or restricted NT	Post-establishment MFN	No ISDS or ISDS limited to the amount of compensation
Second phase (2000s)	BITs with developing countries: No NT or NT subject to national laws. BITs with developed countries: (i) full post-establishment NT; (ii) standstill commitment to non-conforming measures	Post-establishment MFN	ISDS covering broader range of investor-state disputes
Third phase (after 2007)	Pre-establishment NT not covered	Pre-establishment MFN MFN not extended to ISDS	Detailed ISDS provisions

Source Author's compilation based on Berger (2013)

balanced. Chi calls this the "Americanization" of Chinese IIAs.[9] It began signing American style IIAs that included detailed provisions, broader coverage, a more self-contained structure and higher enforceability. For example, for investor-state arbitration, Chinese third generation IIAs often include provisions on the statute of limitations, the constitution of tribunals, consolidation and costs.[10] However, at the same time, recent Chinese IIAs still have some restrictive language regarding the definition of investors. They often cite "substantial business rules", meaning incorporation (without substantial operations) in a partner country is insufficient to fall under the scope of an IIA. Moreover, pre-establishment NT remains excluded from third generation IIAs, although pre-establishment MFN is covered (Table 1).

2.2 *Japan's IIA Policies*

While Japan is known as a major investor in many parts of the world, especially in Asia, it had a surprisingly cautious attitude towards investment inflows until very recently. Until the mid-1970s, inward investment was heavily restricted via the Foreign Capital Law. After joining the Organisation for Economic Co-operation and Development (OECD) in the mid-1960s, investment deregulation started, but progress was slow. It was only in 1980 when the Foreign Capital Law was abolished.

[9]Chi (2015).

[10]Fan (2015).

Japan signed several BITs from the mid-1970s to the late-1990s (first phase). However, it was not as keen to sign BITs with most proposed by its counterparts. Until 2001, Japan signed only nine BITs with the majority of partners are small economies such as Egypt (1977), Sri Lanka (1982) and Bangladesh (1998), with the notable exception of China (1989). Japan's BITs during this period covered only post-establishment NT. But even post-establishment NT provisions were often restrictive. Japan did not have a model BIT and had no preference regarding the specific wording of NT provisions. In other words, it was "flexible" enough to accommodate partner's concerns. Moreover, Japanese BITs during this period did not include clauses on fair and equitable treatment (FET).

One reason Japan did not have a strong interest in BITs in the 1990s was that it had a strong preference for multilateral investment regimes.[11] At the OECD, the ministerial meeting in May 1995 agreed to begin negotiating a Multilateral Agreement on Investment (MAI). The MAI was expected to be a comprehensive and binding investment agreement with 12 sections,[12] covering both pre-establishment and post-establishment. Although the MAI negotiations were initially conducted among OECD countries, it was expected that non-OECD members would later join the agreement. The Japanese government and industry was a strong proponent of the MAI. In fact, a report prepared in 1997 by Keidanren,[13] the largest business association in Japan, emphasized two systemic issues relating with MAI. First, the report argued that MAI should be open for accession by non-OECD members and that Japan should play an important role in bringing in Asian economies, as Japan was then the only Asian country in the OECD. Second, the relationship between the MAI and existing regional and bilateral investment treaties was underscored. Keidanren felt the violation of MAI MFN rules by bilateral or regional agreement (including investment chapter in FTA such as European Union and North American Free Trade Agreement [NAFTA]) should not disrupt the interests of non-treaty members. However, in December 1998, a formal decision to terminate MAI negotiations was made at an informal OECD meeting.[14]

The MAI failure pushed Japan to pursue second generation IIAs. In fact, in November 1998 when the failure of MAI became unavoidable, Japan began negotiating a Japan-Korea BIT (signed in 2002), the very first IIA categorized as second generation. Interestingly, the Japanese Ministry of Economy, Trade and

[11]Stoel et al. (2015).

[12]These included: (i) general provision; (ii) scope and application; (iii) treatment of investors and investments; (iv) investment protection; (v) dispute settlement; (vi) exceptions and safeguards; (vii) financial services; (viii) taxation; (ix) country-specific exceptions; (x) relationship to other international agreements; (xi) implementation and obligations; and (xii) final provisions.

[13]Keidanren (1997).

[14]Several salient reasons for the failure of MAI negotiations included criticism from non-governmental organizations (NGOs) that MAI paid little attention to labor and environmental issues; criticism from developing countries that MAI reflected only developed countries' views; and concerns over the capital flow liberalization triggered by the 1997/98 Asian financial crisis.

Industry felt the Japan-Korea BIT was "equivalent" to the MAI.[15] Likewise, in March 1999, Japan and Vietnam agreed to start some preparatory work for BIT that covers both investment liberalization and protection, unlike its past BITs that covered only the former. However, at this stage, Japan's bilateralism was limited to the investment area.

Meanwhile, there was an attempt made by developed countries including Japan to fully include investment issues under the WTO framework. At the first WTO ministerial conference in Singapore in 1996, ministers agreed to initiate some "exploratory" work in the four Singapore issues—investment, competition policy, transparency of government procurement and trade facilitation—without prejudging the scope of future negotiations. Working Group on the Relationship between Trade and Investment was established for the exploratory work, not negotiations. However, the launch of new round negotiation for trade and investment liberalization became very unlikely by the time when the third WTO ministerial conference was held in Seattle in November/December 1999, which faced the opposition from Non-governmental organizations (NGOs). At the Japan-Singapore Summit on 8 December 1999, only a week after the Seattle ministerial, the two countries agreed to start negotiations for Japan-Singapore EPA, which was Japan's first EPA.

Hence, we should note that Japan's active bilateral and/or regional economic policy began with investment rather than trade. Negotiations on the Japan-Korea BIT and Japan-Vietnam BIT started before negotiations began on its first FTA (the Japan-Singapore EPA). The argument that Japan's engagement in EPA came from its abandoning multilateralism-centric *trade* policy in the late 1990s does not seem to be accurate, because it implies that the shift in Japan's IIA policy was just a side effect of the shift in trade policy because an investment chapter is only one component of an EPA. For Japan, it was investment, not trade, that seriously needed bilateral agreements after multilateralism because unlikely. In fact, some argue that investment, not trade, is the core component of Japanese EPAs.[16]

2.3 Comparative Analysis of China and Japan

A comparison of the evolution of Chinese and Japanese IIAs is summarized in Table 2. Several important observations can be drawn from the comparison.

First, there is some commonality between the two countries. Each country's IIA policy evolved over time. Basically, it begins at a "No BIT" stage with FDI highly restricted, with more restrictive IIAs were signed early on. More recent IIAs are more liberal. Change occurred by stage or phase rather than as a steady or constant development. In other words, IIAs signed during the same stage are more or less

[15]See: http://www.meti.go.jp/policy/trade_policy/asia/s_korea/html/jkbia_gaiyo.html.

[16]Hatch (2004).

Table 2 Summary of the development of China and Japan international investment agreements (IIAs)

China	Japan
No BIT (1949–1978) • Restrictions on foreign direct investment (FDI)	No BIT (1950s–mid 1970) • Restrictions on FDI
First generation (1978–1998) • Reform and opening up; to attract FDI • Growth of BIT, but conservative approach (FDI importer perspective)	First generation (1976–2001) • Expansion of FDI inflows and large declines in FDI outflows • Passive negotiators in the BITs, restrictive approach (BITs mainly proposed by the counterparty)
Second generation (1998–2007) • 'Going global' strategy; began to become FDI exporter, more liberal view on investment protection; • Pro-investor BITs (FDI exporter perspective)	Second generation (2002-onward) • FDI exporting country • Pro-investor IIAs (FDI exporter perspective)
Third generation (2007-onward) • Characteristics of both inflow and outflow of FDI • More balanced and more detailed BITs and FTAs	

Source Author's compilation

similar. The change in stage is more evident in China, which used model BITs. But Japan also shows clear phases in the evolution of its IIAs.

Second, while more recent China and Japan IIAs are more liberal, the level of liberalization achieved in Chinese and Japanese an IIA differs significantly. For example, both China and Japan started to engage in BITs in the mid-1970s upon partner requests. However, the first Japanese BITs give more substantial investment liberalization and protection than those involving China. This has an important implication. Since preferred restrictions vary across Northeast Asia, bilateral or regional IIA negotiations between or among them tend to be challenging. In fact, as we will see later, the 1989 China-Japan BIT was never re-negotiated.

It is interesting that what triggered more liberal IIAs varies across countries. The investment position (whether FDI importer or exporter) is critical for determining IIA policy because more investment security is needed for FDI exporting countries. If a country wants to protect investments in partner countries, it should offer reciprocity. China's shift to second generation IIAs clearly came once it started to invest abroad, especially in Africa. The external environment also affects IIA policies. The MAI failure made Japan realize that an alternative to the multilateral approach was necessary. For Japan, even as it massively invested in Asia in the 1990s, multilateral investment negotiations were more important than BITs.

3 IIAs Between China and Japan

3.1 The 1989 China-Japan Investment Protection Treaty

Negotiations for the Investment Protection Treaty started in 1982 with the BIT signed 27 August 1988 and entered into force 14 May 1989. Both China and Japan IIA policy were in their respective first phases. While Japan was already an active player in international investment by the 1980s, especially after the 1985 Plaza Accord, its IIA policy was not proactive.

Naturally, the 1989 BIT was not ambitious. Since first generation IIAs of the two countries did not usually include pre-establishment NT, it was not covered in the BIT. The post-establishment NT was included, but policies inconsistent with NT is possible for the purposes related to maintaining public order, national security or sound development of national economy. But again, both China and Japan's first generation IIAs included restrictive language when outlining post-establishment NT. Perhaps the two held different views on investor state dispute settlement (ISDS). While Japan's first generation IIAs include ISDS and often mention the International Centre for Settlement of Investment Disputes (ICSID), Chinese first generation IIAs seldom include ISDS. Because China was not a part of the ICSID convention until 1993, it was difficult for China to accept ICSID-based ISDS that covers a wide range of investment dispute problems. As aforementioned, because the scope of ISDS under the China-Japan BIT is limited to the amount of compensation,[17] we can say that the Chinese preference prevailed in this regard.

Article 15 gives the BIT 10-year validity, although it "shall continue in force" unless terminated. Either party could request re-negotiations toward the end of the period, though it never materialized. Apparently, neither wanted it terminated because the investment protection was valued. This is in sharp contrast with the 1980s Chinese BITs with Western European countries, which were replaced by new ones in the early 2000s (for example, the 1983 China-Germany BIT was replaced with a new BIT in 2003). The 1989 China-Japan Investment Protection Treaty remains in force, despite the CJK investment treaty becoming effective in 2014 (see following section).

Meanwhile, the original BIT between China and Korea was signed in 1992. It was initially effective for 5 years, but extended each year by one year. While the 1992 BIT was not particularly ambitious, it was replaced by a new BIT in 2007 after successful renegotiations. While only the amount of compensation can be submitted to dispute settlement under the old BIT, there is no such restriction under the 2007 BIT. FET was also included in the new BIT. However, it does not cover post-establishment NT. Again, Chinese preference prevailed.

---

[17]ISDS on the amount of compensation under the 1989 BIT follows the ICSID convention, though China was not a part of ICSID by that time. ICSID Convention entered into force for China on 6 February 1993.

In short, many Chinese BITs signed in the 1980s and 1990s were renegotiated and replaced by new BITs—Chinese BITs with Western European countries and the BIT with Korea were renegotiated. In contrast, the 1989 China-Japan BIT was not renegotiated and remains in effect. It is shown in Table 3 that the treatment Japan received was not at par with those accorded to, say Korea. In particular, major concerns for Japan included (i) the lack of a prohibition of performance requirement, (ii) the possible introduction of restrictions subject to domestic regulations and laws (such as expropriation, restriction on transfer), and (iii) limited access to an investor-state dispute mechanism. Naturally, by the time the new China-Korea BIT came into effect, Japan felt it was necessary to improve its BIT with China. Because of the large amount of investment assets in China, Japan's business sector was particularly intent on improving the agreement.

Two things stand out on the MFN provisions in the 1989 China-Japan BIT. First, the MFN provision does not include the so-called regional economic integration organization (REIO) exception clause.[18] When the MFN provision in an investment treaty carries an REIO exception, only provisions in other investment treaties can be imported; provisions in other FTAs cannot be used.[19] The China-Japan BIT can conveniently import both provisions in other investment treaties and the investment provisions in FTAs signed by either China or Japan with other partners. Second, MFN provisions in the China-Japan BIT cover both post- and pre-establishment (see Table 3). The treatment accorded nationals and companies of the other contracting party regarding investments, returns and business activities in connection with investment shall be MFN. This implies that better market access related provisions in others IIAs such as provisions on investment liberalization and prohibition of performance requirement can be imported into the China-Japan BIT using MFN. It also applies to judicial access, administrative tribunals and agencies (domestic remedies). However, the scope of international disputes and access to ICSID is not covered by MFN.

3.2 *China-Japan-Korea Trilateral Investment Treaty*

At the China-Japan-Korea trilateral summit meeting in October 2003 in Bali, Indonesia, the three leaders agreed to launch a joint study group of business, government and academia to examine the feasibility of a CJK investment treaty. The feasibility study report was completed in September 2004.[20] By then, the

[18]The absence of REIO exception in the 1989 China-Japan BIT is partly because both China and Japan did not sign any FTA or REIO by that time.

[19]United Nations Conference on Trade and Development (UNCTAD) 2004, The REIO exception in MFN Treatment Clauses, UNCTAD.

[20]The Report of the Joint Study on the Possible Modality of Trilateral Investment Arrangements Among China, Japan, Korea. Available at: http://www.mofa.go.jp/mofaj/gaiko/investment/jck/pdfs/jck_kaigo_04e.pdf.

Table 3 Comparative analysis of investment treaties in Northeast Asia

	China-Japan BIT (1989)	Japan-Korea BIT (2003)	China-Korea BIT (2007)	CJK trilateral investment treaty (2012)
NT (pre-establishment)	No	Yes	No	No
NT (post-establishment)	Yes (discrimination possible for public order etc.)	Yes	Yes	Yes
MFN (pre-establishment)	Yes	Yes (excluding FTAs)	Yes	Yes (excluding FTAs)
MFN (post-establishment)	Yes	Yes (excluding FTAs)	Yes	Yes (excluding FTAs)
Negative list	No	Yes	No	No
FET	Yes (limited scope)	Yes	Yes	Yes
Umbrella clause	No	No	Yes	Yes
Expropriation and compensation	Yes (subject to laws; limited to MFN for compensation for damages)	Yes	Yes	Yes
MFN and NT due to armed conflict, etc.	Yes (limited to NT)	Yes	Yes	Yes
Transfers	Yes (restriction possible based on domestic regulations	Yes	Yes	Yes
ISDS	Yes (limited to the amount of compensation)	Yes	Yes	Yes
State-state dispute	Yes	Yes	Yes	Yes
PR (export restriction)	No	No	No	Yes
PR (local procurement requirement)	No	Yes	Yes (limited)	Yes
PR (local contents requirement)	No	Yes	No	Yes
PR (export-import balance requirement)	No	Yes	No	Yes
PR (export requirement)	No	Yes	No	Yes (limited)

(continued)

Table 3 (continued)

	China-Japan BIT (1989)	Japan-Korea BIT (2003)	China-Korea BIT (2007)	CJK trilateral investment treaty (2012)
PR (domestic sale restriction requirement)	No	Yes	No	No
PR (local senior management requirement)	No	Yes	No	No
PR (local employment requirement)	No	Yes	No	No
PR (regional headquarters requirement)	No	Yes	No	No
PR (R&D requirement	No	Yes	No	No
PR (technology transfer requirement)	No	Yes	Yes (limited)	Yes (limited)
PR (monopolistic supply requirement)	No	Yes	No	No

PR: Performance requirement
Source Author's compilation

difference in preference between China and Japan over the modality of possible trilateral investment treaty became clear. As summarized in Table 4, Japan, together with Korea, felt strong discipline on investment was necessary, while China wanted to maintain some policy space, given its developing country status. It is interesting that both Japan and Korea insisted that the Japan-Korea BIT should be the basis of a CJK investment treaty. As discussed above, the 2002 Japan-Korea BIT was the turning point of Japan's IIA policies. Japan started to sign its second generation BITs after this. The treaty covers both pre-establishment and post-establishment. It employs negative lists, and almost all critical IIA elements are included, except for an umbrella clause. Further, all major performance requirements are prohibited, other than export restrictions (see Table 3). In contrast, China insisted that existing regimes such as the World Trade Organization (WTO) and the 1989 China-Japan BIT had been working well. Due to differences, the launch of official treaty negotiations was delayed. In 2005 and 2006, no formal negotiation was launched, though several low-key intergovernmental meetings were held.

Japan had a strong interest in the trilateral investment treaty, given that renegotiating its bilateral treaty with China was unlikely. This was especially true when the new China-Korea BIT came into effect in 2007. Japan wanted to create a level

Table 4 Negotiation positions for China-Japan-Korea investment treaty

Issues	Position of Japan and Korea	Position of China
Transparency	The principle of transparency as contained in the recently concluded investment arrangements, including the Japan-Korea investment treaty should be incorporated and further strengthened as much as possible	The discipline of the transparency as contained in the relevant rules and provisions in the World Trade Organization should serve as reference
Prohibition of performance requirements	The provision that prohibits performance requirements in recently concluded investment arrangements, including the Japan-Korea investment treaty could be the basis for future deliberation	The prohibition of performance requirements could be further researched in the future
Dispute settlement	The dispute settlement mechanism in recently concluded investment arrangements, including the Japan-Korea investment treaty could be good models for the possible investment arrangement	The dispute settlement mechanism established by China-Japan, China-Korea and Japan-Korea BITs works effectively. The existing mechanism can be strengthened and fully utilized in dealing with disputes concerning investment
Pre-establishment national treatment	Pre-establishment national treatment is essential to the arrangement, as many recently concluded investment arrangements contain this principle and the possible arrangement of the three countries should have the same principle. The difference in economic development should be duly considered and accommodated in a practical manner, e.g. making use of exception clauses in the arrangement	It premature for pre-establishment national treatment to be included in the possible arrangement due to the difference in the development stages of the three countries

Source The Report of the Joint Study on the Possible Modality of Trilateral Investment Arrangements Among China, Japan, and Korea (Available at: http://www.mofa.go.jp/mofaj/gaiko/investment/jck/pdfs/jck_kaigo_04e.pdf)

playing field with Korean industries in the Chinese market. Korea also expected that, by collaborating with Japan, a trilateral treaty could be a stronger treaty than its BIT with China. In fact, as we will see later, the position of Japan and Korea were almost the same on various issues covered by BITs; the two formed a coalition vis-à-vis China. Finally, in January 2007, official negotiations for the CJK investment treaty began. However, progress was slow. This was mainly due to China's reluctance to accept pre-establishment NT to handle national and foreign companies equally in government regulations.[21] After nearly 10 years since the trilateral summit, the CJK investment treaty was signed in May 2012 and came into effect in May 2014.

The CJK investment treaty reflects Japan's preference to a certain degree. In particular, while the focus of dispute settlement was limited to compensation under the 1989 China-Japan BIT, the limitation was removed in the CJK investment treaty. Moreover, the CJK investment treaty sets very clear ISDS procedural guidelines, minimizing the ambiguity of dispute settlement procedures. These cover a wide range of issues from initiating arbitration to award enforcement, which makes the CJK investment treaty "Americanized" (Chi 2015). However, this was no longer controversial for China because the majority of third generation Chinese IIAs has full and detailed ISDS provisions (see Table 1).

Overall, however, Japan was unsatisfied with the CJK investment treaty. First, it covers only post-establishment, not pre-establishment NT. And, unlike the Japan-Korea BIT, it does not use a negative list approach. Second, the transparency provision was strengthened compared with the China-Japan BIT (Article 10). Signatories must provide a reasonable opportunity for public comments on regulations related to investment and consider them before adoption. However, the interval between the announcement of a new regulation and its implementation were best endeavor ("shall endeavor"). Third, performance requirements prohibited under the CJK investment treaty remained limited (Article 7). In addition to the measures listed in WTO Trade-Related Investment Measures (TRIM), only two measures are prohibited by CJK investment treaty: export requirements and technology transfer.[22] Moreover, prohibition is limited to imposing unreasonable or discriminatory measures concerning the two. Hence when a "reasonable" technical transfer request is imposed in a non-discriminatory manner, it would be acceptable as far as the CJK investment treaty is concerned. As seen in Table 3, the Japan-Korea BIT included a much longer list of prohibited performance requirements.

The only reason why Japan eventually signed the CJK investment treaty was that it was still better than the 1989 BIT with China. The prolonged negotiations for the CJK investment treaty did not benefit Japan, as its investors can only rely on the old BIT, which provides weaker investment protection and guarantees lower level of liberalization. Japan preferred concluding the prolonged CJK investment treaty

[21]Yoshimatsu (2014).

[22]When IIAs covers pre-establishment, the prohibition of performance requirement is powerful. This is because the performance requirement is usually imposed when companies decide to make new investment. However, the effectiveness of the prohibition of performance requirement is unclear when IIAs cover only post-establishment. If a host government attempts to impose a performance requirement upon the expansion of existing investment (post-establishment), provisions other than the prohibition of performance requirement, such as FET provisions, seem to be effective enough to prevent the implementation of such performance requirement policies.

negotiations and beginning a new negotiation on the CJK FTA investment chapter. In fact, by 2012, the joint study on CJK FTA was already launched.

The relationship between CJK investment treaty and previous BITs between the three countries requires a careful assessment. It is important to note that the old BITs remain in force. Article 25 (Relation to Other Agreements) of the CJK investment treaty says

> Nothing in this Agreement shall affect the rights and obligations of a Contracting Party, including those relating to treatment accorded to investors of another Contracting Party, under any bilateral investment agreement between those two Contracting Parties existing on the date of entry into force of this Agreement, so long as such a bilateral agreement is in force.
>
> Note: It is confirmed that, when an issue arises between an investor of a Contracting Party and another Contracting Party, nothing in this Agreement shall be construed so as to prevent the investor from relying on the bilateral investment agreement between those two Contracting Parties which is considered by the investor to be more favorable than this Agreement.

One possible reason why the old BITs, especially the 1989 China-Japan BIT, remain in place is the effectiveness of their MFN provisions. As mentioned, the earlier BIT and the 2007 China-Korea BIT does not have an REIO exception, unlike the CJK investment treaty (Article 3.4 (a)) or the 2003 Japan-Korea BIT (see 4.2 for details).

4 Future Prospects of China-Japan Investment Negotiations

4.1 Negotiations Between China and Japan Over a China-Japan-Korea Free Trade Agreement (CJK FTA)

China, Japan and Korea are currently negotiating a CJK FTA, which also includes an investment chapter. At a trilateral summit in October 2009, the leaders of the three countries agreed to launch a joint study group comprising business, government and academia.[23]

The question is whether the CJK investment treaty makes future investment negotiations in Asia easier or not. Some argue the CJK investment treaty can be a basis for future investment negotiations involving both China and Japan, including the CJK FTA—their investment chapter can replicate the CJK investment treaty with limited improvement. However, it is also possible that the CJK investment treaty would make the negotiations for a CJK FTA investment chapter even more difficult, because some "additionality" is required to justify a new agreement.

---

[23]Hamanaka (2014).

From China's perspective, investment is a done deal and authorities believe its investment chapter should basically follow what was agreed in the trilateral investment treaty. From Japan's perspective, however, it is pointless to sign a trilateral FTA given its strong interests in investment issues unless the investment chapter shows a significant improvement. In fact, according to the March 2012 Joint Study Report for the FTA, Japan argued that

> The three countries should conclude as soon as possible the trilateral investment agreement which is being negotiated but far less ambitious in its substance than what the investment chapter of a CJK FTA is expected to be and should then launch negotiations on the investment chapter of a CJK FTA in terms of a high level of investment liberalization, building on the concluded trilateral investment agreement.

The report also underscores the disagreement between the two governments (Table 5). Interestingly, Japan and Korea again formed a coalition vis-à-vis China. Japan wants the CJK FTA investment chapter to go far beyond existing agreements

Table 5 Negotiation position for a China-Japan-Korea free trade agreement (CJK FTA) investment chapter

	Position of Japan and Korea	Position of China
The level of ambition	The essential elements to be covered by the CJK FTA include national treatment (NT) and most favored nation (MFN) at the pre- and post-establishment phases, investor-state dispute settlement (ISDS) procedures for a wide range of scope, prohibition of performance requirements (PR) beyond the trade-related investment measures (TRIM) level, a negative list approach integrated with the services chapter, and any other facilitating elements in a future CJK FTA A future CJK FTA's investment chapter should surpass the level of existing BITs among the three countries including the CJK investment treaty	CJK FTA should look for an investment chapter which would provide better protection, greater transparency and a more effective dispute resolution mechanism, and any other facilitation and promotion elements which could further promote intra-investment flow, including information exchange on investment opportunities and information sharing on laws and regulations in the field of investment Investment promotion and liberalization depend much more on the specific needs of individual countries, their state of economic and legal maturity, and their own development strategies. In future negotiations on the investment chapter, more flexibility should be given to China for adaption and modification in its liberalization process
Scope and coverage	The investment chapter of a CJK FTA should cover all industry sectors, including services sectors, and measures adopted or maintained not only by central governments but also by regional and local governments	The scope and coverage of the investment chapter should be discussed at the negotiation stage being consistent with TRIM, including possible approaches adopted for the negotiations

Source Joint Study Report for an FTA among China, Japan and Korea
Available at: http://www.mofa.go.jp/mofaj/press/release/24/3/pdfs/0330_10_01.pdf

—including the CJK investment treaty and WTO TRIM. It prefers a negative list approach, meaning all sectors will be liberalized unless there are specific reservations. China wants policy flexibility and emphasizes investment facilitation and promotion (such as information exchange) over investment liberalization. It wants to follow TRIM; meaning only "trade related aspects of investment" should be covered with investment liberalization *per se* not on the agenda. While the formal inter-governmental negotiations for the FTA started in November 2012, it remains unclear how far China can go from what was agreed in the CJK investment treaty.

4.2 China's Other IIAs: Can Japan Free-Ride on Others?

As seen, three elements are critical for Japan's IIA negotiations: (i) pre-establishment NT; (ii) detailed ISDS procedures; and (iii) prohibition of performance requirements. Among these, pre-establishment NT is the issue where there is a serious disagreement between Japan and China. So far, China has not signed any IIAs that cover pre-establishment NT. In the recently concluded China-Canada BIT, NT is afforded only for "expansion, management, conduct, operation and sale or other distortion of investment".[24] Moreover, the liberalization commitment by China and Canada under the BIT is not reciprocal.[25] However, China's treaty practice may change in the near future. Three ongoing negotiations need careful examination.

United States (US)–China BIT Negotiations over a proposed US-China BIT is likely to affect Japan's attitude toward investment negotiations vis-à-vis China. While negotiations are ongoing, it is likely that investment liberalization (pre-establishment NT) is included in the BIT.[26]

Japan does not want to fall behind the US by signing the CJK FTA or RCEP with a investment chapter that gives weaker investment protection and that does not guarantee substantial investment liberalization. This would be similar to the 2007 experience where the China-Korea BIT was improved, while the China-Japan treaty was not. Japan does not seem to have large bargaining power vis-à-vis China in investment negotiations because, for example, it does not have an investment screening process for Chinese investment, unlike the US.

Both CJK investment treaty and the China-Japan BIT have MFN provisions. Hence, any better market access given to the US by China under a future US-China BIT, including pre-establishment NT, should be given to Japan (and Korea) as well. In this sense, Japan could "free ride" on the US-China BIT using the MFN in BIT and investment treaty with China.

[24]Schott and Cimino (2015).

[25]Van Harten (2014).

[26]Miner and Hufbauer (2015).

China-Korea FTA As discussed, the 2007 China-Korea BIT does not cover pre-establishment NT (see Table 3). Meanwhile, China-Korea FTA came into force in December 2015. While its investment chapter does not cover pre-establishment NT, an important agreement was made in the annex on "guidelines for subsequent negotiations" (Annex 22-A). Based on this, the two shall start subsequent negotiations not later than 2 years following FTA effectivity and is expected to be concluded within 2 years. The Annex states that "the subsequent negotiation will be conducted based on negative list approach covering pre-establishment phase of investment and trade in services in mode 3". Hence, it is natural to infer that pre-establishment NT will be covered in the renegotiated FTA between China and Korea.

The question is whether Japan can free-ride on the future China-Korea FTA investment chapter. There is no FTA covering both Japan and China at this stage. Therefore, Japan cannot import provisions using its FTA MFN provisions. However, as discussed, the 1989 China-Japan BIT has MFN provisions without REIO exception. Hence, arguably, Japan can free-ride on the China-Korea FTA investment chapter based on its old 1989 BIT, still in place after the launch of CJK investment treaty.

European Union (EU)-China BIT/FTA There are currently 26 BITs between China and EU members. However, the Lisbon Treaty recognizes EU competence over investment issues. This means that Brussels, not each capital, that should negotiate investment treaties. Hence all 26 BITs will be replaced by a single EU-China BIT. Negotiations continue, but pre-establishment NT will likely be covered, just like the US-China BIT.[27]

While the immediate goal of the two sides is to sign stand-alone treaties on investment rather than an FTA (Tams 2015), it seems that China has a strong interest in negotiating EU-China FTA for geo-political considerations.[28] The proposed BIT can be a stepping stone to an FTA, but China may be more willing to commit substantial investment liberalization under the FTA. Either way, Japan can free-ride, because the 1989 BIT has an MFN clause without REIO exception.

In summary, when new or re-negotiated Chinese BITs have a better investment market access provisions, Japan can import them into CJK investment treaty, using its MFN. When new or re-negotiated Chinese FTA have a better investment market access provisions, Japan can import them into 1989 China-Japan BIT, using its MFN (without REIO exception). One important reservation is that the ISDS under 1989 BIT is limited to the amount of compensation for expropriation and its MFN scope is also limited to domestic remedies. This implies that there is no guarantee that a better investment market access in other IIAs such as pre-establishment NT is actually given to Japan, because of the lack of enforcement mechanism.

---

[27]Garcia-Gallardo and Jin (2015).

[28]Zhang (2015).

5 Conclusion

The "IIA relationship" between China and Japan is complex, which is a typical example of the noodle bowl of IIAs. The 1989 BIT between China and Japan still stands. The CJK investment treaty, in force since 2014, is better than the 1989 BIT, but Japan is not entirely satisfied about the outcome. For Japan, pre-establishment NT and prohibition of various types of performance requirements are the most important negotiation items, but the CJK investment treaty insufficiently addressed those problems. However, because CJK investment treaty has MFN provisions (with an REIO exception rule), a better outcome for market access may result from future BITs (not FTAs) such as US-China BIT and China-EU BIT, the provisions of which can be imported into the CJK investment treaty.

So far, China has not signed any IIA that covers pre-establishment NT. There are several important ongoing IIA negotiations involving China. Those with the US and EU will likely cover pre-establishment NT. While the December 2015 China-Korea FTA does not cover pre-establishment NT, it has an important annex which stipulates guidelines for subsequent negotiations. These will be based on a negative list approach covering pre-establishment NT and shall be conducted within 2 years. Therefore, it is likely that the FTA will have pre-establishment NT by 2017 or 2018.

Japan does not have a strong incentive to conclude an FTA investment chapter with China (such as a CJK FTA and RCEP) in a hasty way, because the country can already free-ride on the negotiation outcome of not only BITs but also FTAs signed by China with others, using the MFN provision in the 1989 China-Japan BIT that does *not* contain an REIO exception rules. In other words, while the substance of the original BIT is poor, its MFN clause is of use. In a long run, however, Japan needs a FTA investment chapter with China that covers both MFN[29] and ISDS for two reasons. First, the 1989 China-Japan BIT has MFN without the REIO exception rules, but it does not include ISDS, which is not covered under MFN provisions. Hence, even though the 1989 China-Japan BIT can import better market access provisions from other BITs/FTAs, it may face implementation problems. Second, the CJK TIT is not effective in importing investment provisions from other FTAs such as those in China-Korea FTA and China-EU FTA because of the REIO exception rule. The timing of when a future FTA investment chapter between Japan and China will likely be after the conclusion of China's BIT negotiations with the US and Europe, because, then, Japan can request that an investment chapter better than those agreements be included in the FTA.

[29]The fact that an FTA investment chapter has pre-establishment MFN provisions is more important than the substance of the chapter. In this case, non-conditional or automatic MFN is necessary for Japan. Some Chinese IIAs have conditional MFN provisions, which means that more favorable treatment could be given to future treaty partners. Whether this is extended to previous IIA partners is subject to negotiations. For example, see Article 5 para 2 in Agreement on Investment of the Framework Agreement on Comprehensive Economic Co-operation between China and ASEAN.

Acknowledgements The author would like to thank Julien Chaisse, Sufian Jusoh and Tomoko Ishikawa for useful comments. A preliminary version was published as "Dynamics of Investment Negotiations between China and Japan: The China-Japan-Korea Trilateral Investment Treaty and Beyond", IDE Discussion Paper.

References

Berger, Alex. 2008. China and the global governance of foreign direct investment, the emerging liberal bilateral investment treaty approach. DIE discussion paper 2008/10.

Berger, Axel. 2013. Investment rules in Chinese preferential trade and investment agreements: Is China following the global trend towards comprehensive agreements?

Chi, Manjao. 2015. *A long march towards compatibility, coherence and consistency: The future of China's investment agreements*. ZeuS.

Fan, Kun. 2015. *Investment treaty practice in Northeast Asia: Comparison of China, Japan and Korea*. Mimeo.

Garcia-Gallardo, Ramon., and Jin, Xiao. 2015. The EU-China bilateral investment treaty. China Law Insight. King & Wood Mallesons. http://www.kwm.com/en/knowledge/insights/eu-china-bilateral-investment-treaty-20150414.

Hamanaka, Shintaro. 2014. TPP versus RCEP: Control of membership and agenda setting. *Journal of East Asian Economic Integration* 18: 163–186.

Hatch, Walter. 2004. Japan's agenda for Asian regionalism: Industrial harmonization. *Not Free Trade, The Japanese Economy* 32: 86–97.

Hodgson, Mélida. 2015. The trans-pacific partnership investment chapter sets a new worldwide standard. *Columbia FDI Perspectives* 160: 1.

Keidanren. (1997). Keidanren's views on MAI negotiations. https://www.keidanren.or.jp/english/policy/pol057.html.

Miner, Sean., and Hufbauer, Gary Clyde. 2015. State-owned enterprises and competition policy: The US perspective. In *Towards a US-China investment treaty, Peterson institute for international economics (PIIE) Briefing* 15–1.

Schott, Jeffrey, and Cimino, Cathleen. 2015. The China-Japan-Korea trilateral investment agreement: Implications for US policy and the US-China bilateral investment treaty. In *Towards a US-China investment treaty, Peterson institute for international economics (PIIE) Briefing* 15–1.

Stoel, J.T., T. Ishikawa, and M.G. Jacobson. 2015. Japan's ambitious international investment agreement policy-laying the groundwork for future disputes? *Transnational Dispute Management (TDM)* 12: 1.

Van Harten, Gus. 2014. Canada's non-reciprocal BIT with China: Would the US or Europe do the same? Columbia FDI Perspectives No. 136.

Yoshimatsu, Hidetaka. 2014. Trade politics in Northeast Asia: The development of the trilateral free trade agreement. RCAPS Working paper series. http://www.apu.ac.jp/rcaps/uploads/fckeditor/publications/workingPapers/RWP_14001.pdf.

Zhang, Xiaotong. 2015. Treading carefully in the minefield of the EU-China investment treaty. http://europesworld.org/2015/04/01/treading-carefully-minefield-eu-PRC-investment-treaty/#.VtZgoGfVyUk.

A Baseline Study for RCEP's Investment Chapter: Picking the Right Protection Standards

Junianto James Losari

1 Introduction

Countries in Southeast Asia have concluded numerous International Investment Agreements (IIAs) at an unprecedented rate during the last three decades. Often, this leads to parallelism—overlaps of various legal frameworks, including Bilateral Investment Treaties (BITs), regional investment agreements, and investment chapters in various Free Trade Agreements (FTAs)—that potentially adds a layer of complexity.[1] Where multiple regimes exist, some studies suggest that companies increasingly structure their investments in such a way so as to enjoy benefits from the best regime.[2]

In international trade law, the spaghetti bowl[3] phenomenon was predicted to potentially create trade diversion and exclusive clubs in the global trading system. However, the creation of investment diversion due to numerous IIAs is less clear, and it is beyond the scope of this paper to analyze the issue. It seems clearer that the spaghetti bowl phenomenon in investment law allows investors to pick and choose the most favorable IIA to bring a claim or to use the most-favored nation (MFN) clause to incorporate more favorable protection standards from other IIAs.

This chapter is based on the author's research project with the Economic Research Institute for ASEAN and East Asia (ERIA) which was published in Losari (2015, pp. 225–260).

Junianto James Losari is a lawyer at Allen & Overy, LLP in Singapore. This chapter was written before he assumed his role at the firm, and it does not reflect the opinion of the firm in any way. Any mistakes or errors are of the author's alone.

[1]UNCTAD (2013, pp. 105–107). See also Chaisse (2015, pp. 563–638).
[2]Lovells (2015).
[3]Bhagwati (1995, p. 4).

J.J. Losari (✉)
Allen & Overy, LLP, Singapore, Singapore
e-mail: james@losari.org

J. Chaisse et al. (eds.), *Asia's Changing International Investment Regime*,
International Law and the Global South, DOI 10.1007/978-981-10-5882-0_9

Should we then strive to consolidate the various IIAs? While some argue this to be the ideal move, previous attempts to conclude a multilateral investment agreements has not shown any success yet.[4] Instead, we are witnessing the rise of regional investment agreements. One of the most important agreements based on the size of the economies involved is the Trans-Pacific Partnership (TPP) which may never enter into force after the United States' decision to pull out of the agreement. This paper does not focus on the TPP, but the other regional agreement that ASEAN and its six dialogue partners—Australia, China, India, Japan, Korea and New Zealand (collectively the **RCEP negotiating states**)—are negotiating, the Regional Comprehensive Economic Partnership (RCEP).[5] The 16 states involved in the RCEP negotiation already have more than 80 IIAs among themselves, either in the form of BITs, investment chapter of bilateral and plurilateral FTAs, as well as regional investment agreements.[6] RCEP could be an opportunity to consolidate the overlapping legal frameworks that can potentially address some of the issues arising from the abovementioned spaghetti bowl phenomenon of IIAs.

In this chapter, I assess several main investment protection provisions in the main IIAs among the RCEP negotiating states and analyze the level of protection granted to foreign investors and policy space granted to state parties. In Sect. 2, I explain about the nature and purpose of IIAs and how these affect the standards that states should adopt in their agreement. Section 3 contains the main analysis which examines the objective of the investment protection provisions and subsequently assesses the standards that strike an appropriate balance between investment protection and preservation of state parties' policy space. The methodology that will be used is a comparative study between the provisions in RCEP negotiating states' main IIAs and the provisions in the recent investment agreements such as the TPP's Investment Chapter and the EU-Canada Comprehensive Economic and Trade Agreement (CETA), as well as a case study on how arbitral tribunals have interpreted the various standards. Based on this, I will suggest the standards that should be considered for the RCEP's investment chapter. In Sect. 4, I will conclude and make recommendations.

2 Nature and Purpose of IIAs

This chapter explains the importance of indicating clearly the purpose of an IIA in the text of the agreement by looking at the formulation of the purpose in existing IIAs and how arbitral tribunals perceived it.

Understanding the purpose of an IIA at the outset is beneficial for the negotiation process as well as for the interpretation of the agreement at a later stage when disputes arise. By understanding the purpose of their IIA, the negotiating states can

---

[4]For further elaboration of the attempts, see Koschwar (2009, pp. 367–375).

[5]Some RCEP negotiating states are parties to the TPP negotiations, including Australia, Japan, New Zealand, Brunei Darussalam, Malaysia, Singapore, and Vietnam.

[6]UNCTAD (2013), *supra* note 2 at 106–107.

better customize the agreement to advance such objective and purpose. This will also be relevant in determining the baseline method by using the purpose of the relevant IIA as a yardstick of the ultimate goal that seeks to be achieved.

The lack of clarity in most investment protection clauses, especially those in the existing BITs of the RCEP negotiating states, allows arbitral tribunals to exercise their discretion broadly in interpreting the clauses. In some cases where a BIT's purpose was not clearly enunciated, some tribunals simply read the purpose of the BIT as "to encourage and protect investment"[7] or "to promote greater economic cooperation".[8] Such a liberal interpretation of the purpose, if applied into the interpretation of a clause may put states at a disadvantaged position, especially if the measure that they take have legitimate reasons in spite of affecting some investors.

The Preamble of the ASEAN Comprehensive Investment Agreement (ACIA),[9] one of the most comprehensive IIAs as regards the content, stipulates its purpose as to create conducive investment environment that will enhance freer flow of capital, goods and services, technology and human resources and eventually overall economic and social development in the region. The ASEAN Economic Community Blueprint further provides that it seeks to create a competitive single market and production base.[10] Ewing-Chow et al.'s study explains that production networks in several sectors have been established within ASEAN, but the IIAs remain useful to prevent backsliding of the countries' commitments and ensure that freer flow can be achieved to create an even stronger production networks.[11] This paper does not elaborate further on whether investment treaties affect actual investment flows.[12] However, it is important for an IIA to clarify that besides creating conducive investment environment, the state parties recognize states' right to regulate in the public interest and with respect to certain important policy goals, e.g. protection of human rights, maintenance of health, labor and/or environmental standards.[13]

One of the RCEP's guiding principles of negotiation is to have broader and deeper engagements with significant improvements. The guiding principle for the investment chapter contains the following objective:

> RCEP will aim at creating a liberal, facilitative, and competitive investment environment in the region. Negotiations for investment under RCEP will cover the four pillars of promotion, protection, facilitation and liberalization.

---

[7] *Azurix v. Argentina*, ICSID Case No. ARB/01/12, Award, 14 July 2006 at 307.

[8] *LG&E v. Argentina*, ICSID Case No. ARB/02/1, Decision on Liability, 3 October 2006 at 124.

[9] *ASEAN Comprehensive Investment Agreement*, 26 February 2009 (*entered into force on 29 March 2012*).

[10] Declaration on the ASEAN Economic Community Blueprint, signed on 20 November 2007; ASEAN, ASEAN Economic Community Blueprint (ASEAN Secretariat, 2008), 6.

[11] Ewing-Chow et al. (2014, pp. 134–138).

[12] There have been separate studies on this topic. It is acknowledged that establishing a clear link between changes of FDI flows and the existence of investment treaties is difficult.

[13] UNCTAD (2015, p. 142).

Such an objective should be translated clearly and clarified further in the final text of the RCEP's investment chapter to avoid discretionary interpretation of tribunals.

3 Searching for Appropriate Standards and Developing a Baseline Study

While the RCEP's investment chapter is projected to have different pillars, this study focuses on only the investment protection provisions of IIAs mentioned in Table 1 (Reviewed IIAs). This study does not look at BITs among the RCEP negotiating states because the provisions tend to be lacking clarity thus allowing arbitral tribunals to exercise their discretion in interpretation which may result into diverging interpretations. Further, some of the BITs are becoming obsolete as they have been terminated.[14] On the other hand, most of the reviewed IIAs are more advanced as they have clarified some of these provisions and attempted to strike a balance between investment protection and states' right to regulate.

Governments have also realized that their existing IIAs (particularly the earlier generation BITs) often do not specify about the right of states to regulate certain matters for public purposes, such as protection of health, safety or the environment. Often, these measures affect foreign investments in ways that constitute violation of protection guarantees in the IIAs despite the legitimate reasons to take them.

Nevertheless, investment protection provisions are important because they can contribute to the creation of conducive investment environment. Having investment protection provisions magnifies the member states' commitments in upholding the rule of law in the region. This is especially important given that some RCEP negotiating states are ranked low in the 2016 Corruption Perception Index (CPI) (Table 2).[15]

Half of the RCEP negotiating states are ranked in the bottom half ranks of the CPI. In fact, the states are similarly ranked in the bottom half of the Rule of Law Index, demonstrating a positive correlation between corruption and rule of law in a country. This highlights the importance of maintaining investment protection provisions to provide assurance to foreign investors that their investment will be protected despite the fact that the rule of law in the countries may not be the strongest yet. In relation to this, I will analyze how the investment protection provisions in ASEAN + Dialogue Partners' FTAs provide an assurance that the states will uphold the rule of law, at least as regards foreign investors and their investments. I will focus on the plurilateral IIAs because they are more advanced and clearer than the bilateral IIAs (Table 3).

---

[14]Bland and Donnan (2014). According to an Indonesian official who prefers to remain anonymous, as of early 2016, Indonesia has provided notification to discontinue 21 BITs, one BIT was mutually terminated, one BIT expired, and another BIT was discontinued by the counterpart.

[15]According to the World Justice Project's Rule of Law Index, absence of corruption is one of the indicators for the assessment of the rule of law in a country. For further information, see World Justice Project, World Justice Project Rule of Law Index (2015), http://worldjusticeproject.org/sites/default/files/roli_2015_0.pdf, at 25.

Table 1 Free trade agreements with investment chapter/international investment agreements among ASEAN member states + dialogue partners (reviewed IIAs)

No.	Name	Date of entry into force
ASEAN + dialogue partners		
1	ASEAN comprehensive investment agreement	29 March 2012
2	ASEAN–Australia–New Zealand free trade agreement [AANZFTA] investment chapter	10 January 2012 for all members
3	Agreement on investment of the framework agreement on comprehensive economic cooperation between the association of Southeast Asian nations and the people's republic of China [ASEAN–China investment agreement]	1 August 2010
4	2009 Agreement on investment under the framework agreement on comprehensive economic cooperation among the governments of the member countries of the association of Southeast Asian nations and the republic of Korea [ASEAN–Korea investment agreement]	1 September 2009
Singapore + dialogue partners FTAs		
5	Singapore–Australia FTA	28 July 2003
6	Singapore –India comprehensive economic cooperation agreement	1 August 2005
7	Agreement between Japan and Singapore for a new-age economic partnership	30 November 2002
8	Korea–Singapore FTA	2 March 2006
9	Agreement between New Zealand and Singapore on a closer economic partnership	18 August 2011
Malaysia + dialogue partners FTAs		
10	Malaysia–Australia FTA	1 January 2013
11	Malaysia–New Zealand FTA	1 August 2010
12	Malaysia–India comprehensive economic cooperation agreement	1 July 2011
13	Malaysia–Japan economic partnership agreement	13 July 2006
Thailand + dialogue partners FTAs		
14	Thailand–Australia FTA	1 January 2005
15	Thailand–New Zealand closer economic partnership	1 July 2005
16	Thailand–Japan economic partnership agreement	1 November 2007
Philippines + dialogue partners FTA		
17	Philippines–Japan economic partnership agreement	11 December 2008
Indonesia + dialogue partners FTA		
18	Japan–Indonesia economic partnership agreement	1 July 2008

3.1 Scope and Coverage

The provisions on scope and coverage have been used by governments to regulate the investments which are entitled to the benefits of the agreement. These provisions include the definition of investments and investors, admission clause, and explicit exclusion of certain investments. For the purpose of this analysis, I focus on admission clauses.

Table 2 2016 Corruption perception index ranks of the RCEP negotiating states

Ranking among RCEP	Country	Global ranking (176 countries and territories)
1	New Zealand	1
2	Singapore	7
3	Australia	13
4	Japan	20
5	Brunei Darussalam	N/A; 38 (2013)
6	South Korea	52
7	Malaysia	55
8	India	79
9	China	79
10	Indonesia	90
11	Philippines	101
12	Thailand	101
13	Vietnam	113
14	Laos	123
15	Myanmar	136
16	Cambodia	156

Source Tranparency International, "Corruption Perceptions Index 2016", available at: https://www.transparency.org/news/feature/corruption_perceptions_index_2016

Table 3 Snapshot comparison of investment protection provisions in investment chapters of ASEAN member states + dialogue partners FTAs

	ASEAN–Korea	ASEAN–China	AANZFTA	ACIA
Covered investment, e.g. approval in writing	✓	✓ (Only Thailand)	✓ (Only Thailand and Viet Nam)	✓
NT (both pre- and post-establishment)	✓	Only post-establishment	✓	✓
MFN (both pre- and post-establishment)	✓	✓ (Excludes ISDS)	No	✓ (Excludes ISDS)
FET (Limited scope: denial of justice)	✓	✓	✓	✓
Expropriation	✓ (No annex)	✓ (Exception for land and compulsory licenses (CL))	✓ (Annex, and exception for land and CL)	✓ (Annex, and exception for land and CL)
Prohibition on performance requirement	✓	–	✓	✓
Freedom of transfer and its exception	✓	✓	✓	✓
Balance of payment/prudential measures	✓	✓	✓	✓
General exceptions	✓	✓	✓	✓
Denial of benefits	✓	✓	✓	✓
ISDS	✓	✓	✓	✓

Admission clauses govern the entry of investments into host states.[16] In some IIAs, the clause requires investments to be admitted in accordance with the host state's national laws, whereby the relevant government can still change its domestic laws. Although this type of clause seems to put a lot of discretion on the host state, it remains useful to prevent the host state from refusing admission by disregarding its domestic laws. While some argue that this type of admission clause is useful to protect sensitive industries, others argue that it may lead to rent seeking and corruption.[17] This type of provision is vague but does not necessarily harmful to foreign investors. After all, without pre-establishment commitment, states have the prevailing right to determine who are allowed to invest in their territories.

Most of the reviewed IIAs contain admission clauses.[18] Some of them provide an additional requirement. For example, Article 4(a) of the ACIA provides the following:

> "**covered investment**" means, with respect to a Member State, an investment in its territory of an investor of any other Member State in existence as of the date of entry into force of this Agreement or established, acquired or expanded thereafter, and has been admitted according to its laws, regulations, and national policies, and where applicable, specifically approved in writing[1] by the competent authority of a Member State;

Footnote 1 of the provision further provides, "[f]or the purpose of protection, the procedures relating to specific approval in writing shall be as specified in Annex 1 (Approval in Writing)". It is pertinent to obtain such a specific approval because without it, the investment may not be protected at all.[19]

Such an approval requirement may be burdensome for investors. In certain countries, it may potentially be abused by some government officials. However, the ACIA provides a solution in its Annex 1 that clarifies the specific procedure for approval. This is partly how an IIA can increase governance in the host state, thus contributing to a better investment climate (Table 4).

In RCEP negotiation, if the negotiating states want to incorporate the 'approval in writing requirement', they should include the clarification about the requirement and if possible, improve it further by listing each host state's focal point which will be responsible for the issuance of such approvals, as well as procedures involved.

---

[16]Ibid. at 146.

[17]Pollan (2006, pp. 140–141).

[18]Some IIAs which do not have an admission clause include the Indonesia–Japan Economic Partnership Agreement, the Thailand–Japan Economic Partnership Agreement, and the Philippines–Japan Economic Partnership Agreement.

[19]*Yaung Chi Oo Trading Pte Ltd. v. Government of the Union of Myanmar*, ASEAN Case No. ARB/01/1 (31 March 2003), ASEAN Arbitral Tribunal (ICSID Additional Facility Rules).

Table 4 Various types of admission clause

Type	Approval in writing requirement without clarification	Admission of investments according to the host state's laws and regulations	Approval in writing requirement with specific rules about the approval
Example	Article 3(3) ASEAN-China investment agreement	Article 2(2) trilateral investment agreement (China-Japan-Korea)	Annex 1 of the ACIA

3.2 *Performance Requirements*

A performance requirements clause lays an obligation on host states not to impose certain requirements on foreign investors, such as local content requirements, trade-balancing requirements, or export controls. This clause can also be categorized as an investment facilitation clause as it helps foreign investors to freely choose how they want to run their businesses in the most efficient way.

The RCEP negotiating states should consider including a clause on prohibition of performance requirements in order to create a more liberal investment environment. Investors need the freedom to determine their production processes, including goods and services involved to gain more efficiency. If some of the negotiating states are not ready to make certain commitments, they may create a list of non-conforming measures. However, this should be temporary and phased out.

Since performance requirements can be passed easily by governments, perhaps RCEP should look into the possibility of imposing an obligation on member states to create a domestic review mechanism to deal with investors' allegations of the host state's performance requirements. Arguably, this can contribute further to governance, provided the mechanism is fast and impartial so that the issue does not need to be brought before investor-state tribunals (Table 5).

3.3 *National Treatment (NT)*

NT's application requires a comparative analysis between the treatment granted by the host state to its domestic investments or investors and the treatment granted to foreign investors.[20] In order to create a level playing field between foreign and domestic investors, the host states must provide no less favorable treatment to foreign investments or investors than to domestic investments or investors.

Besides functioning as an investment protection provision, the NT clause also functions as an investment liberalization provision if pre-establishment right is provided. This can be in the form of market access commitments, such as allowing

[20]UNCTAD (2007, p. 36).

Table 5 Various types of performance requirements clause

Type	Incorporation of the WTO TRIMs *mutatis mutandis*	WTO TRIMs + possibility of future additional commitments	Specific stipulation of all prohibited performance requirements	Resolution of performance requirements issue by domestic review
Example	"The provisions of the WTO agreement on trade-related investment measures which are not specifically mentioned in or modified by this agreement, shall apply, mutatis mutandis, to this agreement unless the context otherwise requires." *ASEAN-Korea investment agreement Article 6*	Member states shall undertake joint assessment on performance requirements no later than 2 years from the date of entry into force of this agreement. The aim of such assessment shall include reviewing existing performance requirements and considering the need for additional commitments under this article. *ACIA Article 7(2)*	*TPP Article 9.10*	Proposed innovation

foreign equity ownership in certain sectors which were previously closed to foreign investors.

Normally a member state has a schedule (reservation list) of measures that will not constitute NT violation. For example, Article 9 of the ACIA provides:

1. Articles 5 (National Treatment) and 8 (Senior Management and Board of Directors) shall not apply to:

   (a) any existing measure that is maintained by a Member State at:

      (i) the central level of government, as set out by that Member State in its reservation list in the Schedule referred to in para 2;
      (ii) the regional level of government, as set out by that Member State in its reservation list in the Schedule referred to in para 2; and
      (iii) a local level of government;

   […]

Despite the fact that such flexibilities for NT clause might be needed to preserve policy space of the host states, a long list of reservations may reduce the scope of protection under this standard, and thus not favorable to foreign investors. The reviewed IIAs mostly only have a NT clause for post-establishment.

RCEP should have a NT clause to provide sufficient guarantee to foreign investors that they will not be treated less favorably than domestic investors. In addition, it should also contain pre-establishment commitments to fulfill the objective of RCEP in pushing for further liberalization (Table 6).

Table 6 Various types of NT clause

Type	Post-establishment NT clause	NT clause with both pre-establishment and post-establishment protection
Example	"Each party shall, in its territory, accord to investors of another party and their investments treatment no less favorable than it accords, in like circumstances, to its own investors and their investments with respect to management, conduct, operation, maintenance, use, sale, liquidation, or other forms of disposal of such investments." *ASEAN-China investment agreement, Article 4*	"Each member state shall accord to investors of any other member state treatment no less favorable than that it accords, in like circumstances, to its own investors with respect to the **admission, establishment, acquisition**, expansion, management, conduct, operation and sale or other disposition of investments in its territory." *ACIA Article 5(1)*

3.4 Most-Favored Nation Treatment (MFN)

An MFN treatment clause in an IIA is meant to create a level playing field between all foreign investors of different nationalities. It can apply to conditions of entry and operation of foreign investors.[21] However, in practice, the MFN clause in the primary IIA—under which a dispute is brought—is mostly used by investors/claimants to incorporate/import more favorable substantive provisions[22] or rules of dispute settlement[23] from a third-party agreement (secondary IIA) into the primary agreement.

In *Al-Warraq v Indonesia,* the tribunal allowed the claimant to incorporate an FET clause from Indonesia's other BITs through the Organisation of Islamic Conference Agreement's MFN clause.[24] Nevertheless, in *CMS v. Argentina*, the claimant's attempt to eliminate the emergency exception clause in the primary agreement, the US-Argentina BIT, by virtue of the MFN clause was rejected.[25] Even so, questions might arise with regard to two different agreements with different treaty exceptions where one has less than the other. Can an MFN clause operate to eliminate treaty exceptions contained in the primary agreement? In order to deal with this, newer IIAs such as the CETA explicitly limits the applicability of the MFN clause only to treatment, instead of substantive obligations.

Besides substantive provisions, investors have also attempted to import more favorable rules of dispute settlement. However, this practice is controversial.[26]

[21]UNCTAD (2010, p. 14).

[22]*Hesham Talaat M. Al-Warraq v Indonesia,* UNCITRAL Arbitration, Final Award, 15 December 2014 at 551, 554–555; see also *Bayindir Insaat Turizm Ticaret Ve Sanayi AS v. Islamic Republic of Pakistan*, ICSID Case No. ARB/03/29, Award, 27 August 2009 at 227–235.

[23]*Emilio Augustin Maffezini v. The Kingdom of Spain*, ICSID Case No. ARB/97/7, Decision of the tribunal on the objections of Jurisdiction, 25 January 2000 [*Maffezini*] at 56, 62–63.

[24]*Al-Warraq v Indonesia, supra* note 18 at 554–555.

[25]UNCTAD (2010, p. 24).

[26]For further reading, Ewing-Chow and Ng (2010).

Table 7 Various types of MFN clause

Type	No MFN clause	Broad MFN clause	MFN clause with carve-out on dispute settlement provisions	MFN clause with restricted application
Example	*AANZFTA*, except in Article 7 on compensation for losses	*ASEAN-Korea Investment Agreement, Article 4*	"For greater certainty: (a) this Article shall not apply to investor-State dispute settlement procedures that are available in other agreements to which member states are party;" *ACIA Article 11(2)*	"For greater certainty, the "treatment" referred to in Paragraph 1 and 2 does not include investor-to-state dispute settlement procedures provided for in other international investment treaties and other trade agreements. Substantive obligations in other international investment treaties and other trade agreements do not in themselves constitute "treatment", and thus cannot give rise to a breach of this article, absent measures adopted by a party pursuant to such obligations." *CETA Article X.7(4)*

While some tribunals were willing to incorporate rules of dispute settlement from secondary treaties by virtue of an MFN clause,[27] other tribunals have been reluctant.[28] Following these decisions, more recently concluded IIAs include a special clause to carve out the application of MFN clauses to rules of dispute settlement.

Most ASEAN + Dialogue Partner Investment Agreements have an MFN clause that explicitly excludes its application to provisions on ISDS. This is an addition to the conventional exception found in most MFN clauses, namely the exception relieving parties to the IIA from the obligation to confer MFN treatment granted under other agreements as may be agreed by the parties.

The MFN clause in RCEP should provide clarity. It also makes sense to adopt the MFN Clause of the CETA to ensure that foreign investors do not incorporate substantive provisions in the older IIAs which are vague or disregard the state's policy space (Table 7).

[27]*Maffezini, supra* note 19 at 62–63; *Impregilo S.p.A. v. Argentine Republic*, ICSID Case No. ARB/07/17, Award, 21 June 2011 at 104–108; *Hochtief AG v. Argentina*, ICSID Case No. ARB/07/31, Decision on Jurisdiction, 24 October 2011, at 75.

[28]*Plama Consortium Ltd. v. Republic of Bulgaria*, ICSID Case No. ARB/04/15, Decision on Jurisdiction, 8 February 2005 at 202, 215; *Salini Costruttori S.p.A and Italstrade S.p.A. v. The Hashemite Kingdom of Jordan*, ICSID Case No. ARB/02/13, Decision on Jurisdiction, 29 November 2004 at 112.

3.5 Fair and Equitable Treatment (FET)

FET clauses often lack a precise meaning and have raised lots of controversies leading to multiple interpretations by arbitral tribunals.[29] Most BITs do not define the standard or substantive protection granted by FET.

This type of FET clause is considered to incorporate an independent or autonomous FET standard.[30] Under this standard, past tribunals analysed whether a government's measure: (1) was "arbitrary, grossly unfair, unjust, or idiosyncratic"; (2) "involved a lack of due process leading to an outcome which offends judicial propriety"[31]; (3) "substantially changed the legal and business framework under which the investment was decided"[32]; and (4) "in breach of representations made by the host State which were reasonably relied on by the claimant".[33]

Some other IIAs link the standard with CIL. In *Merrill & Ring*, Canada argued that a CIL-linked FET clause refers to the standard of protection that was developed by the *Neer* case[34] with a high threshold to demonstrate violation.[35] However, several tribunals opined that CIL evolves, and the standard is broader and protects against "all such acts or behaviour that might infringe a sense of fairness, equity and reasonableness".[36]

Due to the diverging approaches, states have attempted to clarify the standard, including by limiting the standard only to denial of justice, specifically the due process principle.[37] The clause limits broad interpretation of the standard and the treatment appears to be procedural,[38] as the due process principle requires a state: (1) to provide prior notice to the relevant party whom it applies its coercive power, and (2) to provide an opportunity for the party to contest the application before an international tribunal, including the right of legal representation.[39] Similar standard

---

[29]UNCTAD (2007, *supra* note 16 at 28).

[30]Vandevelde (2010, p. 49).

[31]*Waste Management, Inc. v. United Mexican States*, ICSID Case No. ARB(AF)/00/3, Award, 30 April 2004 [*Waste Management*] at 98.

[32]*Sempra Energy International v. Argentina*, ICSID ARB/02/16, Award, 28 September 2007 [*Sempra Award*] at 303; *Enron Corporation and Ponderosa Assets, L.P. v. Argentine Republic*, ICSID Case No. ARB/01/3, Award, 22 May 2007 [*Enron Award*] at 264.

[33]*BG Group Plc v. Argentina*, UNCITRAL, Award, 24 December 2007 [*BG Group*] at 297.

[34]*Merrill & Ring Forestry LP v. Canada*, Award, 31 March 2010 [*Merrill & Ring*] at 121; *see also* Vandevelde (2010, *supra* note 26 at 192–3).

[35]*Neer v. Mexico*, 4 R. Int'l Arb. Awards, 15 October 1926, 4 at 61–62; *Gami Investments, Inc. v. Mexico*, UNCITRAL (NAFTA), Final Award, 15 November 2004 at 116, 123,125,127.

[36]Ibid., at 210 and 213.

[37]ACIA Article 11(2).

[38]Bjorklund (2005, p. 809).

[39]Vandevelde, *supra* note 26 at 49–50.

Table 8 Various types of FET clause

Type	Autonomous FET	CIL-linked FET	Enhanced FET
Example	"Investments of investors of either contracting party shall at all times be accorded fair and equitable treatment…" *Vietnam–Malaysia BIT, Article 2(2)*	"This Article prescribes the customary international law minimum standard of treatment of aliens as the minimum standard of treatment to be afforded to investments of investors of the other party. The concepts of "fair and equitable treatment" and "full protection and security" do not require treatment in addition to or beyond that which is required by the customary international law minimum standard of treatment of aliens." *Japan–Philippines Economic Partnership, Article 91*	"[F]air and equitable treatment requires each member state not to deny justice in any legal or administrative proceedings in accordance with the principle of due process…" *ACIA Article 11(2)*

has also been incorporated in the TPP although it is arguable that the standard in the TPP covers broader measures due to the word "includes" (Table 8).[40]

The RCEP negotiating states should consider whether they want to provide a broader FET protection or one that is limited to denial of justice. Whatever the option taken, it is pertinent for the negotiating states to provide this clearly in the agreement so as to provide more certainty both to the states and investors.

3.6 Expropriation

As countries acknowledge that direct expropriation can only be done on a non-discriminatory basis, for a public process, in accordance with the due process of law, and against the payment of compensation,[41] the cases of expropriation before investor-state tribunals now mostly involve indirect expropriation.

Expropriation clauses in older IIAs tend to be vague and do not explain what constitutes indirect expropriation. As a result, different tribunals have been developing different approaches of what constitutes indirect expropriation.

Arbitral tribunals have developed three approaches in determining when an indirect expropriation occurs based on the expropriation clauses in various BITs.

[40]TPP Article 9.6(2)(a).

[41]UNCTAD (2007, *supra* note 16 at 44).

First, the *sole effect* doctrine proposes that a measure or a set of measures constitutes indirect expropriation when it has a permanent character, or substantially deprives the investor's property rights, or conflicts with the investor's investment-backed expectations.[42] The second approach examines "whether such actions or measures [of the host state] are proportional to the public interest presumably protected thereby and to the protection legally granted to the investments." (emphasis added)[43] The last approach as developed in *Methanex* provides that a government measure will not be expropriatory and no compensation shall be owed to investors, when the measure is: (1) non-discriminatory, (2) in accordance with due process, and (3) for public purpose.[44]

Due to the diverging approaches in defining indirect expropriation, states have inserted a clearer guidance. For example, Annex 2 of the ACIA elaborates the factors to assess whether a governmental measure constitutes indirect expropriation. Its para 4 provides that—non-discriminatory measures of a Member State that are designed and applied to protect legitimate public welfare objectives, such as public health, safety and the environment, do not constitute an indirect expropriation. The ACIA also carves out the expropriation of land and the issuance of compulsory licenses in accordance with the Agreement on the Trade-Related Intellectual Property Rights (TRIPS) from the protection under the expropriation clause. This is a way to provide governments with more policy space. TPP Annex 9-B also provides a similar clarification. RCEP should also consider to include such an annex to provide more clarity.

3.7 Transfers and Its Exceptions

All of the reviewed IIAs contain clauses on guarantee of transfers relating to a covered investment and that such transfer can be made freely without delay into and out of the host state's territory. Without the ability to repatriate funds back to their home states, foreign investors will definitely refrain from investing in such host states. Further, these clauses contain a list of exceptions under which the host state may prevent or delay a transfer as long as it is done in an equitable, non-discriminatory and good faith manner. The difference among the clauses mainly lays on the list of exceptions. Such a list of exceptions is important because in certain circumstances, the host state can be under pressures to take necessary measures, e.g. to prevent an abrupt capital outflows from the country during a

---

[42] *LG&E Energy Corp v. Argentine Republic*, ICSID Case No. ARB/02/1, Decision on Liability, 3 October 2006 [*LG&E*] at 190; Dolzer and Schreuer (2008, pp. 65–93); Dugan et al. (2008, p. 455).

[43] *Tecnicas Medioambientales Tecmed S.A. v. The United Mexican States,* ICSID Case No. ARB (AF)/00/2, Award, 29 May 2003 at 122.

[44] *Methanex Corporation v. United States of America*, Final Award on Jurisdiction and Merits, 3 August 2005 [*Methanex*] Part IV Chapter D at 7; Weiler (2005, pp. 918–919).

financial crisis as it can worsen the situation in the country. RCEP also needs to provide this guarantee of transfer and such a list of exceptions.

3.8 *Treaty Exceptions*

Governments use treaty exception clauses as a policy tool to strike a balance between investment protection and the safeguarding of other values or objectives considered to be fundamental to the countries concerned, e.g. public health.[45] The clause provides a host state with significant room to manoeuvre when facing circumstances that may justify derogation from its IIA obligations.[46] If the host state successfully invokes the treaty exception, it is exempted from liability of its breaches.

However, the invocation of a treaty exception clause is complex as can be seen in the invocation of the essential security exception in several cases involving Argentina.[47] The issue was whether the treaty exception clause is the same as the necessity defence under CIL as prescribed by Article 25 of the Articles on Responsibility of States for Internationally Wrongful Acts (ILC Articles).[48] In the Argentinian cases, the different tribunal came with diverging interpretations.[49]

Argentina argued that the treaty exception clause (Article XI) was a self-judging provision. The main difference between a self-judging provision and the necessity defence is the latter requires the fulfilment of the cumulative conditions prescribed in Article 25 of the ILC Articles, while the former provides the host state with discretion to determine what is necessary in light of a certain crisis.[50] While some tribunals found that a successful invocation of the necessity defense under CIL does not affect the host state's duty to compensate for the material loss caused by its measure,[51] the tribunal in *LG&E* found that the CIL defence allows the state not to

---

[45]Ewing-Chow and Fischer (2011, pp. 6–7).

[46]Dugan, Wallace, et al., *supra* note 37 at 179.

[47]*CMS Gas Transmission Co. v. Republic of Argentina*, ICSID Case No. ARB/01/08, Award, 25 April 2005 [CMS Award] at 349-352; *CMS Gas Transmission Co. v. Argentine Republic*, ICSID Case No. ARB/01/8, Decision on Application for Annulment, 21 August 2007 [CMS Annulment]; *LG&E, supra* note 37; *Sempra Award, supra* note 28 at 366–368; *Sempra v. Argentine Republic*, Decision on Argentina's Application for Annulment of the award, 10 June 2010 [Sempra Annulment]; *Enron Award, supra* note 28 at 324–326; *Enron v. Argentine Republic*, Decision on the Application for Annulment, 30 July 2010 [Enron Annulment]; *Continental Casualty Co. v. Argentine Republic*, ICSID Case No. ARB/03/9, Award, 5 September 2008 [Continental] at 183.

[48]*2001 Articles on Responsibility of States for Internationally Wrongful Acts (including official Commentary)*, 53 UN GAOR Supp. (No. 10) at 43, U.N. Doc. A/56/83 (2001) [ILC Articles].

[49]Schill and Briese (2009, p. 62), Kurtz (2008).

[50]Martinez (2012, p. 184).

[51]*CMS Award, supra* note 42 at 388–390; *Enron Award, supra* note 42 at 345; *Sempra Award, supra* note 42 at 394.

compensate investors for losses sustained during a period of crisis.[52] Conversely, the successful invocation of a self-judging provision or a treaty exception clause will arguably protect the state from any claims of compensation because the breach of the IIA will be precluded.[53]

Among the reviewed IIAs, the ACIA provides the most comprehensive types of exceptions, including (1) exceptions to transfer or funds, (2) measures to safeguard balance of payments, (3) general exceptions, and (4) security exceptions. These exceptions have never been invoked in investment arbitration cases, we are yet to see how tribunals will interpret them. Since the general exception clause is similar to the General Agreement on Tariff and Trade (GATT) 1994 Article XX exception (word-by-word with minor modifications), it can be expected that some tribunals might refer to the WTO cases for interpretation.[54]

Another type of general exception clause is also present in some of the reviewed IIAs. For example, ACIA Article 4 provides a general carve out of the following: (i) any taxation measures, except for transfers and expropriation, (ii) subsidies or grants provided by a Member State, (iii) government procurement, (iv) services supplied in the exercise of governmental authority by the relevant body or authority of a Member State, and (v) measures adopted or maintained by a Member State affecting trade in services under the ASEAN Framework Agreement on Services (AFAS).

RCEP should consider incorporating these treaty exceptions to balance investment protection and states' legitimate right to regulate. At the same time, it provides more clarity and certainty to foreign investors regarding the scope of the host states' right to regulate. This can be provided in the investment chapter, or in the exceptions chapter of the agreement.

3.9 Denial of Benefits

This clause is inserted into IIAs to prevent treaty shopping and nationality planning by investors—both domestic and foreign.[55] The clause can be found in more recent IIAs such as Article 19 of the ACIA.

Corporations normally structure their companies in such a way to ensure that their investments are protected by a certain IIA, and law firms have been openly advising for this.[56] While some tribunals have allowed this type of corporate structuring,[57] in certain cases where the structuring is done much later for the

[52] *LG&E, supra* note 37 at 264.

[53] *CMS Annulment, supra* note 42 at 146; *Enron Annulment, supra* note 42 at 414.

[54] For further discussion, see Kurtz, *supra* note 44.

[55] UNCTAD (2014, p. 16).

[56] Smith (2014).

[57] *Tokios Tokelės v. Ukraine,* ICSID Case No. ARB/02/18, Decision on Jurisdiction, 29 April 2004 at 56.

purpose of bringing a dispute, tribunals rejected the claim and found them abusive.[58] However, if investment protection is considered as part of contribution to the creation of the rule of law in the country, such protection should be granted to all foreign investors.

The ACIA's denial-of-benefit clause can be used as a good starting point for RCEP. However, the governments may need to clarify further the clause by providing factors considered to determine the existence of 'substantive business operations'. This phrase has been interpreted by several tribunals, including those using the term 'substantial business activities'.[59] Substantial or substantive means 'of substance and not merely of form'. Some investment-related activities and the employment of a small but permanent staff have been considered sufficient to fulfill this requirement.[60] Even a holding company may carry substantial business activities. However, if the holding company's activities were simply to hold assets of its subsidiaries, then it would not fulfill such requirement.[61] In addition, the denial-of-benefit clause also excludes investments from home states without any diplomatic relations with the ASEAN members.

3.10 Dispute Settlement—Investor-State Dispute Settlement (ISDS)

All of the reviewed IIAs contain both the state-to-state dispute settlement and ISDS mechanisms. The latter has been subject to scrutiny of many countries for several reasons.

First, some developed countries argued that they do not need ISDS mechanism because they have fair and competent courts. While this may be true, in reality, investments do not go only to developed countries, but increasingly to developing countries, including those with judiciary systems which are perceived problematic. In fact, the 16 states involved in negotiating RCEP are becoming both capital importing and capital exporting countries. For this reason, they also have the interests to ensure that their investors who go abroad have direct access to reliable judiciary.

Second, some commentators argue that ISDS exposes governments to expensive litigation. It may be true, but this can be resolved by ensuring that ISDS is done only as a last resort. For this reason, the creation of a dispute prevention mechanism

[58] *Phoenix Action, Ltd. v. The Czech Republic*, ICSID Case No. ARB/06/5, Award, 15 April 2009 at 142.

[59] *Limited Liability Company Amto v. Ukraine*, Arbitration Institute of the Stockholm Chamber of Commerce, Case No. 080/2005, Final Award, 26 March 2008 at 61–62, 69.

[60] Ibid. at 69.

[61] *Pac Rim Cayman v. El Salvador*, ICSID Case No. ARB/09/12, Decision on the Respondent's Jurisdictional Objections, 1 June 2012 at 4.72, 4.74, and 4.78.

in each respective member of RCEP can solve this issue. The mechanism is meant to prevent a conflict from escalating to a dispute, and it is to be implemented as investor after-care services. Further, the RCEP members must ensure transparency by publishing the procedure to use such a mechanism. An example of this mechanism can be seen in the Republic of Korea's Office of the Foreign Investment Ombudsman.[62]

Third, some commentators argue that the ISDS mechanism leads to various interpretations—often contradicting—of investment standards by different arbitral tribunals. This can be addressed in RCEP by the inclusion of a joint-interpretation mechanism, as could be found in Article 40 (2) and (3) of the ACIA. The joint-interpretation mechanism does not exist in most of the reviewed bilateral FTAs. Under this mechanism, the tribunal or a disputing party may request a joint interpretation on any provision of the ACIA that is in dispute. Thus, member states to the IIA can ensure that the agreement will be interpreted in accordance with their intentions.

Another suggestion to improve the current ISDS mechanism is to create an independent appellate body to review the decisions taken by ad hoc tribunals.[63] There has been a proposal to create an International Investment Court as a permanent appeals mechanism to resolve widespread and difficult questions of law and interpretation that could eventually lend greater legitimacy to the regime.[64] In fact, TPP Article 9.23(1) provides possibility for the parties to consider whether to subject awards to a future appellate mechanism (if developed). Even more advanced than the TPP, the European Union-Vietnam Free Trade Agreement's investment chapter establishes an investment tribunal system along with a permanent appeal tribunal to hear appeals from the awards issued by the Tribunal.[65] Nonetheless, there are concerns that an appeal mechanism could undermine the 'finality' of the arbitral award, 'repoliticize' the process, and that the added 'layer' would replicate the difficulties in the current system.[66] Although finality may be compromised, but ensuring increasing governance in the system and more harmonized interpretation—especially when the clause in the IIAs are identical or very similar—should prevail over such concern.

All the suggestions mentioned above can be considered by the RCEP negotiating states to improve and address the concerns that they have with the current ISDS mechanism.

---

[62]The office was established in October 1999, for further information: http://www.i-ombudsman.or.kr/eng/index.jsp.

[63]Sauvant and Ortino (2013, p. 49).

[64]Bishop (2006, p. 17), Crawford (2006, p. 13).

[65]Articles 12 and 13, Section 3, of the Investment Chapter of the European Union-Vietnam Free Trade Agreement.

[66]Sauvant and Ortino, *supra* note 58 at 49.

3.11 Monitoring Mechanism

Aside from the standards mentioned above, it is important to have a monitoring mechanism to ensure that RCEP will be fully implemented by its members. The ACIA can be used as a starting point to develop this mechanism. The ACIA designates the ASEAN Investment Area Council to coordinate and review the implementation of the agreement. However, it neither explain further the monitoring mechanism nor what implementation means. The ASEAN Scorecard endeavored to review the so-called implementation—ratification and transposition of international agreements into domestic laws. Unfortunately such definition does not demonstrate real implementation. Real implementation goes beyond that. For example with regard to market access, implementation should also look into whether investors are granted market access according to the relevant member state's commitment in its schedule.

For the investment chapter of RCEP, the negotiating states must consider to include a more advanced monitoring mechanism such as the Trade Policy Review (TPR) Mechanism in the World Trade Organization (WTO). This mechanism is done regularly to ensure compliance with the WTO agreements. The TPR report is prepared by the WTO Secretariat based on the policy statements of the member under review and a report of the Secretariat's TPR division. The policy statements issued will contain measures of the member states that may not be in compliance with the agreement. This is a far more comprehensive mechanism compared to that of the ACIA. It can promote more transparency and can alert the member states of their non-compliant measures. In the long run, this mechanism can promote better implementation of the agreement.

3.12 Utilizing the Consolidation Opportunity

The existence of various IIAs among the RCEP negotiating states poses an issue of parallelism which can potentially add complexity as regards the applicable regime of investment protection in the region. This problem is true especially for the governments.

On the other hand, foreign investors may not find this as an issue, but rather as an opportunity to pick and choose the IIA that grants the best treatment. If this is the case, concluding new agreements—that balances between investment protection and the states' right to regulate—might become useless as investors would most likely opt for the IIA provides them better protection. Therefore, RCEP should seek to consolidate and simplify the complex and multiple regimes.

In order to do this, RCEP's investment chapter should contain a provision to further effect this consolidation by terminating the existing IIAs among the RCEP negotiating states upon the entry into force of RCEP. Despite not solving this issue

in the context of ASEAN, Article 47 of the ACIA can be used as a template to improve further. For example, the clause in RCEP can be worded as follows:
Article [X]
Transitional Arrangements Relating to the other International Investment Agreements

1. Subject to paragraphs 2 and 3 of this Article [X], nothing in this Agreement shall derogate from the existing rights and obligations of a Member State under any other international agreements to which it is a party.
2. Upon the entry into force of this Agreement, the International Investment Agreements among the Member States (as provided in Annex [Y]) shall be terminated.
3. Notwithstanding the termination of the IIAs mentioned in Annex [Y], the Reservation List and Non-Conforming Measures of those agreements shall apply to the liberalization provisions of this Agreement's Investment Chapter, *mutatis mutandis,* until such time the Reservation List of this Agreement's Investment Chapter comes into force.

With such a clause, the region will have one harmonized investment rules regime that is applicable in all 16 member states for all investors from these states and potentially resolve the issue of parallelism.

4 Conclusion

Many commentators have viewed RCEP as China's response to the TPP, although looking at the chronology, this may not necessarily be the case. While the TPP was already signed on 4 February 2016, it is not clear when RCEP will be signed. Understandably, the negotiation among 16 states may not be easy, not to mention the lack of capacity in some ASEAN member states. In the investment chapter, this can mean that the level of commitments–liberalization, promotion, facilitation and protection—may be lower as each negotiating state may have different interest. In particular, the lower level of commitments might be seen in the rights of pre-establishment under the NT clause.

Nevertheless, RCEP can still add value to the existing investment protection regimes in the region if the negotiating states can successfully refine the various provisions in their existing IIAs to provide more clarity and to ensure that balance can be strike between investment protection and states' right to regulate. It is also a great opportunity to consolidate various existing IIAs among the negotiating states and come up with a refined agreement applicable in all members. This has to be done properly. Otherwise, the efforts in negotiating RCEP will be futile.

I also note that the "race to the bottom" may occur since different states may have different priorities and interests. Thus, it will be challenging to strike a higher level of commitments compared to the existing IIAs. It is notable that the objectives of the negotiating states affect their attitude in approaching the negotiation. Therefore, one of the ways to avoid the risk is to clearly set out the objectives of RCEP. In addition, the negotiating states can also derive some inspiration and align the standards in RCEP with the best practices, including the new generation IIAs, such as the TPP and the CETA as explained above.

References

Barbara, Koschwar. 2009. Mapping investment provisions in regional trade agreements: Towards an international investment regime? In *Regional rules in the global trading system*, 367–375, ed. Antoni Estevadeordal, Kati Suominen and Robert Teh. Cambridge: Cambridge University Press

Ben, Bland, and Shawn Donnan. 2014. Indonesia to terminate more than 60 bilateral investment treaties. *Financial Times*. London. http://www.ft.com/cms/s/0/3755c1b2-b4e2-11e3-af92-00144feabdc0.html#axzz35Qatebp7. Accessed 21 Oct 2014.

Bjorklund, Andrea. 2005. Reconciling state sovereignty and investor protection in denial of justice claims. *Virginia Journal of International Law* 45: 809.

Chaisse, Julien. 2015. The shifting tectonics of international investment law—structure and dynamics of rules and arbitration on foreign investment in the Asia-Pacific region. *George Washington International Law Review* 47: 563–638.

Doak, Bishop. 2006. The case for an appellate panel and its scope of review. In *Investment treaty law* ed. Federico Ortino, Audley Sheppard, and Hugo Warner, Current Issues 1: 15.

Dugan, Christopher F., Don Wallace Jr, et al. 2008. *Investor-state arbitration*, 455. New York: Oxford University Press.

Herbert Smith, Freehills. 2014. Indonesia update: What are the possible consequences of termination of Indonesia's bilateral investment treaties? Jakarta. http://www.herbertsmithfreehills.com/-/media/Files/ebulletins/2014/20140512.

Hogan, Lovells. 2015. Risk and return: Foreign direct investment and the rule of law. http://www.biicl.org/documents/625_d4_fdi_main_report.pdf?showdocument=1.

Jagdish, Bhagwati. 1995. U.S. trade policy: The infatuation with free trade agreements discussion paper series no. 726: 4.

James, Crawford. 2006. Is there a need for an appellate system? In *Improving the international investment law and policy regime* ed. Ortino et al., Options for the Future, 13.

Jürgen, Kurtz. 2008. Adjudging the exceptional at international law: Security, public order and financial crisis, Jean Monnet Working Paper 06/08.

Losari, Junianto James. 2015. Searching for an ideal international investment protection regime for ASEAN + dialogue partners (RCEP): Where do we begin? In *East Asian integration*, ed. Yan Ing Lili, 225–260. Jakarta: ERIA.

Martinez, Elizabeth A. 2012. Understanding the debate over necessity: Unanswered questions and future implications of annulments in the argentine gas cases. *Duke Journal of Comparative and International Law* 23: 184.

Michael, Ewing-Chow, and Geraldine Fischer. 2011. ASEAN IIAs: Conserving regulatory sovereignty while promoting the rule of law? *TDM* 8: 6–7.

Michael, Ewing-Chow, and W. Ng. 2010. Caveat emptor: Three aspects of investment protection treaties. *Asian Yearbook of International Law* 14 (2008).

Michael, Ewing-Chow, Junianto James Losari, and Melania, V. Slade. 2014. The facilitation of trade by the rule of law: The cases of Singapore and ASEAN. In *Connecting to Global Market*, ed. Jansen M. Jallab. WTO, 134–138. http://www.wto.org/english/res_e/booksp_e/cmark_chap9_e.pdf.

Rudolf, Dolzer, and Christoph Schreuer. 2008. *Principles of international investment law*, 65–93. New York: Oxford University Press.

Sauvant, Karl P., and Federico Ortino. 2013. *Improving the international investment law and policy regime: Options for the future*, 49. Ministry for Foreign Affairs of Finland: Publication.

Stephan, Schill, and Robyn Briese. 2009. "If the state considers": Self-judging clauses in international dispute settlement. *Max Planck UNYB* 13: 62.

Thomas, Pollan. 2006. *Legal framework for the admission of FDI*. Eleven International Publishing, Netherlands [Pollan], 140–141.

UNCTAD. 2007. *Bilateral investment treaties 1995–2006: Trends in investment rulemaking*, 36. Geneva: United Nations [UNCTAD 2007].

UNCTAD. 2010. *Most-Favoured-Nation Treatment: UNCTAD Series on Issues in International Investment Agreements II*, 14. Geneva: United Nations [UNCTAD 2010].

UNCTAD. 2013. *World Investment Report 2013: Global Value Chains: Investment and Trade for Development*. UN Publication.

UNCTAD. 2014. *IIA Issues Note: Recent Developments in Investor-State Dispute Settlement (ISDS)*, No. 1, p. 16.

UNCTAD. 2015. *World Investment Report 2015: Reforming International Investment Governance*, 142. UN Publication (2015) [UNCTAD 2015].

Vandevelde, Kenneth J. 2010. A unified theory of fair and equitable treatment, N.Y.U. *Journal of International Law & Politics* 43: 49.

Weiler, Todd. 2005. Methanex Corp. v. U.S.A.: Turning the Page on NAFTA Chapter Eleven? *Journal of World Investment and Trade* 6: 918–919.

World Justice Project, World Justice Project Rule of Law Index 2015, 25. http://worldjusticeproject.org/sites/default/files/roli_2015_0.pdf.

'One Belt, One Road': China's New Strategy and Its Impact on FDI

Jun He

1 Introduction

In September of 2013, China's President Xi Jinping gave an important speech in Kazakhstan and advocated to jointly build Silk Road Economic Belt, enhancing the connectivity of policy, transport, trade, currency and the heart of people; in October, President Xi clearly put forward that China is committed to enhance the connectivity with ASEAN and willing to develop marine cooperative partnership with ASEAN, jointly building the 21st Century Marine Silk Road.[1] The Vision and Actions on Jointly Building the Silk Road Economic Belt and the 21st Century Marine Silk Road consists of New Silk Road Economic Belt and 21st Century Marine Silk Road, hereinafter referred to as One Belt One Road (OBOR) with three major lines: the north line starts from Beijing, through Russia, to North Europe; the middle line connects Beijing and Paris, traversing the Central Asia, Western Asia and Europe; the south line starts from Quanzhou in the east, through Southeast

[1]http://news.gmw.cn/2014-09/25/content_13359997.htm.

J. He (✉)
Foreign Economic Cooperation Center, Ministry of Agriculture of the People's Republic of China, Beijing, People's Republic of China
e-mail: hejun@agri.gov.cn

J. Chaisse et al. (eds.), *Asia's Changing International Investment Regime*, International Law and the Global South, DOI 10.1007/978-981-10-5882-0_10

Asia, South Asia and East Africa, to Italy in the west.[2] It passes 64 countries[3] with over 4 billion people, which are all important areas for China's agriculture investment because they all have rich agricultural resources. Among them there are 43 Asian nations, taking up 67% of the total country number along the OBOR and ranking the 1st in areal distribution.[4] The OBOR run through the continents of Asia, Europe and Africa, connecting the vibrant East Asia economic circle at one end and developed European economic circle at the other, and encompassing countries with huge potential for economic development. The Silk Road Economic Belt focuses on bringing together China, Central Asia, Russia and Europe (the Baltic); linking China with the Persian Gulf and the Mediterranean Sea through Central Asia and West Asia; and connecting China with Southeast Asia, South Asia and the Indian Ocean.[5] The 21st Century Maritime Silk Road is designed to go from China's coast to Europe through the South China Sea and the Indian Ocean in one route, and from China's coast through the South China Sea to the South Pacific in the other. Most countries along the OBOR are emerging economies and developing countries, covering countries and regions of Central Asia, South Asia, West Asia, Southeast Asia and Central East Europe and other areas.

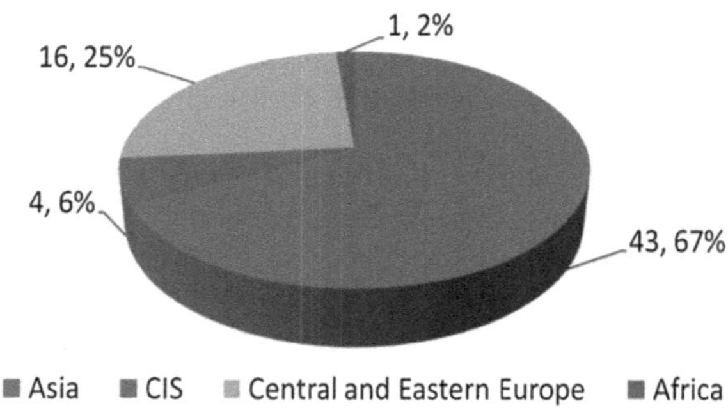

China's Share of Investment in OBOR

---

[2]http://news.xinhuanet.com/fortune/2014-08/11/c_1112013039.htm.

[3]Source: http://www.cssn.cn/gj/gj_gwshkx/gj_jj/201504/t20150408_1578096.shtml.

11 South Asian countries: Indonesia, Malaysia, the Philips, Singapore, Thailand, Brunei, Vietnam, Laos, Burma, Cambodia, east Timer; 7 South Asian countries: Nepal, the Kingdom of Bhutan, India, Pakistan, Bangladesh, Sri Lanka, Maldives; 6 Central Asian countries: Kazakhstan, Turkmenistan, Kyrghyzstan, UZ, Tajikistan, Afghanistan; 18 West Asian countries: Iran, Iraq, Georgia, Armenia, Azerbaijan, Turkey, Syria, Jordan, Israel, Pakistan, Saudi Arabia, Bahrain, Qatar, Yemen, Omen, the United Arab Emirates, Kuwait, Lebanon; 16 Central and East European countries: Albania, Bosnia and Herzegovina, Bulgaria, Croatia, Chech, Estonia, Hungry, Latvia, LTU, Macedonia, Republic of Montenegro, Romania, Poland, Serbia, Slovakia, Slovenia; 4 CIS countries: Russia, The Republic of Belarus, Ukraine, Moldova; 1 other Asian country: Mongolia; 1 African country: Egypt. (note: 43 Asian countries, 16 Central and East European countries, 4 CIS countries, 1 African country, 64 in total.)

[4]http://baike.baidu.com/link?url=DlaxaIHb5fkqQQc1qxkKrxnmdA8vS3UdJmBDwDxFQiYKAFObBHMK5BB91XhtVHgANbBhJhnAA-LB4sMieYn_H0yoZNsWnxllZcxWc54z4LFCedkbcxNQZNGPUAU2CdPD_qHqSQ3DRLJkBORFxFGj1q.

[5]http://news.xinhuanet.com/gangao/2015-06/08/c_127890670.htm.

In Post 2008 Financial Crisis Era, China, as one of the leading engines of the world economic growth, will take full advantage of its capacity, technology and capital, experience and mode.[6] The OBOR will become a growth source of the Asia-Pacific region and even the whole world, connecting Central Asia, South Asia, West Asia, Southeast Asia, etc., promoting regional exchange and complementary advantages, establishing and improving the depth of the supply chain, industry chain and value chain cooperation in Asia and Pacific, thus bringing the regional cooperation of Asia-Pacific to a new level.[7]

In 2015, the OBOR strategy is fully implemented. The strategy built under China's advocation has entered into a stage of practical cooperation, and the countries along the Belt and Road have not only realized the regional connectivity, but also built a new trade and economic corridor, bringing more cooperation opportunities in economy, finance, non-government contact, culture and other fields, and making them get more economic growth, more market and better infrastructure.[8] Now China's economy is closely connected with the world economy.[9] China will be committed to the basic policy of opening-up, build a new pattern of all-round opening-up, and integrate itself deeper into the world economic system. The Initiative will enable China to further expand and deepen its opening-up, and to strengthen its mutually beneficial cooperation with countries in Asia, Europe and Africa and the rest of the world. China is committed to shouldering more responsibilities and obligations within its capabilities, and making greater contributions to the peace and development of mankind.

In recent years, China has sped up the implementation of international agriculture cooperation in trade and investment, between the 60 countries along the OBOR provided a large market.[10] Stimulated by the initiative, 2015 is the first year for Chinese capital to flow into countries overseas, or to create 750 billion yuan of oversea agricultural investment market.[11] China's grain output increased for the 12th consecutive year, but grain import also increased greatly every year. Under the frame of OBOR, China will accelerate to carry out oversea agricultural investment, to achieve the bilateral agricultural development and to improve the situation along OBOR by allocating agricultural resource at a global scale. China will also be committed to create a mutually beneficial environment for agriculture, by actively participating global agricultural treatment, strongly enhancing regional cooperation, and putting a new global agricultural cooperative strategy into force and helping improve other developing countries' capacity of agricultural production. China will contribute to recreate an international rule, which is good to domestic agricultural development and global market stability. OBOR is an exact opportunity for China

[6]http://news.xinhuanet.com/comments/2015-03/28/c_1114791557.htm.

[7]http://news.xinhuanet.com/fortune/2015-02/20/c_1114410808.htm.

[8]http://news.xinhuanet.com/fortune/2015-02/20/c_1114410808.htm.

[9]http://www.sdpc.gov.cn/gzdt/201503/t20150328_669091.html.

[10]http://news.xinhuanet.com/world/2015-06/08/c_127888759.htm.

[11]http://news.xinhuanet.com/2015-06/08/c_1115537556.htm.

to promote oversea agricultural investment, improve international agricultural rule and maintain stability of global market.

For example, the Central Asia countries in Asia-Pacific region have been suffering from a low-efficient production, labor shortage and extensive mode of operation, although they are all vast and sparsely populated areas with concentrated flat land and rich species resource. In Central Asia, Kazakhstan has the largest cultivated land but lowest unit output of cereal. Its output of wheat accounts 80% of the total grain output, but its unit output is 1 t/hec, only one fifth that of China's, thus having a great growth potential.[12] Southeast Asia also has a great agricultural investment potential with fertilized soil and low land cultivation rate in some countries. This area has various and rich crop germplasm resource and is suitable to develop tropical agriculture with sufficient sunshine and rainwater. It also has a long coastline and rich fishery resources. The grain shortage in provinces of Southwest China is 25 million tons, while the grain output capacity of the Southeast Asia countries neighboring these provinces can reach 20 million tons.[13] If the problems of agricultural production and trade can be solved in this area, then Southeast China can realize their regional grain balance.

Compared with the countries along the OBOR, China enjoys advantages in capital, technology, talent output and other field. China has been investing overseas agriculture for decades, but compared with other countries or other fields of China, it is still far behind in both investment scale and growth speed. Oversea agricultural cooperation is an important part of OBOR initiative, and a crucial way to efficiently improve China agricultural capacity of global competitiveness, resource allocation, market control and international influence.

In the background of One Belt One Road, this paper will focus on China's Agricultural FDI in Asia. It will be explored from two aspects, one is characteristic and the other is opportunity. Since One Belt One Road is an important fulcrum of Asia regional economic development, there will be huge opportunities for Agricultural FDI. Main Features of China's Direct Investment in Asian agriculture will be described. At last, the conclusion and suggestion will be given.

2 One Belt One Road, Important Fulcrum of Asia and Future Regional Economic Development

After entering 21st Century, one voice occurred across the world: the Asia Century, that means by the middle of 21st century, Asia is likely to lead the global economy integration, showing an obvious development advantage in many fields including population scale and economy size, and meanwhile shouldering more responsibilities

---

[12]http://view.inews.qq.com/a/20150609A00BU800.

[13]http://view.inews.qq.com/a/20150609A00BU800.

in environment, ecology and resource consumption.[14] From the second half of 20th century to the beginning of 21st century, Asian countries represented by Japan, Singapore, ASEAN, China and India, have experienced several round of economic development and power rise, but compared with the achievements and position that Britain, American and some European countries got in history or at present, these Asian countries still show obvious weakness in many aspects related to economic development such as institutional improvement, business environment and the inclusiveness and sustainability of development.

However, it is doubtless that Asian area has a huge economic growth speed and potential, huge cooperative space based on its geographical characteristic and industrial structure, and huge capacity to promote healthy competition and joint growth with other countries during globalization.

It can be said that the vision and actions which are aiming at Asian regional cooperation contains two major meanings: The first is that the countries along the Belt and Road should promote common development by mutual cooperation. One Belt One Road is a new field and way for regional cooperation and South-South Cooperation. The Silk Road Spirit of peace and cooperation, openness and inclusiveness, mutual learning and mutual benefit is not in conflict with the existing institutional cooperation within this region. Complex and profound changes are taking place in the world. The underlying impact of the international financial crisis keeps emerging; the world economy is recovering slowly, and global development is uneven; the international trade and investment landscape and rules for multilateral trade and investment are undergoing major adjustments; and countries still face big challenges to their development. The initiative to jointly build the Belt and Road, embracing the trend towards a multipolar world, economic globalization, cultural diversity and greater IT application, is designed to uphold the global free trade regime and the open world economy in the spirit of open regional cooperation. It is aimed at promoting orderly and free flow of economic factors, highly efficient allocation of resources and deep integration of markets; encouraging the countries along the Belt and Road to achieve economic policy coordination and carry out broader and more in-depth regional cooperation of higher standards; and jointly creating an open, inclusive and balanced regional economic cooperation architecture that benefits all.[15] The initiative encourages a westward open-up, promotes the development of west China as well as inland countries and regions like Central Asia and Mongolia, and pushes an idea of inclusive development under globalization; meanwhile, China will actively provide its qualified productivity and advantaged industries westward, which will bring the countries along the Belt and Road benefits first. The initiative will adhere to the openness and inclusiveness spirit and refuse closeness, stiffness or exclusiveness mechanism. It is a continuity and upgrade of the existing cooperation rather than a start. Parties concerned can

[14]http://www.chinanews.com/gj/2014/05-05/6133548.shtml.

[15]http://news.xinhuanet.com/fortune/2015-03/29/c_127633221.htm.

connect all these existing and planned cooperation projects to form a package cooperation and bring out an integrated effect of one plus one more than two.

The second is to promote the development of the countries along the Belt and Road by utilizing all resources and elements across the world beneficial to their development. The initiative was proposed by China, but it is in fact a mutual benefit initiative, which will help surrounding countries share more profits from economic growth. It is also open to all regions and countries and the countries along the ancient land or marine Silk Road and China's friendly neighboring countries can also take part in. Central Asia, Russia, South Asia and Southeast countries can join in first, and for a long time, Middle East and East African countries, as the joint part of One Belt One Road can also join in the cooperation together with some countries of Europe, CIS and Africa. In the future, many projects in the initiative may involve more countries and entities with stronger openness. The concept of "economic belt" is an innovation of regional economic cooperative mode, and the economic corridors such China, Russia and Mongolia corridor, New Europe–Asia continental bridge, China–Central Asia, Bengal–Burma and China to Indo–China Peninsula economic corridors, all radiate their economic growth to surrounding countries.[16] Jointly building the Belt and Road is in the interests of the world community. Reflecting the common ideals and pursuit of human societies, it is a positive endeavor to seek new models of international cooperation and global governance, and will inject new positive energy into world peace and development. The initiative to jointly build the Belt and Road, embracing the trend towards a multipolar world, economic globalization, cultural diversity and greater IT application, is designed to uphold the global free trade regime and the open world economy in the spirit of open regional cooperation.[17]

Therefore, the vision and actions is an open strategy with characteristics of globalization and inclusiveness and Asian countries will play a crucial role during this process.

3 Main Features of China's Direct Investment in Asian Agriculture

It is in a fast-development period. From 2009 to 2013, the average growth rate of flow reached 62.52%, higher than 14.3% that of the whole industry during the same period with investment way shifting from being dominated by Greenfield to both Greenfield and Brownfield.[18]

---

[16]http://paper.people.com.cn/gjjrb/html/2015-06/01/content_1571260.htm.

[17]http://www.chinanews.com/gn/2015/03-28/7166565.shtml.

[18]http://www.agri.cn/V20/ZX/nyyw/201505/t20150511_4586583.htm.

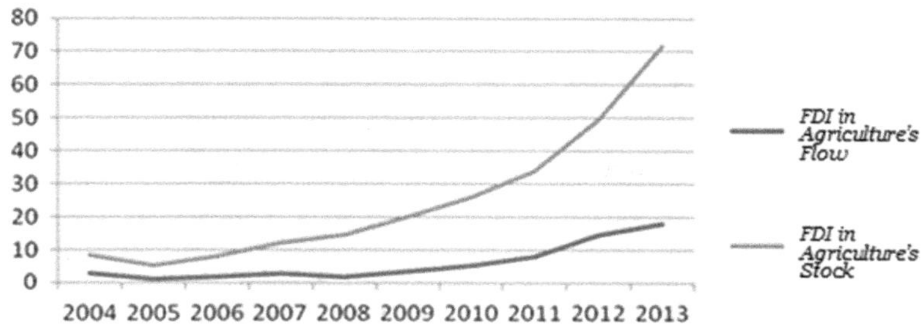

Source Made by the author

3.1 *Wide Investment Coverage and Complete Industrial Structure*

By the end of 2014, Chinese corporations had invested to established 266 agricultural corporations in Asian region, covering 25 countries with investment rate of 55.32%.[19] China has established 122 corporations in Laos, Cambodia, Burma, Indonesia, Vietnam and Thailand, where China carried out the most investment activities. In term of industry category, it covers all industries including agriculture, forestry, farming, fishery, service and manufacturing and business scope involves all steps such as producing, processing, logistics, warehousing and selling. For example, Tianjin JULONG, as such a group, has separately built a first palm plantation and palm oil crushing plant in 2006 and 2011. In order to ensure shipping, the group also has its own dock and created its own brand of palm oil named OilKu based on its self-produced crude palm oil in 2013, finally entering the local market successfully. Now, the group has several palm plantations and successively built 3 palm oil crushing plants with 8,000 oversea staff, over 80% of the total number. Complete industry structure and chain can help corporations mitigate risks and obtain more profits.[20]

3.2 *Concentrated Corporation Investment with Relatively Small Average Investment Scale*

By the end of 2013, the oversea agricultural corporations China set in Asia accounted 56.9% of the total.[21] Seem from the investment scale, the cumulative

[19]http://opinion.hexun.com/2016-05-10/183773154.html.

[20]http://www.julongchina.com/newshow.asp?id=545.

[21]http://www.askci.com/news/201401/04/041126135281.shtml.

Table 1 The agricultural investment by Chinese enterprises in main countries of "One Belt One Road" region

Country	Invest stock (10,000 dollars)	Proportion (%)	Enterprise quantity	Proportion (%)
Indonesia	48,647.11	26.39	21	8.33
Laos	18,541.33	10.06	31	12.30
Viet Nam	12,385.00	6.72	18	7.14
Thailand	11,775.03	6.39	12	4.76
Cambodia	9,524.25	5.17	21	8.33
Myanmar	6,914.74	3.75	21	8.33
Proportion in countries of OBOR	107,787.46	58.48	124	49.2

Data Source Agricultural Investment Information Collection System of Ministry of Agriculture, edited by author

investment in Asian agriculture by China reached 4.489 billion dollars, 49.31% of the total, according to preliminary data of the end of 2014. In general, China's investment in Asian area is concentrated (see Table 1), especially in six countries, where the total investment volume was up to 58.48% (if Russia was counted, it would be 82.55%), and corporation number 49.2%. This concentration in one hand reflect an agglomerate effect of FDI, namely corporations tend to invest in countries with better infrastructure under the same condition, while one the other hand, it shows China's huge investment potential in One Belt One Road region.

In terms of monomer investment scale, the invest stock of China varies, in which 23 enterprises are over 20 million dollars, up to 9.1%; 5–20 million is 71, accounting 28.2%; and less than 5 million is 158, taking up 62.7%.[22] So the agricultural enterprises China set in Asia is small with nearly 2/3 of invest storage are below 5 million dollars. Their average investment scale is 7.313 million dollars, lower than other areas of those 9.136 million dollars.

3.3 *Good Investment Effects with Obvious Geographical and Regional Advantages*

Seeing from the three lines of One Belt One Road, China gives stronger investment in south line, while relatively weak in middle and north lines. By the end of 2013, among the total 252 enterprises, south line has 144 enterprises, accounting 57.2%; middle 27, taking up 10.7%; north 81, up to 32.1%.[23] For scale, the average investment in south line is 8.26 million dollars, middle and north are 7.298 million

[22]http://www.globalview.cn/html/zhongguo/info_1760.html.

[23]http://www.cctvcchina.com/article.asp?ID=964.

Table 2 The agricultural investment and operation of Chinese enterprises in ASEAN (ten thousand US dollars, one enterprise)

Countries	Annual revenue in 2013	Quantity of established enterprise	Accumulative investment by 2013
Singapore	222,170.99	2	4,410.25
Indonesia	36,692.5	21	48,647.11
Viet Nam	22,506.25	18	12,385
Thailand	39,688.47	12	11,775.03
Brunei	185	3	1,059
Myanmar	314	21	6,914.74
Cambodia	24,962.11	21	9,524.25
Laos	10,604.27	31	18,541.33
Malaysia	2,291.47	8	4,267.73
Total	359,415.06	137	117,524.44

Data Source Agricultural Investment Information Collection System of Ministry of Agriculture, edited by author

and 5.664 million separately; for profit, the average revenue of the three lines are 25.186 million, 5.15 million and 4.676 million, with obvious differences.[24]

The effect of investment in One Belt One Road region is better than in other regions, and Southeast Asia is the region with best effect. Southeast Asia, as China's major investment object in south line, by the end of 2013, has absorbed agricultural investment up to 1.175 billion dollars, taking up 29.7% of the total, much higher than other One Belt One Road regions. There are 11 countries in Southeast Asia, and China invested in 9 countries of them except east Timer and the Philippines, coverage rate up to 81.8% (Table 2).

At the same time, enterprises need to improve their agricultural investment effect on the whole. Their economic revenue will be restricted by uneven political condition, inconsistent policy, industrial protection barrier and weak agriculture basis of target countries and coupled with enterprises' weak strength and various risks in nature, politics and economy.

The provincial distribution of the invested countries is extremely unbalanced, for which geography is a key factor affecting enterprises' decision besides their agricultural competition, openness of economy and operation capacity in those provinces. According to an incomplete statistic, the plants set by Yunnan, Hainan and Guangdong all gathered in Southeast Asia.[25] Yunnan has put all its agricultural investment in South Asia. Yunnan Agricultural Reclamation Group Co., Ltd has set

[24]http://www.cctvcchina.com/article.asp?ID=964.

[25]http://theory.southcn.com/nydkt/kandian/200511050205.htm.

a rubber investment corporation in Laos, built 18 rubber planting pilot demonstrative bases and now some of the rubber plantation have enter its production period.[26] Yunnan's oversea agricultural investment added more jobs for local people and enhanced its substituted development and infrastructure construction. It also improved farmers' skills by training, advancing local economic development, and bringing out a good economic and social benefit. Enterprises in Guangxi Zhuang Autonomous region also put most investment in Southeast Asia. Taking Forward Agricultural Technology International Cooperation Co., Ltd as an example, it developed industrial agricultural growing of mainly grain and energy crops like rice and cassava and some commercial crop like fruits and vegetables in Cambodia under a mode of "enterprise + base + association + farmer", which helped enhance the regional grain security globally, and at the same time improved local farmers technical level, increasing production.[27]

3.4 An Important Position and Broad Investment Prospect of Planting Industry

Chinese enterprises invested in such products including cereal, commercial crop, forestry, vegetables and horticultural plants. For example, Tianjin put 90% of its invest stock in planting, including oil palm and other oil crops; Most of the 36 agricultural companies invested by Yunnan are engaged in planting grain crops like rice and commercial crops like rubber, sugarcane, tea and coffee, along with a few enterprises invested to build factory locally for processing agricultural products; There are 57.14% marine fishing oversea enterprises invested by Fujian enterprises, which among the left 42.82%, there are 66.7% engaged in planting vegetables and horticultural crops and 33.3% engaged in cereal and other crops.[28] What's more, the production of rice and oil palm ranked top 2 among other agricultural products China invested in Asia and most of these products are sold locally or exported to other countries.[29] For example, in 2013, Chinese enterprises produced 553,000 tons of rice overseas, among which 295,000 tons were sold in local countries and 152,000 tons were exported to European countries.[30]

Currently, Chinese investment in Asian planting is concentrated with over 68 enterprises being set in South Asia, up to 82.1%.[31] Besides, it also concentrated in grain crops such as rice and commercial crops like oil palm and natural rubber,

---

[26]http://news.xinhuanet.com/fortune/2015-11/25/c_1117258800.htm.

[27]http://www.forwordland.com/html/about/aboutus/.

[28]http://www.fiet.gov.cn/.

[29]http://www.sinosure.com.cn/sinosure/xwzx/rdzt/ckyj/ckdt/xyzt/ncpxy/163958.html.

[30]http://www.chinariceinfo.com/news/market/201312/7562.html.

[31]http://www.chinairn.com/report/20160321/090820851.html.

while it has not completely excavated the potential in other regions and products. For example, India is the important area of potato production and Turkey has a rich source of condiment, and China has a large demand for both, but invested in neither. With the further development of One Belt One Road strategy and deeper agricultural cooperation with neighboring countries around Asia, Asian regions like Southeast, South and Central Asian countries all have a strong investment potential, worthy of more attention.

4 Conclusion and Suggestions

Through above analysis of data and cases of some enterprises, we know that regions like Southeast, Central and South Asia are crucial regions and countries for Chinese foreign agricultural investment.

Now, Chinese enterprises' investment is in a fast development period, but also still in an initial stage in terms of development level. The FDI in agriculture is faced with problems of capital shortage, financing difficulty, lack in experiences of global operation and various investment risks compared with other industries, so we must jointly promote agricultural investment cooperation and long-term agricultural development by well treating the relationship between China and host countries in politics, diplomacy and economy, and utilizing the new round of global trading relation restructuring and each country's participation in One Belt One Road initiative.

First, accelerate the top-level design and effectively play the resultant force of multiple or bilateral cooperation mechanism.

China and Asian countries are suggested to share their views on connecting the vision and actions on One Belt One Road with multiple or bilateral cooperation mechanisms, such as ASEAN, SCO and the recent passed TPP, together with the investment and trade rules, providing strategic and project plan for regional agricultural investment. China should formulate the cooperation plan with Asian countries according to resource endowment, investment basis and agricultural development need of each country and region, playing their geographic advantage, improving the uneven distribution of investment objects, enhancing the cooperation effect of south line of One Belt One Road and optimizing the cooperative layout of each line.

China should speed up investment facilitation, eliminate investment barriers, and push forward negotiations on bilateral investment protection agreements and double taxation avoidance agreements to protect the lawful rights and interests of investors. We should also solve problem related to work visa, investment environment, financing demand, favored policy and so on, and further play the constructive role of international forums and expos in regions and sub-regions along the Belt and Road, as well as Boao Forum For Asia, China–ASEAN Expo, China–Eurasia Expo, Euro–Asia Economic Forum, China International Fair for Investment and Trade (CIFIT), China-South Asia Expo, China Arab States Expo, Western China International Fair, China-Russia Expo and Qianhai Cooperative Forum, to support local governments and people along the Belt and Road to cultivate its historical and cultural heritage and jointly hold specialized activities in investment, trade and cultural exchange. China also advocated establishing an International Leadership Forum of the Belt and Road.

Second, develop the investment subject and enhance investment cooperation between China and host countries as well as transnational enterprises.

Besides encouraging and supporting Chinese enterprises to expand their investment and cooperation in Asian agriculture, China is also advised to improve agriculture related enterprises' competition by marketing and mode of investing, merger and recombining and change the condition of small investment scale and low efficiency; meanwhile, China should stick to the idea of inclusive development to increase its cooperation with local enterprises and deepen their cooperation fields, forming a complementary advantage. On one hand, China should gradually create a number of transnational agricultural enterprises with global competition in host countries, and on other hand, keep more profits in host countries to add more jobs for local people and advance local agriculture development. According to different situations of different countries, we can develop various kinds of agricultural investment such as from trade cooperation to agricultural investment, land leasing to ordered producing, and from building subsidiaries to jointly operating with local enterprises, which can evade risks and improve efficiency.

China should enhance cooperation of industrial chain with related countries, push the synergetic development of related industries of upstream and downstream, and improve industrial supporting capacity and the overall competitiveness of regional industries, and expand the open-up of service industry to each other, actively cooperate with countries concerned to build overseas economic and trade cooperation zones and cross-border economic cooperation zones, to promote the development of industrial clusters. China welcomes enterprises of each country to invest in China, and encourages its enterprises to participate in infrastructure construction and industrial investment in countries along the Belt and Road.

Third, notice investment risks and establish a standard and systematic risk evaluation and defensive mechanism for oversea agricultural development.

Southeast Asia has a good investment environment generally, but some countries with a huge potential for agricultural investment have no such good environment. Laos has 8 million hectare of potential arable land, while the actually cultivated land is only 0.8 million, with a huge potential for land cultivation but a poor infrastructure such as agricultural water conservancy and transportation. Burma has over 18 million hectare arable land with 8 million to be cultivated, but it has a poor investment environment and huge politician and economic risks.[32] Cambodia also has 4 million lands uncultivated among the total 6.7 million because of its poor infrastructure.[33] Thailand has rich fishery resources with better investment

[32]http://opinion.caixin.com/2015-08-17/100840536.html.

[33]http://opinion.caixin.com/2015-08-17/100840536.html.

environment. Countries like the Philips, Vietnam and Indonesia all have a rich fishery resource and good investment environment but with certain politician and economic risks. Central Asia has a rigid land utility rule, where the land property belongs to the government and foreign enterprises only have the right to use the land, and its management about foreign contract workers is also rigid. It also has many problems such as crumbling infrastructure, incomplete industry chain and backward agricultural development. In recent years, different countries expressed the strong willingness to cooperate in agriculture with China, but the various risks in politics, economy and nature worth our notice. Thus, for Chinese enterprises, they should establish a standard and systematic risk evaluation and defensive mechanism for oversea agricultural development supported by departments of commerce, diplomacy and agriculture, as well as policy research and consulting institutions and industrial associations. They should enhance the contact with oversea agricultural investment enterprises and encourage them to actively participate in investment risk evaluation. They should also monitor or predict the risks from politics, economy, society and natural disasters of host countries to provide service or guidance for oversea investment.

Forth, innovate the way of oversea agricultural investment, advance government's public service and gradually improve enterprises' international operation capacity and level.

International agricultural investment is still developing and will be enhanced towards deeper cooperation about entities and capital for a long time, which will put forward a higher requirement for investment way innovation, public service and enterprises' operation and management ability. For this, it is suggested that China should change its traditional FDI mode dominated by planting and manufacturing, actively bring international capital in foreign agricultural investment activities and support enterprises to broadly extend their ways of merger investment, technical cooperation and order agriculture to fields of processing, circulating and trading. At the same time, governments of each country should establish a public service supporting system for interacting and information sharing strengthen the statistical analysis on international primary agricultural products and the establishment of international agricultural investment information platform, and research to establish a *China Oversea Agricultural Investment Guide*. We should also analyze host countries' agricultural resource condition such as land, water and labor, as well as agricultural economic development level, comprehensive cost and incentive policy about agricultural investment, infrastructure and monitoring or incentive policy about foreign investment, to provide guidance and support for our oversea agricultural investment, and create a more convenient operating environment for regional agricultural cooperation by setting policies of finance, insurance and tax.

China should stress the idea of ecological civilization in investment and trade and jointly build a green Silk Road by enhancing cooperation in ecological environment, biodiversity and climate change, as well as support China's oversea enterprises to operate according to the regional management principle through actively helping local development, adding more jobs, improving people's life and undertaking social responsibilities.

The Role of Pacific Rim FTAs in the Harmonization of International Investment Law: Towards a Free Trade Area of the Asia-Pacific

Mark Feldman, Rodrigo Monardes Vignolo and Cristian Rodriguez Chiffelle

1 Introduction

The fragmented international investment law regime—which is composed of thousands of treaties—is harmonizing in two fundamental respects. First, in the near future, five agreements could govern a very substantial share of global investment: a U.S.-China bilateral investment treaty ("BIT"), an EU-China BIT, and three "mega-regional" free trade agreements ("FTAs"): the Transatlantic Trade and Investment Partnership ("TTIP"), the Trans-Pacific Partnership ("TPP"), and the Regional Comprehensive Economic Partnership ("RCEP"). Second, in addition to the development of a small number of major agreements, a convergence in State practice across treaties also is contributing to the harmonization of international investment law. Such convergence is reflected in a number of areas of recent treaty practice. Specifically, recent treaties often include: liberalization commitments; detailed clarifications of substantive obligations (such as the content of the fair and equitable treatment obligation, which does not establish a blanket obligation to avoid "unfair" treatment in an ordinary sense, and the compensation standard for expropriation, which should be prompt, adequate, and effective); provisions

An earlier version of this chapter was commissioned and published by the International Centre for Trade and Sustainable Development (ICTSD) and the World Economic Forum for the E15 Initative Task Force on Investment Policy: http://e15initiative.org/themes/investment-policy/.

M. Feldman (✉)
Peking University School of Transnational Law, Shenzhen, China
e-mail: mfeldman97@gmail.com

R. Monardes Vignolo
Trade and Investment, Permanent Delegation of Chile at the OECD, Paris, France

C. Rodriguez Chiffelle
Trade and Investment Policy, World Economic Forum, Geneva, Switzerland
e-mail: Cristian.RodriguezChiffelle@weforum.org

J. Chaisse et al. (eds.), *Asia's Changing International Investment Regime*,
International Law and the Global South, DOI 10.1007/978-981-10-5882-0_11

authorizing host States to deny treaty benefits to shell companies (to avoid so-called "treaty shopping")[1]; and regulatory transparency commitments, which obligate Parties to make investment-related laws and regulations publicly available.

As the international investment law regime harmonizes, the Pacific Rim region, for several reasons, is particularly well placed to serve as the regime's center of gravity.[2]

First, recent State treaty practice in the Pacific Rim reflects a significant—and increasing—amount of support for investment liberalization: The NAFTA States, the Pacific Alliance States, the ASEAN States, and China have included market access protections in recent agreements.

Second, investment law harmonization in the Pacific Rim largely would be achieved through the negotiation of FTAs, rather than BITs. Achieving investment law harmonization through FTAs is a timely development, given the ability of FTAs—which include investment chapters alongside other chapters such as trade in services and trade in goods—to develop complementary trade and investment disciplines that can be applied to increasingly intertwined trade and investment activities. FTAs also provide additional opportunities for investment liberalization by setting out reserved sectors in a single set of annexes, which apply both to investment and trade in services activities.

Third, as first observed by APEC in 2014, the TPP and RCEP agreements can serve as pathways toward an even larger regional instrument: a Free Trade Area of the Asia-Pacific ("FTAAP") agreement. APEC economies have contemplated such an agreement for many years, and APEC has begun to take concrete steps supporting the development of an FTAAP following the issuance in 2014 of The Beijing Roadmap for APEC's Contribution to the Realization of the FTAAP. APEC recently reaffirmed its commitment to an FTAAP in the 2015 APEC Leaders Declaration, where the heads of State "reiterate[d]" their "belief that the FTAAP should be pursued as a comprehensive free trade agreement by building on ongoing regional undertakings." With respect to the development of an FTAAP investment chapter in particular, the APEC Investment Experts' Group ("IEG")—which has worked on investment initiatives since 1994—could play an important role. Prospects for achieving agreement on an FTAAP investment chapter will, in significant part, depend on the extent to which the TPP and RCEP texts ultimately reflect a convergence of views on investment law issues by the Parties to those agreements.

The TPP and RCEP agreements would be very significant "paths" to an FTAAP. The TPP agreement covers 12 APEC member economies,[3] representing

---

[1]On the practice of treaty-shopping and its treatment by investment tribunals, see Chaisse (2015a, pp. 225–306).

[2]See generally Chaisse (2015b, pp. 563–638) (discussing the case of mega-regionals in the Asia-Pacific region and how they reshape international investment rules and arbitration with a systemic dimension).

[3]Original P4 Agreement signatories Brunei-Darussalam, Chile, New Zealand and Singapore (2005), plus the United States, Australia, Peru and Vietnam (joined negotiations in 2008), Malaysia (2010), Canada and Mexico (2012) and Japan (2013). The Trans-Pacific Partnership was signed in Auckland on February 4th, 2016.

almost 40% of global GDP and 28% of global FDI inflows in 2014.[4] An RCEP agreement would cover the 10 ASEAN members[5] as well as Australia, China, India, Japan, Korea, and New Zealand, representing 30% of global FDI inflows in 2014.[6] The resulting FTAAP—depending on the size of the negotiating group—would represent approximately 50% of global FDI inflows.

Fourth, with respect to the development of an FTAAP, a U.S.-China BIT could bridge remaining differences between the TPP (which includes the United States but not China) and the RCEP (which includes China but not the United States).

This chapter demonstrates that, taken together, these key elements—the TPP and RCEP agreements, a U.S.-China BIT, recent ASEAN and Pacific Alliance treaty practice, the development of an FTAAP, and a potential role for APEC in supporting that development—establish the Pacific Rim region as the natural center of gravity for a rapidly harmonizing international investment law regime.

This chapter proceeds, first, by discussing the fragmented nature of the existing international investment law regime and the role that Pacific Rim FTAs could play in contributing to the harmonization of that regime. The chapter then addresses the significance of achieving investment law harmonization through FTAs (which cover both trade and investment activities) rather than through BITs (which do not extend to trade activities). Next, the chapter argues that the Pacific Rim region is well positioned to serve as the centre of gravity for a harmonizing investment law regime, as illustrated in particular by the TPP and RCEP agreements, which could serve as pathways toward an even larger FTAAP agreement. Finally, the chapter addresses the additional support for Pacific Rim investment law harmonization that has been provided by the recent Pacific Alliance agreement.

2 Harmonizing a Fragmented International Investment Law Regime

An investment regime that is composed of thousands of investment treaties can fairly be characterized as "fragmented."[7] But a fragmented regime need not be an "incoherent" regime.[8] As observed by Stephan Schill, a fragmented investment treaty regime nevertheless can give rise to "a substantive rather than deliberative

[4]United Nations Conference on Trade and Development, World Investment Report 2015, p. 6.

[5]ASEAN member States are Brunei-Darussalam, Cambodia, Indonesia, Laos, Malaysia, Myanmar, Philippines, Singapore, Thailand and Vietnam.

[6]United Nations Conference on Trade and Development, World Investment Report 2015, p. 6.

[7]See, e.g., Sauvant and Ortino (2013, p. 28) (characterizing the international investment regime as "highly fragmented").

[8]*Cf.* UNCTAD IIA Issues Note No. 5, Towards a New Generation of International Investment Policies: UNCTAD's Fresh Approach to Multilateral Investment Policy-making (July 2013) ("At the international level, policy-making faces multiple challenges… [including] how to deal with a fragmented treaty regime characterized by overlaps and incoherence").

multilateralism"; the regime can "multilateraliz[e] on the basis of bilateral treaties" through the development of "increasingly uniform standards of investment protection [.]."[9]

As discussed below, active treaty practice—both bilateral and regional—indeed has brought the international investment regime substantially closer to uniformity. But such convergence is far from complete, and, in our view, the potential remains for a much greater level of harmonization, to be achieved through the completion of the major treaty negotiations outlined above: a U.S.-China BIT, and EU-China BIT, and the TTIP, TPP, and RCEP FTAs. Those major agreements, in turn, have been made possible by the active, and converging, bilateral and regional treaty practice of the individual States negotiating them, in particular the NAFTA States, the ASEAN States, the Pacific Alliance States, and China.

One key aspect of a fragmented treaty regime is the "overlapping, supporting, and possibly conflicting"[10] obligations that arise when treaty proliferation creates the "spaghetti bowl" effect, which, as recently characterized by APEC, poses "complex new challenges to regional economic integration and to business."[11] The less predictable outcomes associated with the spaghetti bowl effect are particularly significant in the investment arbitration context, where divergent interpretations of substantive obligations and procedural requirements by tribunals have been frequently criticized.[12]

---

[9]Schill (2009, pp. 496, 500).

[10]Yu (2011, pp. 953, 978) (quoting Simon Lester and Bryan Mercurio, Introduction to Bilateral and Regional Trade Agreements: Case Studies, at 2 (2009)).

[11]Beijing Roadmap for APEC's Contribution to the Realization of the FTAAP, attached as Annex A to the 2014 APEC Leaders' Declaration. The costs and complexity associated with overlapping treaties also has been referred to as the "noodle bowl." *See, e.g., The Noodle Bowl*, The Economist (Sept. 3, 2009) ("The more overlapping deals there are, the more complex the rules and the higher the costs. Those who follow Asia's FTA mania refer to this as the 'noodle bowl'").

[12]*See, e.g.*, Anna Joubin-Bret (2015) (referring to "concerns about the inconsistency of awards rendered by investment-treaty arbitration tribunals"). As one example of divergent interpretations by investment arbitration tribunals, in the context of a "legitimate expectations" obligation, *see Glamis Gold Ltd. v. United States*, UNCITRAL, Award (8 June 2009), ¶ 799 (a "threshold condition" for a legitimate expectations claim is the "active inducement of a quasi-contractual expectation"); *PSEG Global Inc. v. Republic of Turkey*, ICSID Case No. ARB/02/5, Award (19 Jan. 2007) ¶ 241 ("[l]egitimate expectations by definition require a promise of the administration on which the Claimants rely"); *Saluka Investments B.V. v. Czech Republic*, UNCITRAL, Partial Award (17 March 2006) ¶ 329 ("the Claimant's reasonable expectations to be entitled to protection under the Treaty need not be based on an explicit assurance from the Czech Government," but rather could be based on an expectation that the State would act in "a consistent and even-handed way"); *Joseph C. Lemire v. Ukraine*, ICSID Case No. ARB/06/18, Decision on Jurisdiction and Liability (21 January 2010) ¶ 267 (the "Claimant could expect a regulatory system for the broadcasting industry which was to be consistent, transparent, fair, reasonable, and enforced without arbitrary or discriminatory decisions").

The conclusion of U.S.-China and EU-China BITs, the three mega-regional FTAs (TTIP, TPP, and RCEP), and even an FTAAP, would not eliminate the fragmented nature of the international investment law regime. In some instances, those treaties could further complicate—rather than simplify—the regime by adding another layer of rules to an existing investment law structure.[13] Divergent interpretations of substantive obligations and procedural requirements by tribunals likely would continue, at least to some extent.[14]

But the conclusion of those major agreements nevertheless would harmonize the international investment law regime to a very significant extent. Based on recent State practice, although important differences certainly would remain across treaties, the agreements likely would reflect significant convergence on many key investment law issues. The agreements also would include updated provisions that likely would be viewed favorably by investors, such as market access protections, more developed provisions on performance requirements and state-owned enterprises, and a wider selection of arbitration rules. In addition, similar to the current state of NAFTA Chapter 11, US-CAFTA-DR Chapter 10, and Energy Charter Treaty case law, a substantial body of jurisprudence could develop under each of the major agreements, with the potential for some form of appellate body oversight.

We agree with Professor Schill that a regime composed of "uniform rules on investment protection" would be preferable to a "conglomerate of fragmented and diverging bilateral rules."[15] An investment law regime governed in significant part by five agreements—a US-China BIT, an EU-China BIT, and the TTIP, TPP, and RCEP agreements—likely would reflect substantial—although certainly not complete—movement in the direction of uniformity. The opportunity to then achieve investment law harmonization on a regional, Pacific Rim level through the development of an FTAAP—which could cover as many as 25 economies representing more than half of global FDI inflows–is both significant and realistic, and thus merits close consideration.

---

[13] *See, e.g.*, Alschner (2014, p. 271) ("Regional investment agreements typically add an extra treaty layer to the already existing BITs resulting in vertical overlap of investment treaties for the contracting parties").

[14] In some instances, even identical treaty language has been interpreted in strikingly different ways by investment arbitration tribunals. For example, in the context of NAFTA Article 1105(1), *compare Glamis*, *supra* note [ ], ¶ 22 ("the standard for finding a breach of the customary international law minimum standard of treatment remains as stringent as it was under *Neer*"), *with Bilcon v. Canada*, UNCITRAL, Award on Jurisdiction and Liability (17 March 2015) (characterizing as "particularly apt" the *Waste Management* interpretation of NAFTA Article 1105(1), under which "'arbitrary, grossly unfair, unjust or idiosyncratic'" conduct violates the provision) (quoting *Waste Management Inc. v. Mexico*, ICSID Case No. ARB(AF)00/3 (30 April 2004), ¶ 98).

[15] Schill, *supra* note [], at 500.

3 Investment Law Harmonization Through FTAs: A Timely Reflection of Trade/Investment Convergence

The last global financial crisis caused both trade and investment flows to plummet. Although investment flows have been recovering since then, they have been growing more slowly and remain below pre-crisis levels (global FDI inflows were USD 1.397 trillion in 2005–07 (pre-crisis) and USD 1.228 trillion in 2014).[16] This situation can be improved by different factors, such as stronger national policies to enhance business climates, facilitating investments, and removing obstacles and barriers to FDI.[17] However, such progress is hindered by the fragmentation of FDI regulation at the international level. The fragmentation, and thus greater complexity, of investment regulation raises difficulties not only for businesses but also for countries administering these rules. Even the G20 has acknowledged that while the active negotiation of regional trade agreements ("RTAs") and BITs "has promoted trade and investment liberalization and facilitation, it also results in 'fragmentation' in global trade and investment governance regimes, to which G20 needs to respond."[18]

On the other hand, the emergence of Global and Regional Value Chains (GVCs) in the global marketplace has increased the relevance of having inter-twined trade and investment policies to boost economic growth to its full potential. The development of cross-border supply networks, the evolution of Multinational Enterprises from asset-based corporations to network-based businesses, the inclusion of services into GVCs, the innovations in information and communications technology (ICTs), and the increasing fragmentation of production have highlighted the inter-relation between FDI and trade. With the current economic slowdown, FDI and global trade have become crucially important for fostering economic growth by expanding the productive capacity of the economy, creating jobs, increasing income and transferring knowledge.

Against this background, policy makers faced new challenges for developing the necessary tools to reap the benefits of FDI for boosting economic growth. The ICT revolution has internationalized supply chains, which has created a tight supply-side linkage between trade and FDI.[19] This increasing complexity is emerging directly from the activities of MNEs and their business strategies that include the expansion of networks of parents and vertically-related subsidiaries, through which flow goods

---

[16]United Nations Conference on Trade and Development, World Investment Report 2015, p. 18.

[17]According to the G20 declaration for 2015 priorities, one of the main policy goals is "...bringing together the reforms that tangibly improve the investment climate and to unlock private sector investments both for infrastructure and SMEs..." https://g20.org/wp-content/uploads/2014/12/2015-TURKEY-G-20-PRESIDENCY-FINAL.pdf.

[18]Message from President Xi Jinping on 2016 G20 Summit in China http://www.g20.org/English/China2016/G202016/201512/P020151210392071823168.pdf.

[19]World Economic Forum. Foreign Direct Investment as a key driver for Trade, Growth and Prosperity: The case for a Multilateral Agreement on Investment.

—intermediate and final—services, capital, technology and cross-border data. These developments reaffirmed that trade and investment are no longer separate issues; but two sides of the same coin.

In this context, at the Antalya Summit in 2015, the G20 leaders indicated that the trade ministers meeting would be held regularly and a supportive group would be established. In accordance with that guidance, in January 2016 China launched the G20's trade and investment permanent working group, which highlights the importance of FDI and global trade not only in the Pacific Rim, but globally.[20]

The fragmentation caused by the proliferation of BITs and FTAs raises the question of whether the time has finally come to build a single international regime which would allow countries to apply one set of rules to FDI flows and investment in general. Such harmonization could be achieved incrementally, relying significantly on regional and plurilateral treaty practice, which recently has been active in the context of so-called "mega-regional" trade agreements (TPP, TTIP, and RCEP).[21] Achieving investment law harmonization primarily through FTAs, rather than BITs, would be particularly significant, for two reasons:

(a) First, FTAs and RTAs are better to address the interaction between trade and investment and also better to acknowledge the new complexities of the global trading system, by incorporating new investment disciplines and provisions on trade in goods, trade in services, intellectual property and the digital economy. FTAs and RTAs should combine and balance those different aspects of FDI and global trade. This new reality has been better captured in next-generation FTAs which link investment disciplines with all other "trade-side" sections of the agreement.[22]
(b) Second, achieving harmonization largely through FTAs creates significant opportunities for investment liberalization, given that reserved/carved-out sectors typically are negotiated as part of a single set of annexes which apply to both services and investment. Under such a framework, momentum for services liberalization can have a cascading effect on investment liberalization. As discussed below, active FTA treaty practice in the Pacific Rim region could contribute significantly to such momentum.

---

[20]Ministry of Commerce, People's Republic of China (http://english.mofcom.gov.cn/article/newsrelease/significantnews/201602/20160201251500.shtml).

[21]One advantage of approaching investment law harmonization at a regional level is the regional orientation of many production networks. See, e.g., Stephenson (2016). E15 Initiative. Geneva: International Centre for Trade and Sustainable Development (ICTSD) and World Economic Forum, at 6 ("existing evidence tends to show that most production networks are regionally oriented and concentrated around three hubs: North America, Europe, and East Asia").

[22]*See, e.g.*, Alford (2013, pp. 35, 39) (observing that preferential trade agreements with investment chapters "mitigate the risks associated with trade and investment that are critical for successful global chains of supply. The preferential trade component of such agreements makes it comparatively cheaper for multinational corporations to secure supply chain inputs from the host country, while the investment protections protect against the political risks associated with large capital investments").

The emergence of GVCs has made evident the necessity of a coherent and multilateral set of rules for governing not only investment, but also to regulate the interactions with trade disciplines. In this context RTAs and other plurilateral initiatives can play a key role in the Asia Pacific region in further harmonizing investment provisions and also to reach the full potential of FDI, given that trade provisions are better aligned with investment in the context of FTAs and RTAs, rather than BITs which do not include trade related aspects. The negotiation of mega-regional agreements such as TPP and RCEP reflect an important effort to achieve harmonization of investment provisions in the Pacific Rim.

4 The Pacific Rim as the Center of Gravity for a Rapidly Harmonizing International Investment Law Regime

The Pacific Rim region is well positioned to serve as the center of gravity for a rapidly harmonizing 21st century international investment law regime. Significant gains in investment liberalization are being made in the region; recent treaty practice primarily has occurred through FTAs rather than BITs; the TPP and RCEP agreements can serve as pathways to an FTAAP; a U.S.-China BIT can bridge remaining differences between the TPP and RCEP; and APEC—including the APEC IEG—can play a key role in supporting harmonization efforts in the region. Although challenges to harmonization remain significant—in particular, as discussed below, with respect to performance requirements, free transfers, state-owned enterprises, transparency in dispute settlement, and the potential development of a standing investment court—the scope of such challenges has narrowed considerably.

4.1 Significant Momentum for Investment Liberalization

Over the past decade, International Investment Agreements ("IIAs") have become increasingly controversial and their legitimacy challenged, mainly because of the protection aspect of those treaties, including ISDS. More generally, civil society and other stakeholders have voiced broader concerns about the impacts of policies that attract FDI on the liberalization of domestic regimes through measures such as privatization and deregulation. However, as the scrutiny of ISDS intensifies, an opportunity arises to highlight the liberalization aspect of IIAs in a positive manner.

Concurrent with the rapid expansion of "post-establishment model" BITs in the early 1990s (which accorded protections to investments once they were established), two main exceptions, which included pre-establishment/market access rights, appeared: The WTO's General Agreement on Trade in Services (GATS) and the North American Free Trade Agreement (NAFTA). Those agreements include market access commitments that cover, respectively, a commercial presence in the territory of the other country for investment in the services sector (mode 3 GATS) and the pre-establishment phase of foreign investments generally, including investments in services (NAFTA).

In general terms, FTAs which have followed or have been based in the NAFTA approach do not treat investment in an isolated manner and have regulated all aspects of it, by including provisions on environment, labour standards and services. For example, in NAFTA, services which do not entail a permanent commercial presence (and thus do not entail an investment) are regulated in a specific chapter which disciplines only cross-border trade, while mode 3—commercial presence—is captured by the investment chapter. The latter has the advantage of establishing one set of rules for investments across all economic activity, including investment in services.[23]

Under the NAFTA approach, countries made their liberalization commitments through the listing of non-conforming measures for services and investments, including standstill and ratchet provisions. The agreements also provide countries with the opportunity to safeguard policy space in sectors where they want to keep future policy space, regardless of their current non-conforming measures (in practice this has been referred to as "annex II" of the services and investment chapters of the FTA).

NAFTA was the first to set such an approach on a regional basis and, 20 years later, has become the model for many countries beyond its original membership, including several Latin American countries. Hence, the pre-establishment model is now the preferred approach not only for Mexican FTAs, but also for FTAs signed by Chile and Peru, all of which are today TPP signatories. The Pacific Alliance, which is discussed later in this paper as a harmonization example, incorporates the same structure. Other TPP members such as Australia and New Zealand also have a similar approach when negotiating FTAs, and in general many of the countries that have already negotiated an FTA with the United States today follow a similar approach.

This is also true particularly in the current treaty negotiations in the Pacific Rim, as these regional negotiations do not only include investments as such, but also incorporate, *inter alia*, disciplines on cross-border trade in services, financial services, e-commerce, State-owned enterprises, and labour and environment provisions. This constitutes a healthy attempt to address this complex global trade scenario where those issues are interrelated, acknowledging that FDI does not happen in a vacuum. The potential for the two Pacific Rim mega-regional FTAs—TPP and RCEP—are to serve as pathways to an even larger FTAAP as discussed below.

[23]The exception to this rule is financial services, since investment in financial institutions is governed by a specific chapter covering both financial sector investments and cross-border trade in financial services.

4.2 The TPP and RCEP Agreements as Pathways to an FTAAP

In 2014 and 2015, the APEC economic leaders "reaffirmed" their commitment to an FTAAP and supported "The Beijing Roadmap for APEC's Contribution to the Realization of the FTAAP," which called for pursuing an FTAAP "by building on current and developing regional architectures" and identified the TPP and RCEP as "possible pathways to the FTAAP." The Beijing Roadmap observed that the "proliferation of regional RTAs/FTAs has created favourable liberalizing momentum," but, at the same time, has "resulted in a 'spaghetti bowl' effect," which poses "complex new challenges to regional economic integration and to business."[24] The APEC economic leaders agreed to "[l]aunch a collective strategic study on issues related to the realization of the FTAAP by building on and updating existing studies and past work[.]."[25]

Notably, APEC economies have contemplated regional integration generally, and an FTAAP in particular, for many years. More than 20 years ago, in 1994, APEC economic leaders announced their commitment to achieve "free and open trade and investment in the Asia-Pacific no later than the year 2020." Earlier efforts on investment included several iterations of APEC's "Investment Facilitation Plan" (IFAP),[26] the negotiation of the "APEC Model Measures for Investment Agreements" at the end of the last decade (as a set of non-binding recommendations for the content of investment agreements within the APEC region) and a 2011 update of the "APEC Non-Binding Investment Principles" endorsed by all APEC economies.[27] Advancement and capacity-building on investment disciplines and standards at APEC is led by the APEC IEG, which, since 1994, has met two to three times each year.[28]

Over the last twenty years, the IEG, which comprises experts on investment and officials responsible for investment policies in all APEC member economies, has worked on initiatives to promote a favourable investment climate including ensuring more transparent dispute resolution mechanisms and simplified business regulations. More recently, the IEG has expanded to stimulate investment on social and environmental sustainability, and continues to assist APEC's Committee on Trade and Investment (CTI) to encourage and facilitate free and open investment in the region. If formal FTAAP negotiations are further advanced, the IEG's efforts could also play a significant role in advancing the investment dimension of the FTAAP.

---

[24]Beijing Roadmap for APEC's Contribution to the Realization of the FTAAP, attached as Annex A to the 2014 APEC Leaders' Declaration.

[25]Ibid.

[26]http://publications.apec.org/publication-detail.php?pub_id=1413.

[27]Attached as Annex 2.

[28]http://www.apec.org/Groups/Committee-on-Trade-and-Investment/Investment-Experts-Group.aspx.

The Pacific Economic Cooperation Council (PECC)—a "non-profit, policy-oriented, regional organization dedicated to the promotion of a stable and prosperous Asia-Pacific" and "one of the three official observers of the APEC process"[29]—recently analysed alternative roles that the RCEP and TPP agreements could play as pathways to an FTAAP. According to the PECC, the "simplest paths" to an FTAAP "would involve the conclusion of the RCEP, the coming into force of TPP and the enlargement of one or the other to cover the region."[30] Another potential path, however, "would be to create a new 'umbrella agreement' to complement RCEP and the TPP."[31]

For any path to an FTAAP, an "early, difficult choice" would concern "the definition of an FTAAP negotiating group."[32] "RCEP membership is based on ASEAN's FTA partners, while the TPP represents self-selected APEC economies."[33] Four non-members of APEC are participating in the RCEP negotiations,[34] while four APEC members are not participating in either the TPP or RCEP processes.[35]

As outlined by the PECC, three potential approaches to defining FTAAP membership would be as follows: (i) limit membership to the 21 APEC member economies, "since the FTAAP concept arose in APEC," (ii) as a "more inclusive option," include both the 21 APEC member economies and the four non-members of APEC that are participating in the RCEP negotiations, and (iii) limit membership to the 17 economies that are both APEC members and participating in the TPP and/or RCEP negotiations: "this group has demonstrated the greatest commitment to regional trade and has accumulated the most experience with regional and sub-regional institutions."[36] Under the first approach, the FTAAP member countries' combined FDI inflows would be USD 652 billion (53% of world FDI inflows), based on 2014 figures; under the second approach, combined FDI inflows would be USD 690 billion (56% of world FDI inflows); under the third approach, combined FDI inflows would be USD 525 billion (43%).[37]

One factor weighing in favour of limiting FTAAP membership to APEC member economies would be APEC's central role over the past 20 years in supporting the development of an FTAAP. Reinforcing that central role by limiting FTAAP membership to APEC member economies could heighten prospects for appropriate APEC groups (in particular, the APEC CTI and APEC IEG) to play an active role in supporting further development of an FTAAP.

---

[29]PEEC, State of the Region, Introduction.

[30]PEEC, State of the Region, p. 31.

[31]Ibid.

[32]PEEC, State of the Region, p. 36.

[33]PEEC, State of the Region, pp. 36–37.

[34]Cambodia, India, Laos, and Myanmar. PEEC, State of the Region, p. 36.

[35]Papua New Guinea, Hong Kong, Russia, and Chinese Taipei. PEEC, State of the Region, p. 36.

[36]PEEC, State of the Region, pp. 36–37.

[37]See Annex 1.

Also with respect to the potential participation of non-APEC members in the development of an FTAAP, India merits close attention. An RCEP negotiating State that is not a member of APEC—but which recently expressed interest in the possibility of joining[38]—India recently issued a model investment treaty that reflects very significant departures from recent investment treaty practice.[39] Another RCEP negotiating State that recently has adopted a distinctive approach to investment issues, Australia, also must be considered. Australia's case-by-case approach to investor-State dispute settlement most recently was reflected in the China-Australia Free Trade Agreement, in which the Parties agreed to investor-State dispute settlement with respect to a limited set of obligations while, at the same time, agreeing to "conduct a review of the investment legal framework between them" and to subsequently "commence negotiations on a comprehensive investment chapter."[40]

With the notable exceptions of India and Australia,[41] recent treaty practice by many TPP Parties and RCEP negotiating States reflects substantial investment law convergence in the Pacific Rim region, and thus improves prospects for the TPP and RCEP to serve as key building blocks for an FTAAP agreement. Regarding investment liberalization, recent State practice increasingly adopts a negative list approach and includes market access commitments (including recent practice by China—e.g. in the Shanghai Free Trade Zone and in a joint U.S.-China statement on their BIT negotiations—as well as recent practice by Chile, Korea, Peru, and Singapore). Substantive obligations also show trends of convergence; for example, with respect to fair and equitable treatment, current practice reflects consistent efforts to clarify the scope of the standard, including language confirming that the obligation (i) is not violated by the mere breach of separate provisions found in other agreements, and/or (ii) does not include protections beyond the scope of customary international law. On transparency, Pacific Rim States have included regulatory transparency provisions in many recent agreements and, increasingly, have included additional provisions on transparency in their dispute settlement procedures. A historic overview, and particular examples of recent treaty practice by TPP Parties and RCEP negotiating States, and examples from the TPP final text, are discussed below.

---

[38]See Rudd and Munjal (2015) (referring to India's "newly expressed interest in Apec").

[39]*See, e.g.*, Hanessian and Duggal (2015).

[40]China-Australia Free Trade Agreement Article 9.9.

[41]Like India and Australia, the European Commission recently supported a significant departure from recent investment treaty practice by recommending the establishment of a "permanent investment court with tenured judges." Concept Paper, Investment in TTIP and beyond—the path for reform, p. 11, *available at* http://trade.ec.europa.eu/doclib/docs/2015/may/tradoc_153408.PDF . Such a departure from existing investment treaty practice likely will raise challenges for TTIP investment chapter negotiators. More generally, by adopting such a distinctive approach to investment, the EU, like India and Australia, has rendered the achievement of investment law harmonization in the near term more challenging.

5 Recent Treaty Practice by TPP Parties

For the negotiation of this free trade agreement, TPP members have followed the NAFTA approach for the inclusion of investment disciplines.[42]

For some of the TPP members, this negative list approach does not constitute a departure from their past investment policy, given that Canada, Mexico, Peru, Chile, Singapore and Australia are countries which already have negotiated investment chapters with the US following this structure of negotiations. Also, Japan and New Zealand have experience negotiating with the same approach. However, a major shift in investment treaty practice happened for countries such as Brunei Darussalam,[43] Malaysia and Vietnam. For these countries, TPP was the first time that they followed a negative list approach and included pre-establishment commitments based on non-discriminatory treatment (NT and MFN) for foreign investors and their investments.

5.1 Advancing Investment Liberalization: The Genesis of the Trans-Pacific Partnership

The Trans-Pacific Strategic Economic Partnership (better known as the Pacific 4 or P4) Agreement, which came into force in January 2006 and was negotiated between Brunei-Darussalam, Chile, Singapore, and New Zealand, is the first multi-party free trade agreement linking Asia, the Pacific and the Americas.[44] These negotiations were launched by Chile, Singapore and New Zealand on the side-lines of the APEC Leader's Summit in 2002 in Los Cabos, Mexico. Subsequently, Brunei Darussalam joined as a member in 2005 after attending a number of rounds as an observer of the negotiation process.

In addition to the goal of boosting trade and investment among P4 countries, the FTA was negotiated with the intention of becoming an important vessel for economic integration in the Asia-Pacific region beyond its original member countries, and hence adopted a framework that would welcome new membership after the entry into force of the Agreement. In this context, the P4 was conceived as an "open agreement" providing the possibility of accession of third parties with the objective

[42]https://medium.com/the-trans-pacific-partnership/investment-c76dbd892f3a#.fvfjglhzo.

[43]Brunei as an original member of the P4 FTA had already negotiated a Services Chapter with a negative list approach, which includes liberalization commitments on mode 3 (commercial presence) for investments in the services sector. In practice, this proved to be a difficult exercise at the time, which portrays the high complexity that negotiating a full agreement with this approach (such as the TPP) brings for countries like Brunei, Malaysia and Vietnam. This would be also an important hurdle for an FTAAP, considering other countries which still lack negative-list/pre-establishment framework negotiating experience.

[44]http://www.mfat.govt.nz/Trade-and-Economic-Relations/2-Trade-Relationships-and-Agreements/Trans-Pacific/2-P4.php.

of promoting the creation of a major strategic alliance for the liberalization of trade and investment in the Asia-Pacific region. Specifically, Article 20.6 of the P4 Agreement establishes that other APEC economies or other States can join the Agreement on the terms agreed by the Parties.

On this basis, in 2008, the Office of the United States Trade Representative (USTR) announced that the United States would participate in the subsequent negotiations of the P4 Agreement, specifically in those related to the pending chapters of investment and financial services negotiations, which were not included in the original P4 Agreement. Later that year, the P4 countries and the United States announced the launch of negotiations for the U.S. to join the Trans-Pacific Strategic Economic Partnership Agreement,[45] which started the formal process that in time became the TPP negotiations.

At the time, USTR Susan Schwab stated that "(…) while the United States is the first additional country to seek to join the four original members of the Trans-Pacific Strategic Economic Partnership, we are confident that other countries in the region will ultimately embrace the benefits of participation. This high-standard regional agreement will enhance the competitiveness of the countries that are part of it and help promote and facilitate trade and investment among them, increasing their economic growth and development."[46] At that moment, the focus of the U.S. accession to P4 shifted from an 'investment and financial services chapters'-only approach, to a participation in the full FTA, which soon brought the opening and renegotiation of all P4 chapters into a new landmark agreement known as the TPP.

During the APEC summit of 2008, Australia, Peru and Viet-Nam formally expressed their interest to join the negotiations of the initial P4, and one year later the President of the United States of America announced, during his first trip to Asia, "…the United States' intention to engage with the Trans-Pacific Partnership countries to shape a regional agreement, with broad-based membership and with the highest standards of an agreement of the 21st Century."[47]

5.2 *Structure of the TPP's Investment Chapter*

For the investment section, TPP countries followed the NAFTA negative list approach for scheduling their services and investments commitments regarding National Treatment, Most Favoured Nation, Performance Requirements, Senior Management and Board of Directors and Market Access for commercial presence for the services sector. The scope of the Investment Chapter includes investments in

[45] https://ustr.gov/schwab-statement-launch-us-negotiations-join-trans-pacific-strategic-economic-partnership-agreement.

[46] https://ustr.gov/schwab-statement-launch-us-negotiations-join-trans-pacific-strategic-economic-partnership-agreement.

[47] http://www.sice.oas.org/whatsnew_pending/TTP_Congress_e.pdf.

all sectors of the economy, excluding only investments in the financial sector, which is dealt with in a specific and separate chapter for the cross-border supply of financial services and investment in financial institutions.

The Investment Chapter encompasses investments in the pre-establishment and post-establishment phase, granting rights not only to foreign investors which are already established, but also to foreign investors who are seeking to invest in the territory of the other country. Pre-establishment commitments are those which grant foreign investors non-discriminatory (NT and MFN) treatment with respect to the establishment and acquisition of their investments.

TPP Parties consolidated their commitments by listing their current non-conforming measures in the different sectors of their economies (Annex 1 reservations) and locking in those sectors in which no reservations have been taken (stand-still effect). The TPP Parties also commit to automatically capture in the agreement future liberalization of measures (ratchet effect). Policy space on sensitive sectors is still preserved by reservations on future measures, as set out in Annex 2 of non-conforming future measures.

In addition, market access commitments for investments in services on a negative-list approach also provide for the right of entry for foreign investors in the services sector, aligning market access commitments and lists of non-conforming measures for investment and services involving commercial presence. Countries which have followed this approach for the first time face many challenges in order to be able to list their non-conforming measures and to determine the scope of their future reservations for specific sectors in which, whether a current non-conforming measure is in force or not, there is a need for further policy space to regulate activity within such sectors in the future.

It is important to stress that TPP investment liberalization builds on previous commitments made by the other TPP members who have been following this approach in past FTA and RTA practice. Co-existence of agreements means that TPP commitments will not supersede prior commitments, and bilateral FTAs will not be terminated. Instead, TPP commitments will cohabit with liberalization made in past agreements. However, in practice, those later commitments reflect the current level of market openness of those countries and, by definition, need to be equal to or broader than past commitments included in previous FTAs.

TPP investment commitments provide a major opportunity to foster harmonization of investment liberalization in the Asia Pacific Region, especially since the agreement builds on previous FTAs among TPP partners and consolidates a deeper integration process among them, creating the most important free trade zone in the region, not only for investments, but for trade in general.

5.3 Standards of Protection

The TPP investment chapter also achieved major progress in advancing harmonization on standards of protection of investments in Pacific Rim treaty practice.

Several provisions adopted in the TPP confirm that a significant number of Asia Pacific countries have a common understanding on key elements of investment protection. In this regard, obligations on free transfers of capital (including specific exemptions added in the TPP), the prohibition on imposing specific mandatory performance requirements, the inclusion of specific standards for the treatment of foreigners in cases of civil strife, and the concept of denial of benefits provide examples of the improvements in harmonization of Asia-Pacific investment treaty practice made by TPP.

Regarding the relationship between fair and equitable treatment ("FET") and the minimum standard of treatment ("MST") obligation, the TPP expands the applicability of the widely-adopted NAFTA approach to FET, which views FET as falling within the MST obligation, which itself is tied to customary international law ("CIL"). That approach had been confirmed by the NAFTA Parties in 2001, in a NAFTA Free Trade Commission ("FTC") interpretation which clarified the relationship between FET, MST, and CIL under the NAFTA.[48] Prior to the conclusion of the TPP, most, but not all, of the TPP negotiating Parties had adopted the NAFTA approach to FET, either in FTA negotiations with the United States or in other IIA negotiations.[49] With the conclusion of the TPP, three additional Pacific Rim countries—Brunei-Darussalam, Vietnam and Malaysia—now follow the NAFTA approach to FET, which further harmonizes treaty practice on a fundamental international investment law issue.

Regarding the expropriation obligation, TPP has reaffirmed the commonly accepted features of direct expropriation, ensuring that in case of an expropriation TPP Parties will have acted with a public purpose, in accordance with due process of law, and subject to prompt, adequate and fully realizable and transferable compensation. Furthermore, improvements have been made in establishing guidance for arbitral tribunals in order to determine situations that may constitute indirect expropriation, which could further support investment law harmonisation in the Pacific Rim. First, the guidance provided by the TPP regarding measures that could have effects equivalent to a direct expropriation is an important addition, which is complemented by having a shared view among TPP Parties regarding measures that can constitute an indirect expropriation.

The TPP also underscores that countries can regulate in the public interest, including on health, safety, financial stability, and environmental protection, although not with the same level of specificity that other regional proposals are bringing forward, such as the European Union's Trans-Atlantic Trade and Investment Partnership (TTIP) proposal. On this particular point, one controversial aspect was TPP's inclusion of a dispute settlement carve-out for measures related to tobacco control in order to protect public health, prompted by recent ISDS cases

[48]*See* Interpretation of the Free Trade Commission of Certain Chapter 11 Provisions, July 31, 2001, http://www.state.gov/documents/organization/38790.pdf.

[49]Canada, Mexico, Australia, Chile, Peru and Singapore adopted the NAFTA approach to FET in FTA negotiations with the United States; Japan and New Zealand adopted the approach in FTA negotiations with countries that followed the NAFTA approach.

which led to heavy public criticism in some TPP countries. It will be interesting to follow if such a provision will be replicated in future Asia-Pacific treaty practice, and in other regional agreements.

The TPP investment chapter also includes enhancements with respect to Investor-State Dispute Settlement (ISDS). These include consolidation provisions and specific safeguards for discouraging abusive and frivolous claims, including the potential award of costs and attorneys' fees to the respondent government. Consolidating the trend of including transparency provisions as the general practice for investment arbitration proceedings, the TPP investment chapter mandates that arbitration hearings and documents are open and available to the public and that interested non-parties, such as trade unions and NGOs, are eligible to participate in the proceedings by submitting amicus curiae briefs. The chapter also includes the possibility that an investor's home government and other TPP Parties present submissions to the arbitral tribunal on issues of TPP treaty interpretation, in accordance with the non-disputing Party submissions provision.

The TPP also includes innovative procedural features, such as language reaffirming the binding nature of joint interpretations issued by the TPP Free Trade Commission, and obligations to address discriminatory measures that provide advantages to foreign State-owned enterprises, including clarifications that TPP investment disciplines apply to SOEs and other persons exercising delegated governmental authority.[50]

Unlike the TPP, text of an RCEP agreement is not currently available; however, consideration of recent treaty practice of RCEP negotiating Parties can inform analysis of the extent to which the TPP and RCEP agreements can serve as pathways toward an FTAAP.

6 Recent Treaty Practice by RCEP Negotiating Parties

Given that the RCEP is an "ASEAN-led trade agreement,"[51] recent ASEAN treaty practice can offer important insights into the kinds of provisions that likely would be included in a final RCEP text. The recent investment treaty practice of another RCEP negotiating State, China, reflects positions that are largely consistent with ASEAN practice. Categories of recurring provisions in ASEAN and Chinese treaty practice that reflect, and contribute to, an increasing level of harmonization in international investment law are discussed below.

[50]United States Trade Representative, the Trans-Pacific Partnership. https://medium.com/the-trans-pacific-partnership/investment-c76dbd892f3a#.rayh31t8k.

[51]Hiebert and Hanlon (2012).

6.1 Advancing Investment Liberalization

Provisions supporting investment liberalization appear consistently in recent ASEAN treaty practice, both when setting out the goals of a particular treaty and in substantive obligations. National treatment and most-favoured-nation obligations in those agreements normally extend protections to the "admission," "establishment," and "acquisition" of investments.[52] The ASEAN-China Investment Agreement includes pre-establishment protections under the most favoured nation treatment, but not the national treatment obligation.[53] More recently, however, China has agreed to include pre-establishment protections within the scope of the national treatment obligation under a U.S.–China bilateral investment treaty,[54] which provides additional momentum for the harmonization of market access protections in investment treaties.

6.2 Standards of Protection

Recent ASEAN investment treaties consistently place limitations on the scope of the fair and equitable treatment obligation, as many of these treaties include language clarifying that a breach of another provision of the treaty, or of another agreement, does not establish a breach of the fair and equitable treatment obligation.[55] The ASEAN-Australia-New Zealand and ASEAN-Korea agreements include the additional clarification that the scope of the fair and equitable treatment obligation is limited to protections available under the customary international law minimum standard of treatment.[56] China also has consistently placed limitations on the fair and equitable treatment obligation in its recent investment treaties.[57]

Recent ASEAN investment agreements also consistently provide for prompt, adequate, and effective compensation for expropriation. For example, the original ASEAN Investment Agreement provides that compensation for expropriation must be "paid without delay," "be equivalent to the fair market value of the expropriated

[52] See, e.g., ASEAN Investment Agreement art. 5 and art. 6; ASEAN-Korea art. 3 and art. 4; ASEAN-Australia-New Zealand FTA, chapter 11, art. 4.

[53] *Compare* ASEAN-China art. 5 (including the "admission," "establishment," and "acquisition" of investment in the most-favoured-nation obligation) *with* ASEAN-China art. 4 (not including the "admission," "establishment," or "acquisition" of investment in the national treatment obligation).

[54] *See* Joint U.S.-China Economic Track Fact Sheet of the Fifth Meeting of the U.S.-China Strategic and Economic Dialogue (July 12, 2013) ("The [U.S.-China] BIT will provide national treatment at all phases of investment, including market access ('pre-establishment')").

[55] See ASEAN Investment Agreement art. 11(3), ASEAN-China art. 7(3), ASEAN-Korea art. 5(3), ASEAN-Aus-NZ art. 6(3).

[56] ASEAN-Aus-NZ art. 6(2), ASEAN-Korea art. 5(2)(c).

[57] See, e.g., China-Mexico BIT art. 5, China-Canada BIT art. 4, China-Korea-Japan Investment Agreement art. 5.

investment," and "be fully realisable and freely transferable [.]"[58] ASEAN's agreements with China,[59] Korea,[60] and Australia and New Zealand[61] include similar provisions.

Provisions on regulatory transparency also have been consistently included in recent ASEAN investment agreements. For example, under the ASEAN-China Investment Agreement, the Parties commit to "make available through publication all relevant laws, regulations, policies and administrative guidelines that pertain to, or affect investments in its territory."[62] ASEAN's agreements with Australia and New Zealand,[63] and with Korea,[64] include similar transparency commitments. ASEAN has also included provisions on transparency in arbitral proceedings in the ASEAN Investment Agreement, as well as the ASEAN-Australia-New Zealand agreement.[65]

With respect to China and opportunities for the harmonization of investment rules, the transparency of investment dispute settlement proceedings remains an issue to watch. In the China-Canada BIT, for example, the Parties agreed that "[a]ny Tribunal award" under the dispute settlement section "shall be publicly available."[66] With respect to "all other documents" submitted to, or issued by, a tribunal, such documents will be made publicly available if a "disputing Contracting Party"—i.e. the respondent in an investor-State case—"determines that it is in the public interest to do so and notifies the Tribunal of that determination."[67] More recently, in the China-Australia FTA, the Parties agreed in a side letter to enter into consultations, within one year of the entry into force of the agreement, on the applicability of the UNCITRAL Transparency Rules to disputes submitted to arbitration under the China-Australia investment chapter.[68] Thus, under both the China-Canada BIT and the China-Australia FTA, a wide range of outcomes is possible with respect to the level of transparency of dispute settlement proceedings brought by investors against China.

[58]ASEAN Investment Agreement art. 14.

[59]ASEAN-China art. 8.

[60]ASEAN-Korea art. 12.

[61]ASEAN-Australia-New Zealand art. 9.

[62]ASEAN-China art. 19.

[63]ASEAN-Australia-New Zealand Chap. 11 art. 13.

[64]ASEAN-Korea art. 8.

[65]See ASEAN Investment Agreement art. 39, ASEAN-Australia-New Zealand art. 26.

[66]Canada-China BIT art. 28.

[67]Ibid.

[68]*See* Letter from Andrew Robb, Minister for Trade and Investment, to Gao Hucheng, Minister of Commerce (17 June 2015), available at http://dfat.gov.au/trade/agreements/chafta/official-documents/Documents/chafta-side-letter-on-transparency-rules-applicable-to-investor-state-dispute-settlement.pdf.

6.3 Responses to "Treaty Shopping"

China, like the ASEAN States, recently has been including in its investment agreements denial of benefits provisions, which authorize host States to deny treaty benefits to shell companies.[69] Such provisions have been developed in response to concerns over 'treaty shopping," i.e., the practice of establishing a corporate presence in a jurisdiction solely to gain access to certain treaty protections.

6.4 A U.S.-China BIT as a Bridge Between the TPP and RCEP Agreements

When evaluating prospects for achieving harmonization of the international investment law regime in the Pacific Rim region, the ongoing U.S.-China BIT negotiations must be considered at the centre of the exercise. The negotiations bring together the world's two largest economies, one of which (the United States) is a signatory of the TPP, while the other (China) is participating in the RCEP negotiations.

As noted above, with respect to investment liberalization, the United States and China have announced that the national treatment obligation under a U.S.-China BIT will include market access protections and that the agreement will be negotiated on a negative list basis. With agreement already reached on market access coverage for national treatment, three issues to watch for in the US-China BIT negotiations will be performance requirements, free transfer obligations, and the transparency of dispute settlement proceedings. On those issues, China's recent BIT with Canada—another NAFTA Party whose model investment treaty resembles the U.S. model BIT in many respects—provides noteworthy approaches. For performance requirements, the Canada-China BIT limits protections to those set out in Article 2 and the Annex of the WTO Agreement on Trade-Related Investment Measures ("TRIMS").[70] Regarding free transfer obligations, the Canada-China BIT allows a Contracting Party to adopt or maintain "measures that restrict transfers when the Contracting Party experiences serious balance of payment difficulties," subject to certain limitations,[71] which is consistent with latest recommendations of the IMF.[72] Regarding the transparency of arbitral proceedings, as noted above, under the China-Canada BIT tribunal awards must be made publicly available, but public access to any other documents will require a determination by the respondent

[69]See, e.g. China-ASEAN Investment Agreement art. 15, China-Korea-Japan Investment Agreement art. 22, China-Australia FTA art. 9.6.

[70]Canada-China BIT art. 9.

[71]Canada-China BIT art. 12.

[72]Ostry et al. (2010).

in each investor-State dispute that making a certain set of documents publicly available "is in the public interest [.]."[73]

Given the size of the two economies and their respective roles in TPP and RCEP, a BIT between the US and China will provide significant insights into whether, and how, harmonization of international investment law in the Pacific Rim region can be achieved. The TPP, plus the finalization of RCEP and a US-China BIT—involving many of the world's largest economies and covering very substantial investment flows—could serve as fundamental stepping stones not only towards an FTAAP in the Pacific Rim region but also, on a broader scale, towards global harmonization of the investment system. An EU-China BIT and TTIP agreement also would play key roles in that process.

With respect to recent EU treaty practice in particular, an additional challenge to Pacific Rim investment law harmonization that must be addressed is the recent EU proposal to establish an Investment Court System in ongoing and future investment treaty negotiations, with a view toward establishing a permanent, multilateral international investment court. In September 2015, the European Commission released an Investment Court System proposal,[74] a final version of which subsequently was presented to the United States as part of the ongoing TTIP negotiations.[75] In recent negotiations with the EU, Canada and Vietnam have agreed to such an investment court system.[76] The ongoing TTIP and EU-China BIT negotiations will serve as valuable indicators of future Pacific Rim treaty practice with respect to the potential use of international courts—rather than international arbitration—to resolve international investment disputes.

7 Pacific Alliance: Investment Law Harmonization in the Pacific Rim Gains Additional Momentum

The harmonization of international investment law in the Pacific Rim region has gained additional momentum with the emergence of the Pacific Alliance, a regional economic integration process involving four Pacific Rim States: Chile, Colombia,

[73] Canada-China BIT art. 28.

[74] *See* European Commission, Press Release, Commission proposes new Investment Court System for TTIP and other EU trade and investment negotiations, September 16, 2015, http://europa.eu/rapid/press-release_IP-15-5651_en.htm.

[75] *See* European Commission, Trade, EU finalises proposal for investment protection and Court System for TTIP, November 12, 2015, http://trade.ec.europa.eu/doclib/press/index.cfm?id=1396.

[76] *See* European Commission, Press Release, CETA: EU and Canada agree on new approach on investment in trade agreement, February 29, 2016, http://europa.eu/rapid/press-release_IP-16-399_en.htm; European Commission, News archive, EU-Vietnam Free Trade Agreement Now Available Online, February 1, 2016, http://trade.ec.europa.eu/doclib/press/index.cfm?id=1449 ("The Vietnam agreement includes all of the key provisions of the new Investment Court System for EU trade and investment negotiations proposed by the European Commission").

Mexico, and Peru. The Pacific Alliance promotes the exchange of trade, investment, innovation and technology with the world, with special emphasis on the Asia-Pacific region. The Pacific Alliance agreement was finalized quickly and is seen as a global example of how like-minded countries can swiftly agree on a comprehensive, 21st century FTA. Significantly, the agreement includes 32 official observer countries, including many Pacific Rim States: Australia, Canada, China, India, Japan, New Zealand, Singapore, South Korea, and the United States. New Zealand recently announced its desire to either become a member of, or negotiate an FTA with, the Pacific Alliance.

Investment liberalization under the Pacific Alliance agreement, while not ground-breaking, nevertheless is significant because it builds upon the bilateral FTAs of its member countries, using them as a starting point for further liberalization of investments and taking into account their current commitments. By embarking on this exercise, the Pacific Alliance States also strive to update the standards of protection and liberalization to the most forward-thinking trends. Notably, the Pacific Alliance has incorporated into their market access NT and MFN commitments the latest liberalization efforts made by each one of its members, locking in that liberalization through the listing of non-conforming measures on a negative list basis.

Just like the P4 at the beginning of the century, the Pacific Alliance is an initiative which is open for new membership, providing an opportunity to foster further harmonization in the region. The Agreement has followed the NAFTA approach, by including a services chapter which deals with cross-border supply of services, an investment chapter which includes all types of investments in all sectors (including mode 3) for pre-establishment and post-establishment protection, and a specific chapter for financial services (cross-border supply of financial services and investments in financial institutions).

Finally, Pacific Alliance member countries have restated their approach in the context of standards of protection, by reaffirming their shared understanding of key provisions such as the MST obligation (which, following the NAFTA approach, is tied to CIL) and indirect expropriation (identifying common criteria for situations that might constitute an indirect expropriation).

Like the TPP, RCEP, and U.S.-China BIT, the Pacific Alliance can advance the development of investment law harmonization in the Pacific Rim region by reaffirming the shared understanding of a group of Pacific Rim States on fundamental investment law issues.

8 Conclusion

For policymakers interested in the harmonization of the international investment law regime, the building blocks for such a project already exist in the Pacific Rim region. The TPP and Pacific Alliance agreements, as well as the ongoing RCEP and U.S.-China BIT negotiations, provide key opportunities for a large number of

Pacific Rim States to reach agreement on investment law obligations and investor-State dispute settlement provisions. One important first step towards harmonization of the regime would be to consider the extent to which the TPP and RCEP texts reflect a convergence of State views on investment law issues.

A U.S.-China BIT can help to bridge textual differences between the TPP (which includes the United States but not China) and RCEP (which includes China but not the United States). In that respect, challenges to concluding a U.S.-China BIT can serve as reliable indicators of challenges to bridging the TPP and RCEP investment chapter texts. For a U.S.-China BIT, provisions on performance requirements, free transfers, state-owned enterprises, and transparency of documents and hearings could be particularly challenging to negotiate, given recent treaty practice of the two States.

In response to such challenges to harmonization, Pacific Rim States could consider several potential strategies. The China-Australia FTA provides one approach, where the Parties agreed to an investment chapter with ISDS, while also agreeing to hold further negotiations on additional, unresolved investment issues. Second option would be follow the "opt-in" approach reflected in UNCITRAL's Mauritius Convention on Transparency, where particularly contentious issues—such as, for example, transparency in dispute settlement—can be addressed in standalone instruments that States can elect to apply to existing treaties on an opt-in basis. Third option would be for APEC to take an active role in attempting to facilitate resolution of remaining differences between the TPP and RCEP agreements, with the APEC IEG focusing on the development of an FTAAP investment chapter.

Regarding APEC involvement in the development of an FTAAP, two complicating factors would need to be considered: (i) potential participation by the four RCEP negotiating States that are not members of APEC (Cambodia, India, Laos, and Myanmar), and (ii) potential participation by the four APEC members that are not participating in either the TPP or RCEP negotiations (Hong Kong (China), Chinese Taipei, Russia, and Papua New Guinea). One reason to limit FTAAP membership to APEC member economies would be to reinforce and reconfirm APEC's central role in the development of an FTAAP. Reinforcing that central role could, in turn, heighten prospects for appropriate APEC groups (in particular, the APEC CTI and APEC IEG) to actively support further development of an FTAAP.

The 2004 US Model BIT provides one example of how an individual instrument can have a very substantial impact on the entire investment law regime. Many of the innovations introduced in that model—including clarifications of the fair and equitable treatment and expropriation obligations, as well as provisions addressing public access to documents—have been included in a wide range of recent treaties. Even greater contributions to the international investment law regime could be made by an FTAAP, which potentially would include, among other States, the U.S., China, India, Japan, Korea, Canada, Mexico, Australia, New Zealand, and the 10 ASEAN States.

The boost that China has given to the G20 process on the issues of FDI and global trade—by launching the G20's first-ever trade and investment working group in 2016, closely followed by a similar effort from the B20 side—is also noteworthy and could play an important role in supporting the further advancement of investment law harmonization. Private sector drive (and demand) is also a key element to advance harmonization, and in this respect the APEC Business Advisory Council (ABAC) could bring to APEC an input similar to what the B20 will bring to the G20, delivering specific recommendations on investment. Business associations and public-private cooperation institutions which work on investment policy, such as the International Chamber of Commerce (ICC) and the World Economic Forum, could also be instrumental in supporting these regional processes.

Regarding the recent European Union proposal to establish an Investment Court System in ongoing and future investment treaty negotiations, that proposal would reshape the ISDS regime in fundamental ways, most notably by eliminating the appointment of arbitrators by disputing parties. One clear advantage offered by the Pacific Rim model for harmonization is the momentum that has been building through more than a decade of active, converging treaty practice by many Pacific Rim States, including the NAFTA States, the Pacific Alliance States, the ASEAN States, Korea, Japan, and China. That momentum establishes the Pacific Rim region as the natural center of gravity for a rapidly harmonizing international investment law regime. Establishing investment law harmonization on a regional, Pacific Rim level could then serve as a platform, potentially, for multilateral harmonization. Recognizing the significant gap that would exist between regional and multilateral harmonization—as illustrated by recent investment treaty models developed by India, Brazil, Russia and South Africa, which depart significantly from the convergence in treaty practice discussed in this paper—multilateral harmonization nevertheless could be achieved either by treaty propagation[77] (as recently illustrated by the impact of the NAFTA FTC 2001 Interpretation and the 2004 U.S. Model BIT on the investment law regime) or by the development of a multilateral instrument.

[77] *See, e.g.*, J. Christopher Thomas, QC, Introductory Comments, The Pacific Rim and International Economic Law: Opportunities and Risks of the Pacific Century, Transnational Dispute Management, 2015, http://www.transnational-dispute-management.com/article.asp?key=2168 (observing that the points set out in the NAFTA FTC's 2001 Interpretation "have found their way into many subsequent treaties throughout the Pacific Rim [, which] is a good example of the phenomenon of 'treaty propagation' whereby an expression of a substantive obligation in one bilateral treaty finds its way into other treaties not necessarily being negotiated by the states who agreed the original text").

Annex 1: Relevant Regional Agreements' Membership, Possible FTAAP Membership and World FDI Inflows (2014)

No.	APEC (21) [FTAAP I]	TPP (12)	RCEP (16)	FTAAP II (25)	FTAAP III (17)
1	United States	United States		United States	United States
2	Australia	Australia	Australia	Australia	Australia
3	Brunei Darussalam	Brunei Darussalam	Brunei Darussalam	Brunei Darussalam	Brunei Darussalam
4	Canada	Canada		Canada	Canada
5	Chile	Chile		Chile	Chile
6	China		China	China	China
7	Hong Kong, China			Hong Kong, China	
8	Indonesia		Indonesia	Indonesia	Indonesia
9	Japan	Japan	Japan	Japan	Japan
10	Malaysia	Malaysia	Malaysia	Malaysia	Malaysia
11	Mexico	Mexico		Mexico	Mexico
12	New Zealand	New Zealand	New Zealand	New Zealand	New Zealand
13	Papua New Guinea			Papua New Guinea	
14	Peru	Peru		Peru	Peru
15	The Philippines		The Philippines	The Philippines	The Philippines
16	Russia			Russia	
17	Singapore	Singapore	Singapore	Singapore	Singapore
18	Republic of Korea		Republic of Korea	Republic of Korea	Republic of Korea
19	Chinese Taipei			Chinese Taipei	
20	Thailand		Thailand	Thailand	Thailand
21	Viet Nam	Viet Nam	Viet Nam	Viet Nam	Viet Nam
22			Myanmar	Myanmar	
23			Cambodia	Cambodia	
24			Laos	Laos	
25			India	India	
FDI Inflow (2014) (in billions of USD; % share in world)					
	652; 53%	345; 28%	363; 30%	690; 56%	525; 43%
	p. 6	p. 6	p. 6	pp. 6, A3–A6	pp. 6, A3–A6

Source World Investment Report 2015, United Nations Conference on Trade and Development, pp. 6, A3–A6

Note These are FDI inflows from the world to countries in the various regional groups and, hence, do not reflect the value of investment actually covered by the investment agreement

Calculations

FTAAP II (APEC + Myanmar, Cambodia, Laos and India)		
Entity	FDI Inflow (billions of dollars)	Share in world (%)
APEC	652	
Myanmar	0.946	
Cambodia	1.73	
Laos	0.721	
India	34.417	
FTAAP II	689.814	56.16
FTAAP III (APEC—HKC, Papua New Guinea, Russia and Taiwan)		
Entity	FDI Inflow (billions of dollars)	Share in world (%)
APEC	652	
Hong Kong, China	103.254	
Papua New Guinea	−0.03	
Russia	20.958	
Chinese Taipei	2.839	
FTAAP III	524.979	42.74

Annex 2: APEC Investment Principles (Updated 2011)

APEC Non-binding Investment Principles

Jakarta, November 1994
Honolulu, November 2011

In the spirit of APEC's underlying approach of open regionalism,
Recognising the importance of investment to economic development, the stimulation of growth, the creation of jobs and the flow of technology in the Asia-Pacific region,
Emphasising the importance of promoting domestic environments that are conducive to attracting foreign investment, such as stable growth with low inflation, adequate infrastructure, adequately developed human resources, and protection of intellectual property rights,
Reflecting that most APEC economies are both sources and recipients of foreign investment,
Aiming to increase investment including investment in small and medium enterprises, and to develop supporting industries,
Acknowledging the diversity in the level and pace of development of member economies as may be reflected in their investment regimes, and committed to ongoing efforts towards the improvement and further liberalisation of their investment regimes,

Without prejudice to applicable bilateral and multilateral treaties and other international instruments,
Recognising the importance of adherence to the WTO Agreement on Trade-Related Investment Measures.

APEC members aspire to the following non-binding principles:

Transparency

– Member economies will make all laws, regulations, administrative guidelines and policies pertaining to investment in their economies publicly available in a prompt, transparent and readily accessible manner.

Consistency of Interpretation and Implementation

– Member economies will seek to ensure consistent interpretation of laws, regulations, administrative procedures and policies governing foreign investment, as well as prompt, transparent, and predictable licensing and approval processes, coordinated across all levels of government.

Non-discrimination

– Member economies will extend to investors from any economy treatment in relation to the establishment, expansion and operation of their investments that is no less favourable than that accorded to investors from any other economy in like circumstances, without prejudice to relevant international obligations and principles.

National Treatment

– With exceptions as clearly provided for in domestic laws, regulations and policies, member economies will accord to foreign investors in relation to the establishment, expansion, operation and protection of their investments, treatment no less favourable than that accorded in like circumstances to domestic investors.

Regulatory Protections

– Member economies will not relax health, safety, labour, and environmental regulations as an encouragement to foreign investment.

Investment Incentives

– With limited and specified exceptions, member economies will avoid the use of investment incentives which distort fair competition within or between their economies, or which are inconsistent with these principles.

Performance Requirements

– Member economies will minimise the use of performance requirements that distort or limit expansion of trade and investment.

Expropriation and Compensation

- Member economies will not expropriate foreign investments or take measures that have a similar effect, except for a public purpose and on a non-discriminatory basis, in accordance with the laws of each economy and principles of international law and against the prompt payment of adequate and effective compensation.

Transfers and Convertibility

- Member economies will maintain their goal of the free and prompt transfer of funds related to foreign investment, such as capital contributions, profits, dividends, royalties, loan payments and liquidations, in freely convertible currency.

Settlement of Disputes

- Member economies accept that disputes arising in connection with a foreign investment will be settled promptly through consultations and negotiations between the parties to the dispute or, failing this, through procedures for arbitration in accordance with members' international commitments or through other arbitration procedures acceptable to both parties.

Protection and Enforcement of Rights

- Member economies will ensure non-discriminatory access to dispute resolution mechanisms, including tribunals, courts, and appeal processes, and, with due regard to judicial independence, will seek to ensure the availability of resources to enable timely delivery and enforcement of judgments and arbitration awards.

Entry and Sojourn of Personnel

- Member economies will permit, in a timely manner, the temporary entry and sojourn of key foreign technical and managerial personnel for the purpose of engaging in activities connected with foreign investment, subject to relevant laws and regulations.

Avoidance of Double Taxation

- Member economies will endeavour to avoid double taxation related to foreign investment.

Investor Behaviour

- Acceptance of foreign investment is facilitated when foreign investors abide by the host economy's laws, regulations, administrative guidelines and policies, just as domestic investors should, and when investors take into account guidelines related to CSR that have been developed by multilateral bodies, as appropriate.

Removal of Barriers to Capital Exports

- Member economies accept that regulatory and institutional barriers to the outflow of investment will be minimised.

References

Alford, Roger. 2013. The convergence of international trade and investment arbitration. *Santa Clara Journal of International Law* 12 (35): 39.

Alschner, Wolfgang. 2014. Regionalism and overlap in investment treaty law: Towards consolidation or contradiction? *Journal of International Economic Law* 17: 271.

Chaisse, Julien. 2015a. The issue of treaty shopping in international law of foreign investment—Structuring (and restructuring) of investments to gain access to investment agreements. *Hastings Business Law Review* 11: 225–306.

Chaisse, Julien. 2015b. The shifting tectonics of international investment law—Structure and dynamics of rules and arbitration on foreign investment in the Asia-pacific region. *George Washington International Law Review* 47: 563–638.

Hanessian, Grant and Kabir Duggal. 2015. The 2015 Indian model BIT: Is this change the world wishes to see? *ICSID Review*.

Hiebert, Murray, and Liam Hanlon. 2012. *ASEAN and partners launch regional comprehensive economic partnership*. Center for Strategic and International Studies.

Joubin-Bret, Anna. 2015. Why we need a global appellate mechanism for international investment law. *Columbia FDI Perspectives*, 146.

Ostry, Jonathan D., et al. 2010. *Capital inflows: The role of controls, IMF staff position note, SPN/10/04*. http://www.imf.org/external/pubs/ft/spn/2010/spn1004.pdf.

Rudd, Kevin, and Sunil Kant Munjal. 2015. Why APEC needs India. *The Straits Times*.

Sauvant, Karl P., and Federico Ortino. 2013. *Improving the international investment law and policy regime: Options for the future*, 28. Ministry for Foreign Affairs of Finland.

Schill, Stephan W. 2009. Multilaterlizing investment treaties through most-favored-nation clauses. *Berkeley Journal of International Law* 27 (496): 500.

Stephenson, Sherry. 2016. Trade governance frameworks in a world of global value chains: Policy options. E15 expert group on global value chains: Development challenges and policy options —Policy options paper. E15 Initiative. Geneva: International Centre for Trade and Sustainable Development (ICTSD) and World Economic Forum, at 6.

Yu, Peter K. 2011. Sinic trade agreements. *U.C. Davis Law Review* 44: 953, 978.

Part III
Towards a Greater Practice of Investment Arbitration in Asia-Pacific?

The Future of Investor-State Arbitration: Revising the Rules?

Rahul Donde and Julien Chaisse

1 Introduction

The significant increase in the number of international investment agreements ("IIAs") over the past two decades has been accompanied by a meteoric rise in the number of investor-state disputes.[1] In 2016 alone 62 investor-state arbitrations were initiated, the second highest number of cases in a single year and significantly up from the 42 arbitrations initiated in 201.[2] Asia itself has witnessed a startling

[1]UNCTAD World Investment Report 2017, accessed by http://unctad.org/en/PublicationsLibrary/wir2017_en.pdf (noting that the number of cases initiated in 2016 (62) were higher than the 10-year average of 49 cases per year); IIA Issues Note No. 2 2016; UNCTAD World Investment Report 2016, accessed by http://unctad.org/en/PublicationsLibrary/wir2016_en.pdf (noting that the number of investor-state arbitrations in 2015 set a new annual high). See also Kollamparambil (2016) (concluding on the basis of empirical analysis that investors initiate a higher number of disputes against countries that have IIAs).
[2]IIA Issues Note No. 2 2016, IIA Issues Note No. 1 2015. See also UNCTAD World Investment Report 2016, accessed by http://unctad.org/en/PublicationsLibrary/wir2016_en.pdf<http://unctad.org/en/PublicationChapters/wir2015ch0_KeyMessage_en.pdf. This is the number of publicly known cases. As a significant number of cases are conducted in a confidential framework, the actual number of disputes is likely to be higher.

R. Donde (✉)
Cabinet Lévy Kaufmann-Kohler, Geneva, Switzerland
e-mail: Rahul.Donde@lk-k.com

J. Chaisse
CFRED, Faculty of Law, The Chinese University of Hong Kong,
Sha Tin, Hong Kong
e-mail: Julien.chaisse@cuhk.edu.hk

J. Chaisse et al. (eds.), *Asia's Changing International Investment Regime*,
International Law and the Global South, DOI 10.1007/978-981-10-5882-0_12

number of investment disputes: about 21% of all investment disputes involve Asian states.[3] The vast majority of claims are against India (21), making it the 11th highest sued country in the world, followed by Kazakhstan (17) and Kyrgyzstan (13).[4] Several authors foretell a greater number of disputes involving Asian parties in the future, mainly because of the rising number of IIAs in parallel with increasing FDI flows in Asia, coupled with a greater awareness of investment rules shown by Asian actors.[5]

While international arbitration remains the preferred mechanism for resolving disputes between an investor and a state,[6] a number of states disenchanted with or simply critical of investment arbitration are proposing viable alternatives.[7] Several states are redefining the current investor-state arbitration framework and its relationship to democratic decision-making. In fact, the EU-Vietnam Free Trade Agreement contemplates the creation of an "investment court" that would resolve disputes between investors and Member States.[8] Other states have chosen to significantly reduce the scope of issues that can be submitted to arbitration,[9] while still others require such disputes to be submitted first to their own domestic courts.[10]

In addition, the G20 released its "Guiding Principles for Global Investment Policymaking" ("G20 Principles") which insist that "[i]nvestment policies should

---

[3]See http://investmentpolicyhub.unctad.org/ISDS/FilterByCountry. See also Chaisse (2013, pp. 187, 202) (concluding that more than 90 investment disputes involving 24 Asia-Pacific states have been filed since 1987). Dr. Chaisse's study did not include cases involving Asian investors, or claims filed in 2014–2016.

[4]See http://investmentpolicyhub.unctad.org/ISDS.

[5]Chaisse (2015, p. 563), Chaisse (2013, p. 187), Malintoppi (2015, p. 12), Kim (2012, p. 399). Luttrell, ISDS in the Asia-Pacific, a regional snap shot.

[6]See generally Vandevelde (2005, p. 157) (noting that foreign investors are increasingly resorting to international arbitration for resolving their disputes with host states).

[7]See Bernasconi-Osterwalder (2014). Retrieved from http://www.iisd.org/publications/investment-treaty-arbitration-opportunities-reform-arbitral-rules-and-processes.

[8]See Press release of the European Commission, available at: http://ec.europa.eu/trade/policy/countries-and-regions/countries/vietnam/. On 1 February 2016, the text of the EU–Vietnam Free Trade Agreement was published, following the announcement of the conclusion of the negotiations. The legal review of the text has now begun and will be followed by translation into the EU's official languages and Vietnamese. The Commission will then present a proposal to the Council of Ministers for approval of the agreement and ratification by the European Parliament. An investment court is also contemplated under the EU–Canada Comprehensive Economic and Trade Agreement (see below). See EU–Canada Comprehensive Economic and Trade Agreement, available at http://trade.ec.europa.eu/doclib/docs/2014/september/tradoc_152806.pdf.

Available at http://trade.ec.europa.eu/doclib/press/index.cfm?id=1409. See also: Daly and Ahmad (2015).

[9]WIR 2016, p. 110 (noting that Indonesia's draft model BIT is 'is characterized by carve-outs, safeguards and clarifications'). See also, UNCTAD (2007) (noting a recent trend of "more circumscribed" IIA dispute settlement provisions, and citing the Malaysia–Pakistan Closer Economic Partnership Agreement (2007) which excludes all disputes concerning national treatment and performance requirements as an example.)

[10]See, for instance, the 2015 Indian Model BIT, which has been analyzed in Chapter 16 [add full reference].

provide legal certainty and strong protection to investors and investments, tangible and intangible, including access to effective mechanisms for the prevention and settlement of disputes, as well as to enforcement procedures".[11] The Principles also emphasise the importance of adequate and modern dispute resolution mechanisms: "[d]ispute settlement procedures should be fair, open and transparent, with appropriate safeguards to prevent abuse."[12] While the ramifications of the Principles are yet to be seen, it is expected that they will have a significant resonance in the Asia-Pacific region.

In this scenario, with Asia also witnessing record foreign investment inflows and outflows,[13] it is timely to review current trends, concerns and recent developments in investment arbitration, particularly as they affect Asia. Section 2 of this chapter briefly introduces IIAs and investment arbitration. Section 3 outlines current trends and concerns, focusing on Asia. Section 4 reviews global developments in the traditional investment arbitration framework and examines their reception in Asia. Section 5 concludes.

2 IIAs and Investment Arbitration

A. IIA Framework

IIAs may be broadly understood as treaties between sovereign states to protect and promote investments made by investors from one state in the territory of the other.[14] They are entered into with the aim of mutual development of both states by *inter alia* promising a stable and predictable business environment. IIAs may take the form of bilateral investment treaties ("BITs") i.e. treaties between two states (such as the India–Australia BIT), or investment chapters in broader economic agreements (like Chap. 9 of the Australia–China Free Trade Agreement).[15]

IIAs are now ubiquitous; the global network of IIAs has grown considerably over the past years. It now consists of 3,327 treaties, 38 of which were concluded in

[11]Following their meeting in Shanghai on 9–10 July 2016 under the Chinese G20 Presidency, G20 trade ministers issued a statement reinforcing their determination to "promote inclusive, robust and sustainable trade and investment growth." At the same time, ministers agreed to the G20 Principles. See Annex III: G20 Guiding Principles for Global Investment Policymaking [available at www.g20.org/]. Nine non-binding Guiding Principles provide guidance for investment policymaking with a view to fostering an open, transparent and conducive global policy environment for investment, promoting coherence in national and international investment policymaking and promoting inclusive economic growth and sustainable development.

[12]See Annex III: G20 Guiding Principles for Global Investment Policymaking.

[13]See WIR 2017; WIR 2016.

[14]See generally Lowenfeld (2003, pp. 123, 129).

[15]See generally Chaisse and Bellak (2015, p. 79).

2016.[16] By the end of 2016, more than 150 economies were engaged in negotiating new IIAs.[17]

Asian states have been prolific in entering into IIAs.[18] More than a half of investment treaties in the world involve at least one Asian state.[19] In 2016 and 2017, three Asian states concluded the highest number of IIAs.[20]

B. Investment Arbitration

Investment arbitration—also known as investor-state arbitration—is a mechanism through which foreign investors may obtain a binding adjudication of their claims against host states that have either violated IIA obligations or, in some circumstances, have breached their contractual commitments or their national foreign investment laws.

As we mentioned above, investment arbitration is by far the most popular mechanism for resolving investor-state disputes. Indeed, investment arbitration is attractive from an investor's perspective as it allows the investor to make a claim without having to rely on its "home state"[21] to initiate inter-state proceedings against the "host state"[22] for a violation of the latter's treaty obligations. This is in stark contrast to the dispute resolution procedures of the World Trade Organization ("WTO") that only allow Member States to initiate proceedings against other Member States in the event of a violation.[23] Investment arbitration is attractive to states too as it improves the perception of the investment climate of the host state, making it easier for the host state to attract foreign investment.[24]

There is no single global forum under which investor-state disputes are conducted. The majority of such disputes are conducted under the procedural framework of the Convention on the Settlement of Investment Disputes between States and Nationals of Other States ("ICSID Convention") and the ICSID Arbitration Rules.[25] The next most popular procedural framework for resolving disputes is the UNCITRAL Arbitration Rules.[26] Unlike ICSID, the UNCITRAL framework has no

[16]See http://investmentpolicyhub.unctad.org/ISDS.

[17]UNCTAD (2016).

[18]See Chaisse (2015, p. 563).

[19]See http://investmentpolicyhub.unctad.org/IIA; Bryan Cave (2015).

[20]See http://investmentpolicyhub.unctad.org/IIA; WIR 2016, p. 101 (noting that Japan, the Republic of Korea and China were the "most active" in concluding IIAs).

[21]'Home state' refers to the investor's state of nationality.

[22]'Host state' refers to the state in which the investment is made.

[23]Sacerdoti (2014, p. 4).

[24]Blythe (2013, pp. 273–290).

[25]IIA Issues Note No. 1 (2017) showing trends in known IIA based investor-state cases from 1987 to 2016; IIA Issues Note No. 2 (2016) (finding that 62% of all known cases have been filed under the ICSID Convention or ICSID Additional Facility Rules).

[26]Allee and Peinhardt (2010, p. 1).

formal or permanent institutional support,[27] and the contracting states to the IIA need not be parties to the ICSID Convention. For states like India that have not ratified the ICSID Convention, initiating a dispute under the UNCITRAL framework usually the only option available to investors.

Investment arbitration awards frequently run into several million US dollars. Despite this, states tend to comply with them, arguably because the economic costs of non-compliance are higher than compliance.[28] For instance, non-payment of an ICSID award may restrict a state's ability to access World Bank funding.[29] Further, in non-ICSID contexts, non-compliance may significantly impact a state's sovereign risk rating, in turn increasing its borrowing costs.[30] Other consequences could be equally severe: in 2012, the U.S. suspended Argentina's preferential trade status due to its failure to comply with two investment arbitration awards.[31]

Having broadly set out the contours of the IIA and investment arbitration framework, we now turn to examine trends, concerns and developments in this framework.

3 Investment Arbitration: Trends and Concerns

C. Global Trends

The first investment arbitration arising out of an IIA was filed in 1987 by a Hong Kong corporation against an Asian state, Sri Lanka.[32] Since then, there have been 767 investment claims.[33] Significantly however, a recent study found that no investment dispute has arisen under more than 90% of the BITs presently in force.[34]

The large number of investment claims have led to a number of studies to identify and analyse trends in investment arbitration. While these studies have not always reached the same conclusion (because of different units of analysis and different sources of data), largely they conclude that most disputes are decided in favour of the state.

---

[27]Some level of institutional support is often provided by the Permanent Court of Arbitration at The Hague.

[28]Allee and Peinhardt (2010, p. 401).

[29]MercoPress, US will vote against loans to Argentina in World Bank and IDB, available at http://en.mercopress.com/2011/09/29/us-will-vote-against-loans-to-argentina-in-world-bank-and-idb.

[30]Viñuales and Bentolila (2012).

[31]See generally, Rosenberg (2013, p. 503).

[32]ICSID, "50 Years of ICSID", available at www.icsid.worldbank.org/apps/ICSIDWEB/Documents/ICSID%20Timeline%20-%20Featured.pdf. See also *Asian Agricultural Products Limited v. Democratic Socialist Republic of Sri Lanka* (ICSID Case No. ARB/87/3), Award, June 27, 1990.

[33]See http://investmentpolicyhub.unctad.org/ISDS; Behn and Langford (2016).

[34]Scott Miller and Gregory Hicks, 'Investor-State Dispute Settlement: A reality Check', available at www.csis.org/analysis/investor-state-dispute-settlement-reality-check-working-paper.

According to a study recently conducted by UNCTAD, 495 investor-state proceedings have been concluded up to 2016. Of these, a quarter were settled, approximately one third were decided in favour of the state and about one fourth were decided in favour of the investor.[35] About half the cases that were favourable to states were dismissed for lack of jurisdiction. Where cases moved beyond jurisdiction to the merits (i.e. where a tribunal made a determination of whether the state breached any of the IIAs substantive obligations), 60% were decided in favour of the investor and 40% in favour of the state.[36]

In another study, Franck and Wylie observed that states "win"[37] approximately 60.4% of the time and investors "win" approximately 39.6% of the time.[38] Miller and Hicks came to largely similar conclusions: about one-third investment claims settle amicably, and for those that are not settled, states generally win twice as many times as investors. Further, they conclude that when investors do prevail, they are usually awarded a small fraction of their initial claim—usually less than 10% of the amounts claimed.[39]

The most recent study of 676 public international investment arbitrations filed from the 1990s too reached similar conclusions: cases are settled about one-third of the time, and states win more than one-third of disputed cases.[40]

While this empirical analysis has been criticised by some, it cannot be denied that states are more likely to be successful than investors in investment arbitration, a conclusion that undermines arguments that the investment arbitration system is biased in favour of investors.[41]

D. **Trends in Asia**

Unlike the global trends in investment arbitration considered above, it is difficult to identify particular trends in investment arbitration in Asia. Prominent scholars have reached often contradictory conclusions.

In terms of the likely number of investment claims involving Asia, in 2012, Nottage and Weeramantry predicted that there would be few Asia-centric claims possibly because of "institutional barriers", including costs and a paucity of experienced counsel and arbitrators in Asia, rather than any specific "cultural aversion" to adversarial forms of dispute resolution (such as arbitration).[42] A study conducted a few months later, however, reached a different conclusion. On the basis

---

[35]WIR 2017, IIA Issues Note No. 2 2016.

[36]WIR 2017, IIA Issues Note No. 2 2016.

[37]A 'win' is defined as the awarding of US$1 or more, even if *de minimus* or less than the investor's unrecovered expenses. Franck and Wylie (2015, p. 459).

[38]Franck and Wylie (2015).

[39]Scott Miller and Gregory Hicks, 'Investor-State Dispute Settlement: A reality Check', available at https://www.csis.org/analysis/investor-state-dispute-settlement-reality-check-working-paper.

[40]Wellhausen (2016, pp. 117–135).

[41]For an analysis of the limits of empirical research in answering legal questions see Van Harten (2011, p. 33).

[42]Nottage and Romesh Weeramantry (2012, p. 19).

of the higher number of claims seen in 2011, it predicted that the future would see more claims against Asian states as well as claims being made by Asian investors.[43]

In 2015, Chaisse conducted a comprehensive review of investor-state claims involving the Asia-Pacific. Like the other studies mentioned above, he noted a sharp jump in 2011 (10 claims, compared to five each year over the previous decade), which was maintained in 2012 and 2013 (13 claims each). He observed that the growth in investment claims could be explained by increased FDI, a larger number of IIAs as well as a better understanding of these instruments by both Asian states and Asian investors. He too predicted an increasing number of claims involving Asia.[44] Other authors have come to the same conclusion, while still others submit that it is simply too early to tell whether investor-state arbitration will proliferate in the region.[45]

Few studies have been conducted examining claims brought by Asian investors. Salomon and Friedrich observe that 29 investment arbitrations have been brought by investors in the East Asia and Pacific Region, 22 of which were under the ICSID Convention.[46] 19 investment arbitrations were based on an IIA, two of these on the ASEAN Agreements.[47] They note that after a period of decline in the 1990s where only one claim was brought, there were nine new cases between 2000 and 2010, and 16 cases from 2010 to 2015.[48] Overall, 92 cases have been initiated by Asian claimants, 49 of which (53.2%) have been initiated in the past five years alone.[49]

In terms of subject-matter, oil, gas and mining has traditionally been the dominant sector for claims in Asia. The last few years however have seen a considerable increase in the number of disputes in other sectors (construction, electricity etc.) possibly as a result of the industrial diversification in Asia.[50]

In terms of outcome, a recent study concluded that states in Asia won 14 out of the 45 disputes considered. States in the Middle East and North Africa as well as Europe (and the former Soviet Union) are found to win significantly more often than Asian states.[51] Latest statistics however indicate that Asian states have won 37 (53.6%) out of the 69 disputes that concluded with a known decision on the merits.[52]

---

[43]Kim (2012, p. 399).

[44]Chaisse (2015, p. 563).

[45]Nakagawa (2007, pp. 837–867).
doi: 10.1093/jiel/jgm032.

[46]Salomon and Friedrich (2015, pp. 800, 837).

[47]Ibid.

[48]Ibid. 838.

[49]See http://investmentpolicyhub.unctad.org/ISDS.

[50]See http://investmentpolicyhub.unctad.org/ISDS; Bryan Cave (2015).

[51]Welhausen (2016, pp. 117–135).

[52]See http://investmentpolicyhub.unctad.org/ISDS.

E. Concerns

The findings outlined above should lead one to conclude—or at least seriously question—the perception that investor state arbitration does not favour investors over states. By contrast however, there has been increasing criticism of investment arbitration as being "pro-investor". The popular press has carried several (oft-misleading) articles on investor-state arbitration[53] alleging for instance that "secret trade courts"[54] pose a "real threat to the national interest from the rich and powerful".[55]

Nearly every aspect of investment arbitration has come under criticism. Concerns have been expressed about the biased interpretation of IIA provisions in favour of investors, the lack of predictability and transparency of arbitral proceedings, as well as the independence and impartiality of arbitrators.[56] Other serious concerns include suggesting that investment arbitration has a "chilling effect" on a state's regulatory power[57] and that foreign investors are allowed to circumvent the operation of domestic law and national courts through the process.[58]

Unfortunately, these criticisms have had a particular resonance in Asia. Non-governmental organizations have fanned the belief that Asian states fail to enact bona fide regulatory measures because of a perceived or actual threat of investment arbitration. Indonesia's termination of its IIAs, and India's new model BIT have both been linked to the so-called "pro-investor" interpretation of IIA provisions by investment tribunals.[59] Australia's earlier rejection of investment arbitration too can be traced to a belief that investment arbitration was biased towards investors.[60, 61]

It not within the scope of this chapter to respond to these criticisms; this has been comprehensively done elsewhere,[62] and has even formed the subject-matter of a survey conducted by the International Bar Association to ascertain whether the

---

[53]See for instance, Ikenson (2014), The Economist (2014).

[54]New York Times (2004).

[55]Monbiot (2013).

[56]Eberhardt et al. (2012), Van Harten (2012, p. 1), Ikenson (2014).

[57]Brown (2013, p. 1) (noting that IIAs "do indeed prevent some countries from developing or enforcing effective environmental policies").

[58]See Schill (2015).

[59]Trakman and Sharma (2014a, b); Press Release from the Government of India, Model Text for the Indian Bilateral Investment Treaty (2015) http://pib.nic.in/newsite/PrintRelease.aspx?relid=133411 (noting that "during the last few years, significant changes have occurred globally regarding BITs, in general, and investor-state dispute resolution mechanism in particular").

[60]Tienhaara and Ranald (2011).

[61]See generally, Nottage (2011, p. 5), Tietje et al. (2014) Study prepared for the Minister of Foreign Trade and Development Cooperation, Ministry of Foreign affairs, The Netherlands; UNCHR (2003).

[62]See, for instance, Gloria et al. (2016, pp. 1–36).

criticism was justified.[63] It suffices to say here that most of these concerns are over stated. In any event, significant attempts have been made to address them through the various reform mechanisms discussed below.

4 Recent Developments

The criticism of ISDS outlined above has led to an evolution of international investment law—both in the substantive protections offered to investors as well as in the procedural framework of investment arbitration.[64] While most developments are incremental and address only some aspects of the system, others, such as the establishment of a permanent investment court, result in an entirely new system for investor-state disputes.

These developments are particularly relevant for Asia for several reasons. First, the "backlash"[65] against investment arbitration has been severe in this region, with several Asian states substantially reforming their IIAs as a result.[66] Others are either delaying ratification of IIAs,[67] renegotiating them,[68] or terminating them altogether.[69] Second, by dominating global investment flows, and entering into an increasing number of IIAs, Asian actors are now in a position to act as global rule-makers in international investment law.[70] There is "little doubt" that Asian states "are becoming focal points in rule-making in international investment law."[71] Third, Asian states are already involved in a significant number of investment disputes, running into billions of dollars and concerning increasingly sensitive

[63]IBA Subcommittee on Investment Treaty Arbitration, Report on the Subcommittee's Investment Treaty Arbitration survey May 2016.

[64]WIR 2016, p. 116. For a detailed review of substantive developments see UNCTAD (2016).

[65]Langford et al. (2016) (providing a historical overview of the narrative of 'legitimacy crisis' in the field of investment arbitration). See generally, Waibel et al. (2010).

[66]Sri Lanka has announced its intention to move away from traditional IIAs, inter alia because of the "bitter lessons" learned from investment arbitration. See http://unctad-worldinvestmentforum.org/wp-content/uploads/2014/10/Malalgoda.pdf. The same is the case with India, which substantially revised its earlier model IIA in light of the ruling against it in the White Industries arbitration. See Press Release from the Government of India, Model Text for the Indian Bilateral Investment Treaty (2015) http://pib.nic.in/newsite/PrintRelease.aspx?relid=133411 noting that "during the last few years, significant changes have occurred globally regarding BITs, *in general, and investor-state dispute resolution mechanism in particular*".

[67]Haftel and Thompson (2013, p. 355).

[68]This is the case with India, which has begun renegotiating its IIAs. See http://isds.bilaterals.org/?india-wants-new-foreign-investment&lang=en.

[69]This is the case with India and Indonesia. *See*, for instance, Bland and Donnan (2014); Trakman and Sharma (2014a, b).

[70]Schill (2016).

[71]Ibid.

issues.[72] Some developments, such as transparency and third party participation, could thus be usefully adopted in on-going proceedings to quell criticism that investment arbitration is a "closed" process. Fourth, the number of claims against Asian states is expected to rise in the future. Asian states should thus pay close attention to recent developments to make sure that the oft-competing state and investor interests are adequately balanced.

It is not possible to review all the current developments in investment arbitration in this chapter. Instead, we touch on a few procedural developments that will likely have the strongest repercussions in Asia. Some of these developments—such as controlling treaty interpretation—already exist within the Asian investment arbitration framework. Others, however, are notably absent.

A. **Control of Interpretation**

As we mentioned above, one of the serious criticisms of the current investment arbitration framework is that investment tribunals interpret IIAs with a "pro-investor" bias which is not what states had in mind when they negotiated and entered into those IIAs. It is also argued that at the time states entered into IIAs, they were not fully aware of the implications of the structure and language of treaty provisions.[73]

To address this concern, recent IIAs contemplate joint interpretations by the states party to the IIA in question.[74] Arbitral tribunals are bound by such interpretations, although whether an interpretation would also apply to a pre-existing dispute remains to be seen.[75] Several states including Canada, Chile, Mexico, the US as well as the European Union now include express provisions in their IIAs allowing for binding joint interpretations of the IIA.[76]

It is heartening to note that some Asian IIAs such as the ASEAN Comprehensive Investment Agreement ("ACIA") between ten major Asian nations[77] and the ASEAN-Australia-New Zealand FTA ("AANZ") already contain such provisions.[78] In fact, some Asian states have gone a step further by not only controlling the

[72]Australia for instance has faced claims concerning its tobacco regulations. *See also* Kim (2012, p. 399).

[73]See Wälde (2009, pp. 724, 737).

[74]Gaukrodger (2016).

[75]Eleni Methymaki and Antonios Tzanakopoulos (forthcoming).

[76]See US CAFTA-DR, Art. 10.22 (3) and 19.1(3), available at https://ustr.gov/trade-agreements/freetradeagreements/cafta-dr-dominican-republic-central-america-fta/final-text; EU–Canada Comprehensive Economic and Trade Agreement, Art. X.27 and X.42, consolidated text available at http://trade.ec.europa.eu/doclib/docs/2014/september/tradoc_152806.pdf.

[77]Brunei, Cambodia, Indonesia, Lao People-s Democratic Republic, Malaysia, Myanmar, Philippines, Singapore, Thailand and Vietnam.

[78]ACIA, Art. 40(3) ("A joint decision of the Member States, declaring their interpretation of a provision of this Agreement shall be binding on a tribunal, and any decision or award issued by a tribunal must be consistent with the joint decision"); AANZ, Art. 27(3) ("A joint decision of the Parties, declaring their interpretation of a provision of this Agreement shall be binding on a tribunal, and any decision or award issued by a tribunal must be consistent with that joint decision.").

interpretation of the IIA, but also controlling its *application*. For instance, if an investor challenges a regulatory measure under the China-Australia FTA ("ChAFTA"), the respondent state may issue a "public welfare notice" specifying why it believes that the measure falls within the exceptions provided in the FTA.[79] The arbitration proceedings are then suspended, triggering a 90-day consultation period with the other treaty party.[80] If the state parties agree that the challenged measure is excluded from the FTA, their decision would bind the investment tribunal.[81] If the treaty parties are unable to agree whether the measure is excluded within 90-day period, the matter would be decided by the investment tribunal, which is not to draw any adverse inference from the non-issuance of a public welfare notice by the respondent or from the absence of any decision between the treaty parties as to whether the measure falls within the scope of the exception.[82]

B. Counterclaims

Investment arbitration is commonly perceived as being biased towards investors.[83] It is assumed that the state must always adopt a defensive position when faced with an investment claim[84] and can, at best, only hope to defeat the claims of an investor.[85] Recent developments are, however, altering this perceived asymmetry, with counterclaims becoming increasingly common. 28 counterclaims are known to have been raised so far, 13 of which have been filed in the past six years.[86] Further, most recent treaties contemplate counterclaims.

The Asian experience with counterclaims is somewhat mixed. On the one hand, four Asian states have initiated counterclaims, with Indonesia so far being the only successful counterclaimant in its dispute with a Saudi Arabian investor.[87] Further, provided certain conditions are met, the Trans Pacific Partnership ("TPP") allows counterclaims,[88] as does the Agreement for the Promotion, Protection and Guarantee of Investments Among Member States of the Organisation of the Islamic

[79]Measures that are non-discriminatory and that have been taken for 'legitimate public welfare objectives' of public health, safety, the environment, public morals or public order are excluded. See ChAFTA, Art. 9.11.5.

[80]ChAFTA, Arts. 9.11.5–9.11.6.

[81]ChAFTA, Art. 9.18.3.

[82]ChAFTA, Art. 9.11.8.

[83]See generally Waibel et al. (2010).

[84]Lalive and Halonen (2011, pp. 141, 154–55).

[85]Lalive and Halonen (2011, p. 479).

[86]Popova and Poon (2015, p. 223).

[87]*Hesham Talaat M. Al-Warraq v The Republic of Indonesia*, UNCITRAL, Award (15 December 2014).

[88]TPP, Art. 9.18.2: '"When the claimant submits a claim pursuant to para 1(a)(i)(B), 1(a)(i)(C), 1(b)(i)(B) or 1(b)(i)(C), the respondent may make a counterclaim in connection with the factual and legal basis of the claim or rely on a claim for the purpose of a set off against the claimant."'

Conference, which comprises a large number of Asian states. On the other hand, most Asian IIAs do not contemplate counterclaims, at least expressly.[89]

C. **Transparency**

A serious concern voiced about the existing ISDS system is the lack of transparency. Recently however, there has been a global movement towards increased transparency and third party participation in investment arbitration,[90] even among those states that have been traditionally reluctant to transparency. For instance, Ecuador now regularly publishes information about progress of its investment cases on its government websites.[91] A similar policy is being followed by the Czech Republic.[92]

In 2014, the UNCITRAL Rules on Transparency in Investor-State Arbitration came into effect. These Rules apply to all UNCITRAL arbitrations initiated under IIAs concluded after 1 April 2014, unless the parties to the IIA agree otherwise. They also apply to arbitrations under existing IIAs, provided the parties to those treaties consent to their application. The Rules chart new ground concerning public access to ISDS. They cover issues ranging from disclosure of the initiation of arbitral proceedings, to specifying the documents to be disclosed, to requiring open hearings and publication of awards. Further, the Rules are not limited to arbitrations conducted under the UNCITRAL Arbitration Rules; rather they are available for both institutional and other ad hoc investment arbitration proceedings. The Stockholm Chamber of Commerce for instance has issued a practice note which call for the application of the Transparency Rules in investment arbitration.[93]

In another noteworthy development, in 2015, states agreed on a Convention on Transparency in Treaty-Based Investor-State Arbitration ("Transparency Convention").[94] The Convention is designed to extend the scope of application of the UNCITRAL Transparency Rules, by providing a mechanism by which states can agree to the application of the Transparency Rules to UNCITRAL arbitrations

---

[89]For a review of counterclaims in Asian IIAs, see Trisha Mitra and Rahul Donde Claims and Counterclaims under Asian Multilateral Investment Treaties in: L. Choukroune (Ed.), Judging the State in International Trade and Investment Law: Modern Sovereignty, the Law and the Economics, Springer, 2016.

[90]See generally, UNCTAD Series on Issues in International Investment Agreements II Transparency 2011 at http://unctad.org/en/PublicationsLibrary/unctaddiaeia2011d6_en.pdf; Kaufmann-Kohler (2013, pp. 305, 308).

[91]www.iisd.org/itn/2016/02/29/state-strategies-for-the-defence-of-domestic-interests-in-investor-state-arbitration-julia-calvert/.

[92]www.iareporter.com/articles/the-czech-republic-updates-on-fifteen-investment-treaty-disputes/.

[93]www.sccinstitute.com/media/72819/scc-application-of-mauritius-convention-and-uncitral-rules-on-transparency.pdf.

[94]United Nations Convention on Transparency in Treaty-based Investor-State Arbitration (adopted on 10 December 2014, opened for signature on 17 March 2015). See also UN (2014a), United Nations Convention on Transparency in Treaty-based Investor-State Arbitration, General Assembly, 69th session, Resolution A/69/116 (18 December 2014).

instituted under pre-April 2014 IIAs. While only Canada, Switzerland and Mauritius have ratified the Convention so far,[95] more States are likely to do so in the near future. 16 countries have signed the Transparency Convention till date, but none from the Asia-Pacific.[96]

It is now a foregone conclusion that investment arbitration should be conducted in an open, transparent manner. Given the public dimension of investment disputes, and the growing interest of civil society, Asian states would do well to make their investment disputes more transparent. While a few Asian states have taken steps in this direction, others are lagging behind.[97]

D. **State-State Dispute Settlement**

Most IIAs contain two dispute resolution clauses: one permitting investor-state arbitration (for resolving disputes between the investor and the host state) and the other permitting arbitration between the signatory states (for resolving disputes concerning the interpretation and/or application of the IIA). State-state dispute resolution provisions are not commonly used to resolve investor-state disputes. This position has, however, changed recently with state-state dispute resolution emerging as a viable option through which states can exercise greater control over the interpretation and application of disputed IIA provisions.[98] States have initiated claims against their counterparty in response to investor-state disputes that they were facing at the time. In *Peru v. Chile* for instance, state-state arbitration was initiated to define the temporal limits of the Peru-Chile BIT.[99] Similarly, in *Ecuador v. United* States, a tribunal was called on to define the scope of the Contracting Parties' obligations under the US-Ecuador BIT.[100]

Some Asian IIAs include state-state dispute resolution as the only dispute resolution mechanism—not one in addition to ISDS. For example, Australia's agreements with the United States and Malaysia, and the Philippines' with Japan, subject all investment disputes to state–state dispute settlement.

Asian states should review and consider state-state dispute resolution mechanisms in their existing (and new) investment treaties to ascertain whether, and how, these provisions can be effectively used in an investor-state context.

---

95 www.uncitral.org/uncitral/en/uncitral_texts/arbitration/2014Transparency_Convention_status.html.

96 www.uncitral.org/uncitral/en/uncitral_texts/arbitration/2014Transparency_Convention_status.html.

97 For instance, while the ACIA and the AANZ contain transparency obligations, China is more reluctant. See Zhao and Yun (2014, pp. 150–163), Hsu (2012, pp. 243, 256).

98 Potestà (2013, pp. 753–770).

99 See discussion of this case in Bernasconi-Osterwalder (2014).

100 *Ecuador v. United States*, PCA Case No. 2012-5, Request for Arbitration, ¶ 1 (Perm. Ct. Arb. 2011). See generally Roberts (2011, p. 1).

E. **Appeals Mechanism**

Decisions of arbitral tribunals in investment arbitration are final, and usually subject only to very limited grounds of review.[101] As mentioned above, the current ISDS system has been criticised as there is no corrective mechanism if tribunals get their decisions wrong. The ability to appeal decisions was one of the key concerns raised by both businesses and non-governmental organizations.[102]

In this context, the establishment of an appellate mechanism has regained currency.[103] The EU-Vietnam FTA as well as the Canada-EU FTA both contemplate the creation of an Investment Court (examined below), as well as an appeal tribunal. Other IIAs too contemplate the creation of an appellate mechanism under which the correctness of a decision of an arbitral tribunal can be contested. The US-Singapore FTA contemplates the creation of an appeals mechanism,[104] as does India's new model BIT.[105] The TPP refers to the possibility of an 'appellate mechanism for reviewing awards rendered by investor-state dispute settlement tribunals' being 'developed in the future',[106] and this possibility is also left open in the ChAFTA under which China and Australia are to commence negotiations for an appellate and review mechanism for hearing questions of law arising out of arbitral awards issued under that Agreement. There is thus "a real possibility" that a regional investment appeals body will be established in the near future.[107]

F. **Investment Court**

Another development of considerable importance is the Investment Court System ("ICS") which would altogether replace the current investment arbitration framework. This system is contemplated in the EU-Vietnam FTA as well as the Canada-EU FTA.[108]

---

[101]In the ICSID context, grounds for annulment are specified in Article 52 of the ICSID Convention. In non-ICSID context, the grounds for review would be the same as those for international commercial arbitration, which usually exclude a full review of the merits. See generally, Fouret and Mourre (2015).

[102]European Commission Concept Paper, 'Investment in the TTIP and Beyond' 8.

[103]Proposals for an appeals mechanism were considered by ICSID in 2004 and by the OECD in 2005. See generally Parra (2014, p. 9), Yannaca-Small (2008, p. 223).

[104]See, for example, Article 15.19(10) of the United States–Singapore FTA, available at https://ustr.gov/sites/default/files/uploads/agreements/fta/singapore/asset_upload_file708_4036.pdf.

[105]India Model BIT, Art. 29.

[106]TPP, Art. 9.22(11).

[107]Sam Luttrell, ISDS in the Asia-Pacific: A Regional Snap-Shot.

[108]Both these treaties are awaiting domestic approvals and subsequent ratification.

Under this approach, amicable resolution is favoured and settlement can be agreed at any time, including after arbitration proceedings have commenced.[109] Where a dispute cannot be resolved amicably, the claimant may submit a request for consultations to the other party which must usually take place within 60 days.[110] Six months after the submission of this request for consultations, the claimant can submit a claim to the Tribunal of First Instance ("the Tribunal").[111]

The Tribunal is composed of 15 judges, appointed on a permanent basis, with five judges being nationals of a Member State of the EU, five judges being nationals of Vietnam (in the EU-Vietnam FTA) and a further five judges being nationals of third countries.[112] Three judges would hear each individual dispute, with one judge from the EU, one from Vietnam and one from a third country.[113]

The Tribunal is to issue its award within 18 months of the submission of the claim.[114] Any party dissatisfied with the award may approach the Appellate Tribunal on specific grounds including errors in the application or interpretation of applicable law and "manifest errors" in the establishment of the facts, including the establishment of relevant domestic law.[115] The Appellate Tribunal is empowered to uphold, modify, or reverse an award.[116]

The reception that the ICS will have in Asia is yet unknown. In fact, some prominent Asian commentators have expressed their strong discontent with the ICS.[117] However, as the EU and Canada have expressed their strong support for the proposal,[118] and as they are both currently negotiating investment agreements with important Asian states,[119] it is likely that—at least for some Asian states—ICS will replace the traditional investment arbitration framework.

[109]EU-Vietnam FTA, Art. 4.

[110]EU-Vietnam FTA, Art. 4(4).

[111]EU-Vietnam FTA, Art. 7(1).

[112]EU-Vietnam FTA, Art. 12(2).

[113]EU-Vietnam FTA, Art. 12(6).

[114]EU-Vietnam FTA, Art. 27(6).

[115]EU-Vietnam FTA, Art. 28(1).

[116]EU-Vietnam FTA, Art. 28(2)-(3).

[117]Sornarajah (2016).

[118]Joint statement: Canada-EU Comprehensive Economic and Trade Agreement (CETA) available at http://europa.eu/rapid/press-release_STATEMENT-16-446_en.htm.

[119]For instance, Canada and India are presently negotiating a 'Foreign Investment Promotion and Protection Agreement', as are the EU and China.

5 Conclusion

Asia is in the midst of unprecedented economic growth. Foreign investment inflows and outflows are at historic highs. Investment protection instruments like IIAs continue to be critical to the investment framework of the region. In addition, the G20 Principles explicitly place foreign investment very high in terms of international economic policy by indicating that the G20 has "the objective of (i) fostering an open, transparent and conducive global policy environment for investment, (ii) promoting coherence in national and international investment policymaking, and (iii) promoting inclusive economic growth and sustainable development."[120] The combination of favorable regional and global drivers suggest that investment flows and investment policies will gain in importance in the years to come as a key driver of the world economy.

A vast majority of Asian IIAs provide for investment arbitration, both as an element of the regional trade and investment treaty architecture as well as a practical means for resolving disputes. Over 21% of all investment disputes involve Asian states, and these numbers are likely to rise.

Investment arbitration has however been facing a considerable backlash, which is leading to a recalibration of substantive investment disciplines as well as dispute settlement procedures. This backlash has been particularly significant in Asia, with some Asian states exiting from the system altogether and others altering it in material ways.

Several reforms to the present investment arbitration framework have been proposed to reaffirm state control while at the same time retain investor interest. These reforms are particularly significant for Asia, and it is heartening to note that some Asian states are adopting a more refined approach towards investment arbitration. Asia is, however, lagging in some respects. Having considerable investment jurisprudence before them, Asian states are uniquely placed now to benefit from the experiences of others. Besides, the increase of Asia-centric investment flows places Asian states in an increasingly important position to determine the future of global investment governance. This is certainly an exciting time for those dealing with international investment law, particularly in the Asia-Pacific region.

References

Allee, T., and C. Peinhardt. 2010. Delegating differences: Bilateral investment treaties and bargaining over dispute resolution provisions. *International Studies Quarterly* 54: 1.

Allee and Clint Peinhardt. 2011. "Contingent credibility: the impact of investment treaty violations on foreign direct investment," *International Organization* 63: 401–432.

[120]Annex III: G20 Guiding Principles for Global Investment Policymaking.

Behn, Daniel, Berge Tarald Laudal, and Malcolm Langford. 2016. Poor states or poor governance? Explaining outcomes in investment treaty arbitration. Considering investment claims up to May 2016.

Bernasconi-Osterwalder, Nathalie. 2014. State-state dispute settlement in investment treaties. www.iisd.org/sites/default/files/publications/best-practices-state-state-dispute-settlement-investment-treaties.pdf.

Bland, B., and S. Donnan. 2014. Indonesia to terminate more than 60 bilateral investment treaties. *Financial Times*. www.ft.com/cms/s/0/3755c1b2-b4e2-11e3-af92-00144feabdc0.html#axzz42JTevYOq.

Blythe, Stephen. 2013. The advantages of investor-state arbitration as a dispute resolution mechanism in bilateral investment treaties. *The International Lawyer* 47: 273–290.

Brown, Julia. 2013. International investment agreements: Regulatory chill in the face of litigious heat? *Western Journal of Legal Studies* 3: 1.

Bryan Cave. 2015. International investment arbitration in Asia: Year in review. www.lexology.com/library/detail.aspx?g=ecb1496d-a05a-4841-a2c6-703ac8494813.

Chaisse, Julien. 2013. Assessing the exposure of Asian states to investment claims. *Contemporary Asia Arbitration Journal* 6 (187): 202.

Chaisse, Julien. 2015. The shifting tectonics of international investment law—Structure and dynamics of rules and arbitration on foreign investment in the Asia-Pacific region. *George Washington International Law Review* 47: 563.

Chaisse, Julien., and Christian, Bellak. 2015. Navigating the expanding universe of investment treaties—Creation and use of critical index. *Journal of International Economic Law* 18: 79.

Daly, M.J., and T. Ahmad. 2015. The EU-Vietnam FTA: What does it all mean? What does it mean for the future? Kluwer Arbitration Blog. http://kluwerarbitrationblog.com/2015/12/14/the-eu-vietnam-fta-what-does-it-all-mean-what-does-it-mean-for-thefuture/.

Eberhardt, Pia, et al. 2012. Profiting from injustice: How law firms, arbitrators and financiers are fuelling an investment arbitration boom. Corporate Europe Observatory (CEO). http://corporateeurope.org/sites/default/files/publications/profiting-from-injustice.pdf.

Fouret, Julien, and Castal Di Mourre (2015), *Enforcement of investment treaty arbitration awards: A global guide. Globe Law and Business*, 1st ed.

Franck, Susan, and Linsey Wylie. 2015. Predicting outcomes in investment treaty arbitration. *Duke Law Journal* 65: 459.

Gaukrodger, D. 2016. The legal framework applicable to joint interpretive agreements of investment treaties. OECD working papers on international investment. OECD Publishing, Paris http://dx.doi.org/10.1787/5jm3xgt6f29w-en.

Gloria, Maria A., et al. 2016. A response to the criticism against ISDS by EFILA. *Journal of International Arbitration* 33: 1–36.

Haftel, Y.Z., and A. Thompson. 2013. Delayed ratification: The domestic fate of bilateral investment treaties. *International Organization* 67: 355.

Hsu, Locknie. 2012. Asian treaty-makers and investment treaty arbitration: Negotiating with a wary eye. *Contemporary Asia Arbitration Journal* 5 (243): 256.

ICSID, 50 Years of ICSID. www.icsid.worldbank.org/apps/ICSIDWEB/Documents/ICSID%20Timeline%20-%20Featured.pdf.

Ikenson, Dan. 2014. Eight reasons to purge investor-state dispute settlement from trade agreements. www.forbes.com/sites/danikenson/2014/03/04/eight-reasons-to-purge-investor-state-dispute-settlement-from-trade-agreements/.

Kim, Joongi. 2012. A pivot to Asia in investor-state arbitration: The coming emergence of asian claimants. *ICSID Review* 27: 399.

Kaufmann-Kohler, Gabrielle. 2013. Non-disputing state submissions in investment arbitration: Resurgence of diplomatic protection? In *Diplomatic and judicial means of dispute settlement*. ed. Laurence Boisson de Chazournes and others, 305, 308. www.arbitration-icca.org/media/1/13571333245800/diplomatic_protection_and_investment_arbitration_kaufmann-kohler.pdf.

Kollamparambil, Umakrishnan. 2016. Bilateral investment treaties and investor state disputes. ERSA working paper.

Lalive, P., and L. Halonen. 2011. On the availability of counterclaims in investment treaty arbitration. *Czech Yearbook of Public & Private International Law* 479.

Langford, Malcolm, et al. 2016. Storm in a teacup? The international investment regime and state backlash. In *The changing practices of international law: Sovereignty, law and politics in a globalising world*, ed. Thomas Gammeltoft-Hansen and Tanja Aalberts. Cambridge: Cambridge University Press.

Lowenfeld, Andreas. 2003. Investment agreements and international law. *Columbia Journal of Transnational Law* 42 (123): 129.

Malintoppi, Loretta. 2015. Is there an 'Asian way' for investor-state dispute resolution. *KLRCA Newsletter* 19: 12. http://klrca.org/downloads/newsletters/2015Q3newsletter.pdf.

MercoPress, US will vote against loans to Argentina in World Bank and IDB. http://en.mercopress.com/2011/09/29/us-will-vote-against-loans-to-argentina-in-world-bank-and-idb.

Methymaki, Eleni, and Antonios,Tzanakopoulos (forthcoming). Masters of puppets? Reassertion of control through joint investment treaty interpretation. In *Reassertion of control over the investment treaty regime*, ed. Andreas Kulick. Cambridge: Cambridge University Press. http://ssrn.com/abstract=2740127.

Miller, Scott, and Gregory, Hicks. Investor-state dispute settlement: A reality check. https://www.csis.org/analysis/investor-state-dispute-settlement-reality-check-working-paper.

Mitra, Trisha, and Rahul Donde (forthcoming). Claims and counterclaims under Asian multilateral investment treaties. In *Judging the state in international trade and investment law: Modern sovereignty, the law and the economics*, ed. Leila Choukroune. Berlin: Springer.

Monbiot, George. 2013. The real threat to the national interest from the rich and powerful. *The Guardian*.

Nakagawa, Junji. 2007. No more negotiated deals? settlement of trade and investment disputes in East Asia. *Journal of International Economic Law (JIEL)* 10: 837–867. doi:10.1093/jiel/jgm032.

New York Times. 2004. The secret trade courts. Editorial.

Nottage, Luke, and J. Romesh, Romesh Weeramantry. 2012. Investment arbitration in Asia: Five perspectives on law and practice. *Arbitration International* 28: 19.

Nottage, L. 2011. The rise and possible fall of investor-state arbitration in Asia: A skeptic's view of Australia's gillard government trade policy statement. TDM 5. www.transnational-dispute-management.com, www.transnational-dispute-management.com/article.asp?key=1767.

Parra, Antonio. 2014. Advancing reform at ICSID. *Transnational Dispute Management* 11: 9.

Popova, I.C., and F. Poon. 2015. From perpetual respondent to aspiring counterclaimant? State counterclaims in the new wave of investment treaties. *BCDR International Arbitration Review, Kluwer Law International* 2: 223.

Potestà, M. 2013. State-to-state dispute settlement pursuant to bilateral investment treaties: Is there potential? In *International courts and the development of international law: essays in honour of Tullio Treves*, ed. Boschiero, N and others, 753–770. The Hague, The Netherlands: T.M.C. Asser Press.

Rachel L, Wellhausen. 2016. Recent trends in investor–State dispute settlement. *Journal of International Dispute Settlement* 7(1): 117–135. https://doi.org/10.1093/jnlids/idv038.

Roberts, Anthea. 2011. *Harvard International Law Journal* 55: 1, www.harvardilj.org/wp-content/uploads/2014/03/HILJ_55-1_Roberts.pdf.

Rosenberg, Charles. 2013. The intersection of international trade and international arbitration: The use of trade benefits to secure compliance with arbitral awards. *Georgetown Journal of International Law* 44: 503.

Schill, Stephan. 2015. Reforming investor-state dispute settlement (ISDS): Conceptual framework and options for the way forward. E15 initiative Geneva: International Centre for Trade and Sustainable Development (ICTSD) and World Economic Forum. www.e15initiative.org/.

Schill, Stephan. 2016. Changing geography: Prospects for Asian actors as global rule-makers in international investment law. Columbia FDI Perspectives No. 177. http://ccsi.columbia.edu/files/2013/10/No-177-Schill-FINAL.pdf.

Sacerdoti, Giogio. 2014. Trade and investment law: Institutional differences and substantive similarities. *Jerusalem Review of Legal Studies* 9: 4.

Salomon, Claudia, and Sandra Friedrich. 2015. Investment arbitration in East Asia and the Pacific. *Journal of World Investment and Trade* 16: 800, 837.

Sornarajah, M. 2016. An international investment court: Panacea or purgatory. Columbia FDI Perspectives No. 180. www.ccsi.columbia.edu/files/2013/10/No-180-Sornarajah-FINAL.pdf.

The Economist, The arbitration game. 2014.

Tienhaara, Kyla, and Patricia Ranald. 2011. Australia's rejection of investor-state dispute settlement: Four potential contributing factors. www.iisd.org/itn/2011/07/12/australias-rejection-of-investor-state-dispute-settlement-four-potential-contributing-factors/.

Tietje, et al. 2014. The impact of investor-state-dispute settlement (ISDS) in the transatlantic trade and investment partnership. Study prepared for the Minister of Foreign Trade and Development Cooperation, Ministry of Foreign affairs, The Netherlands.

Trakman, Leon, and Kunal Sharma. 2014. Indonesia's termination of the Netherlands–Indonesia BIT: Broader implications in the Asia-Pacific? Kluwer Arbitration Blog. http://kluwerarbitrationblog.com/2014/08/21/indonesias-termination-of-the-netherlands-indonesia-bit-broader-implications-in-the-asia-pacific/.

Trakman, Leon, and Kunal Sharma. 2014. Why is Indonesia terminating its bilateral investment treaties? www.eastasiaforum.org/2014/09/20/why-is-indonesia-terminating-its-bilateral-investment-treaties.

UNCHR. 2003. High commissioner for human rights, human rights, trade and investment. UN doc E/CN.4/Sub.2//2003/9, 35.

UNCTAD. 2016. *Taking stock of IIA reform*, 1. No: International Investment Agreement Issues Note.

UNCTAD. Investor state dispute settlement, UNCTAD series on issues in international investment agreements II. http://unctad.org/en/PublicationsLibrary/diaeia2013d2_en.pdf.

Vandevelde, Kenneth J. 2005. A brief history of international investment agreements' (2005) 12 *U.C. Davis Journal of International Law & Policy* 12: 157.

Van Harten, Gus. 2011. Summary of G. Van Harten, "The use of quantitative methods to examine possible bias in investment arbitration" and "Reply" [to Franck, Garbin, and Perkins] in the Yearbook on International Investment Law & Policy (2011). All Papers, Paper 33.

Van Harten, Gus. 2012. Arbitrator behaviour in asymmetrical adjudication: An empirical study of investment treaty arbitration. *Osgoode Hall Law Journal* 50: 1. http://digitalcommons.osgoode.yorku.ca/cgi/viewcontent.cgi?article=1036&context=ohlj.

Viñuales, J.E., and D. Bentolila. 2012. The use of alternative (non-judicial) means to enforce investment awards. In *Diplomatic and judicial means of dispute settlement: Assessing their interactions*, ed. Boisson de Chazournes, L., and others. The Hague: Brill.

Waibel, M., et al. 2010. The Backlash Against Investment Arbitration: Perceptions and Reality. In: Michael Waibel and others (eds), *The backlash against investment arbitration*. Kluwer Law International.

Wälde, T. 2009. Interpreting investment treaties: Experiences and examples. In *International investment law for the 21st century: Essays in honour of Christopher Schreuer*, ed. C. Binder and others, 724, 737. Oxford: Oxford University Press.

Yannaca-Small, Katia. 2008. Improving the system of investor-state dispute settlement: The OECD governments' perspective. In *Appeals mechanism in international investment disputes* ed. Karl P. Sauvant and Michael Chiswick-Patterson, 223. Oxford: Oxford University Press.

Zhao, Jun, and Liu Yun. 2014. The Transparency Reform in International Investment Arbitration and China's Reactions. *Journal of Zhejiang University* 44: 150–163.

Investor-State Dispute Settlement (ISDS) Cases in the Asia-Pacific Region—The Record

Martina Francesca Ferracane

Abstract The inclusion of Investor-State Dispute Settlement (ISDS) clauses in bilateral trade and investment agreements and in multilateral free trade agreements has recently been a matter of serious debate and it remains a topic dealt under close scrutiny amongst policy-makers. This chapter provides a detailed analysis of the ISDS cases involving countries in the Asia-Pacific region. It points out which countries are most actively involved, a sectoral analysis of the disputes and relevant information regarding the outcome of the cases, including the amounts sought and awarded by tribunals. A regional analysis of ISDS cases is extremely timely given the undergoing reform efforts of the system, as it results evident from the recently agreed text for a Trans-Pacific Partnership (TPP).

1 Introduction

The ISDS mechanism is an international arbitration procedure, which is already contained in more than 3,000 agreements worldwide. In particular, ISDS clauses are included in more than 90% of Bilateral Investment Treaties (BITs) in force today, but also Free Trade Agreements (FTAs) and other arrangements, such as the ASEAN Comprehensive Investment Agreement. Such provision enables investors to bring a case before an international arbitration tribunal if they consider that the host country has violated the rights granted them by an investment agreement. These rights include, inter alia, protection against discrimination, direct and indirect expropriation, unfair and inequitable treatment and restrictions on movement of capital.

The ISDS mechanism was a response to calls by international investors for stronger protection of their investments in countries whose judiciary was deemed

M.F. Ferracane (✉)
Institute of Law and Economics, Hamburg University, Hamburg, Germany
e-mail: martina.ferracane@ile-graduateschool.de

J. Chaisse et al. (eds.), *Asia's Changing International Investment Regime*,
International Law and the Global South, DOI 10.1007/978-981-10-5882-0_13

not fully independent from the government. An international arbitration was considered a more neutral framework than national courts to ensure enforcement of the host state's obligations towards investors.[1] Moreover, it was also seen as a more flexible instrument than State-to-State disputes.[2]

Today, however, this mechanism has been increasingly used to file claims among developed countries and, indeed, 40% of the cases initiated in 2014 have been against developed countries, compared with an historical average of 28%.[3] Beyond the potential for bias of domestic courts, the preference for international arbitration is to relate to the fact that the arbitrators chosen are specialized in ISDS cases and therefore considered more competent in addressing those cases and to the fact that the arbitration process is often more flexible and rapid than the alternative of a national court procedure.

In order to analyze the record of the ISDS cases in the Asia-Pacific region, the paper proceeds as follows: the first section will examine and compare outward FDI stock and the number of filed ISDS disputes on both a global and regional stance; the second part will take a closer look at the evolution of ISDS proceedings on a country basis; the outcome and the awards of the cases, on the one hand, and a debate on ISDS with regards to current and future trade and investment agreements will be analyzed in the third and fourth section respectively, before concluding with some final remarks.

2 The Record

The first multilateral instrument for resolving investment disputes between investor and State—the International Centre for Settlement of Investment Disputes (ICSID)—was established by the World Bank in 1966. As of today, 161 countries have ratified the ICSID Convention to become Contracting States.[4] However, the earliest attempt to compile statistics on investor-State cases was an initiative of the United Nations Conference on Trade and Development (UNCTAD) and covers cases initiated from 1987. Today, there is still no official public registry for all ISDS cases and several arbitration forums do not maintain a register of the claims.[5] Therefore, any analysis of this instrument has to rely on the limited set of information publicly available.

According to the latest data available, the overall number of known ISDS claims up to the year 2015 is 696.[6] The number of cases has been growing firmly since

[1]Latek and Puccio (2015).

[2]US Trade Representative (2015).

[3]UNCTAD (2014a).

[4]The updated list is available at the ICSID website at the link https://icsid.worldbank.org/apps/ICSIDWEB/about/Pages/Database-of-Member-States.bak.aspx.

[5]UNCTAD (2014b).

[6]Data retrieved from the Investment Dispute Settlement Navigator in May 2016. Available at http://investmentpolicyhub.unctad.org/ISDS.

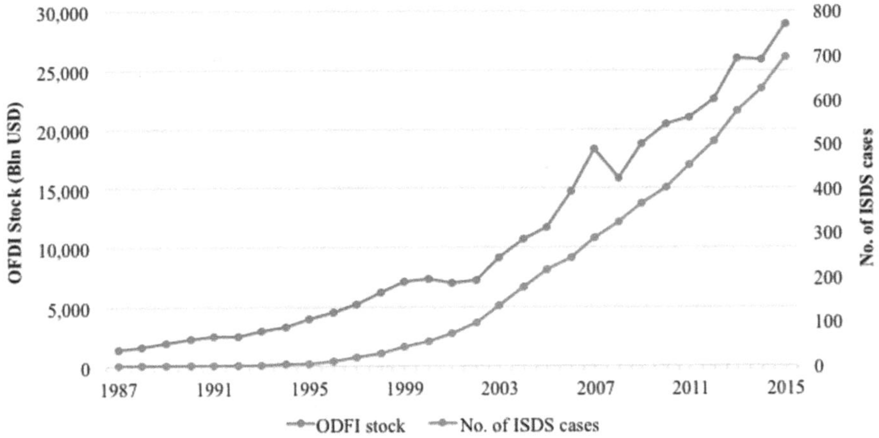

Fig. 1 Outward FDI stock and number of ISDS cases, 1987–2015. *Source* Own calculations based on UNCTADstat and Investment Dispute Settlement Navigator. Data retrieved in May 2016. *Note* The OFDI value for 2015 is estimated using average growth rate for the period 1987–2014

1987, reflecting the likewise steady growth of the amount of investment stock in the world (Fig. 1). While less than 100 cases were initiated in the period 1987–2002, the accumulated number of cases nearly tripled by 2007 and doubled again by 2013. Similarly, the stock of Foreign Direct Investment (FDI) globally has increased tenfold since 1990.

That is also the case when the analysis is restricted to the economies in the Asia-Pacific region, where the growth of the ISDS cases and the growth of outward stock of FDI largely follow the same trend (Fig. 2).

Overall, investors from Asia-Pacific countries have started only 4% of all ISDS cases. More specifically, they initiated 24 cases out of the 696 ISDS recorded by the end of 2015. Their participation in investment disputes has been significantly less than proportional to the share of the Asia-Pacific region in global FDI stock. In fact, in the same period around one fifth of the global stock of FDI came from the Asia-Pacific region.

2.1 *The Growth of Dispute Intensity*

Relatively few cases were initiated globally in the first decade for which data is available. In fact, only 19 ISDS cases had been brought to international arbitration courts by 1997—of which none was initiated by investors from Asia-Pacific countries (Fig. 3).

During the late 1990s, the number of cases started to raise, with a sharp increase in the last decade. That has not been the case for economies in Asia-Pacific, whose

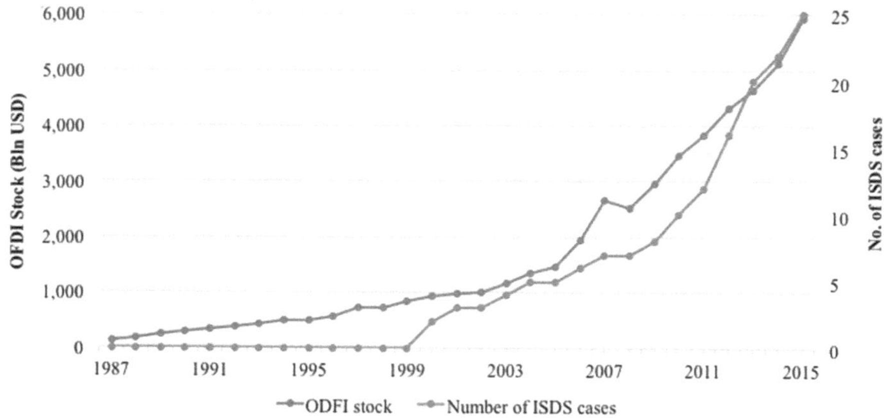

Fig. 2 Outward FDI stock and number of ISDS cases started by investors from the Asia-Pacific Region, 1987–2015. *Source* Own calculations based on UNCTADstat and Investment Dispute Settlement Navigator. Data retrieved in May 2016

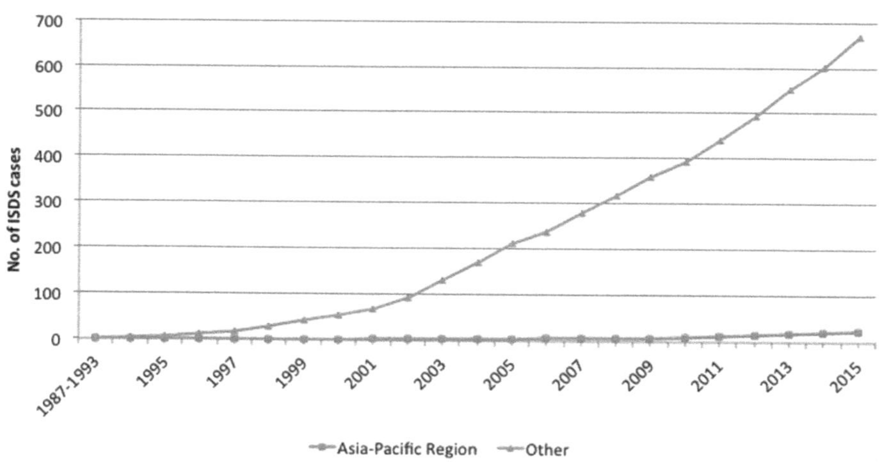

Fig. 3 ISDS cases filed by investors from Asia-Pacific countries versus the rest of the world, 1987–2015. *Source* Own calculations based on Investment Dispute Settlement Navigator. Data retrieved in May 2016

participation remained relatively modest. The first registered case filed by an Asia-Pacific country was only in the year 2000. The year 2013 saw the highest number of cases filed by investors from the Asia-Pacific region (4 cases), while the peak globally was in 2015 (with a total of 70 cases started).

More than half of the cases started by investors in Asia-Pacific are filed against a country in the Asia-Pacific region. In total, there have been 15 intra-regional cases.

Of the 24 cases initiated by investors based in Asia-Pacific, 14 were filed with the International Centre for Settlement of Investment Disputes (of which 2 cases were under the ICSID Additional Facility Rules), 7 under the arbitration rules of UNCITRAL and 2 under the Moscow Chamber of Commerce. For the remaining case, there is no public information available.

2.2 *Cases by Country*

Globally, the United States (US) has brought the highest number of cases to investor-State arbitration (22% of all ISDS cases). It is not surprising that the US is the most frequent initiator of ISDS cases, as it accounts for roughly a fourth of global outward FDI stock.

Of the total 24 cases started by investors located in the Asia-Pacific region, investors from China and Kazakhstan are the most actively involved claimants, with 4 cases each. Investors from Korea, India, Malaysia and Australia have filed 3 cases each, while two cases were brought forward by investors in Singapore and one case by investors in Hong Kong and Japan.[7] As of 2015, all the other countries in the Asia-Pacific region have not started any case. The main respondent to cases started by investors in Asia-Pacific countries has been Kyrgyzstan (4 cases), followed by Indonesia (3 cases) and China (2 cases).

On the other hand, Asia-Pacific countries have responded to 116 cases since 1987. India is the most frequent respondent to ISDS cases (17 cases), followed by Kazakhstan (15 cases) and Kyrgyzstan (12 cases).[8]

2.3 *Sectoral Distribution of the Claims*

When looking at the sectoral distribution of ISDS, it emerges that the majority of cases initiated globally relates to the services sector (about 61% in 2014).[9] These include the supply of electricity or gas, telecommunications, construction, tourism and financial services, among others. The majority of the remaining claims involve investments in the primary sector—including mining, oil and gas (about 28% in 2014). Finally, manufacturing industry represents 11% of the ISDS cases started in 2014.

A detailed analysis of sectoral data shows that the distribution of claims brought against countries in the Asia-Pacific region follows a similar pattern. In the period 1987–2015, 66% of the cases relate to the service sector and include mainly claims

[7]Full list available in Annex 1.

[8]Full list available in Annex 2.

[9]UNCTAD (2015).

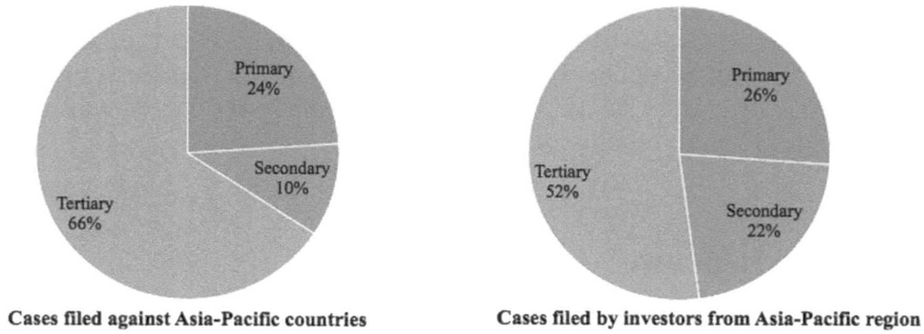

Fig. 4 Sectoral distribution of ISDS cases in the Asia-Pacific region, 1987–2015. *Source* Own calculations based on Investment Dispute Settlement Navigator. Data retrieved in May 2016

on electricity or gas, information and communication, financial activities and transportation (Fig. 4). Of the remaining cases, 24% refers to investments in the primary sector (mainly mining and quarrying), while 10% arise from the manufacturing industry.

When looking instead at cases started by investors originating from countries in the Asia-Pacific region, the representation of cases in manufacturing sectors in somewhat higher (22%), while the services sector covers 52% of the claims.

According to a study by the OECD on 95 concluded cases world-wide, claimants seeking international investment arbitration range from 'an association of retirees' to multi-national companies.[10] More specifically, 22% of the claimants in the sample are either individuals or small corporations, while 48% of the cases in the sample were brought by medium and large enterprises. Of these, 8% are large multinationals. For the rest of the cases in the sample, little or no public information about the claimant was available.

2.4 *The Outcome of Arbitrations*

According to the latest statistics available, the global number of concluded cases reached 356 in 2014.[11] Of these, 37% were decided in favor of the State, 25% in favor of the investor and 28% of the cases settled. The remaining 10% of the cases were either discontinued for reasons other than settlement (8% of the cases) or a treaty breach was found but no monetary compensation was awarded to the investor (2% of the cases).

When considering Asia-Pacific countries as respondents to claims, there is a significantly lower share of cases won by the State (28%) than the global average

[10]Gaukrodger and Gordon (2012).

[11]UNCTAD (2015).

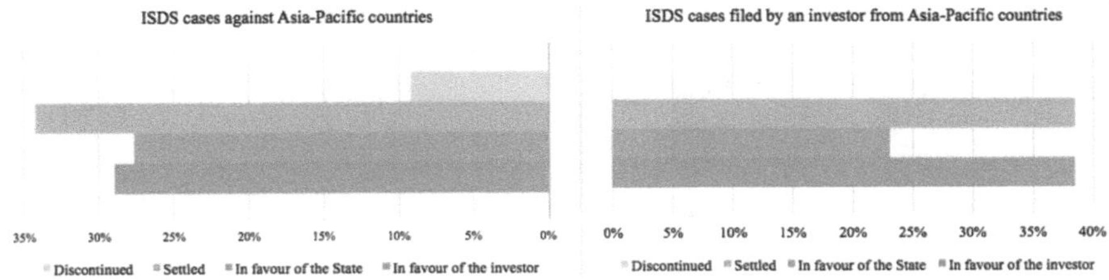

Fig. 5 Outcome of arbitration cases involving Asia-Pacific countries, 1987–2015. *Source* Investment Dispute Settlement Navigator and own calculations as of May 2016

(Fig. 5). The arbitration panel has ruled in favor of the investor in 29% of the cases, while a significant portion of the cases were deemed to be settled before an arbitration ruling (34%). The remaining 9% of the cases were discontinued.

On the other hand, when investors from Asia-Pacific countries have started an ISDS case, the picture changes. It is more likely that the case is awarded to the investor (38% of the cases, as shown in Fig. 5). Nonetheless, in 38% of the cases, the two parties settled in advance of an arbitration ruling, while the arbitration panel has sided with the State in 23% of the cases. No discontinued cases have been reported.

2.5 *Awards*

Information relating to the pecuniary amounts demanded and awarded is not always disclosed on a case-by case basis. In particular, for those cases that do not go through the entire process of the dispute procedure—given an advanced settlement prior to an arbitration ruling—the specific terms of settlement usually remain confidential.

When information on the outcome of the case is available, it emerges that the amount claimed by the investor is not fully awarded and usually only a small percentage of the original claim is indeed awarded. According to an analysis by the Arbitration Institute of the Stockholm Chamber of Commerce (SCC), 61% of the investment awards rendered by the institute were substantially less than the amount claimed, while 28% of the claimants were awarded about half of the claimed amounts and the remaining 11% obtained almost the entire amount claimed.

A study published in the North Carolina Law Review analysing 82 concluded cases reports that the average amount claimed for these cases was US$343.5 million, with an average amount awarded by tribunals of US$10.4 million.[12] A more recent study on an enlarged dataset confirms that on average the inflation-adjusted

[12]Franck (2007).

Table 1 Amount ratio in awards in favour of the investor in ISDS cases against Asia-Pacific countries, 1987–2015

Home state of investor (claimant)	Respondent state	Year	Ratio amount awarded/amount sought
United Kingdom	Sri Lanka	1987	6%
United States	Kazakhstan	1996	n/a
United States	Kazakhstan	2001	44%
United Kingdom	Kyrgyzstan	2003	27%
Italy	Georgia	2005	n/a
Greece	Georgia	2005	50%
Turkey	Kazakhstan	2005	27%
Italy	Bangladesh	2005	50%
Germany	Thailand	2005	25%
Turkey	Kyrgyzstan	2006	34%
Israel	Georgia	2007	50%
Turkey	Georgia	2008	n/a
Germany	Turkmenistan	2009	n/a
Germany	Sri Lanka	2009	100%
Moldova	Kazakhstan	2010	19%
Australia	India	2010	46%
Latvia	Kyrgyzstan	2011	15%
Canada	Mongolia	2011	22%
United Kingdom	Uzbekistan	2011	1%
Korea	Kyrgyzstan	2013	n/a
Kazakhstan	Kyrgyzstan	2013	n/a

For the calculations, the raw sums awarded (without interest rates) have been considered. When not available, they were calculated
Source Investment Dispute Settlement Navigator and own calculations as of May 2016

damage claimed was around US$622 million, while the average amount awarded was around US$16.6 million.[13]

In the case of claimants from Asia-Pacific, investors claimed compensation amounts between US$2.3 million and US$4 billion—when the request was disclosed. However, the amount awarded by tribunals ranged from US$460,000 to US $497 million.[14]

There have been a total of 21 cases against countries in the Asia-Pacific region that have been awarded to the investor. Even though information about the amount sought by the investor is not always clear, it is nonetheless possible to retrieve an overall estimate of the amount initially sought and the amount that the investor has actually been awarded. An overview of the results of the analysis is presented in Table 1. Only in 5 cases, the investor has been awarded more than 50% of the

[13]Franck (2014).

[14]Investment Dispute Settlement Navigator and own calculations as of May 2016.

amount sought, and in only 2 cases the amount awarded to the investor was equal to the one initially sought.

Overall, the ratio between amount sought and the amount awarded by the investor is 39% in the region.

2.6 *The Debate*

Recently, the ISDS mechanism has come under the spotlight during the negotiations of important agreements such as the Comprehensive Trade and Economic Agreement (CETA) between Canada and the EU, the Trans-Pacific Partnership (TPP) and the Transatlantic Trade and Investment Partnership (TTIP) between the United States and the EU.

In a number of countries, there has been opposition to the inclusion of the mechanism in international agreements as it is argued that the system contains flaws that allow investors to challenge domestic health, environmental and social regulations. In particular, the lack of transparency around the mechanism, the inconsistency of certain decisions and the high cost of the procedures are criticized as serious obstacles to ensure the legitimacy of the process.[15]

An often cited example is the case brought against a country in the Asia-Pacific region—Australia—by the tobacco multinational Philip Morris, which challenged the Government's regulation on plain packaging of tobacco products. This case also shows the extent of the challenge of treaty shopping resulting from the global IIAs spaghetti bowl. The US-headquartered Philipp Morris would not be allowed to start an ISDS case against the Australian Government, because of the absence of an ISDS clause in the US-Australia FTA. Yet, the company was able to launch the proceedings via its Asian subsidiary based in Hong Kong, China.[16] In December 2015, the arbitration tribunal concluded that it did not have jurisdiction to hear Philip Morris's claim.[17]

The financial burden of arbitration proceedings and the sovereignty costs associated with the implementation of these treaties have been recently considered by some countries to outweigh the benefits of BITs. Bolivia, Ecuador and Venezuela have terminated several BITs and have withdrawn from ICSID, while the Australian government announced, in spring 2011, that it would no longer include investor-State dispute settlement provisions in its trade agreements. A new Government subsequently weakened this policy and inclusion in each new agreement is considered on a case-by-case basis. ISDS provisions have, in fact, been

[15]European Parliamentary Research Service (2014).

[16]Chaisse and Hamanaka (2014).

[17]The award on jurisdiction and admissibility is available at the following link: http://www.italaw.com/sites/default/files/case-documents/italaw7303_0.pdf.

included in recent agreements, as for example the China-Australia FTA entered into force in December 2015 and the recently signed TPP agreement.

Moreover, South Africa has announced that it will not renew old investment treaties due to their expiry and started to cancel some of its bilateral investment treaties. India is reported to have decided not to include investor-State dispute provisions in future free trade agreements and Indonesia has recently announced that intends to terminate more than 60 bilateral investment treaties.[18]

The inclusion of ISDS in major agreements such as CETA, TPP and TTIP faced serious opposition. However, the negotiating partners have seen the discussions as an opportunity to promote an alternative to the current system by seeking 'an agreement among the parties on a high-standard approach to resolving international investment disputes'—which could therefore serve as a blueprint for future agreements.[19]

Therefore, concrete proposals have been brought forward to improve the ISDS system with the view to strike a balance between investment protection and governments' sovereign right to regulate. On one hand, the investment chapter of the Trans-Pacific Partnership agreement includes a series of provisions aimed at ensuring the government's' ability to regulate in areas of public welfare, financial regulation, environment and health—including with an explicit "tobacco exception" which prevents claims based on tobacco regulations.

The agreement includes a series of safeguards such as binding joint interpretation by the parties; increased transparency by opening the hearings to the public as well as public notices of arbitration, pleadings, submissions and awards; a limitation of investors access to the mechanism (e.g. with an expedited review of frivolous claims); an explicit limitation of remedies to monetary damages; the possibility of third parties intervention by filing amicus curiae submissions; the review of the awards by either domestic courts or international review panels; and consolidation of different arbitration proceedings to avoid parallel proceedings.

However, a major backtrack from a US policy perspective has been the lack of an appellate mechanism, to which post-2000 US IIAs have either required or strongly aspired.[20] The presence of an appellate mechanism has been often advocated as an important tool to correct erroneous arbitral awards if necessary and to lead to a more consistent system by ensuring a uniform interpretation of a specific agreement. This would enhance the legal certainty and predictability of arbitral awards and put an end to cherry-picked interpretations of certain provisions.[21]

On the other hand, the talks on investment protection and ISDS under the Transatlantic Trade and Investment Partnership were put on hold in early 2014, after the European Commission announced it would suspend them in order to solicit public comment on the matter. In November 2015, the European Commission formally transmitted to the Unites States its proposal for 'Investment Protection and

---

[18]ECIPE (2014).

[19]US Trade Representative (2015).

[20]Sampliner (2013).

[21]Ferracane (2015).

Resolution of Investment Disputes'.[22] The proposal aims to fundamentally transform the current arbitration tribunals into a court system. The new Investment Court System (ICS) would be composed of a First Instance Tribunal and an Appeal Tribunal, with publicly appointed judges and with a limited and precisely defined scope. The system also covers a wide range of safeguards similar to those presented in TPP investment chapter. They include full transparency of all documents and hearings, a ban on forum shopping, government control of interpretation, a strict code of conduct for arbitrators, early dismissal of unfounded claims, a losers pays principle to avoid frivolous claims and a system to prevent parallel claims.[23]

While the proposal still needs to be debated with the American counterparts, the ICS has been included in the text of the EU-Vietnam FTA—which was agreed in January 2016. Moreover, the text of the concluded CETA agreement was re-opened to include the new approach on investment protection. In addition to the inclusion of the ICS system, the reviewed CETA text presents a stronger language on the right to regulate of governments, more detailed commitments on ethics of members of tribunal and a commitment to set up a multilateral investment court with a standing appellate mechanism.[24]

In fact, the European Commission has accompanied its actions with the endeavor to bring forward the concept of a permanent International Investment Court, which would represent a multilateral alternative to the current ISDS system. Given the different directions undertaken in the current discussions, the debate remains open and it is not clear whether it will emerge a single alternative system, which is supported internationally.

3 Conclusions

From an analysis of the ISDS cases involving countries in the Asia-Pacific region, it emerges that their participation in investment disputes is less than proportional to their share in global FDI stock. They have initiated a total of 24 cases since 1987 (only 4% of the 696 cases recorded globally by 2015), while their share in the global outward stock of FDI in 2014 was close to 20%.

Investors from China and Kazakhstan started 4 ISDS cases, which is extremely moderate compared to over 130 cases initiated by American companies. Investors from most of the Asia-Pacific countries have not started any case. On the other hand, Asia-Pacific countries have responded to 116 cases of which 15 are intra-regional cases.

The main respondent state among Asia-Pacific countries is India (17 cases), followed by Kazakhstan (15 cases) and Kyrgyzstan (12 cases).

---

[22]The text of the proposal is available at the following link: http://trade.ec.europa.eu/doclib/docs/2015/november/tradoc_153955.pdf.

[23]Ferracane (2015).

[24]European Commission (2016).

Cases filed by investors from the Asia-Pacific are mainly in the tertiary sector (52% of the cases), but the proportion of cases regarding the manufacturing sector and the primary sector remains substantial.

Contrary to the general pattern that can be identified globally, the cases started by investors from Asia-Pacific countries show a higher probability to be awarded to the investor than to the State (38% of the cases). If we consider cases against countries in the Asia-Pacific region, it is most likely that the case would be settled (34%).

For those cases where the claimant is successful, the amount claimed is usually not fully awarded and only a small part of the original claim is awarded. On average, the investors from the Asia-Pacific region have been awarded 39% of the amount sought.

The ISDS mechanism has been at the core of a vigorous debate in the last years, especially since Philip Morris challenged the decision by the Australian Government to impose plain tobacco packaging. The inclusion of an ISDS clause in several agreements has been on the spotlight and a potential obstacle to the conclusion of these FTAs.

Current discussions on concrete proposals to improve the ISDS system are ongoing. Given the reality of increasingly growing investment stemming from developing countries as well as the globalized nature of investment, the results of current discussions around mega-regional trade agreements could serve as a blueprint for future agreements with the view to strike a balance between investment protection and sovereign right to regulate.

The debate, however, remains open and it is not clear whether from the current discussions it will emerge a single alternative system, which is supported internationally.

Annex 1: Ranking of Countries According to the Number of ISDS Initiated by Investors Located in the Country

Home investor	No. of ISDS initiated
China	4
Kazakhstan	4
Australia	3
India	3
Korea, Republic Of	3
Malaysia	3
Singapore	2
Hong Kong, China SAR	1
Japan	1

Source Own calculations based on Investment Dispute Settlement Navigator. Data retrieved in May 2016

Annex 2: Ranking of Countries According to the Number of ISDS Cases Failed Against Them

Respondent state	No. of ISDS respondents
India	17
Kazakhstan	15
Kyrgyzstan	12
Pakistan	9
Georgia	8
Turkmenistan	8
Uzbekistan	7
Indonesia	6
Mongolia	4
Philippines	4
Viet Nam	4
Korea, Republic of	3
Malaysia	3
Sri Lanka	3
Armenia	2
Azerbaijan	2
China	2
Lao People's Democratic Republic	2
Australia	1
Bangladesh	1
Myanmar	1
Tajikistan	1
Thailand	1

Source Own calculations based on Investment Dispute Settlement Navigator. Data retrieved in May 2016

References

Chaisse, J., and S. Hamanaka. 2014. *The investment version of the Asian noodle bowl: The proliferation of international investment agreements*. ADB Working Paper Series on Regional Economic Integration No. 128/2014. https://aric.adb.org/pdf/workingpaper/WP128_Hamanaka_Investment_Noodle_Bowl.pdf.

ECIPE. 2014. Demystifying investor-state dispute settlement (ISDS). ECIPE Occasional Paper No. 5/2014. By Roderick Abbott, Fredrik Erixon, and Martina Francesca Ferracane. http://www.ecipe.org/app/uploads/2014/12/OCC52014__1.pdf.

European Commission. 2016. *CETA: EU and Canada agree on new approach on investment in trade agreement*. Press release on February 29, 2016. http://europa.eu/rapid/press-release_IP-16-399_en.htm.

European Parliamentary Research Service. 2014. *Investor-state dispute settlement (ISDS)—State of play and prospects for reform*, Briefing on January 21, 2014. http://www.europarl.europa.eu/RegData/bibliotheque/briefing/2014/130710/LDM_BRI(2014)130710_REV2_EN.pdf.
Ferracane, M.F. 2015. *Realpolitik in ISDS reform: Will the commission's proposal get us anywhere?* November 2015. http://ecipe.org/blog/realpolitik-in-isds-reform-will-the-commissions-proposal-get-us-anywhere/.
Franck, Susan D. 2007. Empirically evaluating claims about investment treaty arbitration. *North Carolina Law Review*, December 2007. http://papers.ssrn.com/sol3/papers.cfm?abstract_id=969257.
Franck, S.D. 2014. *Using investor-state mediation rules to promote conflict management: An introductory guide*. Washington & Lee Legal Studies Paper No. 2014-13. Washington and Lee University—School of Law, February 2, 2014. http://papers.ssrn.com/sol3/papers.cfm?abstract_id=2389763.
Gaukrodger, D., and Gordon, K. 2012. Investor-state dispute settlement: A scoping paper for the Investment Policy Community. *OECD Working Papers on International Investment*, 2012/03, 17–19. OECD Publishing. http://dx.doi.org/10.1787/5k46b1r85j6f-en.
Latek, M., and L. Puccio. 2015. Investor-state dispute settlement (ISDS)—State of play and prospects for reform. *European Parliament Briefing*. http://www.europarl.europa.eu/thinktank/en/document.html?reference=EPRS_BRI(2015)545736.
Sampliner, G.H. 2013. Arbitration and innovations in recent U.S. investment treaties. In *International Arbitration: Contemporary Issues and Innovations*, ed. J.N. Moore. Martinus Nijhoff Publishers.
UNCTAD. 2014a. *Investor-state dispute settlement: An information note on the United States and the European Union. No. 2*, June 2014. http://unctad.org/en/PublicationsLibrary/webdiaepcb2014d4_en.pdf.
UNCTAD. 2014b. *Recent developments in investor-state dispute settlement (ISDS)*. IIA Issues Note No. 1, April 2014. http://unctad.org/en/PublicationsLibrary/webdiaepcb2014d3_en.pdf.
UCNTAD. 2015. *Recent trends in IIAs and ISDS, No. 1*, February 2015. http://unctad.org/en/PublicationsLibrary/webdiaepcb2015d1_en.pdf.
United States Trade Representative. 2015. *Fact sheet: Investor state dispute settlement*. https://ustr.gov/about-us/policy-offices/press-office/fact-sheets/2015/march/investor-state-dispute-settlement-isds.

Databases

Investment Dispute Settlement Navigator: http://investmentpolicyhub.unctad.org/ISDS.
UNCTADstat: http://unctadstat.unctad.org/wds/.

Breaking the Market Dominance of ICSID? An Assessment of the Likelihood of Institutional Competition, Especially from Asia, in the Near Future

Andrea K. Bjorklund and Bryan H. Druzin

1 Introduction

This chapter examines the possibility of the emergence of an alternative centre for investment arbitration—a very much debated, if not favoured, option in Asian policy circles—from a law and economics angle, conceptualizing investment arbitration in market terms.[1] We argue that, given the current market dominance of the International Centre for Settlement of Investment Disputes (ICSID), the emergence of competition from Asia or from somewhere else should be constrained by network externalities (what is known as network effects in the literature).[2] Network effects arise where the implicit value of a service (or product) increases as the number of other agents using the same service grows. As more users use the service and its utility is enhanced, additional consumers flock to the service, and on it goes, creating a positive feedback loop. When a market has settled upon a single standard for the service with all competitors eliminated or significantly marginalized, the market is

[1]Law and Economics utilizes economic concepts to explain legal processes and their effects. An economic analysis of law may be extraordinarily useful in identifying the economic dynamics that underlie legal institutions. Throughout the discussion, we use terms such as 'market dominance', 'market share', and 'monopoly' that may, at first blush, seem ill-fitted to describe investment arbitration. Conceptualizing the topic in such terms, however, provides a great deal of explanatory power, as we will show.
[2]We use the terms 'network externaities' and 'network effects' interchangeably throughout the discussion.

A.K. Bjorklund
Faculty of Law, McGill University, Montreal, Canada
e-mail: andrea.bjorklund@mcgill.ca

B.H. Druzin (✉)
Faculty of Law, The Chinese University of Hong Kong, Sha Tin, Hong Kong
e-mail: bryandruzin@cuhk.edu.hk

J. Chaisse et al. (eds.), *Asia's Changing International Investment Regime*, International Law and the Global South, DOI 10.1007/978-981-10-5882-0_14

said to have "tipped."[3] Once a market has tipped, it creates a monopoly-type situation that prevents potential rivals from successfully challenging the market dominance of the prevailing standard.[4] The market for investment arbitration seems to have tipped. Because ICSID effectively dominates the investment arbitration service world, which can be understood as a market for specific legal services, network effects are being generated that bolster and entrench this market dominance, limiting and even precluding competition from Asia (or elsewhere).

However, while we feel this model is robust and its impact discernible in the current investment arbitration environment, certain exogenous events could substantially reduce or altogether annihilate the network effect. The possibility of these 'disruptive events' does not contradict the model; rather they make the model more nuanced. Network effects suggest that the robust emergence of an alternative centre for investment arbitration would prove extremely difficult; however, given several unknown factors, it remains a possibility. For example, the European Union has proposed establishing a "permanent" court and Appellate Body in the EU-Vietnam Free Trade Agreement and in the Comprehensive Trade and Economic Agreement between Canada and the European Union (CETA)—and has proposed that a similar body be included in the Transatlantic Trade and Investment Partnership (T-TIP). The question is which institution (or institutions) will host these bodies, and whether these agreements ever enter into force. At present, the European Union has proposed either the Permanent Court of Arbitration (PCA) or ICSID as administrators in T-TIP and in the EU-Vietnam FTA, but ICSID alone has been chosen as the administering institution in CETA; however, in principle, any number of institutions may be selected. Whether or not the European Union becomes a party to the ICSID Convention might play a role in ICSID's continued dominance. Also considered are regional preferences. For instance, Singapore has established itself as a premier centre for commercial arbitration and has recently (January 2017) released rules specific to investment arbitration. It, or some similar institution or even a combination of institutions, may yet succeed in displacing the market dominance of ICSID. Such exogenous factors would short-circuit the network effect pressures in the market for investment arbitration, as would other potentially disruptive events. The conclusion we reach is that network effects are indeed currently at play and powerfully reinforce the market dominance of ICSID. While this dominance is likely to continue in the foreseeable future, the long-term continuation of ICSID's dominance in the market for investment arbitration is by no means guaranteed.

[3]William Page et al. (2000, pp. 952, 960). *See also* Schelling (1978, pp. 92–94, 98–99).

[4]The use of the term 'monopoly' here is carefully deployed. ICSID may be understood as a monopoly in that the network externalities that inhere in the market for investment arbitration inhibit market competition, creating barriers to entry. For all intense and purposes the dynamic functions as a monopoly. ICSID is not, however, a monopoly in the strict sense of a firm strategically engaging in anti-competitive practices.

2 Network Effects Unpacked

The idea of network effects is relatively straightforward. A network effect occurs where the implicit value of a product or service increases as the number of other agents using the product or service grows, which in turn draws more users.[5] The often-used example of a network effect is language.[6] Language is fundamentally predisposed to a network effect.[7] The more people who, for example, speak English, the more useful English is to each one of its speakers. This creates a positive externality. As English grows in popularity, so too does its value, encouraging further growth in a 'snowball-like' fashion.[8] There are numerous other examples of network effects—telephone networks, railway gauges, computer software, credit cards, videotape standards, currencies, electrical outlets, screw thread sizes, even time zones. The dynamic reinforces bourgeoning patterns, causing the patterns to become progressively more entrenched over time, which ultimately gives rise to a monolithic standard. Network effects render a highly interconnected system unable to sustain multiple equilibria for long periods because the force of network effects pushes the market towards a single dominant standard—in this case, a dominant standard in the market for investment arbitration services.

3 How Network Effects Reinforce the Market Dominance of ICSID

The network externalities that underpin and reinforce ICSID are a species of network effects known in the literature as *indirect network effects*.[9] Network effects can emerge with respect to a wide variety of goods or services beyond merely physically networked items, such as telecommunications, or networks that rely on direct interaction between users, as in the case of languages. The literature distinguishes between network externalities that involve direct interaction between network

---

[5]*See* Liebowitz et al. (1998, pp. 671, 671).

[6]For a very good overview of other network effect examples in a wide range of contexts, *see* Ferrell and Klemperer (2006, pp. 46–54).

[7]Lemley and McGowan (1998). ("Language, for example, is the fundamental medium of communication and could be said to have both negligible inherent value to the first speaker and increasing value over the range of additional speakers."); *see also* Liebowitz and Margolis (1994, pp. 133, 136); Aviram (2003, p. 15). For a more in-depth analysis of the network effects of language, *see*, e.g., Church and King (1993, p. 337).

[8]*See* Druzin (2009, pp. 131, 151) (arguing that network effects induce standardization in choice of law and choice of forum clauses in transnational commercial contracts).

[9]As opposed to direct network effects, which derive their force purely from the synchronization value they provide. For a deeper explanation of this distinction, *see* ibid 149–53.

participants (direct network effects) and those that involve "mediation through the marketplace" in the form of decreased costs, etc. (indirect network effects).[10] While less obvious, indirect network externalities can exert significant pressure on a market.

To illustrate the power of indirect network effects, consider taxi cabs in Hong Kong. Virtually every taxi cab in Hong Kong is the identical car model—a Toyota Crown Comfort YXS10. There is, however, no regulatory requirement stipulating that cabbies use this model. The Toyota Crown Comfort YXS10 gained ascendancy as a consequence of indirect network externalities stemming from its widespread use. For instance, because it is widely used, the price of replacement parts for the Toyota Crown Comfort YXS10 is comparatively cheap, auto body shops able to service the vehicle are more numerous, and the automobile is more easily visible as a taxi to potential patrons. Now consider the position of a new taxi driver plugging into this powerful system of indirect network externalities who is theoretically 'free' to select any model of car he or she wishes. The driver will effectively be compelled to purchase the Toyota Crown Comfort YXS10, which in turn further reinforces the car's market dominance. This network effect is indirect—the effect is 'mediated through the marketplace.' Indeed, the advent of the automobile itself is a good example of indirect network effects in action. Initially, the lack of suitable roads during the early days of the automobile was an issue. However, as more people purchased cars, more surfaced roads were built to better accommodate motorized vehicles. With more surfaced roads, the utility of owning a motor vehicle increased, attracting more consumers. And on it went in a self-reinforcing process.

We argue that indirect network effects are manifest with respect to the dominance of the ICSID in the market for investment arbitration. Indirect network effects emerge in primarily three ways. The first relates to a general impression of institutional legitimacy. An arbitration centre's reputation will increase commensurate with growth in its user base. An institution that is a recognized authority will attract more "users," thereby increasing its user base in a self-reinforcing fashion. This appears to be the case with the ICSID, which has experienced escalating growth over the last two decades.[11]

These numbers could of course simply reflect growth in the number of investment arbitration cases, and it is true that in the past several years the filing of non-ICSID Convention cases[12] has also increased. The Pluricourts Centre of Excellence at the University of Oslo has data showing that approximately 38.3% of the 760 registered investment cases have *not* been ICSID Convention cases.[13]

[10] Liebowitz and Margolis (1995a, b, p. 1).

[11] https://icsid.worldbank.org/apps/ICSIDWEB/resources/Documents/ICSID%20Web%20Stats%202016-1%20(English)%20final.pdf (p. 7).

[12] For purposes of this article the term "ICSID cases" refers to cases submitted under the ICSID Convention and its accompanying arbitration rules, but does not encompass other cases administered by ICSID but submitted under other arbitral rules, such as the ICSID additional facility rules or the UNCITRAL rules.

[13] Behn (2016).

The ratio of ICSID to non-ICSID cases varies from year to year. UNCTAD's (2015a, b) Issues Note shows ICSID and non-ICSID cases as having been instituted in approximately equal numbers for some years, but with ICSID cases eclipsing those of its (collective) rivals in others.[14] Overall ICSID's market share seems to be holding steady or even slightly increasing as the total number of cases has increased. Thus, we believe its market-dominant position—with 61.7% of known treaty cases submitted under the ICSID Convention, and even more administered by the Centre under other arbitration rules—is well established.

The fact that ICSID is widely recognized and extensively used provides a certain reassurance to claimants. As of April 2016 ICSID boasted 161 signatory States and 153 States Party to the ICSID Convention.[15] Because contracting member states agree to enforce and uphold ICSID arbitral awards as if they are final judgments of their own courts, actors are confident that ICSID awards will be honoured and enforced. This impression of legitimacy only strengthens as its customer base increases—a classic self-reinforcing process.

The second indirect network effect we identify relates to predictability and familiarity regarding the rules and procedures of the institution. With widespread use, users gain a greater familiarity with the rules and procedures of that particular institution. Indeed, ICSID Convention arbitration is an option—sometimes the only option—in numerous investment treaties. This will feed upon itself in an increasing returns fashion: the more frequently the services of ICSID are utilized, the more familiar these services become to potential users, encouraging more users to opt for ICSID. This is equally true for the lawyers who represent these claimants. The more claimants go to ICSID, the more lawyers advise clients to go to ICSID. The greater the number of cases decided by ICSID Convention tribunals, the more ICSID Convention arbitration is likely to be studied by counsel and recommended as the best option.

A third indirect network effect relates to the general quality and scope of arbitral service. Breadth and expertise of arbitral services are powerful considerations for claimants. Institutions vary in terms of their reputation for competence in dealing with a wide array of legal matters. This reputation also builds on itself. If the institution is perceived as possessing a high degree of competence in specialized areas of dispute, the institution will attract more claimants in these areas, deepening the arbitrators' expertise in these specific economic sectors. To date, ICSID has administered over 550 cases, some 73.6% of which were based on investment treaties,[16] distributed across an impressively wide swath of economic sectors.

These indirect network effects generate self-reinforcing pressure for claimants to take their matters to ICSID, bolstering the market dominance of the arbitration

[14]UNCTAD (2015a, b, p. 5), available at http://unctad.org/en/PublicationsLibrary/webdiaepcb2015d1_en.pdf.

[15]https://icsid.worldbank.org/apps/ICSIDWEB/icsiddocs/Documents/List%20of%20Contracting%20States%20and%20Other%20Signatories%20of%20the%20Convention%20-%20Latest.pdf.

[16]https://icsid.worldbank.org/apps/ICSIDWEB/about/Pages/default.aspx; https://icsid.worldbank.org/apps/ICSIDWEB/resources/Documents/ICSID%20Web%20Stats%202016-1%20%28English%29%20final.pdf, (p. 10).

centre. The presence of indirect network effects in the market for arbitration services is significant because network effect pressures will have the peculiar effect of 'locking in' a standard, rendering it tenaciously resistant to competition. Any assessment of the likelihood of institutional competition from Asia or elsewhere needs to consider the implications of this dynamic.

4 Critical Mass and Penguins

If there are no bounds to increasing returns, a networked market will eventually induce a lock-in situation—"a point is reached after which every agent, regardless of inherent preferences, will select the same technology."[17] Once a monopoly emerges, it becomes locked-in as "no actor is willing to bear the disproportionate risk of being the first adopter of a standard and then becoming stranded in a small network…"[18] This inability to challenge a locked in standard is known as the *start-up problem*. As one scholar observes, any system that "share[s] the characteristics of lock-in, the presence of network externalities, the absence of entrepreneurs who can induce transition, and the absence of a centralized authority that can mandate simultaneous change—could be as vulnerable to path dependence as technological standards."[19] Under such conditions, it is extremely difficult for a new standard to start up and dislodge a standard that is locked in as a result of powerful network effects.

It becomes a problem of critical mass. What is termed *hysteresis effect* plays a crucial role here.[20] The hysteresis effect states that, "the product is only interesting for potential customers if a critical mass of consumers is reached such that the sum of original and derivative utility outweighs the respective costs"[21] of adopting a new standard. A certain chicken and egg paradox emerges: "…many consumers are not interested in purchasing the good because the installed base is too small, and the installed base is too small because an insufficiently small number of consumers have purchased the good."[22] This makes it very difficult to achieve sufficient critical mass. If only "a fraction of the market adopts a new technology, for most users the gains will be below costs."[23] The market will therefore become locked in, with no one willing to bear the costs of switching to a new standard.[24] This has been termed the 'penguin effect': "Penguins who must enter the water to find food often delay

---

[17]David and Shane Greenstein (1990, pp. 3, 6).

[18]Weitzel (2004, p. 16).

[19]Gillette (1998, pp. 813, 820).

[20]Kemper (2010, p. 73).

[21]Ibid 73–74. For this principle, *see* Economides and Himmelberg (1995a, b), Clement et al. (1998), Choi and Whinston (2000).

[22]Economides and Himmelberg (1995a, b, p. 5).

[23]David and Greenstein (1990, pp. 3, 9).

[24]Farrell and Saloner (1986, pp. 940, 940).

doing so because they fear the presence of predators. Each would prefer some other penguin to test the waters first."[25] This dynamic greatly inhibits competition in the market.

5 The Possibility of 'Disruptive Events'

The effects of lock-in, however, may not be quite as robust as the theory projects. Indeed, the inevitability of a lock-in effect is the subject of some debate in the literature. Liebowitz and Margolis question the notion that network effects induce a permanent monopoly, arguing that although there are indeed periods of persistent lock-in where one product dominates the market (they look at the software market), network effect markets will frequently tip towards a new monopoly[26] in a process which they termed it as "serial monopoly."[27]

A variety of considerations can disrupt a lock-in effect. Liebowitz and Margolis, for example, argue that major product innovations and predatory pricing can successfully challenge a lock-in monopoly.[28] Building on this insight, others have noted that network effects do not inevitably result in natural monopolies, and that "[d]ifferences in the quality of competing network goods or in their production costs may offset the relative advantage of the larger network."[29] Thus, the presence of network externalities does "not necessarily result in a winner-takes-all situation: they can be partly or fully be undone by other factors…"[30] Katz and Shapiro contend that if "rival systems have distinct features sought by certain consumers, two or more systems may be able to survive by catering to consumers who care more about product attributes than network size."[31] In such cases, multiple equilibria can be sustained—competition may emerge. In the absence of a regulator that can facilitate (or even mandate) a simultaneous jump to a new network by all the members, some inherent feature provided by the upstart competitor is needed to create an incentive to change that is powerful enough to offset the loss of network access.

Are such incentives on the horizon for investment arbitration?—that is the question we must ask. To be sure, investment arbitration is in the midst of a tumultuous period. The European Union's proposal for the establishment of an investment "court" that

[25]Ibid 943.

[26]Liebowitz and Margolis (2001, p. 227).

[27]ibid 10. See Liebowitz and Margolis (2001, p. 1) (refuting the much cited QWERTY keyboard example of lock-in, claiming that evidence of the superiority of Dvorak, a keyboard competitor to the QWERTY layout, is lacking. *See also* Liebowitz and Stephen Margolis (2001, p. 205), William Cohen (1996, pp. 535, 539–546).

[28]Liebowitz and Margolis (n 24) 110.

[29]Aviram (2003, p. 15). *See also* Liebowitz et al. (2001, pp. 671, 672).

[30]Bekkers (2001, p. 196).

[31]Katz and Shapiro (1994, pp. 93, 106).

includes an appellate body is the most salient example of how investor-state dispute settlement might change over the coming years. Whether this proposal is truly a sea change that will result in a challenge to ICSID's market dominance is unclear. A great deal depends on how broadly the European Union succeeds in implementing its two-tiered investment court and whether, as currently seems likely, ICSID is chosen to be the, or one of the, institutions that hosts the Court, even if those proceedings do not take place under the ICSID Convention. Other exogenous factors might come into play as well; other market actors already vie with ICSID to host investment arbitrations, a trend that one can only expect to continue.

The European Union has concluded two free trade agreements whose investment chapters include proposals for a two-tiered investment court.[32] It has proposed that a similar institution be included in the Transatlantic Trade and Investment Partnership (T-TIP) that it is currently negotiating with the United States.[33] The EU-Singapore Free Trade Agreement, negotiations for which were concluded on 17 October 2014, does not contain the court proposal,[34] but one expects that the EU might re-open negotiations to include a similar mechanism.[35] The European Union

---

[32]*Comprehensive Economic and Trade Agreement (CETA) Between Canada, of the one part and the European Union, of the other part* http://trade.ec.europa.eu/doclib/docs/2014/september/tradoc_152806.pdf, Chapter 8, Section F—Resolution of investment disputes between investors and states (CETA); *Free Trade Agreement between the European Union and the Socialist Republic of Vietnam* (in negotiation), http://investmentpolicyhub.unctad.org/Download/TreatyFile/3563, Section 3 (Resolution of Investment Disputes), Sub-Section 4: Investment Tribunal System (EU-Vietnam FTA).

[33]*Transatlantic Trade and Investment Partnership—European Union's proposal for Investment Protection and Resolution of Investment Disputes*, 12 November 2015 http://trade.ec.europa.eu/doclib/docs/2015/november/tradoc_153955.pdf, Chapter 8, Section 3 (Resolution of Investment Disputes and Investment Court System), Sub-Section 4: Investment Court System (T-TIP proposal).

[34]See *EU-Singapore Free Trade Agreement*, negotiations completed on 17 October 2014, http://trade.ec.europa.eu/doclib/press/index.cfm?id=961, Chapter 9.

[35]See Daly and Ahmad (2015):

> The EU may seek to propose an Asia-wide permanent investment court to resolve disputes arising under the FTAs that the EU is currently negotiating with some Asian States (Malaysia, Thailand, India, Philippines and Japan). While the EU-Singapore FTA, which is pending signature and ratification, does not provide for the creation of a distinct permanent investment court, it does establish a joint committee (known as the 'Trade Committee') comprised of the Parties' Trade representatives with the task to, *inter alia*, oversee the implementation of the FTA, consider amendments to the FTA and issue binding decisions. With these wide powers, the creation of an Asia-wide permanent investment court is not entirely far fetched. The Trade Committee is tasked, after all, to examine whether an appellate mechanism could be created (Article 9.30(1) (c) of the EU-Singapore FTA).

See also Lester (2015):

> [T]here's the question of the yet to be ratified pre-ICS [ie 'Investment Court System'] FTAs that still have old ISDS rules in them, such as (…) the EU-Singapore FTA. Can those really be ratified as currently written, when the new and improved version of ISDS is out there, being sold as a better alternative?

sees the establishment of these courts as nuclei (which would presumably be merged) for a multilateral investment court to which investor-state dispute settlement in all EU investment agreements, at the least, would lead.[36] In the fullness of time, once the European Union has replaced, or has caused its member states to re-negotiate, all extra-EU BITs, they would lead to that multilateral court.[37]

Whether any court under any agreement will ever be established is an open question—the hostility in Europe towards free trade agreements generally and investor-state dispute settlement in particular is unprecedented.[38] Less widespread but still marked opposition can be found in other countries as well—as of April 2016, every remaining U.S. presidential candidate had spoken against the Trans-Pacific Partnership, and President Trump withdrew the United States from it in January 2017.[39] The CETA has been confirmed as a mixed agreement, meaning parts of the pieces of the treaty are a matter of shared competence and thus subject to ratification by the member states. The portions of the treaty subject to EU competence will have provisional effect cmomencing in mid-September 2017,

[36]Schill (2016, pp. 1, 2):

The Commission's proposal to create a permanent investment court is a strong vision and the text presented constitutes the first concrete step towards practical implementation. (…) The proposal breathes the right spirit: to transform investor-state arbitration into a truly public, fully transparent, more predictable and balanced system of global adjudication.

[37]CETA (n 30), art. 8.29; European Commission, 'Commission proposes new Investment Court System for TTIP and other EU trade and investment negotiations', Press release (16 September 2015) (European commission 2015a), available at http://europa.eu/rapid/press-release_IP-15-5651_en.htm.

[38]The European Commission received approximately 150,000 comments when it called for public comment on the proposed inclusion of investor-state dispute settlement in the T-TIP. While a vast majority of those were 'form' comments generated by opponents of investor-state arbitration, some 3,500 were individualized. European Commission, *Report—Online public consultation on investment protection and investor-to-state dispute settlement (ISDS) in the Transatlantic Trade and Investment Partnership Agreement (TTIP)* (Commission Staff Working Document, SWD (2015b) 3 final) 13 January 2015, 3, http://trade.ec.europa.eu/doclib/docs/2015/january/tradoc_153044.pdf.

It is noteworthy, in addition, that the Netherlands recently demanded a referendum on the T-TIP. See http://sputniknews.com/europe/20160415/1038074644/ttip-deal-dutch-referendum.html. and http://www.euractiv.com/section/trade-society/news/dutch-voters-now-demanding-referendum-on-ttip/.

[39]For instance, Democratic presidential candidate Hillary Clinton said about the TPP: 'I want to make sure that I can look into the eyes of any middle-class American and say, "this will help raise your wages". And I concluded I could not' (Grewal 2015); Bernie Sanders was also strongly opposed to the trade deal and stated that '[t]he Trans-Pacific Partnership is a disastrous trade agreement designed to protect the interests of the largest multi-national corporations at the expense of workers, consumers, the environment and the foundations of American democracy. It will also negatively impact some of the poorest people in the world' ('Senator Bernie Sanders: The Trans-Pacific Trade (TPP) Agreement Must be Defeated' http://www.sanders.senate.gov/download/the-trans-pacific-trade-tpp-agreement-must-be-defeated?inline=file); Republic presidential candidates Donald Trump and Ted Cruz were also generally opposed to the trade deal. See Greenberg (2016) http://www.politifact.com/truth-o-meter/statements/2016/mar/10/ted-cruz/ted-cruz-i-always-opposed-tpp-trans-pacific-partne/ and Clayton Youngman (2015), Blanchfield (2017)

but the investor-state dispute settlement mechanism, including the investment court, will not come into effect until it is approved by the individual member states.[40] Given the hostility in many member states to investor-state dispute settlement, it seems unlikely that the agreements would be implemented, at least in the near term. The insertion of the investment court system is unlikely to be enough to satisfy the critics; German judges have placed on the record their negative reaction to the proposal.[41] These very specific hurdles do not take into account the other significant problems facing the European Union—in June 2016 the United Kingdom put to its voters the question of whether to stay in the Union and a majority voted to leave, right-wing nativist political parties in key European states have seen a surge in popular support, the refugee crisis remains staggering, and the fiscal affairs of Greece and certain other member states persistently bad, with corresponding threats to the Eurozone, if not to the European Union itself.

Assuming an investment court is established, one significant question is who will host it. If there is more than one, who will host them? ICSID is certainly a possibility. It is the institution chosen in the CETA,[42] and is one of two institutions proposed (the other is the Permanent Court of Arbitration) in the T-TIP and the EU—Vietnam Free Trade Agreement.[43] The proposal of the court is not fully compatible with ICSID Convention arbitration, although this does not mean that ICSID cannot administer the court's arbitrations—it certainly can, and its qualifications and market position make it eminently qualified to do so. This is the case whether the arbitration unfolds under the ICSID Additional Facility rules (available if either the home state of the investor or the host state of the investment is party to the investment treaty) or under ad hoc arbitration rules, such as the UNCITRAL Arbitration Rules.[44] That arbitration would not, however, be ICSID Convention

---

[40]Politico Pro's Morning Trade: TTIP bogged down in feta cheese—CETA will be a 'mixed agreement', Politico (12 May 2016). The CJEU determined that the investor-state dispute settlement portion of the EU-Singapore investment chapter is subject to mixed competence, a decision applicable to the investor-state dispute resolution portions of other EU free trade agreements as well. Opinion (C-2/15) (16 May 2017). The CJE has yet to determine whether investor-state dispute settlement more generally is compatible with EU law.

[41]*Opinion No. 04/16 on the establishment of an investment tribunal in TTIP—the proposal from the European Commission on 16.09.2015 and 11.12.2015.* For a commentary in English about the letter, see http://canadians.org/sites/default/files/tpp-deutsche-richterbund-opinion-0216.pdf. See *also* 'Germany's judges and public prosecutors reject proposed investment court system in TTIP', *Investment Treaty News* (29 February 2016) https://www.iisd.org/itn/2016/02/29/germanys-judges-and-public-prosecutors-reject-proposed-investment-court-system-in-ttip/.

[42]CETA (n 30) art 8.27(16).

[43]T-TIP (n 24) Investment Chapter, Section 3, art 9.16; EU-Vietnam FTA (n 23) Chapter Eight, Section 3, Sub-Section 4, art 12(18).

[44]How the EU Court proposal will be integrated with the current system of international arbitration, where the court in the place of arbitration has the potential to set aside the award on grounds specified under local arbitration law, is not altogether clear. The assumption is that once the appellate system is in place it will supplant review in local courts, yet it seems that those arbitrations will still have a 'place' for purposes of judicial assistance to arbitration, for example. CETA provides that the disputing party must not seek to set aside the award once the appellate

arbitration, with its concomitant benefits—the most important of which is the requirement that each ICSID Convention state treat ICSID Convention awards as if they were final judgments of courts of that state.[45]

The ICSID Convention stipulates that the only recourse against an ICSID Convention arbitral award is annulment under the ICSID Convention itself[46] and that only states (which would not include the European Union as such) can be adherents.[47] Should ICSID be able to surmount these incompatibilities, perhaps by amendment, perhaps by the addition of a protocol to the ICSID Convention that established a parallel mechanism for investment court arbitrations and which would permit the European Union to become a party, it would reinforce its position of market dominance.

ICSID will face competition whether or not the EU proposal is finalized. The Permanent Court of Arbitration is one institution that one might expect to challenge ICSID's hegemony in investor-state arbitration. Indeed, the PCA is currently overseeing several investor-state arbitrations[48] and has a long pedigree in administering public-international-law based disputes.[49] Another is the Singapore International Arbitration Centre which, under the leadership of its new President, Gary Born, instituted new rules under which investment arbitrations can

(Footnote 44 continued)

body structure is fully in place: 'Upon adoption of the decision [setting out the functioning of the Appellate Tribunal]: a disputing party shall not seek to review, set aside, annul, revise or initiate any other similar procedure as regards an award under this Section'. CETA (n 30) Article 8.28(9)(b). Whether parties will necessarily abide by this stricture, and whether local courts will necessarily dismiss a set-aside application if one is made, may well be put into question. Also unclear is the role that will be played by the Convention on the Recognition and Enforcement of Foreign Arbitral Awards (the New York Convention) (concluded 10 June 1958, entered into force 7 June 1959, 330 UNTS 38; 21 UST 2517; 7 ILM 1046 (1968)), the usual enforcement mechanism in non-ICSID Convention arbitration. Will an award from the first-instance tribunal be enforceable under the New York Convention while an appeal is pending, or will only a post-appeal award (or an award that the losing party has declined to appeal) be enforceable? Will parties continue to resist enforcement on the grounds permited in the New York Convention, or will the language in the investment agreement be viewed as superseding the possibility of resisting enforcement? These questions will be answered by national courts.

[45]*Convention on the Settlement of Investment Disputes between States and Nationals of other States*, 17 UST 1270, 575 UNTS 159 (1966) (ICSID Convention) art 54(1).

[46]Ibid art 52.

[47]Ibid art 67.

[48]Permanent Court of Arbitration, *PCA Case Repository*, http://www.pcacases.com/web/allcases/.

[49]See Permanent Court of Arbitration, *About Us*, http://www.pcacases.com/web/aboutus/:

> Established in 1899 to facilitate arbitration and other forms of dispute resolution between states, the PCA has developed into a modern, multi-faceted arbitral institution that is now perfectly situated at the juncture between public and private international law to meet the rapidly evolving dispute resolution needs of the international community. Today the PCA provides services for the resolution of disputes involving various combinations of states, state entities, intergovernmental organizations, and private parties.

See also Daly (2014, p. 3).

proceed.[50] Singapore has already built, in a relatively short time, an outstanding reputation as a centre for commercial arbitration. The reasons for Singapore's success include the robust support of the Singaporean government, Singapore's status as an Asian transport and commercial hub, and its strong and predicable legal framework.[51] It is also important to underscore the shift of the global economy to the Asia-Pacific region as businesses tend to think and act regionally; regional disputes are increasingly likely to be settled in the Asia-Pacific region as opposed to Europe or North America.[52]

The Kuala Lumpur Regional Center for Arbitration (KLRCA)[53] is another potential challenger in the Asia region. The KLRCA is an international organisation established in 1978 under the auspices of the Asian-African Legal Consultative

[50] *SIAC Investment Arbitration Rules*, http://www.siac.org.sg/our-rules/rules/siac-ia-rules-2017.

[51] According to the SIAC website, the reasons for Singapore's success are as follows:
An independent neutral third-country venue consistently ranked in the top 5 for the least corrupt public sector in the world in the Corruption Perceptions Index. Singapore is also consistently ranked no. 1 for the least corrupt public sector in Asia in the Corruption Perceptions Index.

- A strong multicultural society, with excellent legal and technological expertise as well as language fluency.
- A central location in Southeast Asia with 6,600 scheduled flights a week to 320 cities.
- An open economy and business environment that is host to over 7,000 multinational firms.
- The UNCITRAL Model Law is the cornerstone of Singapore's legislation on international commercial arbitration which is regularly updated to incorporate internationally accepted codes and rules for arbitration.
- A party to the 1958 New York Convention (on enforcement of arbitration awards). Singapore arbitration awards are enforceable in over 150 countries worldwide.
- A strong tradition of the rule of law, supported by a highly skilled judiciary that receives top rankings in international surveys.
- The Courts offer maximum judicial support of arbitration and minimum intervention granting parties full and consistent support in the conduct of international arbitration.
- Parties have a freedom of choice of counsel in arbitration proceedings regardless of nationality.
- There is no restriction on foreign law firms engaging in and advising on arbitration in Singapore.
- Non–residents do not require work permits to carry out arbitration services in Singapore.
- There are excellent facilities and services to support the conduct of arbitration at Maxwell Chambers, Asia's largest fully-integrated dispute resolution complex with state-of-the-art hearing facilities.
- Lower costs than in almost any other major centre of arbitration. http://www.siac.org.sg/2014-11-03-13-33-43/why-siac/arbitration-in-singapore.

[52] See Chaisse (2015, pp. 563–638). See also Choo (2015)[https://singaporeinternationalarbitration.com/2015/06/15/the-rise-and-rise-of-singapore-singapore-as-a-preferred-venue-for-international-arbitration/].

[53] See the official website here: http://klrca.org/.

Organisation (AALCO).[54] The KLRCA was the first regional centre established by AALCO in Asia to provide institutional support as a neutral and independent venue for the conduct of domestic and international arbitration proceedings in Asia. Its caseload has increased considerably in the last five years. In addition, recent investment treaties explicitly refer to the KLRCA for the settlement of investment disputes. In particular, Article 33 of Section B of the 2009 ASEAN Comprehensive Investment Agreement allows them to be referred, *inter alia*, to the KLRCA.[55] The KLRCA's status as an international organisation and its location in Malaysia—a multicultural and state with a true democracy—might also make it attractive to a number of South East Asian and South Asian states.[56]

The PCA, the Singapore International Arbitration Centre, and the KLRCA are not the only potential rivals to ICSID. Indeed, there are far too many to list here. The Stockholm Chamber of Commerce arbitration centre has some specialty in arbitrations involving Russia and former Soviet and Soviet satellite states; Dubai and Mauritius have relatively new arbitration centers. The International Chamber of Commerce Court of Arbitration, the London Court of International Arbitration, and the Hong Kong International Arbitration Centre are all capable of administering investment disputes, though they are better known for commercial cases.

Several Latin American countries, led by Ecuador, have proposed the establishment of a regional arbitral institution to hear investment arbitrations involving members of the Union of South American Nations (UNASUR).[57]

The UNASUR proposal in particular demonstrates the introduction of a preference for regionally based dispute settlement for disputes emanating from that region. Whether any preference for regionally based *investment* arbitration will emerge in Asia is not clear, given the paucity of investment arbitration cases involving Asian states. One might imagine that China, given its "one belt, one road" policy, would seek to establish an Asian arbitration centre. If it were to do so, would it regard Singapore or Kuala Lumpur as an appropriate venue, or would it prefer a Chinese location?

One of ICSID's primary advantages—the virtual automatic enforceability of ICSID awards—should help it to maintain its position, yet even there some uncertainties exist. Romania and the European Union have challenged the enforceability of an ICSID Convention Award in the U.S. Court of Appeals for the

---

[54]See http://www.aalco.int/Scripts/default.asp.

[55]The 2009 ASEAN Comprehensive Investment Agreement is a multilateral investment treaty between all member States of ASEAN, which comprises Brunei, Cambodia, Indonesia, Laos, Malaysia, Myanmar, Philippines, Singapore and Thailand. Section B of the 2009 ASEAN Comprehensive Investment Agreement provides for the resolution of investment disputes between an investor and a member State. For a detailed commentary on the ACUA, see Chaisse and Jusoh (2016, p. 265).

[56]The degree to which the KLRCA is wholly free from political influence remains, however, unclear—a point that should be noted.

[57]See 'UNASUR Arbitration Centre one step closer to being established', *Investment Treaty News* (29 February 2016) 10, http://www.iisd.org/itn/wp-content/uploads/2016/02/iisd-itn-february-2016-english.pdf.

Second Circuit. [58] One of the claims is that the act of state doctrine should render the ICSID Convention award unenforceable because the award imposes liability on Romania in a manner that violates EU laws on state aid.[59] If Romania and the EU were to be successful on their claims, the enforceability of ICSID Convention awards would be undermined even outside EU member states—it is quite clear that the *Micula* case, for example, will not be enforced in the European Union, notwithstanding the ICSID Convention. Incidentally, should the act of state doctrine be found available to be interposed by a state as a defense to enforcement in the ICSID Convention context, logic would suggest that the argument would be available in defenses to the enforcement of New York Convention awards as well. But there are already some limited grounds on which states can challenge the enforcement of New York Convention awards, so the effect on enforceability is much greater vis-à-vis the ICSID Convention.

If and when these challenges to ICSID's hegemony ripen, one might still expect ICSID to remain dominant for many years. The investment treaty network comprises approximately 2,700 treaties currently in force[60] and ICSID Convention arbitration is an option under most of them (and ICSID Additional Facility arbitration is available in some cases as well), whereas the arbitration centers mentioned above are much more rarely included as options, although some treaties would permit the disputing parties to select another set of rules even if they were not listed in the treaty. ICSID is thus well entrenched in the existing network of investment treaties. This widespread treaty 'pre-installment' only reinforces institutional lock-in. If treaties are unilaterally terminated, most have a survival clause providing that the investor may seek the protection of the treaty for a specified period—often 20 years—which suggests that any wholesale change will not come soon.[61]

---

[58] *Ioan Micula et al. v Government of Romania*, Case No. 15-3109-cv (2d. Cir.). The decision below is *Ioan Micula v Government of Romania*, Case No. 15-CV15 MISC 107 (Apr. 28, 2015). The U.S. District Court ordered enforcement of the award on an ex parte basis (which is the process applicable to court decisions of U.S. courts). The crux of the case is the procedure a judgment creditor needs to follow to enforce an ICSID award. The Second Circuit decided a similar case in which it held that the Foreign Sovereign Immunities Act was the only appropriate vehicle for enforcement. *Mobil Cerro Negro Ltd. et al. v. Bolivarian Republic of Venezuela* (2nd Cir. 2017). The same result will ensue in the Micula case, likely obviating, for now, any deicsion on the applicability of the act-of-state doctrine.

[59] *Ioan Micula et al. v Government of Romania*, Case No. 15-3109-cv (Brief for Amicus Curiae the Commission of the European Union in Support of Defendant-Appellant, 2d. Cir., Feb. 4, 2016).

[60] http://investmentpolicyhub.unctad.org/IIA. These 2,700 hundred are the BITs and international investment agreements that have entered into force. Others are pending. At the end of 2014, UNCTAD identified a total of 3,271 international investment agreements. See UNCTAD (2015a, b, p. 106): "The conclusion in 2014 of 31 international investment agreements (IIAs)—18 bilateral investment treaties (BITs) and 13 'other IIAs'—brought the total number of IIAs to 3,271 (2,926 BITs and 345 'other IIAs') by year-end." [footnote omitted].

[61] An open question is the effect on investors' rights if both states to the treaty terminate the treaty, and in so doing terminate the survival clause. Do states retain that power, or does the investor have vested rights that cannot be ousted by such an agreement? For a provocative study of this issue, see Roberts (2015, p. 353).

Second, even if one were to see the shift from the current approach to investment arbitration to the EU court approach, ICSID is likely to play at least some—and possibly a dominant—role there as well. The ICSID Secretariat has already been named as the administrator for CETA investor-state arbitrations even if they do not occur under the auspices of the ICSID Convention.

Third, should there be a growing demand for regionally based investment arbitration, it is not necessarily the case that ICSID cannot dominate that market as well. The ICSID Secretariat staff hail from dozens of countries.[62] ICSID has cooperation agreements with multiple institutions around the world, including CIETAC, SIAC, the HKIAC, and the KLRCA,[63] and many others as well. ICSID thus has venues around the world in which it can administer arbitrations. Indeed, should there be the requisite demand, nothing would stop ICSID from establishing a regional branch, in China or elsewhere.

6 Conclusion

Long-term projections are always hard to make. Will investment arbitration even continue as a viable form of dispute settlement at all? Its availability in some 2,700 extant treaties suggests it will last for some time, but the pace of treaty negotiation has slowed and, as adverted to above, whether the European Union and the United States will continue to negotiate investment treaties is not certain. The European Union's proposal to establish a court could be viewed as saving investment arbitration, but by many critics it will be viewed as not going far enough. "State-friendly" modifications to investment treaties have made it harder for investors to prevail on their claims.[64] Nonetheless, one should recall that at its founding ICSID was expected to administer disputes arising under investment contracts, not investment treaties. Thus, while investment treaty arbitration has eclipsed contract arbitration in ICSID's workload,[65]

---

[62] ICSID *Secretariat*, https://icsid.worldbank.org/apps/ICSIDWEB/about/Pages/Secretariat.aspx ('The Secretariat consists of approximately 70 staff of diverse backgrounds and nationalities').

[63] https://icsid.worldbank.org/apps/ICSIDWEB/Documents/KLRCA%20Agreement%20Announcement%20FINAL.pdf?Mobile=1&Source=%2Fapps%2FICSIDWEB%2F_layouts%2Fmobile%2Fview.aspx%3FList%3D55947ab4-4786-48b9-803c-40abd126dbd5%26View%3D918f21b0-91dc-4b7b-88df-b8291b7c6282%26CurrentPage%3D1.

[64] Lars and Titi (2015, pp. 401–435).

[65] ICSID statistics indicate that overall, the basis of consent invoked to establish ICSID jurisdiction in registered ICSID cases was found in an investment contract between the investor and the host state in only 17.3% of the cases. The basis for consent was found in the domestic law of the host state in 9.3% of the cases while the basis for consent in the other cases was found in a BIT (60.3%) or another investment agreement. In 2015, the basis of consent invoked to establish ICSID jurisdiction in registered ICSID cases was found in an investment contract between the investor and the host state in only 8% of the cases. The basis for consent was found in the domestic law of the host state in 8% of the cases while the basis for consent in the other cases was found in a BIT (46%) or another investment agreement. See ICSID (2016, pp. 10 and 23).

contractual arbitrations will likely continue. ICSID does not have a monopoly over them, either, but the same network externalities and market dominance characteristics apply in that area as well.

In sum, if the European Union's proposals for an investment court gain traction, and if eventually that court crystallizes into a multilateral facility that is headquartered in another institution outside ICSID, that institution could rival ICSID for investment arbitration dominance. Such an event would constitute a 'disruptive event' sufficient to undermine network lock-in. Even aside from the European Union's activities, other existing and even new institutions will continue to compete with ICSID, and one or more of them could eventually erode ICSID's market dominance. Exogenous factors such as national court decisions that undermine the enforceability of ICSID Convention awards could accelerate that process. Other unforeseen events might also undermine the market dominance of ICSID and trigger either a large-scale coalescence around an alternative institution or, rather more likely, the parceling out of investment arbitration among multiple competitors. Such a scenario might mean ICSID remains the single most dominant market force, albeit without a monopoly or quasi monopoly. Yet ICSID's consistent strength and its network-effect-reinforced position of dominance will be hard to unseat.

Acknowledgements The authors wish to thank an anonymous editor for his or her helpful comments. Any mistakes are our own. The core ideas outlined here draw from a more detailed exposition of the theory published as an article with the University of Pennsylvania Journal of International Law.

References

Aviram, A. 2003. A network effects analysis of private ordering. Berkeley Program in Law and Economics, Working Paper Series 15.

Behn, D. 2016. The worst option but for all the others: The performance of investment treaty arbitration in historical context. In *The performance of international courts and tribunals*, ed. Theresa Squatrito, et al. Cambridge University Press.

Bekkers, R. 2001. *Mobile telecommunications standards: GSM*, 196. UMTS: Tetra, and Ermes.

Blanchfield, M. 2017. Donald Trump signs order to withdraw from Trans-Pacific Partnership. Global News, global news.ca/news/3198932/donald-trump-withdraw-tpp-executive-order

Chaisse, J. 2015. The shifting tectonics of international investment law—Structure and dynamics of rules and arbitration on foreign investment in the Asia-Pacific region. *George Washington International Law Review* 47: 563–638.

Chaisse, J., and S. Jusoh. 2016. *The ASEAN comprehensive investment agreement—The regionalization of laws and policy on foreign investment*, 265. London: Edward Elgar.

Choo, J. 2015. The rise and rise of Singapore: Singapore as a preferred venue for international arbitration, Singapore Law Gazette—Arbitration in 2014: Looking Ahead to 2015. https://singaporeinternationalarbitration.com/2015/06/15/the-rise-and-rise-of-singapore-singapore-as-a-preferred-venue-for-international-arbitration/.

Choi, S., and A. Whinston. 2000. The future of the digital economy. In *Handbook on electronic commerce*, ed. M. Shaw, et al.

Church, J., and I. King. 1993. Bilingualism and network externalities. *Canadian Journal of Economics* 26: 337.

Clayton, Youngman. 2015. Trump says China gets an advantage from the Trans-Pacific Partnership, Politifact.

Clement, M., et al. 1998. Netzeffekte und kritische masse. In *Marketing Mit Interaktiven Medien—Stategien Zum Markterfolg*, ed. S. Albers, et al.

Cohen, William E. 1996. Competition and foreclosure in the context of installed base and compatibility effects. *Antitrust Law Journal* 64 (535): 539–546.

Daly, W. Brooks. 2014. In *Evgeniya goriatcheva and hugh a meighen, a guide to the PCA arbitration rules*, 3. OUP. Draft SIAC Investment Arbitration Rules, http://www.siac.org.sg/images/stories/articles/rules/IA%20Rules%20(rev%2020160115).pdf.

Daly M.P., and J. Ahmad. 2015. The EU-Vietnam FTA: What does it all mean? What does it mean for the future? Kluwer Arbitration Blog. http://kluwerarbitrationblog.com/2015/12/14/the-eu-vietnam-fta-what-does-it-all-mean-what-does-it-mean-for-the-future/.

David, P.A., and Shane Greenstein. 1990. The economics of compatibility standards: An introduction to recent research. *Economics of Innovation and New Technology* 1 (3): 6.

David Singh Grewal. 2015. *Why Hillary Clinton Is Right on the TPP*, The Huffington Post. http://www.huffingtonpost.com/david-singh-grewal/why-hillary-clinton-is-ri_b_8295420.html.

Druzin, B. 2009. Buying commercial law: Choice of law, choice of forum, and network externalities. *Tulane Journal of International and Comparative Law* 18 (131): 151.

Economides, N., and C. Himmelberg. 1995. Critical mass and network evolution in telecommunications. In *Toward a competitive telecommunications industry: Selected papers from the 1994 telecommunications policy research conference*, ed. G. Brock.

Economides, N., and C. Himmelberg. 1995. *Critical mass and network size with application to the US FAX market*. Stern School of Business, Discussion paper No. EC-95–11, 5.

European Commission. 2014. *Singapore: The commission to request a court of justice opinion on the trade deal, news archive*. http://trade.ec.europa.eu/doclib/press/index.cfm?id=1185.

European Commission. 2015a. *Commission proposes new investment court system for TTIP and other EU trade and investment negotiations*, Press release. http://europa.eu/rapid/press-release_IP-15-5651_en.htm.

European Commission. 2015b. Report—Online public consultation on investment protection and investor-to-state dispute settlement (ISDS) in the transatlantic trade and investment partnership agreement (TTIP) (Commission Staff Working Document, SWD (2015) 3 final), 3, http://trade.ec.europa.eu/doclib/docs/2015/january/tradoc_153044.pdf.

Farrell, J., and G. Saloner. 1986. Installed base and compatibility: Innovation, product preannouncements, and predation. *The American Economic Review* 76 (940): 940.

Ferrell, J., and P. Klemperer. 2006. *Coordination and lock-in: Competition and switching costs and network effects*, 46–54.

Gillette, C. 1998. Lock-in effects in law and norms. *Boston University Law Review* 78 (813): 820.

ICSID. 2016. *The ICSID caseload—statistics* (Issue 2016–1): 10–23.

Jon Greenberg. 2016. Ted Cruz: "I always opposed the TPP (trans-pacific partnership)", Politifact. http://www.politifact.com/truth-o-meter/statements/2016/mar/10/ted-cruz/ted-cruz-i-always-opposed-tpp-trans-pacific-partne/.

Katz, M., and C. Shapiro. 1994. Systems competition and network effects. *J Econ Perspectives* 8 (93): 106.

Kemper, A. 2010. *Valuation of network effects in software markets: A complex networks approach*, 73.

Lars, A., Markert, and Catharine Titi. 2015. States strike back—Old and new ways for host states to defend against investment arbitrations. In *Yearbook on international investment law & policy 2013–2014*, ed. Andrea K. Bjorklund, 401–435. OUP.

Lemley, M., and D. McGowan. 1998. *Legal implications of network economic effects*. California Law Review 86: 479–494.

Lester, S. 2015. From ISDS to ICS. *International Economic Law and Policy Blog*. http://worldtradelaw.typepad.com/ielpblog/2015/12/from-isds-to-ics.html.

Liebowitz, S.J., and Stephen E. Margolis. 1995. Are network externalities a new source of market failure? *Research in Law and Economics* 17: 1.

Liebowitz, S.J., and S.E. Margolis. 1990. The fable of the keys. *The Journal of Law and Economics* 33: 1.

Liebowitz, S.J., and S.E. Margolis. 1994. Network externality: Uncommon tragedy. *The Journal of Economic Perspectives* 8 (133): 136.

Liebowitz, S.J., and Stephen E. Margolis. 1995b. Path dependency, lock-in and history. *Journal of Law, Economics & Organization* 11: 205.

Liebowitz, S.J., and S. Margolis. 2001. *Winners, losers, and microsoft: Competition and antitrust in high technology*, 227.

Liebowitz, S.J., et al. 1998. Network externalities. In *The new Palgrave dictionary of economics and the law*, ed. Peter Newman, 671.

Roberts, Anthea. 2015. Triangular treaties: The nature and limits of investment treaty rights. *Harvard International Law Journal* 56: 353.

Schelling T.C., 1978. *Micromotives and macrobehavior*, 92–94, 98–99.

Schill, S.W. 2016. Editorial: US versus EU leadership in global investment governance. *The Journal of World Investment & Trade* 17 (1): 2.

UNASUR Arbitration Centre one step closer to being established, Investment Treaty News (2016) 10. http://www.iisd.org/itn/wp-content/uploads/2016/02/iisd-itn-february-2016-english.pdf.

UNCTAD. 2015a., Issues Note No. 1, *Recent Trends in IIAs and ISDS*, 5. http://unctad.org/en/PublicationsLibrary/webdiaepcb2015d1_en.pdf.

UNCTAD. 2015b. *World investment report 2015—Reforming international investment governance*, 106. United Nations.

Weitzel, T., 2004. *Economics of standards in information networks*, 16.

William Page., et al. 2000. Network externalities. In *Encyclopedia of Law and Economics*, Boudwijn Bouckaert and Gerrit DeGeest (ed.), 952.

FSC
www.fsc.org
MIX
Papier | Fördert
gute Waldnutzung
FSC® C083411

Kolibri 360 GmbH
Ferdinand-Jühlke-Straße 7
99095 Erfurt, Deutschland
produktsicherheit@kolibri360.de